CONTENTS

PART I

1. Introduction
Jones, A.P.

2. Background to Sedimentary Facies
Jones, A.P.

3. Guidelines and Recommendations
Jones, A.P., Tucker, M.E. and Hart, J.K.

9

THE DESCRIPTION & ANALYSIS OF QUATERNARY STRATIGRAPHIC FIELD SECTIONS

Technical Guide No. 7

Edited by
A.P. Jones, M.E. Tucker & J. Hart

⊃

Edited by Alison P. Jones, Maurice. E. Tucker and Jane K. Hart

Department of Geography
University of Southampton
Highfield
Southampton SO17 1BJ

© Quaternary Research Association: London 1999

ISSN 0264 9241
ISBN 0 907780 47 4

Printed by: Frontier Print and Design, Pickwick House, Chosen View Road, Cheltenham, Glouc. GL51 9LT.

Recommended reference:
JONES, A.P., TUCKER, M.E. and HART, J.K. (eds) 1999. The Description and Analysis of Quaternary Stratigraphic Field Sections. Technical Guide 7, Quaternary Research Association, London. 295 pp.

Cover photo: field section, Unzen Volcano, Japan (see Figure 6.3, Chapter 6, p.146).

8. Glacial Sedimentology: a Case Study from Happisburgh, Norfolk
Hart, J.K.

9. Ice Facies: a Case Study from the Basal Ice Facies of the Russell Glacier, Greenland Ice Sheet
Knight, P.G. and Hubbard, B.P.

10. Permafrost: a Case Study in Cryostratigraphy, Pleistocene Mackenzie Delta, Western Canadian Arctic
Murton, J.B.

11. Coastal Stratigraphy: a Case Study from Johns River, Washington
Long, A.J., Innes, J.B., Shennan, I. and Tooley, M.J.

List of Contributors (*E-mails given for correspondance w.r.t. relevant chapters*)

Dr. Jane K. Hart   Department of Geography, University of Southampton,
                          Southampton, SO17 1BJ, UK. *J.Hart@soton.ac.uk*

Dr. Bryn P. Hubbard   Department of Geography, U.W. Aberystwyth, Ceredigion,
                          SY23 3DB, UK.

Dr. James B. Innes   Environmental Research Centre, Department of Geography,
                          University of Durham, Durham, DH1 3LE, UK.

Dr. Alison P. Jones   Department of Geography, University of Southampton,
                          Southampton, SO17 1BJ, UK. *a.jones@soton.ac.uk*

Dr. Peter G. Knight   Department of Earth Sciences,University of Keele, Keele,
                          Staffordshire, ST5 5BG, UK. *gga34@cc.keele.ac.uk*

Dr. Simon G. Lewis   School of the Environment, C&GCHE, Francis Close Hall,
                          Cheltenham, GL50 4AZ, UK. *slewis@chelt.ac.uk*

Dr. Antony J. Long   Environmental Research Centre, Department of Geography,
                          University of Durham, Durham DH1 3LE, UK.
                          A.J.Long@durham.ac.uk

Dr. Darrel Maddy   Department of Geography, University of Newcastle, Newcastle.
                          NE1 7RU, UK. *darrel.maddy@ncl.ac.uk*

Philip M. Marren   Department of Earth Sciences, University of Keele, Keele,
                          Staffordshire, ST5 5BG, UK.

Dr. Anne E. Mather   Department of Geographical Sciences, University of Plymouth,
                          Plymouth, Devon, PL4 8AA, UK. *A.Mather@plymouth.ac.uk*

Dr. Julian B. Murton   School of Chemistry, Physics and Environmental Science,
                          University of Sussex, Brighton, BN1 9QJ, UK.
                          J.B.Murton@sussex.ac.uk

Dr. Andrew J. Russell   Department of Earth Sciences, University of Keele, Keele,
                          Staffordshire, ST5 5BG, UK. *gga31@cc.keele.ac.uk*

Prof. Ian Shennan   Environmental Research Centre, Department of Geography,
                          University of Durham, Durham, DH1 3LE, UK.

Prof. Michael J. Tooley   School of Geography and Geology, University of St. Andrews,
                               St. Andrews, KY16 9ST, UK.

Prof. Maurice E. Tucker   Department of Geological Sciences, University of Durham,
                               Durham, DH1 3LE, UK.

Prof. Tadahide Ui   Department of Earth and Planetary Sciences, Hokkaido
                               University, Hokkaido, Japan.

PREFACE

Alison P. Jones

In the past few decades, established and more modern sedimentological techniques have been applied with much success to the generally unlithified clastic sediments of the Quaternary Period. [1] The study of these sediments has spanned more than a century and as a result there is a positive wealth of literature devoted to this research area, and many classic papers written in the earlier part of this century that are still considered cornerstones. Considering this, a technical guide to the description of stratigraphical field sections may seem superfluous; a major conundrum when compiling this guide was whether "Quaternary sedimentology" was synonymous with "sedimentology", or whether there were differences significant enough to merit a specialised technical guide. It is difficult to generalise or make any assumptions about Quaternary sediments since there are inevitable exceptions to every rule. Furthermore, some researchers do not perceive any differences between "Quaternary sediments" and older "pre-Quaternary sediments".

Quaternary sediments in general are unlithified, especially if siliciclastic; however, a significant proportion, especially carbonates, are tightly cemented. Moreover unlithified sediments are not restricted to the Quaternary Period, being found throughout the geological record. Other discriminatory criteria such as diagenesis, tectonics and scale prove equally difficult to apply. Perhaps the only infallible discriminator is the presence of modern artifacts such as beer cans and plastic bottles (Hunt, 1959, Ager, 1993). However, most researchers recognise that there are differences that are not always addressed in standard texts. Interestingly enough, researchers working within Quaternary sedimentology do not necessarily have a scientific background in geology/sedimentology, since a significant proportion have arrived there via other routes such as geography, archaeology, biological sciences and physics.

A further conundrum for this guide was how to cover all the main aspects of field sedimentology so that they could be of use to both the specialist and the generalist from diverse backgrounds, in a limited space, given the fact that the source of literature is so detailed and abundant. Unfortunately the logistic reality of this meant that many important elements have not been covered in any great depth; for instance it is immediately apparent that case studies on a variety of depositional environments are omitted. It must be stressed that this bears no reflection on their relative importance. An important consideration when planning the guide was its relevance to as wide a readership as possible, and therefore a number of the case studies presented here are examples of research typically undertaken by Quaternary scientists.

---

[1] The Quaternary Period is divided into the Holocene and Pleistocene Epochs that started approximately 10,000 yrs BP and approximately 2 million yrs BP respectively, although the beginning of the Pleistocene is the subject of some debate.

Stratigraphic field sections are the focus of sedimentological research and their description becomes of prime importance for a number of reasons. First and foremost, they provide a window into the past history of a field area yielding a wide range of detailed information, that is of interest to a large and diverse body of scientists. Often, this is the only window available. Secondly they provide an effective way of conveying information on the sedimentology of a particular field site through publications to other researchers in the same field, and subsequently allow further interpretations and environmental reconstructions, as well as promoting local, regional, national and international correlations. The adage that 'a picture saves a thousand words' is particularly relevant in this case.

On the whole, Quaternary scientists have applied themselves with vigour to this branch of science, producing an extensive and positive contribution to the literature. However, there are many complexities that face the sedimentologist, and as a result there tends to be a lack of consistency and some confusion in the literature when field descriptions of Quaternary sediments are presented, and with this in mind this Technical Guide was written. The guide brings together all of the relevant information required for field-section description of Quaternary clastic sediments.

Part I is essentially a comprehensive reference section covering the principal trends and themes in sedimentology, and presents a general set of guidelines and recommendations for researchers to follow. Part I can also be used as a rapid reminder section as well as the basis for a literature search, since it provides an extensive bibliography with over 200 references. Part II comprises a series of case studies relating to specific depositional environments, and aims to provide working examples of the application in the field of the techniques outlined in Part I, as well as giving ideas on the format of written descriptions and figures to be used in publications. It also discusses any specifics relating to a particular depositional environment or sedimentary facies. It is hoped that the guide, will encourage standard and accurate application of field techniques and the subsequent presentation of the data collected.

Acknowledgements
First and foremost I would like to thank all of my case study contributors for their good will, enthusiasm, diligence and patience as well as the occasional limerick. Especial thanks go to my co-editors Prof. M.E. Tucker and Dr. J.K. Hart for coming on-board and showing nothing but good will. Their comments and criticisms were unfailingly constructive and for that I am very grateful. I would also like to thank Dr. Rob Kemp who was initially involved with the guide series for his patience and support, and thanks also to Dr. Simon Lewis who took over his role of series editor. I am indebted to Dr. J.F Aitken, Dr. D.R. Bridgland, Prof. H. French, Prof. I. Fairchild, Prof. A. Harvey, Dr. D. McCarroll, Dr. A.

Plater, Prof. S. Self, Dr. P. Sutcliffe, Prof. W. Theakstone, Dr. I. West and Dr. T. Yamamoto for reviewing various chapters. Thanks also go to the researchers who took the time and trouble to reply to my questionnaire. Grateful acknowledgement is made to Tim Aspden and his colleagues in the Cartographic Unit at Southampton University, for their cooperation, good humour and for letting me play a brief role in their friendly working environment. A special mention should be made of Linda Hall who put a good deal of time and effort into helping me compile the guide, was unfailingly patient under difficult circumstances, and produced many excellent figures. General thanks go to the Geography Department at Southampton University, for its interest and support in the guide. Finally, researching in Japan whilst the guide was being compiled presented many administrative difficulties, and I owe a big thanks to my Mum and Dad who carried out a number of the tasks for me in the U.K.

Grateful acknowledgement is made to the following copyright holders for granting reprint permission of the figures and tables shown in brackets. See appropriate figures for full acknowledgments: Blackwell Science (Figs. 2.2, 3.4, Table 3.2); Springer-Verlag (Figs. 2.4, 2.8); Society for Sedimentary Geology (SEPM) (Fig. 2.5); John Wiley (Fig. 2.7), Elsevier Science Pub. (Fig. 3.10) and the Centro Nacional de Informacion Geografica, Madrid (Fig. 4.6).

The field visit was going really well until they started discussing the sediments.

PART I

Chapter 1

INTRODUCTION

Alison P. Jones

1.1 SEDIMENTOLOGY

Geologists this century have looked to modern sediments to enhance their understanding of ancient rock successions, with the consequential emergence of a number of sedimentological schemes (e.g. Miall, 1977, 1978, 1985; Eyles *et al.*, 1983). In the last few decades many sedimentological techniques, in both their original and modified forms, have been applied with much success to the generally unlithified clastic sediments of the Quaternary Period. Many of these techniques have survived a century of rigorous application and are still used today. To accompany them, new techniques have appeared which include for example: sequence stratigraphy (see Section 2.3) and micromorphology (see Section 2.2.1.3).

The evolution of sedimentology in the past few decades has been both rapid and diverse. Researchers working within the discipline have shown considerable adaptability, innovation and philosophical transgression. There has been an intensified interest in the relationships between processes and three-dimensional deposits (see Chapters 6 and 7); increased understanding of such relationships is achieved through the collation of data from process studies, field investigations and physical modelling (e.g. Best, 1996, Peakall *et al.* 1996). Furthermore, theoretical modelling of sedimentary fills is very much concerned with the reality of sedimentary successions in the field, (e.g. Heller and Paola, 1996, Zahela, 1997). This is part of an ever increasing trend in some branches of sedimentology towards *inter-disciplinary* research using a *basin-wide* approach (see Chapters 4 and 6), and is supported by the introduction of such journals as *Basin Research*.

Researchers have sought answers to these increasingly complex problems through the description and analysis of stratigraphic field sections. Paradoxically the techniques involved in the description of field sections have remained relatively unchanged throughout the century, the main development being a move away from essentially one-dimensional vertical profiles towards two- and three-dimensional schemes as seen in the application of architectural elements (see Section 2.1.2). Perhaps, the key point is that stratigraphic field sections have been and continue to be fundamental elements in many areas of research.

1.2 UNDERLYING RATIONALE

The original concerns that initiated this guide are outlined below, some of which apply to the discipline of sedimentology as a whole, whereas others are essentially restricted in application to Quaternary sediments, as discussed earlier in the Preface.

1) Sedimentological techniques at times require some modification or adaptation for use on unlithified sediments, a fact recognised for example by the North American Commission on Stratigraphic Nomenclature who introduced *Allostratigraphy* in 1983 specifically for use on Quaternary sediments.

2) A number of workers have introduced their own modifications which in some instances have varied markedly between publications, suggesting (or otherwise) that with time it has become necessary to modify the original approach.

3) Terminologies, coding and practises that accompany the sedimentological techniques as well as the actual definitions and original concepts are numerous and often confusing.

4) Quaternary sedimentology is multidisciplinary and researchers may lack expertise in one particular area, thus necessitating an extensive literature search and/or collaborative research projects. Representations are made by sedimentologists, palynologists, micropalaeontologists, geochemists, geomorphologists, archaeologists, seismologists and engineers. A diverse body of scientists exists within the discipline of Quaternary sedimentology itself, with researchers usually having expertise in one or more of the various depositional environments.

5) Quaternary sedimentology is essentially a field science, which by its very nature presents many logistical difficulties to the researcher.

1.3 AREAS OF DEBATE

There are a number of fundamental themes that occur throughout sedimentology and have been the subject of long-running debates. These themes are well known, but are cited briefly below since they recur throughout the guide.

1.3.1 Classification

"In its simplest form classification is merely defined as the ordering of entities into groups or classes on the basis of their similarity. Statistically speaking, we generally seek to minimize within-group variance, while maximizing between-group variance"
(Bailey, 1994, p.5).

Classification occurs at all levels of sedimentology whereby sediments can be classified on a regional scale in terms of stratigraphical formations or members, and on a more local scale in terms of architectural elements and/or facies.

1.3.2 Standardisation

"Sciences vary widely in their terminology....fundamental principles common to one field are largely unknown to other fields" (Krumbein and Pettijohn, 1938, p.viii).

The call for consistency in sedimentology is not an original one, there being a number of texts devoted to reviewing and standardising techniques as well as a general call for consistency in other publications.

1.3.3 Complexity

"There is no easy solution to the description and categorization of deposits that occur over a large range of scales and exhibit a wide variety of three-dimensional shapes" (Miall, 1995, p.379).

"Perhaps....the very complexity and variability of fluvial sedimentation will make general facies models so unrealistic as to be often worthless" (Collinson and Lewin, 1983, p.2).

The complexity of sedimentary sequences is manifest within existing literature.

1.3.4 Objectivity

"The standard argument is that interpretive terminologies are to be avoided, because whilst the rocks themselves will not change as observational methods improve, our understanding of them may" (Miall, 1995, p.379).

A recurring theme in sedimentology over the past few decades is the debate centred on the descriptive versus interpretative issue, especially with respect to field terminology used in sedimentological descriptions. Some researchers advocate that there is no reason why terminology should not be objective, explicit and unambiguous (Bridge, 1995). However, another approach is that in principle interpretative terminology should be avoided, but in practise it is not so simple, especially with ever-increasing complexity (Miall, 1995).

1.4 TECHNICAL GUIDE

The purpose of this book is to address these issues and provide a comprehensive reference (Chapter 2) and general guidelines (Chapter 3) to the Quaternary researcher in Part I of the guide, for use within and outside the field. Recognition is also made of the fact that each environmental field area has its own peculiar set of characteristics by including eight case studies presenting specific depositional environments in Part II. However, the general guidelines outlined in Part I can be applied to all of the environments presented in Part II and cross-referencing between the two is therefore expedient. Cross-references (highlighted using a smaller font size) are provided to facilitate this.

1.5 COMPLEMENTARY TEXTS

Benn, D.I. and Evans, D.A. 1997. *Glaciers and Glaciation*. Arnold, London.

Bennett, M.R. and Glasser, N.F. 1996. *Glacial Geology, Icesheets and Landforms*. Wiley, Chichester.

Cas, R.A.F. and Wright, J.V. 1987. *Volcanic Successions*. Chapman and Hall.

Collinson, J.D. and Thompson, D.B. 1982. *Sedimentary Structures*. Allen and Unwin.

Hart, J. K. and Martinez, K. 1997. *Glacial Analysis: An Interactive Introduction*. Routledge, London (CD-ROM).

Lindholm, R. 1987. *A Practical Approach to Sedimentology*. Allen and Unwin.

Miall, A.D. 1996. *The Geology of Fluvial Deposits: Sedimentary Facies, Basin Analysis, and Petroleum Geology*. Springer-Verlag Berlin.

Reading, H.G. 1986. *Sedimentary Environments and Facies*. Second edition. Blackwell Scientific Pub.

Reading, H.G. 1996. *Sedimentary Environments and Facies*. Third edition. Blackwell Scientific Pub.

Ricci Lucchi, F. 1995. *Sedimentographica: Photographic Atlas of Sedimentary Structures.* Second (English) edition. Columbia Uni. Press.

Tucker, M. (ed) 1988. *Techniques in Sedimentology*. Blackwell Sci. Pub.

Tucker, M.E. 1996. *Sedimentary Rocks in the Field.* Second edition. J. Wiley and Sons.

Walker, R.G. (ed) 1984. *Facies Models*. Second edition. Geoscience Canada, reprint series, Airworth Press Ltd.

Walker, R.G. and James, N.P. 1992. *Facies Models: Response to Sea Level Change*. Geological Association of Canada, St. Johns, Newfoundland.

Chapter 2

BACKGROUND TO SEDIMENTARY FACIES

Alison P. Jones

This chapter is essentially a reference section which is continued in Chapter 3, where the current position and accepted practises are outlined in more detail. The main techniques and concepts that are relevant to the field sedimentologist are discussed here, including a brief historical account, the main research papers written, standard definitions and the main elements involved.

2.1 GENERAL SCHEMES

Various schemes have been introduced with the aim of standardising techniques and terminologies used in field sedimentology. The popularity and general acceptance of any particular scheme become apparent with time and are dependent upon a number of factors. Sedimentological schemes tend to be developed with respect to one particular depositional environment, although their application can be broadened with time to include a variety of environments. Relatively few schemes are accepted as international standards; examples are the Udden-Wentworth grain-size scale, Power's (1953) visual comparison charts and Hedberg's (1976) lithological hierarchy. However, there are a number of schemes that are widely used but remain contentious (e.g. Troels-Smith, 1955, Miall, 1977, 1985; Eyles *et al.*, 1983).

Troels-Smith (1955, p.42) introduced his schemes in order to provide the researcher with a system of symbols that recorded completely, accurately and objectively, the component elements and the physical properties of unconsolidated sediments. The application of Troels-Smith's schemes varies globally, being used widely in mainland Europe, but rarely used in the United States. Long *et al.* (see Chapter 11) argue that this is an important scheme and encourage its widespread application within Quaternary sedimentology. However, its use in the UK tends to be restricted to researchers interested in biofacies, particularly in association with sediment coring.

The most cited text regarding architectural elements, facies terminology and coding, applied principally to fluvial deposits, is that of Miall (1977, 1985, 1988, 1990, 1995, 1996) who believed that his approach has clearly proved its usefulness (Miall, 1995). Miall also co-authored the paper of Eyles *et al.* (1983) which discussed lithofacies of glacial diamict successions.

However, a number of researchers have criticised these schemes and in some instances have proposed alternative schemes (e.g. Friend, 1983, Kemmis and Hallberg, 1984, Karrow, 1984, Thomas *et al.*, 1987, Bridge, 1993, 1995; Krüger, 1994).

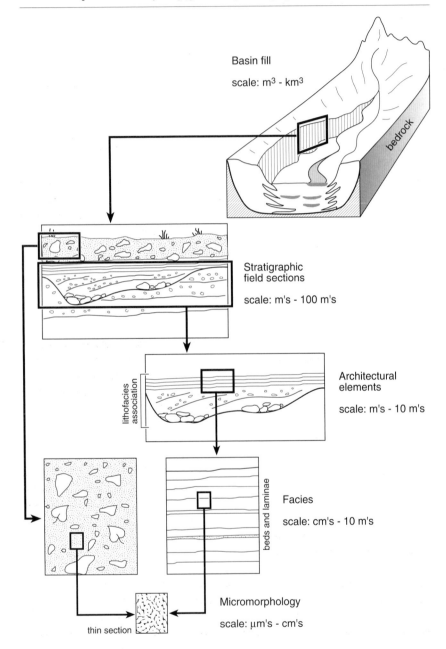

Figure 2.1. *Hierarchies in the sedimentary environment.*

2.1.1 Hierarchies

Hierarchical elements are intrinsic to science, sedimentology being no exception (Figure 2.1) and have appeared in numerous publications over the past few decades (e.g. Alexis *et al.*, 1997, Figure 2.2). For example, McKee and Wier (1953) introduced a quantitative and qualitative terminology to aid the description of field sections and included a hierarchy of cross-stratification. This was followed by Allen (1966) who introduced an hierarchy of bed-form size within Holocene sedimentary environments which consists of five categories [1].

Jackson (1975), following this earlier work, introduced a well-documented hierarchy of bedforms: (1) microforms (e.g. ripples, current lineation), the lifespan of which is much shorter than the periodicity of dynamic events, (2) mesoforms (e.g. dunes, sand waves) which respond to dynamic events such as floods and (3) macroforms (e.g. point bar) which respond to the geomorphological regime of the environment and are relatively insensitive to change with respect to dynamic events such as floods.

Allen in 1966 logged eleven two-dimensional vertical profiles in the Lower Old Red Sandstone in the Forest of Dean. The field evidence comprises various facies and a hierarchical set of bedding contacts (Figure 2.3).

First-order contacts typically bound such entities as individual trough cross-bedding sets, or bundles of plane-bedded laminae genetically associated with cross-strata. Second-order contacts bound clusters of sedimentation units that are genetically related and distinguished from adjacent groupings by facies and/or palaeocurrent direction. Third-order contacts divide groupings of complexes from each other (Allen, 1983, p.249).

2.1.2 Architectural Elements

The concept of architectural elements was born in the 1960's through the work of J. R. L. Allen and basically materialised through the realisation that vertical logs provided limited information on the depositional environment. Collinson and Lewin reported as early as 1983 that 'alluvial architecture' was becoming a major theme in geological sedimentology. It was Allen who introduced the term 'architectural elements' in his 1983 paper, which was later taken up and adapted by Miall (1985, 1988).

Miall (1985) wrote a paper synthesising these earlier ideas, in which he developed Jackson's (1975) hierarchy of bedforms, grouping fluvial deposits into macroforms, mesoforms and microforms. Miall (1985) went on to develop eight basic architectural elements which are defined and described using: nature of lower and upper bounding surfaces, external geometry,

---

[1] Ranging from small-scale ripples to large-scale integrated systems.

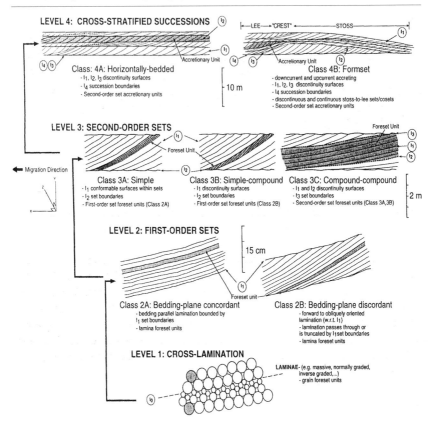

Figure 2.2. *Levels and classes of cross-stratification within the Te Kuiti Group limestones. Examples of important lithological surfaces (I_{0-4}) and foreset/accretionary units (shaded) are included. Arrows show hierarchical arrangements of cross-stratification. Bedform migration direction is from right to left, (from Alexis et al. 1997, p.878, fig. 7). Reprinted by permission of Blackwell Science Ltd.*

scale and internal geometry (Figure 2.4). Many lithofacies types appear in more than one element and multiple lithofacies are found within individual elements. This approach aims firstly to standardise facies assemblages for modelling purposes at the element level, rather than at the level of the entire environment, and secondly, to place much greater emphasis on facies geometries (architecture) than in the past.

Other schemes include: Friend (1983), Friend *et al.* (1979), Miall (1985 and later modifications) and Krüger (1994). Bridge (1995) proposed a new terminology to describe sedimentary sections in two-dimensions if three-dimensions are not available, further to this he believed that there is a need to define geometrical terms (e.g. tabular, sheet) quantitatively.

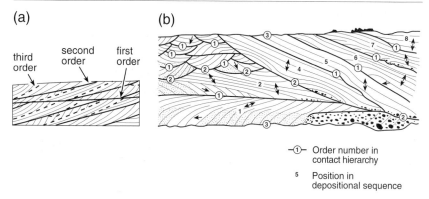

Figure 2.3. Schematic diagram of bounding-surface hierarchies (after Brookfield, 1977 and Allen, 1983).

Architectural elements have been employed by a number of workers in recent years (e.g. Allen, 1965, Friend, 1983, Miall, 1985, Dawson and Bryant, 1987, Marzo *et al.*, 1988, Postma, 1990, Platt and Keller, 1992, Davis *et al.*, 1993, Tirsgaard, 1993, Dreyer, 1994, Eriksson *et al.*, 1995, Brierly, 1996, Hunter *et al.*, 1996). Historically, documentation of architectural elements has been limited to fluvial deposits. However, this concept is being increasingly applied to sediments from other depositional environments (e.g. Platt and Keller, 1992, Davis *et al.*, 1993, Tirsgaard, 1993, Dreyer, 1994, Hambrey, 1994 (p.18), Eriksson *et al.*, 1995).

2.1.3 Facies

Another important consideration when describing sediments in the field is the facies: its definition and use. The original concept of facies in a stratigraphical sense, introduced by Gressly in 1838 has survived to the present day (Teichert, 1958). Walther (1894) defined facies as "the sum total of all primary characteristics of a sedimentary rock, from which the environment of its deposition may be induced." A definition that is still recognised today.

The specified characteristics can be grouped into two main aspects, biological and lithological, which are referred to as biofacies and lithofacies respectively. However, facies have also been identified on the basis of stratigraphic relations, structural form or condition, geographic location or distribution, temporal relation and tectonic situation or control (Weller, 1958).

Facies analysis involves the detailed description of a sedimentary rock unit followed by an interpretation of depositional processes and environmental setting, Lindholm (1987). This

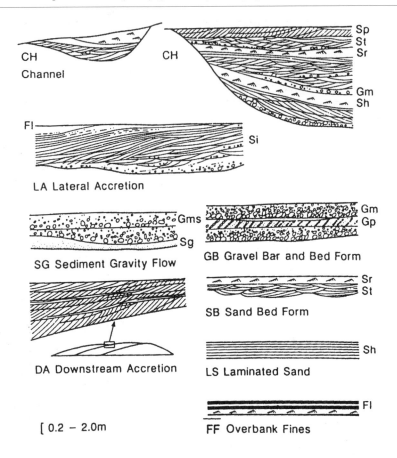

Figure 2.4. *Eight basic architectural elements in fluvial deposits (from Miall, 1996, p.92, fig.4.13). Reprinted by permission of Springer-Verlag.*

approach is supported by many other researchers (e.g. Walker, 1984a, Reading, 1986 and Tucker, 1996).

Coding of facies has become popular in recent years, primarily for ease of logging (Miall, 1977). Other advantages include speedier section drawing, using codes in place of annotation, easier use in written descriptions of sections and producing a rapid visual summary of the field section. Standard codes have been developed for specific depositional environments, the foremost example being Miall (1977), who introduced a lithofacies coding for braided river sediments. Following this, Eyles *et al.* (1983) and Eyles and Miall (1984) introduced a code for glacial deposits. Facies coding is useful for very thick successions of sediments, but care should be taken when devising your own scheme to ensure it is flexible enough to accommodate the unusual (Tucker, 1996).

The concept of sedimentary facies was introduced by Brodzikowski and Van Loon (1991), together with a novel approach to facies coding that consists of a four-level subdivision into: environment, subenvironment, facies and deposit. However, this scheme has not been popular with researchers because it is considered to be too genetic in its approach.

Facies are commonly grouped into facies associations (Figure 2.5), which Tucker (1996 p.128) described as: *comprising sediments generally deposited in the same broad environment, in which there are several different depositional processes operating, distinct subenvironments or fluctuations in the depositional conditions.* (see Section 4.2.7).

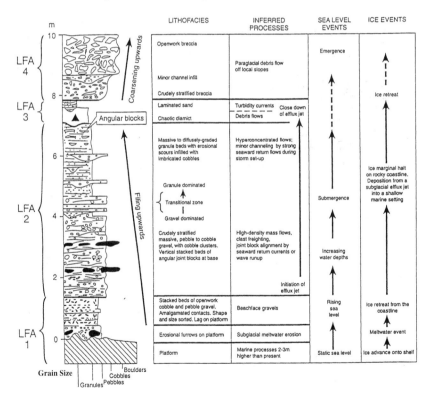

Figure 2.5. *Example of a sedimentary log representing a vertical succession of Lithofacies Associations (LFA 1-4) at Simon's Cove (from McCabe and O'Cofaigh, 1996 p.385, fig.11). Reprinted by permission of SEPM (Society for Sedimentary Geology).*

For example, thick bedded turbidites may be interbedded wih conglomerates, slump sediments and mudstones which may be treated as one association because of the environmental and/or genetic link (Reading, 1986, p.5). Environmental interpretation is made easier by considering an association rather than individual facies. Facies groupings whose genetic/environmental relationship is not necessarily known can be referred to as *facies assemblages* (see Chapters 6 and 10), as distinct from *facies associations* where the genetic/environmental relationship is known.

A facies sequence is defined by Reading (1986, p.5) as a series of facies which pass gradually from one to the other. Care must be taken when using the term sequence in order to avoid confusion with respect to sequence stratigraphy (see Section 2.3). For vertical series of facies the term *succession* may be more appropriate. In terms of scale, facies have been divided according to individual beds (e.g. Macklin and Lewin, 1986, Lewin *et al.*, 1991), bedsets (e.g. Thomas *et al.*, 1982, Harvey, 1990) and depositional environments (e.g. Eyles and Miall, 1984). On a smaller scale, Ryder and Church (1986) grouped sediments into facies and subfacies.

2.2 PHYSICAL PROPERTIES OF SEDIMENTS

The physical properties of sediments can be divided into two main categories: sediment texture and sedimentary structures.

2.2.1 Sediment Texture

Texture refers to the grain size and its distribution, the morphology and surface features of grains, and the fabric of sediment (Tucker, 1996, p.41), all of which are measurable in the field and/or laboratory. A number of studies have emphasised the importance of specific textural indices in terms of providing information on Quaternary palaeoenvironments, including: gravel shape (e.g. Gale and Hoare, 1991), roundness (e.g. Macklin and Lewin, 1986), fabrics (e.g. Hicock *et al.*, 1996, Todd, 1996) and clast lithology (e.g. James, 1991). Statistical measures of grain size are also used to gather information on a deposit, the main ones being median and mean grain-size, standard deviation (sorting), skewness and kurtosis (e.g. Lindholm, 1987).

The term diamict/diamicton is commonly found in descriptions of glacial sedimentary successions (see Figure 2.6), although it is not restricted to these environments. Sedimentary rocks with particle size ranging from clay to boulder dimensions are termed diamictites and their unlithified equivalents are diamicton (e.g. Flint *et al.*, 1960, Kemmis and Hallberg, 1984, Bailey *et al.,* 1990).

Figure 2.6. *Photograph of typical homogeneous diamicton, Dinas Dinlle, North Wales.*

2.2.1.1 Grain Size
The Udden-Wentworth scale is now internationally accepted as the standard grade-scale for sediments, although the scale has been adapted in some research fields, for example, volcanology. The Udden grade-scale was introduced in 1898 and advocated by Krumbein and Pettijohn (1938); it was the first true geometric scale developed for soils and sediments. Udden's grade-scale was later modified and extended by Wentworth in 1922, who retained the geometric interval and added descriptive terms to the intervals. In 1934, Krumbein applied a logarithmic transformation equation to the Wentworth grade-scale to produce a phi scale, which was developed in order to simplify the application of statistics to sedimentary data. For logistical purposes these grade scales are all based on unequal class intervals wherein each interval bears a fixed-size ratio to the preceding and succeeding interval. The b axis is frequently used to represent grain-size measurements in the field, although it is argued by some workers that it does not sufficiently represent grain-size differences or changes, and that all three axes should be considered. Sieving is the most commonly used method in the laboratory for sorting sediment into grain-size classes and determining grain-size distribution.

2.2.1.2 Grain Morphology
1) Particle roundness: there are a number of problems associated with the measurement of roundness, since it is often confused with sphericity and shape (e.g. Wentworth, 1919, King and Buckley, 1968). Roundness is often grouped under the general heading 'grain morphology' along with shape (or form) and sphericity (e.g. Tucker, 1996), or alternatively

under the general term 'grain shape' (e.g. Barret, 1980, Boggs, 1987, Graham, 1988). Roundness is basically concerned with the curvature of the corners of the grain and the most common method of ascribing roundness to particles is by comparison to standard images. Krumbein (1941) presented a chart of 10 classes of pebble images for visual roundness, followed by Powers (1953) who named and redefined six roundness grades and introduced visual comparison charts based on the Wadell (1932) method for determining roundness.

The first quantitative measure of roundness was introduced by Wentworth (1919), who went on to modify his technique in 1922 using the diameter of the sharpest corner. Cailleux (1947) reintroduced Wentworth's earlier technique, which is widely known as the Cailleux index. Kuenen (1956) modified this technique by using the b axis as opposed to the a axis.

2) Particle form: grain shape includes the form (overall shape), sphericity and surface texture (laboratory measurement) of a grain. Form is determined by the various ratios of the long, intermediate and short axes and how closely the grain shape approaches a sphere. Sphericity is commonly expressed using mathematical measures (e.g. Wadell, 1932). Particle shapes are often described by comparison to the four major classes erected by Zingg (1935): oblate, equant, bladed and prolate.

2.2.1.3 Micromorphology

The term micromorphological analysis is used by Quaternary sedimentologists for a technique that is essentially the equivalent of thin-section petrology, which is routinely used by geologists (e.g. van der Meer *et al.*, 1992, Menzies and Maltman, 1992, van der Meer, 1993). This technique is commonly used by soil scientists and is being increasingly taken up by glacial sedimentologists. A thin-section is taken from a block of unlithified sediment that has been hardened using a resin. The *in situ* micromorphological features can then be investigated using a standard petrological microscope. Micromorphologies can also be studied using a scanning electron microscope (SEM).

2.2.1.4 Fabrics and Sorting

Texture refers to the size, shape and the mutual arrangement (packing and fabric) of the component elements of a sedimentary rock (Pettijohn, 1957); fabric includes the orientation and packing of the grains. Particles can be either clast-supported, sometimes referred to as grain-supported, or they can be matrix-supported. Palaeocurrent parameters include the inclination direction/azimuth of foresets, orientation of ripple-crests, as well as channels and scours which may indicate the direction of an erosive current. The imbrication of gravel clasts[2] and the preferred orientation of particles through the action of water (Figure 2.7), ice (e.g. Holmes, 1941, Glen *et al.*, 1957, Harrison, 1957, Andrews, 1971) or wind,

---

[2] overlapping pebbles that generally dip upstream

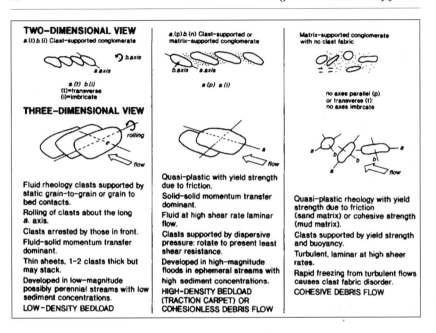

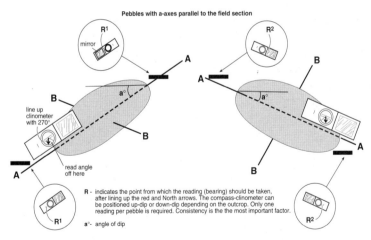

Figure 2.7. Table showing process deduction from the orientation of disc-and blade shaped clasts (from Todd, 1996, p.302, fig. 9.2). Reprinted by permission of J. Wiley. Diagram below shows measurement in the field of orientation and dip of pebbles.

can also be used to give palaeocurrent direction. Theoretically, elongated particles within a flowing medium will orientate themselves to attain a position of minimum torque: this medium may be ice, water, subglacial sediment or any viscous sediment. For a lone particle positioned parallel to the flow, slight velocity variations in the fluid will tend to rotate the particle into a transverse alignment; however, if a number of clasts impinge on each other in the fluid, the transverse orientation produces many collisions and so a longitudinal orientation is more stable (Rusnak, 1975). Fabrics result from both depositional and/or post-depositional processes.

2.2.1.5 Sediment Colour
Describing sediment colour requires a standard colour chart, the most widely used being the Munsell Soil Colour Chart, which is based on a three parameter colour system. The first element (e.g. 0YR) refers to the hue, which is defined in terms of the wavelength of light. The second term (e.g. 4/) is the value (brightness) which is based on the relative amount of black versus white. The third term (e.g, /3) is the chroma (saturation), which is based on the relative amount of pure colour versus neutral grey. Colour is influenced by (1) rock-forming minerals, (2) grain size, (3) the amount and oxidation state of iron present, (4) the amount and type of organic matter present and (5) moisture.

2.2.1.6 Clast Lithological Analysis
Provenance is the source area or areas of the grains within a deposit, in essence the nature of the rocks from which the material has been derived (e.g. Critelli *et al.*, 1997). Within geology the use of provenance was well established by the beginning of this century, principally through sedimentary petrology and clast lithological analysis (pebble counting). Bridgland (1986, p.3) outlined some specific uses for clast lithological analysis of Quaternary sediments which include: the effects of weathering and pedogenesis on different rock types, tracing transport routes, differentiating fluvial deposits from overlying colluvial accumulations (e.g. McGregor and Green, 1983), down-valley and cross-valley lithological variability (e.g. Green *et al.*, 1982), and in order to assess any changes in load composition during transport and after deposition (e.g. Frostick and Reid, 1980).

2.2.1.7 Lithology/Rock type
The two main characteristics of lithology are composition-mineralogy and grain size, whereby rocks are divided into four main lithological groups: terrigenous clastics, biochemical-biogenic-organic deposits, chemical precipitates and volcaniclastics (Tucker, 1996).

2.2.2 Sedimentary Structures

Sedimentary structures are well documented in a number of texts (e.g. Pettijohn and Potter, 1964, Conybeare and Crook, 1968, Carver, 1971, Reineck and Singh, 1980, Allen, 1982, Leeder, 1983, Boggs, 1987, Lindholm, 1987, Selley, 1988, Collinson and Thompson, 1989, Taira *et al.*, 1992, Ricci Lucchi, 1995), and they are produced by physical, chemical and/or biogenic processes before, during and after deposition. Ricci Lucchi (1995) pointed out that in classical stratigraphy, the bed has two characterisations: geometry (three-dimensional form in which two-dimensions prevail on the third one (thickness)) and rock type, which he referred to as the "container and content," respectively. A bed therefore represents an event or series of events in sedimentation and is our fundamental reference representing the base line for stratigraphy and sedimentology. A considerable problem in sedimentological descriptions is that recognition of most sedimentary structures occurs in two dimensional sections, but almost all sedimentary structures are three dimensional.

2.2.2.1 Sequences and Cycles

Sediments are commonly arranged into distinct units which may repeat themselves in a stratigraphic section (e.g. Bouma, 1962, Allen, 1964). Symmetry is often used to distinguish between the terms cycle and sequence, but there is no well-defined difference between the terms (Ricci Lucchi, 1995). Tucker (1996, p.129) referred to "thin repeated units, on a scale of 1-10 m," as cycles or parasequences, which make up sequences in sequence stratigraphy (see Section 2.2.4). Cycles/parasequences can be described as thinning-up or thickening-up with respect to vertical changes in the thickness of beds, and fining-up or coarsening-up with respect to vertical changes in grain size within the cycles.

2.2.2.2 Depositional Structures

1) Bedding: (also referred to as stratification and layering), is defined as layers of sediment (each a bed) over 1 cm thick that may be lithologically different in texture and structure, from that above and below and generally has parallel bedding planes. Lamination is similarly defined, but the laminae are less than 1 cm thick. The main bedding types are: massive, flat (also referred to as horizontal, planar and parallel), graded, inclined, cross and deformed. By far the most complex bedding is that of cross and deformed; both types of bedding require detailed examination and detailed measurement of a number of criteria, together with a more specific classification.

2) Massive bedding: refers to a bed where there is an apparent absence of any form of sedimentary structure and is also referred to as 'structureless'. However, the existence and occurrence of genuine ***massive bedding*** is disputed. A number of researchers have pointed out that bedding which appears massive to the naked eye is in fact bedded or bioturbated

etc., as revealed by X-radiography (Hamblin, 1965), or by etching and staining methods (Boggs, 1987, Tucker, 1996).

3) Flat bedding: (also referred to as horizontal bedding, planar bedding and parallel bedding[3]) is described as bedding which parallels the major bedding surface and may grade, via sub-horizontal bedding, into cross bedding, but there are no critical angles of dip which separate these categories. ***Flat bedding*** is thought to result from two basic scenarios: strong traction currents (upper plane-bed phase lamination) and weak traction currents/suspension (lower plane-bed phase lamination).

4) Graded bedding: sediment carried in turbulent suspension such as turbidity flow and fluvial currents is subject to internal sorting which may subsequently be preserved as ***graded bedding***. This term implies a vertical change in grain size within a bed. There are several kinds of graded bedding, including normal grading (fining upwards) and reverse (or inverse) grading (coarsening upwards). The term 'fining-up/coarsening-up succession or unit' is normally applied to a change in grain size within a group of beds (see Figure 7.9) as opposed to grading, which refers to a change in grain size within a specific bed.

5) Inclined bedding: sediments are deposited as ***inclined bedding*** passively (i.e. deposition from suspension on to an existing slope) and actively (lateral accretion or progradation of large-scale bedforms such as point bars or Gilbert-type deltas). Subaqueous flat, inclined and cross-bedding have been classified according to original dip values: 0-2°, 1-30°, and 1-34°, respectively (Thomas *et al.*, 1987). Thomas *et al.* (1987) introduced the terms '*inclined heterolithic stratification (IHS) and inclined stratification*' to replace certain existing terms concerning large-scale, waterlain, lithologically heterogeneous and homogeneous siliciclastic sedimentary deposits (figure 2.8). They went on to define (p.172) IHS as follows: "deposits consist of inclined units that are separated by inclined surfaces produced by either non-deposition or erosion."

6) Cross-stratification: ***cross-bedding*** (Figure 2.9) consists of inclined bedding, bounded by subhorizontal surfaces (see Figures 7.11 to 7.15). McKee and Weir (1953) recognised three main types of cross-stratification, based on the character of the lower bounding surface of the set, and referred to them as simple, planar and trough cross-stratification. Simple cross-stratification is classified as any set of cross-strata whose lower bounding surfaces of sets are non-erosional. Planar and trough cross-stratification are similarly classified, but have planar surfaces of erosion and curved surfaces of erosion respectively. Cross-bedding is mostly produced by four different processes.

---

[3] Parallel bedding can be suddivided into even, wavy, curved, continuous and discontinuous (Campbell, 1967) and therefore is not technically flat bedding.

a) Formed from unidirectional water currents, as for example within fluvial, deltaic and shallow-marine environments (storm currents), rivers and deltas. (see Allen, 1963, 1966, 1968; Cant, 1982, Collinson and Thompson, 1989, Tucker, 1996).

b) Formed from oscillatory water-currents, as within wave and tidal environments (see Weimer *et al.*, 1982, Walker, 1984b).

c) Formed by air currents (wind), as within desert and coastal backshore environments (see Collinson and Thompson, 1989).

d) Formed from unidirectional hot gaseous and particulate currents, primarily those found in pyroclastic surges (see Sparks, 1976, Cas and Wright, 1987).

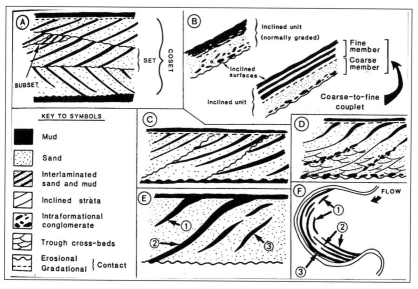

Figure 2.8. *Diagram showing proposed nomenclature for the description of inclined heterolithic stratification (IHS). IHS sets (A, C, D and E) may range in thickness from <1 to 30m. (F) plan view of bar showing three possible types of along-strike continuity (1-3), (from Thomas et al., 1987, fig 1). Reprinted by permission of Springer-Verlag.*

2.2.2.3 Erosional Structures

Erosional surfaces assuming a curved (concave-up) basal profile are referred to as ***scours*** and can be formed in fluvial, glacial, lacustrine, slope, coastal, submarine and volcanic settings. Different scales and forms of scour exist, for example flutes, obstacle scours, wave-produced scours, and scour-and-fill.

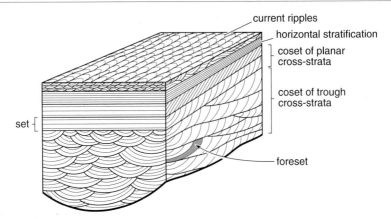

Figure 2.9. *Terminology for cross-bedding (adapted from McKee and Wier, 1953 and Campbell, 1976).*

Scour-and-fill and channels can normally be identified from a strong contrast between the filling material and the substratum. A number of different channel-fill elements have been identified (e.g. Ramos *et al.*, 1986). Channel structures range in width and depth from a few centimetres to thousands of metres and are generally thought to be sites of sediment transport for long periods of time. On the other hand scours usually form during a single erosive event and consist of smaller-scale asymmetrical troughs from a few centimetres to metres wide, commonly having a steep upcurrent slope and a more gentle downcurrent slope (Boggs, 1987). The long axis of a scour points downcurrent and is usually elongate in plan view. Friend (1983) suggested using a non-genetic term such as 'hollow' to describe such features and outlined definitive and genetic criteria.

2.2.2.4 Bounding Surfaces
All bounding surfaces of large-scale features such as facies and architectural elements, boundaries that delimit cycles/parasequences and individual beds, and parting planes that subdivide beds into constituent parts or laminae, represent physical discontinuities. The nature of these boundaries, especially unconformities, is important in terms of palaeoenvironments, since it can indicate a major phase of erosion, exposure and/or biological activity.

2.2.2.5 Deformed Bedding
Deformation structures (see Sections 3.2.4.2, 8.2.4, 8.3, 10.6.2) include faults, thrusts, shear zones, convolutions, folds and fabrics (e.g. Hart and Boulton, 1991, Lunkka, 1994, McCabe and O'Cofaigh, 1996). Deformation can result directly or indirectly from various processes, such as dewatering, density contrasts, slumping, current drag, subglacial deformation, proglacial deformation, volcanics and large-scale tectonics.

The phrase *soft sediment deformation* (Sims, 1973, Brodzikowski and Van Loon, 1980, Owen, 1995, Mohindra and Bagati, 1996) reflects a wide range of deformation types as well as a range of sediment conditions; if possible, a more specific term should be used (Maltman, 1984). Dewatering structures are formed by water escaping vertically and laterally from porous sediments to regions of lower hydrostatic pressure and in so doing can displace grains and/or entrain solid particles (elutriation) along its path. Loading structures may result from an inverted density stratification, when a material of higher density (e.g. sand) rests on a less dense material (e.g. liquefied clay) causing instability. The sand tends to sink and the mud to inject upwards producing load and flame structures, respectively (Figure 2.10). The shearing action of currents moving in the same direction that sediments were deposited can deform and in some cases overturn surficial saturated sediments, typically cross-bedded sands. The general term 'slump structures' has been applied to structures produced by deformation resulting from the lateral displacement of unconsolidated and typically saturated sediments under the influence of gravity and, in some cases, earthquake trigger mechanisms (Jones and Omoto, *submitted, see* Figure 2.10).

Figure 2.10. Ball-and-pillow structures with flames of clay, Nakayamadaira Basin, Japan.

Deformation associated with active glaciers (see Section 8.2.4) is known as glaciotectonic deformation; *proglacial glaciotectonic deformation* takes place at the glacier margin and *subglacial glaciotectonic deformation* occurs beneath the glacier. Additionally, deformation associated with ice decay at the glacier margin is known as dead-ice tectonics. This latter phenomenon is mostly associated with dead-ice collapse features such as kettle holes, sediment gravity flows, and the injection of saturated subglacial sediments up through crevasses (crevasse infills or diapirs).

Proglacial deformation consists mostly of compressive styles of deformation, including open folds and reverse faults. This results mostly from frontal pushing by the glacier. Subglacial deformation is dominated by simple shear and longitudinal extension (Hart and Boulton, 1991, Hart and Roberts, 1994). Characteristics of this type of environment are: folds, tectonic laminae, augens and boudins.

2.3 STRATIGRAPHY

When studying sediments in a spatial and temporal context, a system is required that encapsulates the relationships between different bodies of sediment, or more specifically different sedimentary units within field sections. In effect the sedimentary units need to be classified and later correlated. The recognised procedure for the classification of bodies of sediment on a regional scale is the principle of stratigraphy (see Chapter 8), where a stratigraphic unit is defined as.

"A naturally occurring body of rock or rock material distinguished from adjoining rock on the basis of some stated property or properties. Commonly used properties include composition, texture, included fossils, magnetic signature, radioactivity, seismic velocity and age" (North American Commission on Stratigraphic Nomenclature, 1983, p.847).

A lithostratigraphic unit is a *"defined body of sedimentary, extrusive igneous, metasedimentary or metavolcanic strata which is distinguished and delimited on the basis of lithic characteristics and stratigraphic position. A lithostratigraphic unit generally conforms to the law of superposition and commonly is stratified and tabular in form...recognised and defined by observable rock characteristics...lithification or cementation is not a necessary property; clay, gravel, till and other unconsolidated deposits may constitute a valid lithostratigraphic unit"* (NACSN, 1983, p.855).

Units are named according to their perceived rank in a formal lithological hierarchy (Hedberg, 1976)[4].

---

[4] Additional units in the hierarchy include tongue/lentil, supergroup and subgroup (refer to Miall, 1990, p.90-91).

| Supergroup |
| Group |
| Formation |
| Member |
| Bed |

A Formation is defined as "the smallest mappable or traceable unit...generally varies in maximum thickness from a few metres to several hundreds of metres" (Whittaker *et al.*, 1991).

A bed is the smallest formal lithostratigraphic unit of sedimentary rocks (NACSN, 1983). Whittaker *et al.* (1991) believed that it is rarely worth giving a formal name to every individual bed.

A particular type of lithostratigraphic unit may be formed by stratigraphic events which have widespread depositional effects within a very short time-span (e.g. volcanic ash falls). They may have chronostratigraphic significance and this led to the concept of 'event stratigraphy' (Miall, 1990).

Chronostratigraphy is the classification of strata by age, which may be determined by a number of means, e.g. radiometric dating, amino acid dating, pollen dating, unconformities etc. A chronostratigraphic unit is defined as *"a body of rock established to serve as the material reference for all rocks formed during the same span of time"* (NACSN, 1983, p.849).

Morphostratigraphy is an approach which includes both landform and lithology. The classic model of this approach is the Alpine model, where four outwash terraces were mapped and linked with end-moraines (Penck and Bruckner, 1909), and they were thought to represent four glacial phases. Bowen (1978) disputed the use of morphostratigraphy as a feasible technique. Morphostratigraphical units are regarded with an informal status and are not recognised by the NACSN.

Biostratigraphy is based on the fossil content of rock bodies. The basic unit in biostratigraphic classification is the biozone, of which there are several kinds, i.e. interval, assemblage and abundant biozones (NACSN, 1983).

Pedostratigraphy is defined as *"a body of rock that consists of one or more pedologic horizons developed in one or more lithostratigraphic, allostratigraphic, or lithodemic units and is overlain by one or more formally defined lithostratigraphic or allostratigraphic units"* (NACSN, 1983, p.850).

The NACSN (p.849) guide recognised the difficulty of applying stratigraphical principles to Quaternary deposits, a view emphasised by the following statement

"Many upper Cenozoic, especially Quaternary deposits are distinguished and delineated on the basis of content, for which lithostratigraphic classification is appropriate. However, others are delineated on the basis of criteria other than content. To facilitate the reconstruction of geological history, some compositionally similar deposits in vertical sequence merit distinction as separate stratigraphic units, because they are the products of different processes; others merit distinction because they are of demonstrably different ages. Lithostratigraphic classification of these units is impractical and a new approach, **allostratigraphic** *classification, is introduced."*

An allostratigraphic unit is a mappable stratiform body of sedimentary rock that is defined and identified on the basis of its bounding discontinuity and the ranking of allostratigraphic units is similar to that of lithostratigraphic units.

| Allogroup |
| Alloformation |
| Allomember |

North (1996) believed that allostratigraphy is in effect an extension of Miall's architectural element analysis and is a more natural method of subdividing sediments for interpretative purposes than the conventional lithostratigraphy. Posamentier and James (1993) and North (1996) outlined the relationship between allostratigraphy and sequence stratigraphy. In general, researchers have been reluctant to employ allostratigraphy, although the general principle can be seen in some studies (e.g. Maizels, 1987, Jones, 1995, Walker, 1995, Eyles *et al.* 1998, Rhee *et al.*, 1998). However, the application of sequence stratigraphy has been more popular (e.g. Martini and Brookfield, 1995).

Sequence Stratigraphy, an increasingly popular way of dividing up the stratigraphic record, including the Quaternary, is on the basis of unconformities into sequences. A sequence is defined as a succession of relatively-conformable, genetically-related strata bounded by an unconformity or its correlative conformity (Wilgus *et al.*, 1988, Van Wagoner *et al.*, 1990, Emery and Myers, 1996, Miall, 1997). An unconformity (the sequence boundary) is a surface separating younger from older strata along which there is evidence of subaerial exposure with a significant hiatus. It will pass laterally (basinwards) into a conformity. A sequence can usually be divided into several systems tracts (defined as a linkage of contemporaneous depositional systems), deposited during a specific part of a cycle of relative sea-level change, i.e., lowstand (LST), transgressive (TST), highstand (HST), shelf-margin wedge (SMWST) and forced-regressive (FRST) systems tracts. Apart from the sequence boundary, other key surfaces are the transgressive surface (ts) (which may be coincident . with the sequence boundary in more proximal (landward) parts of a basin) at the base of the TST, and the maximum flooding surface (mfs), that separates the TST from the HST. In more distal parts of the basin, there is commonly a condensed section (cs) equivalent to the upper part of the TST, the mfs and the lower part of the HST. Some sequences are composed of several or many metre-scale cycles, termed parasequences (defined by flooding surfaces at their bases), and then the systems tracts are defined by the stacking patterns of the parasequences. Sequences within an area are generally named by letters or numbers, or a combination of both, working from the base upwards.

Cycle Stratigraphy and Sequence Stratigraphy
Quaternary sediments of certain depositional environments, such as shoreline clastic and carbonate, deltaic, fluvial and lacustrine, are commonly arranged into distinct units which are repeated several or many times in the succession. Thin repeated units, on a scale of 1-10 metres, are usually referred to as cycles, or in sequence stratigraphic terminology, parasequences or high frequency sequences. They were deposited over timespans of several 10's to 100's of 1000's of years. Sedimentary cycles vary considerably in composition and facies depending on the depositional environment. Some cycles are alternations of lithologies e.g., mudrock-sandstone in shallow-marine, fluvial and deltaic successions. Other cycles show systematic upward changes in grain-size, e.g., a coarsening-up, as in deltaic mudrock to sandstone cycles, or a fining-up, as in meandering-stream sandstone to mudrock cycles. There may be systematic upward changes in the thickness of beds within cycles too (thinning-up or thickening-up). Many cycles show a general shallowing-upwards of the facies and are the result of repeated transgressions and regressions through rises and falls of relative sea-level. The presence of cycles within a succession can usually be seen in the field by close observation of the facies, although rarely it is only revealed after a detailed graphic log has been made. The boundaries between cycles should be examined carefully; distinct horizons may occur here. In many case the top of a cycle is an emergence horizon such as a palaeosoil. The tops of some cycles were not subaerially exposed, but show evidence of shallowing and a pause in deposition represented by intense bioturbation or local lithification. The base of a cycle is usually a flooding surface. Thus there may be a thin gravel or conglomerate of material reworked from the top of the underlying cycle and evidence of erosion (a sharp, scoured surface), and/or a muddy bed reflecting the deeper-water conditions of the transgression initiating the new cycle. There is much scope for applying sequence stratigraphy to Quaternary successions, where many consist of several high-frequency sequences produced by glacioeustatic changes in sea-level; other cycles, however, are the result of movements on major faults and earthquake deformation cycles (e.g. Shennan *et al.*, 1996, Long *et al.*, this guide) or autocyclic mechanisms (sedimentary processes such as tidal-flat progradation and lateral migration of meandering streams). However, the application of sequence stratigraphy to non-marine successions, such as fluvial

and glacial facies, is still being developed and has been controversial, since there are several other factors, such as climate, uplift, sediment supply and autocyclic processes, in addition to relative sea-level/base-level changes which control the stratigraphic record in non-marine environments. The application of sequence stratigraphy in the field is discussed by Tucker (1996).

Chapter 3

GUIDELINES AND RECOMMENDATIONS

Alison P. Jones, Maurice E. Tucker and Jane K. Hart

This chapter aims to provide a set of guidelines for the Quaternary field sedimentologist: a formidable task given that sedimentology is such a complex area of research with a number of highly contentious issues, as well as being accommodated by a diverse body of scientists. Feedback from researchers (Appendix 2) working in different fields (whose views and comments received in answers to a questionnaire have been taken into account in compiling this chapter), served to emphasise that field practise has to be flexible enough to accommodate not only the individual requirements of the field worker and their personal preferences, but also the varying nature of the field that the research is being carried out in.

3.1 FIELD STAGE

3.1.1 Description of Stratigraphic Field Sections: Procedure

Summary recommendations for field-section description are given below. Further information is provided for the terms in *bold lower case* in Section 3.2.

1) Often, one of the most difficult problems facing the field sedimentologist is the location of suitable field sections. Some studies lend themselves more easily to sediment exposures than others, for example active glacial environments and volcanic terrain. In most cases a thorough reconnaissance of the proposed field area is necessary and the choice of field area may indeed be influenced by available exposures. If a researcher is investigating a published field section then location is obviously much easier[1]. Field exposures are commonly found in the following areas: active/recent glacial areas and volcanic terrain, coastal sections, river banks and cliffs, waterfalls, slope scars, areas of construction especially roads, quarries and gravel pits. Many of these are labelled on the small-scale maps of areas that have been surveyed in detail (e.g. Ordnance Survey Maps (U.K.)), but aerial photographs may be more useful in areas that have not been surveyed in such detail (e.g. Svalbard, Spitsbergen).

2) Field safety is of paramount importance to Quaternary researchers who conduct a great deal of their research in the field, often in remote, dangerous and inaccessible areas (see Sections 6.5.4 and 11.4). Each field area and environment has its own set of potential hazards, but there are a number of simple guidelines that can be followed in all field areas.

---

[1] This emphasises the importance of including accurate locations (with specific grid references where possible) when describing field sites.

It is often stipulated that field work should never be carried out alone. However, the reality is that researchers often find themselves alone in the field and they should therefore take the following precautions: notify the appropriate people of your fieldwork location and if possible carry some form of communication such as a cellular phone or radio.

Make sure that you have the appropriate equipment as well as ensuring that it is in a suitable condition before setting out to the field. A hard hat is an essential piece of equipment at field sections exceeding 2 m in height. Ropes, harnesses and/or ladders should be used for scaling big sections. A first-aid kit is also recommended and in some cases a survival kit (e.g. map bearings for base camp, compass, whistle, flare, survival sack and rations). Remember to correct your compass to true north if necessary.

Enquire about any local conditions relevant to your field site, such as tide times in coastal areas and diurnal flood levels of glacial rivers, as well as local weather forecasts.

3) On the whole Quaternary research can be carried out with low tech. equipment, the most important of which is probably the trowel; however, high tech. additions such as GPS[2] are gradually making their way into the field kit. Other vitally important pieces of equipment are: field hammer, spade, sample bags, waterproof field notebook and pen, some scale measure (metre rule), compass-clinometer and camera. Additional equipment may include coring devices, GPR[2], surveying equipment, box samplers, resin/lacquer, callipers and grids. Laminating relevant diagrams and tables is a useful way of preserving them in the field. Some form of official identification is recommended, which states who you are and what you are doing. Remember that permission should always be secured before entering private property.

4) Once a suitable section has been located, the following information should be recorded in field notebooks: map sheet, grid reference or GPS reading, geomorphological landform (the amount of detail will depend on the aims of the research), orientation, elevation; for future reference it may be useful to note the date, time and weather. Before and/or after cleaning the section photograph any well-preserved, well-developed and unusual structures for further analysis or simply to have photographs for future reference. Also, the construction of a *photomosaic* for reference during and/or following field investigations is useful. Remember to record the exact position, orientation and film number of each photograph and if a visible scale marker cannot be placed in the field of view, make a note of the scale of the photographic subject.

---

[2] Global Positioning Systems
[3] Ground Penetrating Radar

5) View the outcrop from a distance and trace in outer margins to scale (this may be estimated or measured) and then draw in the large-scale features such as faults, folds, cycles etc. Cleaning the section may precede or proceed this task, depending on the field site; normally it should precede any sketching. Cleaning free faces is vitally important and a significant amount of time may have to be devoted to this - remember when cleaning, work from the top of the section downwards.

6) Traverse the outcrop, making a note of initial facies and facies associations if possible. Trace in bounding surfaces and select *vertical profiles for logging*. Access may be a problem with thick vertical successions and a ladder, roping up or digging successive steps into the section may be required. *Physical properties* can be measured both in the field and the laboratory and include: *general texture, grain size, particle roundness, particle form, fabric and sorting, sediment colour, clast lithological analysis, rock type and sedimentary structures.* Various schemes may be used at this stage to standardise and abbreviate descriptions, for example, Miall (see Chapter 7)); Troels-Smith (see Chapter 11) and others (see Chapters 4, 6, 9 and 10).

7) Trace in any geometries and *architectural elements* as appropriate (see Chapter 6). If the section is two-dimensional use orientation data to infer a third dimension[4]. Measure specific geometries such as the width and depth of channel units.

8) Determine a more specific *sampling strategy* for any field measurements to be made (e.g. grain size, palaeocurrents) and mark sample points on the outcrop profile. Determine a *sampling strategy* for *in situ sampling* and for sediments being returned to the laboratory; collect and place samples in clearly labelled bags. Mark sample points on the outcrop profile field-sketch.

9) Interpret the section using all of the information, diagrams, logs and data collected in the field, together with any laboratory results. Finalise *facies and facies associations* designation and if appropriate, develop and outline a *formal stratigraphy* or correlate with an established stratigraphy.

---

[4] This obviously raises the issue of applicability of architectural element schemes, since palaeocurrent data are not easy to synthesise in the field.

3.2. DESCRIPTION OF STRATIGRAPHIC FIELD SECTIONS: FURTHER INFORMATION

3.2.1 Photomosaics

Photographs can be used after field work has been carried out for supplementary information and later reference (see Figures 6.8, 7.14a and 7.19). Another approach is to relinquish first-hand field evidence and describe field sections based exclusively on photomosaics. This has obvious disadvantages and is discouraged for a number of reasons: photos may present distorted images of the facies and without a field investigation, colour cannot be accurately described; textures cannot be classified, and many other valuable insights will be unattainable. The implementation of field investigations and photomosaics collectively will produce the best results. An outline of the methodology for annotated photomosaics can be found in Miall (1995), building on the original work by Allen (1983). Some researchers suggested that field section profiles should be drawn on photograph overlays and subsequently checked in the field (e.g. Miall, 1996 p.98). However, in most circumstances this can entail two or three field investigations at one particular site and, given time and logistical constraints, a single field investigation proceeded by reference to photographs is more than justified. Some important points to remember when constructing a photomosaic are listed below.

1) Remember to use a visible scale reference and mark photographic sites on your outcrop profile.

2) A reference line (baseline) is usual when using photomosaics, for example a length of levelled string. For more accurate field sketches a grid of string can be erected across the whole section face.

3) Photographing the section may precede or proceed any cleaning or both.

4) Researchers photographing the whole outcrop and later constructing a photomosaic should use a camera that minimises distortion.

5) The photographer should move parallel to the section along a traverse that is equidistant from the section.

3.2.2 Vertical Profiles and Logging

Bouma (1962) is often cited as demonstrating the first successful application of graphic logs to a succession of turbidites, and sedimentary logging in the field is now considered to be a standard procedure, graphic logs being a popular means of relaying information through publications (see Figures 4.8, 4.10, 8.2 and 8.14). In the past few decades however, there has been an ever increasing move away from these essentially one dimensional vertical profiles, towards two- and three-dimensional schemes. However, sedimentary logging has a number of unique applications outlined below, and its use is particularly recommended in field sections with significant vertical variation.

1) They are a relatively rapid method of recording information from a section.

2) Logs can be laid side by side for comparison and correlation of different localities and also allow rapid visual comparisons to be made.

3) The vertical successions of facies displayed in the logs are important with respect to environmental reconstruction.

4) Logs highlight gradual trends, particularly vertical ones, e.g. of grain size.

5) They provide a comprehensive summary of exposures that are too large-scale to record in field-section sketches. Similarly they can provide a summary of specific environments, acting as models.

6) They provide a useful means of relaying information through publications.

The drawing of sedimentary logs (see Figure 3.13) varies according to the location and the researcher, but there are a few standardised recommendations.

1) Field workers can use a pre-prepared logging sheet (Figure 3.1), or graph paper.

2) Bed thickness is drawn to scale in the vertical column: between 1:5 and 1:10 for precise work or 1:50 and 1:100 (i.e. 1 cm on the log sheet equals: 5cm, 10 cm, 0.5 m and 1 m) (Tucker, 1996).

3) The width of the column is a measure of the grain size.

4) Various symbols can be added to convey further information regarding lithology, sedimentary texture, sedimentary structures and nature of boundaries (Figure 3.2).

Log sheet							Date:	
Location:			Scale 1:	GPS/GR			Sheet	of
Height/depth	Thickness (m)	Bed number	Samples/photos	Lithology	Grain size and sedimentary structures		Remarks	
					Clay Silt	Sand ꜰ ᴍ ᴄ Gravel		

Figure 3.1 *Log sheet*

5) Sedimentary logging should always be from the base upwards, using the base as a zero mark. However, it can sometimes be useful to place zero at the top, if for example the researcher is describing individual palaeosols, coring sediment, or they require a stable marker that can be found at a later date. Archaeologists traditionally place a zero mark at the top of a section, an important consideration for collaborative projects.

3.2.3 Sampling Strategy

"If a sample is worth collecting it is worth collecting well" (Krumbein and Pettijohn, 1938, p.11).

Most sedimentary properties can be measured in the field and it is advisable to do so; however, sediments can be collected for further analysis in the laboratory. Traditionally samples are collected and returned to the laboratory for the purpose of: further grain size analysis (e.g. Friedman, 1967, Visher, 1969, Folk, 1974, Glaister and Nelson, 1974, McManus, 1988, Duck, 1994, Konert and Vandenberghe, 1997), geochemistry (e.g. Lewin *et al.*, 1977, Peart and Walling, 1982, Lewin and Macklin, 1986, Fairchild *et al.*, 1988), SEM (e.g. Krinsley and Doornkamp, 1973, Trewin, 1988), micromorphology (e.g, van der Meer, 1993), palynology, absolute dating (e.g. Smart and Frances, 1991) etc.

There are a number of considerations when selecting sample sites, some of which are listed below.

1) Field section descriptions and samples of recent/ancient sediments are limited to available exposures, although shallow cores can also be used.

2) Available exposures are often obscured by slumping, vegetation etc.

3) Lateral and vertical grain-size variations are common.

4) Grain-size variations within facies occur, especially in diamictons.

5) Possible bias occurs when sampling towards distinctive facies, provenance rocks etc.

6) Field logistics, such as access to sections or the distance that samples have to be transported back to the laboratory, need to be considered.

7) Diagenetic alteration is an important factor since sediment sequences vary with time due to degree of weathering, lithification/compaction, slumping, etc.

Sedimentary structures

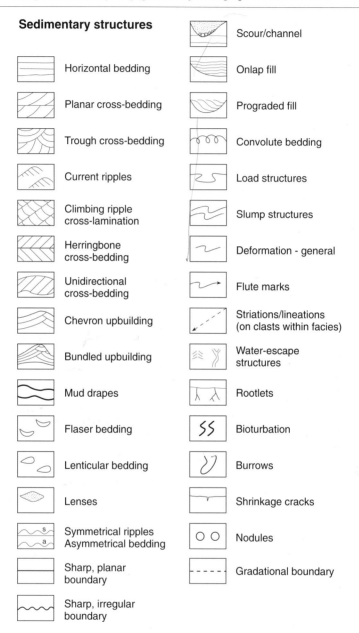

Horizontal bedding	Scour/channel
Planar cross-bedding	Onlap fill
Trough cross-bedding	Prograded fill
Current ripples	Convolute bedding
Climbing ripple cross-lamination	Load structures
Herringbone cross-bedding	Slump structures
Unidirectional cross-bedding	Deformation - general
Chevron upbuilding	Flute marks
Bundled upbuilding	Striations/lineations (on clasts within facies)
Mud drapes	Water-escape structures
Flaser bedding	Rootlets
Lenticular bedding	Bioturbation
Lenses	Burrows
Symmetrical ripples Asymmetrical bedding	Shrinkage cracks
Sharp, planar boundary	Nodules
Sharp, irregular boundary	Gradational boundary

Figure 3.2. Symbols for sediment textures and sedimentary structures

Textures and lithology

Symbol	Label
△	Diamicton
	Gravel
▲▲ ▲▲	Breccia
	Sand
	Silt
	Clay
	Carbonate mud
	Calcareous
~ ~	Marl
■	Peat
	Volcaniclastic
E	Evaporite
	Normal grading
	Inverse grading

Symbol	Label
	Clast-supported
	Matrix-supported
OOO	Imbrication/ clast fabric

Others

	Plant fragments
	Shell fragments
⊕	Coral
✖	Algae
~	Rip-up clasts
	Thickening/thinning-up successions
F——F	Fault
▬	Thrust plane
↗	Azimuth
↙↗	Trend

There is not an all encompassing sampling strategy that can be applied by Quaternary scientists. Instead, field workers develop their own strategy that provides a representative picture of the field section under consideration. There are, however, a number of standard sampling procedures (e.g., BSI, 1997) that can be applied during sample collection; these are listed below. Recommended sample sizes are given in Table 3.1.

Indice	Sample size
Grain size	Mean maximum grain size; 10 largest clasts per sample
	Mean grain size of gravel >50 clasts per sample
	Bulk sample for grain size analysis
Roundness and shape	>35 clasts per sample
Fabric and sorting	>30 clasts per sample
Clast lithology	>100 clasts per sample

Table 3.1 *Recommended sample sizes.*

Bulk samples (see Gale and Hoare, 1992)
Bulk samples are often made up of composite samples, collected in order to represent the facies being sampled. The sampling strategy will depend upon the individual facies, heterogeneous facies requiring more widespread sampling.

a) Volumetric (bulk) samples of subsurface and/or surface sediments.
This is a common method of sampling sands. Bulk sampling of gravels is more problematic due to the large sample size required if the principle of equivalent sample sizes (to grain size) is adhered to (Kellerhals and Bray, 1971). Most contributors collected bulk samples of 5kg for coarse grain-sizes and 0.5kg for finer grain-sizes. The following weights of typical sandy gravel are recommended in order to obtain between 300 to 500 clasts[5].

After Bridgland (1986, p.8)

Grain size range (mm)	Weight (Kg)
8.0 - 16.0	10 - 15
11.2 - 16.0	20 - 25
16.0 - 32.0	30 - 50

[5] Necessary for clast lithological analysis. With respect to roundness, grain size and form for which smaller samples are required, divide the weight by 6.

The following weights are recommended in order to obtain *ca.* 100 clasts

After Gale and Hoare (1992, p.732)

Maximum particle diameter (mm)	Approx. minimum sample size (kg)
2.0 (Till)	1.0
6.0 (Glaciofluvial gravel)	1.0
9.0 (Modern fluvial gravel))	1.0
50.0 (Till)	18.0
50.0 (Glaciofluvial gravel)	23.0
50.0 (Modern fluvial gravel)	31.0

b) *In situ* sampling

More detailed observations than those possible in the field may be required, or the field worker, perhaps for safety reasons etc., may want to gather as much information from a section in as short a time as possible. There are a number of techniques that can collect a segment of the sedimentary succession exposed in a field section, which is then observed in detail back in the laboratory; these include: sediment coring, box coring, lacquer peeling and to some extent micromorphology (e.g. van der Meer *et al.*, 1994). All of these devices do use, or have the option of using, lacquer/resin to fix the sediments. There are a number of different lacquers available on the market that can be used; for more information see Bouma (1969).

Sediment coring is widely used for subsurface sampling, but can also be used for field sections such as slackwater successions, to allow a more detailed examination in the laboratory. A length of drain-pipe pushed into soft sediments can provide a useful and relatively quick core sample. For an account of sedimentary coring see Chapter 11.

Box cores can be taken using metal or plastic containers that are pushed into the sediment and removed. Equipment does exist for this specific purpose, for example, the 'Senckenberg box', and the 'Reineck box' (Collinson and Thompson, 1989). Researchers have the option of fixing the sediment with a lacquer.

Lacquer peels can be taken from section faces (Bouma, 1969). An outline of this technique is found in Collinson and Thompson (1989, p.201): the section should be cleaned and levelled and then sprayed with a dilute solution of lacquer. The surface of the section can be ignited allowing the lacquer to penetrate more deeply if using a lacquer such as acetone, with volatile organic solvents. Several sprayings may be necessary in order to harden the surface layer and additionally, several layers of lacquer-soaked bandage/gauze are plastered onto the surface in order to strengthen it for removal. When the lacquer is completely dry the peel can be removed, using a rigid board for support. The surface can be fixed with further spraying, after excess sediment is carefully removed.

2) *Individual clasts*
There are a number of methods that can be used to select individual clasts (e.g. Wolman, 1954, Kellerhals and Bray, 1971).

a) Grid sampling in which the grid points mark the clasts to be measured.

b) Survey tape or metre rule where a clast is measured at intervals (e.g. 10 cm) across a defined distance (e.g. 2 m).

c) Transect sampling where all the clasts lying under the ruler or string are measured

3.2.4 Architectural Elements

"Architectural methods are based on the two- and three-dimensional mapping of large outcrops, using outcrop profiles" (Miall, 1995, p.75). In situations where only two dimensional outcrops occur, the third dimension can be inferred with careful use of orientation data (based on cross-bedding and bounding surfaces).

Miall (1985) proposed eight basic architectural elements, which he later modified (Miall, 1988, 1995). Although this scheme was originally set-up for fluvial sediments, the following components can be used for all deposits when recording architectural elements in the field (after Miall, 1985).

1) Nature of lower and upper bounding surface: erosional or gradational; planar, irregular, curved (concave-up or convex-up).

2) External geometry: sheet, lens, wedge, scoop, U-shaped fill.

3) Scale: thickness, lateral extent parallel and perpendicular to flow direction.

4) Lithology: lithofacies assemblage and vertical sequence.

5) Internal geometry: nature and disposition of internal bounding surfaces; relationship of bedding and first- to second-order surfaces to these surfaces (parallel, truncated, onlap, downlap).

6) Palaeocurrent patterns: orientation of flow indicators relative to internal bounding surfaces and external form of element.

Field researchers may feel that they need to erect their own classification systems. This is fine as long as it is outlined sufficiently in any publication (see Section 6.5.5).

3.2.5 Facies

Facies are intended to aid the sedimentologist by providing a means by which strata can be classified into units, followed by the detection of any vertical and lateral arrangements of these units. Facies cannot be classified until all the data have been collected and assimilated; this may include laboratory data. The field worker may want to define tentative groupings in the field and verify these later on.

Facies divisions should be made on field evidence of the divider and not on information collected by another worker. These divisions include facies and facies associations (see Sections 4.2.8 and 6.5.5). It is generally better to over subdivide rather than under-subdivide sediments into facies.

With respect to facies coding, since the codes are an additional source of information together with written descriptions and field section drawings, a compromise must be reached in terms of relaying enough information through the codes and keeping them relatively simple to avoid confusion and laborious writings (see Sections 7.5 and 7.6). There are a number of criticisms levelled at prevailing schemes, particularly with respect to interpretative elements. Perhaps the scheme presented in Graham (1988) offers the best compromise (Table 3.2).

3.3 MEASUREMENT OF THE PHYSICAL PROPERTIES OF SEDIMENT

The background, definitions and areas of debate concerning the physical properties of sediments, are outlined in detail in the previous chapter. Individual field studies should take into account and measure a number and preferably all of the properties outlined below.

3.3.1 Sedimentary Texture

3.3.1.1 General texture
Textural groups are presented in Figure 3.3, based on the relative proportions of gravel, sand and mud in sediments which can be used for detailed classification purposes in the

Code	Lithofacies	Sedimentary structures
Gms	Massive, matrix-supported gravel	None
Gm	Massive or crudely bedded gravel	Horizontal bedding, imbrication
Gt	Gravel, stratified	Trough crossbeds
Gp	Gravel, stratified	Planar crossbeds
St	Sand, medium to coarse, may be pebbly	Solitary (theta) or grouped (pi) trough crossbeds
Sp	Sand, medium to coarse, may be pebbly	Solitary (alpha) or or grouped (omicron) planar crossbeds
Sr	Sand, very fine to coarse	Ripple marks of all types
Sh	Sand, very fine to very coarse, may be pebbly	Horizontal lamination, parting or streaming lineation
Sl	Sand, fine	Low angle (10°) crossbeds
Se	Erosional scours with intraclasts	Crude crossbedding
Ss	Sand, fine to coarse, may be pebbly	Broad, shallow scours including eta cross-stratification
Ssc, Shc, Spe	Sand	Analogous to Ss, Sh, Sp
Fl	Sand, silt, mud	Fine lamination, very small ripples
Fsc	Silt, mud	Laminated to massive
Fcf	Mud	Massive with freswater molluscs
Fm	Mud, silt	Massive, dessication tracks
Fr	Silt, mud	Rootlet traces
C	Coal, Carbonaceous mud	Plants, mud films
P	Carbonate	Pedogenic features

Table 3.2. *Lithofacies codes (from Graham, 1988, p. 8, table 2.2). Reprinted by permission of Blackwell Science.*

Code	Lithofacies	Sedimentary structures
Dmm	Matrix-supported, massive	Structureless mud/sand/pebble admixture
Dmm(r)	Dmm with evidence resedimentation	Initially appears structureless but careful cleaning, macro-sectioning, or X-ray photography reveals subtle textural variability and fine structure (e.g. silt or clay stringers with small flow noses). Stratification less than 10% of unit thickness
Dmm (c)	Dmm with evidence of current reworking	Initially appears structureless but careful cleaning, macro-sectioning, or textural analysis reveals fine structures and textural variability produced traction current activity (e.g. isolated ripples or ripple trains). Stratification less than 10% of unit thickness
Dmm (s)	Matrix-supported, massive, sheared	Dense, matrix supported diamict with locally high clast concentrations. Presence of distinctively shaped flat-iron clasts oriented parallel to flow direction, sheared
Dms	Matrix-supported, stratified diamict	Obvious textural differentiation or structure within diamict. Stratification more than 10% of unit thickness
Dms (r)	Dms with evidence of resedimentation	Flow noses frequently present; diamict may contain rafts of deformed silt/clay laminae and abundant silt/stringers and rip-up clasts. May show slight grading. Dms (r) units often have higher clast content than massive units; clast clusters common. Clast fabric random or parallel to bedding. Erosion and incorporation of under-lying material may be evident
Dms (c)	Dms with evidence of current reworking	Diamict often coarse (winnowed) interbedded with sandy, silty and gravelly beds showing evidence of traction current activity (e.g. ripples, trough or planar cross-bedding). May be recorded as Dmm, St, Dms, Sr etc. according to scale of logging. Abundant sandy stringers in diamict. Units may have channelised bases
Dmg	Matrix-supported graded	Diamict exhibits variable vertical grading in either matrix or clast content; may grade into Dcg
Dmg (r)	Dmg - with evidence of resedimentation	Clast imbrication common

field/laboratory. Diamicton (see Sections 6.5.5.3, 8.1 and 10.6.2) refers to unlithified deposits and is defined as "any non-sorted or poorly sorted sediment that contains a wide range of particle sizes," (INQUA Commission on genesis and lithology of Quaternary deposits).

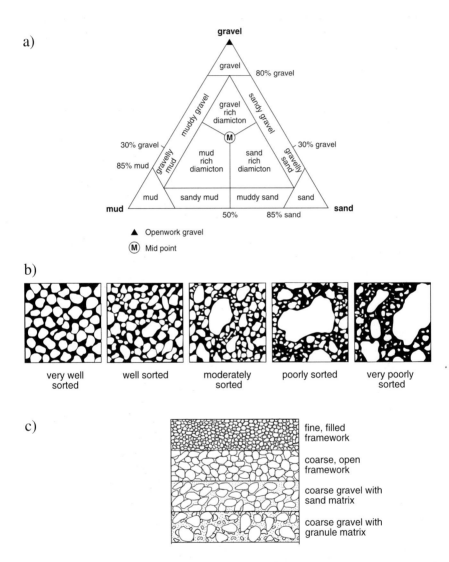

Figure 3.3. *a) Classification of sediment textures, b) Sorting textures and c) Textural terminology.*

3.3.1.2 Grain Size

The standard classification scheme for grain size is the Udden-Wentworth (Figure 3.4). Regarding fine-grained sediments, reference can be made to a visual comparator chart either in the form of simple images or a more realistic comparator, constructed from previously collected samples. Coarse-grained sediments can be measured directly using callipers and a measuring tape for boulder-sized clasts. The researcher may want to determine the maximum grain size, whereby the ten or so largest clasts are measured (e.g. Bluck, 1967, Allen, 1981, Graham, 1988, p.13). The sorting of coarse-grained sediment into grain-

Udden-Wentworth (1922)	phi	mm	Friedman & Sanders (1978)
	-11	2048	V. large — Boulder
	-10	1024	Large / Medium — Boulder
	-9	512	Small
Cobbles	-8	256	
	-7	128	Large / Small — Cobbles
————	-6	64	V. coarse
	-5	32	Coarse
Pebbles	-4	16	Medium — Pebbles
	-3	8	Fine
———— Granules	-2	4	V. fine
V. coarse	-1	2	V. coarse
Coarse	0	1 microns	Coarse
Medium — Sand	1	500	Medium — Sand
Fine	2	250	Fine
V. fine	3	125	V. fine
	4	62	V. coarse
	5	31	Coarse
	6	16	Medium — Silt
	7	8	Fine
———— Clay	8	4	V. fine
	9	2	Clay

Figure 3.4. *Grain-sizes of Udden and Wentworth (1922) and Friedman and Sanders (1978), from McManus, 1988, p. 74, table 3.4). Reprinted by permission of Blackwell Science.*

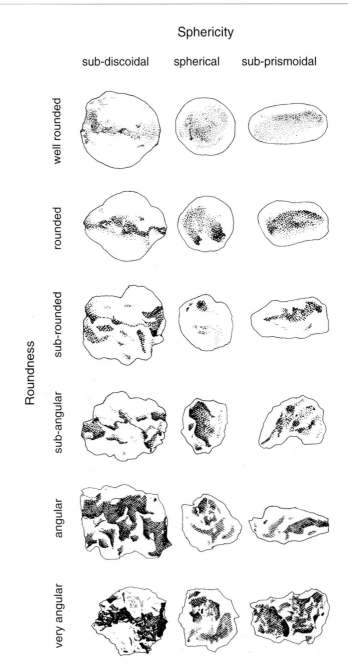

Figure 3.5. Standard image of particle roundness (adapted from Krumbein, 1941 and Powers, 1953).

classes, may be required in the field since some indices (e.g. Kuenen, 1956), require measurement of a specific range of grain sizes. In this instance coarse-grained sieves may be useful. Some workers determine the modal clast size simply by observation in the field or from photographs; however direct measurements are recommended.

3.3.1.3 Grain Morphology
In the field, roundness can be estimated by comparison to a visual comparison chart (Figure 3.5). Some workers do estimate roundness and sometimes shape from photographs; however, direct field measurements are recommended.

1) Mathematical measurements of roundness can be made using for example, the Cailleux (1947) and Kuenen (1956) index. The radius of curvature of the pebble (Appendix 1) and its corresponding intermediate-axis can be recorded in the field.

Kuenen index $= \dfrac{2r}{b}$ Cailleux index $= \dfrac{2r}{L} \times 1000$

r = radius of curvature (mm) r = radius of curvature (mm)
b = b axis (mm) L = length of the longest (a) axis (mm)

2) Usually roundness values are plotted as histograms and/or the roundness is quantified:

a) Powers (1953) assigned values to roundness intervals to enable statistical analysis:

Class	Roundness Indices
Very angular	0.12 - 0.17
Angular	0.17 - 0.25
Sub-angular	0.25 - 0.35
Sub-round	0.35 - 0.49
Round	0.49 - 0.70
Well round	0.70 - 1.00

b) **RA** value which refers to the percentage of clasts which are **very angular** or **angular.**

3) Grain shape can be classified using the ratios between the three axes after Zingg (1935) (Figure 3.6).

4) The C_{40} index can be calculated using: the percentage of clasts with c:a axes ratio of less than or equal to 0.4 (Sneed and Folk, 1958, Benn and Ballantyne, 1993) (Figure 3.7).

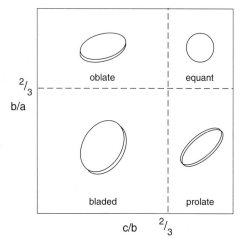

Figure 3.6. *Particle shape (adapted from Zingg, 1935).*

size

3.3.1.4 Micromorphology

A sample of unconsolidated sediment is removed from the field section using a Kubiena tin and knife, and later impregnated with resin before being cut and ground into a thin section, from which the micromorphological structures can be recorded (e.g. Murphy, 1986, Roberts, 1991, van der Meer, 1993). Great care must be taken not to disturb the sample when collecting, and it can take up to one hour just to collect one sample. Label the tin (sample site and orientation w.r.t. section) and secure with tape after the sample has been taken. Remember to note down the point of extraction on the field sketches and/or photograph the site. The samples are then left to dry out in the laboratory for about 6 weeks.

3.3.1.5 Fabrics and Sorting

1) Points to remember when recording fabrics and palaeocurrent directions:

a) record the precise position in the stratigraphic section.

b) record the bed geometry, texture and facies.

c) record the local structural dip.

d) a minimum of 25 measurements at each sample site is necessary to provide statistically significant small samples (Miall, 1990).

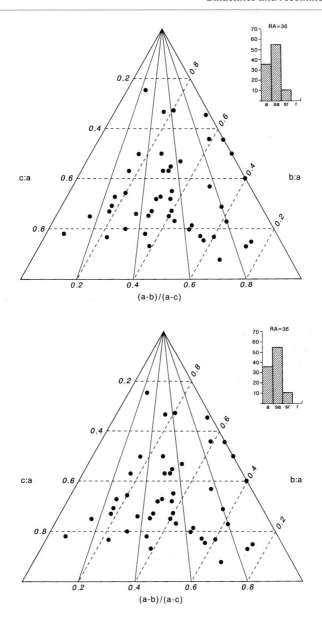

Figure 3.7. *Roundness diagrams from a) supraglacial debris and b) debris-rich basal ice from Matanuska Glacier, Alaska (from Hart, 1995).*

2) Preferred orientation (fabric) of clasts

Clasts and other fragments should have elongation ratios of at least 1.5:1 if they are to be measured regarding preferred orientations. Pebbles may lie parallel or normal to currents/flow direction; check this by looking at other structures.

Fabric is calculated by measuring the direction and dip of the clasts. The dip is defined as the angle between the plane the clast lies in and the horizontal plane, and this is measured using a clinometer (see Figure 2.7). The orientation of the clast is measured with a compass. Fifty clasts are normally measured, although twenty-five clasts are accepted as the minimum amount (Andrews, 1971). Usually the easiest way to measure fabric is to remove the clast from the face and then insert a pencil in its place. Then measure the direction and dip from the pencil.

When taking fabric measurements, the site for investigation must be chosen carefully, since clasts must be taken in a relatively small area to avoid any lateral or vertical facies changes. This is because most environments were active to some degree and depositional processes change quickly in time and space. Care must be taken to ensure that the clasts are removed from the true, i.e. *in situ* deposit and not a modern slump covering the face. It is advisable to clean the surface of the face with a spade before beginning the measurements. The fabric results can be plotted in one of three ways (Figure 3.8):

a) the simplest way is to plot the fabrics on a *Rose diagram*. This is a circular histogram, where the orientation is divided into classes, and the number within each class is recorded as the distance from the centre. This method plots the orientation only and not the dip (see Sections 4.2 and 4.6).

b) the *polar diagram* is more sophisticated than the rose diagram because it gives you information about both orientation and dip. However, it provides no quantitative data on fabric strength. It consists of a circular grid, on which the orientation is plotted around the circle, and the dip is indicated by the distance from the centre.

c) a more detailed method is to plot the points on an *equal-area stereonet*; this is a common technique in structural geology and crystallography and presents the data in three dimensions (Figure 3.8). The orientation and dip of each clast is plotted as lineations (points) on a lower hemisphere equal-area stereonet (Schmidt Net). The data are then contoured at appropriate intervals. Although this method takes longer to construct than the rose or polar diagram, the results are far more valuable because they indicate the statistical significance (or otherwise) of any preferred direction. This is normally done using Kamb's (1949) method. In this method the contouring area (density of points) **A** is chosen so that, if the population lacks a preferred orientation, the number of points are expected to fall within a given area.

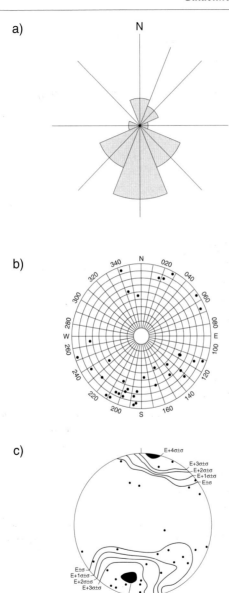

Figure 3.8. *Fabric diagrams a) rose diagram b) polar diagram and c) contoured stereonet, from the Happisburgh diamicton - see Chapter 8, figure 8.7, samples taken from 2600 m along the section and 1 m from the base.*

A is three times the standard deviation of the number of points **N** that will actually fall within the area under random sampling of the population. Observed densities that differ from the expected density **e/A** by more than two or three times the standard deviation σ are then likely to be significant. The observed densities are therefore contoured at intervals of **2σ**, the expected density **e** for no preferred orientation being **3σ**. To calculate the parameters, the following equation is used:

$$\sigma / e = \quad ((1 - A) / NA)^{1/2}$$

where **e = NA**, and $\sigma / e = 1 / 3$ and **A** is expressed as a fraction of the area of the hemisphere.

An additional tool for analysing fabric data is to calculate the strength of the preferred orientation. In recent years, eigenvalue analysis has been used for till deposits (Mark, 1973, Dowdeswell and Sharp, 1986). Eigenvalues (E1, E2 and E3) summarise fabric strength along the three principal directions of clustering and thus provide a quantitative value of fabric strengths. The eigenvalue results are initialised (divided by the number in the sample) so that sites with different numbers of data points can be compared (S1, S2 and S3). A fabric with no preferred orientation (weak fabric) would have equal eigenvalues, whilst a strong fabric would have a high value in the direction of maximum clustering (S1) which is usually the ice movement direction, and a low value in the direction of least clustering (S3) (see Chapter 8).

3) Palaeocurrent analysis

The direction of dip of the foreset (foreset azimuth) as well as the magnitude of the dip should be measured. The dip of the bounding surface of the cross-bed set should be recorded also. The average direction of foreset dip is a measure of the average local flow direction and can be calculated directly from three dimensional exposures using a compass-clinometer. For two dimensional exposures (De Celles *et al.*, 1983), true foreset dip can be calculated by measuring two apparent dips and using a stereographic projection. It is important to appreciate that tectonism, tilting and deformation, may have changed the orientation or shape of the sedimentary structure being measured. The removal of the tilting effect is straight forward (e.g. see Graham, 1988, Collinson and Thompson, 1989, Tucker, 1996).

4) Measurement of cross-stratification:

a) determine whether the structure has been formed by water or wind.

b) is the cross-stratification planar or trough? It is assumed that the inclination of foreset directions is downcurrent in ripples and cross-stratification.

c) if planar cross-bedding the palaeocurrent direction is simply given by the direction of maximum angle of dip. If measuring from a three-dimensional exposure or two-dimensional where a bedding plane surface can be made accessible, then measurement is simple and can be made directly. If a one dimensional exposure, then only the dip of the exposed bedding can be measured. This has obvious disadvantages and possible inaccuracies.

d) with trough cross-stratification it is essential to have a three-dimensional exposure, or one with a visible bedding plane. It is essential that the direction down the trough axis is evident and can be measured. However, DeCelles *et al.* (1983) introduced two new methods of palaeocurrent determination from 2-D and 3-D exposure of trough cross-stratification and presented a useful field scheme.

e) ripples have steeper lee-sides downstream and palaeocurrents can be easily measured. The crest orientation and, if visible, the dip of internal cross-lamination, should be measured in wave-formed ripples.

3.3.1.6 Sediment Colour
A number of contributors commented that their perception of colour is rarely matched by the description given by Munsell's chart, which would suggest that a standard chart is therefore a necessity. Obviously field measurements of colour are more difficult since moisture is known to affect the colour of sediments and cannot be eliminated in the field. Fresh exposures of sediment are important when recording colour, so care must be taken to remove any weathered material. However, the colour of the weathered surface should also be recorded as this provides important information on the mineralogy etc.

3.3.1.7 Clast Lithology
Recommendations and techniques concerning pebble counting were outlined in detail in Bridgland (1986). Any pebbles should be broken with a hammer in order to observe fresh surfaces and small rock comparators can be taken into the field which are made from previously collected rock samples. Bridgland (1986) suggested measuring a minimum of 250-300 clasts for statistical viability and, for more detailed work, a minimum of 500 clasts is recommended (see Section 4.2).

3.3.1.8 Rock Type
At times, the standard rock-type classification schemes are difficult to apply to unlithified Quaternary sediments, especially since lithology is seldom verified at a later date in the laboratory. Laboratory analysis will be easier in the future as new and existing techniques are developed, for example micromorphology of unlithified sediments (see Section 3.3.1.4).

However, lithology is a fundamental component in sedimentology; therefore lithological classifications are encouraged. Rock type can be classified using standard schemes or the classification scheme presented below (Figure 3.9, Table 3.3).

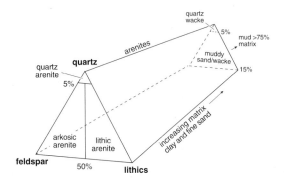

Figure 3.9. *Classification of sandstones (adapted from Folk et al., 1970 and Williams et al., 1982).*

Sedimentary textures		Rock type
Mud absent		Grain*stone*
Mud present	grain-supported	Pack*stone*
	mud-supported	Wacke*stone* (> 10% grains)
		Mud*stone* (<10% grains)
Original components were bound together during deposition		Bound*stone*

Table 3.3. *Classification of **carbonate rocks** based on sedimentary textures (after Dunham, R.J. 1962). This classification system can be used for lithified and carbonate unlithified rocks. The term **stone** can be used but if the reader explicity wishes to avoid using a term associated with lithified sediments, it can be replaced with texture.*

Conglomerates and breccias are coarse siliciclastic sediments which are sometimes referred to variously as rudites, breccio-conglomerates, diamictites, and mixtites (e.g. see Whitten and Brooks 1972, Tucker, 1996). Breccias are generally poorly sorted and commonly consist of angular clasts derived from a restricted source. There are various types of breccia: megabreccia (very large blocks), fault breccia, cemented breccia, volcanic breccia, bone breccia and collapse breccia. Coarse siliciclastics were traditionally classified as being intra/extra formational and named para/ortho conglomerates. However, currently these terms are less popular. Instead conglomerates should be described using a number of criteria:

1) epiclastic (secondary) or pyroclastic (volcanic) (see Chapter 6).

2) fabric: clast-supported (orthoconglomerate) or matrix-supported (paraconglomerate). Clast-supported fabric is also referred to as the gravel framework.

3) matrix volume: a conglomerate with no matrix is described as openwork and a conglomerate with >15% matrix is classified as a diamicton (if the matrix comprises some proportion of mud and sand).

4) matrix type: the term matrix when used in association with conglomerates can refer to any size of sediment that is fine enough to fill the interstitial spaces between the gravel framework (note that matrix when applied to sandstones refers to material less than 0.03 mm).

5) clast lithology and other textures: are the clasts of a single dominant lithology or mixed lithology? sometimes referred to as oligomictic (or monomictic) conglomerates and polymictic conglomerates respectively.

3.3.2 Sedimentary Structures

3.3.2.1 Cycles
Cycles are also referred to as cyclothems and rhythms and in sequence stratigraphy as parasequences (see Sections 2.2.2.1, 2.3). When describing cycles in the field attention should be paid to the internal features of the cycles, the cycle boundaries and the overall stacking patterns of the associated cycles within a field section (see Tucker, 1996). The thickness of cycles and the smaller-scale units within them should be recorded. Key properties to make a note of are:

1) internal changes in the cycle facies: note vertical changes in texture, especially grain-size and rock-type and sedimentary structures.

2) upper and lower boundaries: look for erosive and exposure surfaces; for example, channel-floor lag deposits and soil horizons.

3) stacking patterns: note any variation between the cycles; for example: thickness, facies and nature of the boundaries.

3.3.2.2 Bedsets

A simple descriptive scheme for use in the field that requires minimal classification was introduced by Campbell in 1967, who used the term laminaset and bedset to describe sets of laminae and beds. A bedset *"consists of two or more superposed beds characterized by the same composition, texture and sedimentary structures. This unit is bounded above and below by bedset surfaces"* (Campbell, 1967, p.20). The term 'composite bedset' refers to a group of alternating beds of different composition. Bedsets can be classified by the terminology outlined in Figure 3.10 (see Sections 6.5.5 and 10.3).

Beds and laminae are subdivided based on Ehlers and Blatt (1982) after Ingram (1954) and McKee and Wier (1953): a lamina is a stratum less than 1cm thick, very thin beds (1-5 cm), thin beds (5-10 cm), medium beds (10-60 cm), thick beds (60-120 cm) and very thick beds (>120 cm). Care must be taken to ensure that the vertical cross section of the bed is measured and not simply the exposed bed thickness.

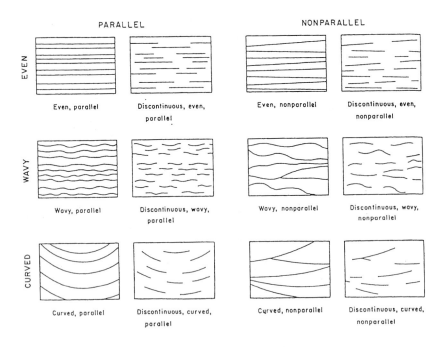

Figure 3.10. *Descriptive terms used for the configuration of bedding, (from Campbell, 1967, p.18, fig. 2). Reprinted by permission of Elsevier Science Publishers, Amsterdam.*

3.3.2.3 Graded Bedding

There are various types of graded bedding (Figure 3.11), although normal and inverse grading are the most common. A distinction should be made as to whether the unit is (see Section 6.4):

1) content graded, where the mean grain size of sediment varies.

2) coarse-tail graded, where only the coarsest grain size varies and the matrix remains homogeneous throughout.

3) gravitationally (or buoyancy) graded, where there is a contrast in density between the largest clasts and the matrix.

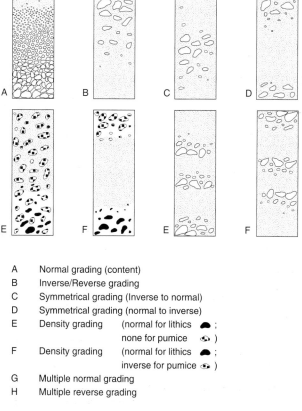

A	Normal grading (content)		
B	Inverse/Reverse grading		
C	Symmetrical grading (Inverse to normal)		
D	Symmetrical grading (normal to inverse)		
E	Density grading	(normal for lithics ● ;	
		none for pumice ◌)	
F	Density grading	(normal for lithics ● ;	
		inverse for pumice ◌)	
G	Multiple normal grading		
H	Multiple reverse grading		

Figure 3.11. *Graded bedding (adapted from Pettijohn et al., 1972).*

3.3.2.4 Cross-Stratification
In the field cross-beds are described and classified according to a number of criteria (Figure 3.12) (see Section 7.2.4).

1) Solitary or grouped: solitary sets are bounded by other types of bedding or cross-bedding, whereas grouped sets are cosets consisting entirely of one cross-bedded type.

2) Scale: forms thinner than 5 cm (Miall, 1990) and < 6 cm (Tucker, 1996) are referred to as ripples, small-scale forms or cross-lamination. Allen (1984) used 4 cm (height) to distinguish between ripples and dunes. Ashley (1990) used 4 cm to distinguish between small and medium subaqueous dunes.

3) Cross-bedding scale: is the bedding large scale, if so is it aeolian, fan or deltaic (Gilbert-type)?

4) Set thickness: measure the set thickness, coset thickness, cross-bed/lamina thickness, maximum angle of dip and direction of dip of cross-strata.

5) Discordant or concordant: foresets are discordant where they terminate at the base of the set and concordant where the cross-beds are parallel to the lower bounding surface.

6) Shape: is the shape of the foresets tabular or trough?

7) Dip-angle: measure the dip-angle of the foreset relative to the bounding surface and the variance between sets.

8) Texture: homogenous cross-beds are those composed of foresets whose mean grain size varies by less than two phi classes. Heterogeneous may contain widely varying grain size, including interbedded sand and gravel/mud.

9) Minor internal structures: note any minor internal structures such as synsedimentary faults and slumps.

10) Mud: are there mud drapes or interbedded mud horizons? If so classify as flaser, lenticular or wavy bedding.

11) Surfaces: look for reactivation surfaces, which represent minor erosion surfaces on bedforms that were abandoned by a decrease in flow strength and then reactivated at some later time.

12) Evidence of wave/tidal currents: herring-bone cross-stratification, mud drapes on the cross-beds, lenses of reversed flow cross-lamination, unidirectional cross-lamination is

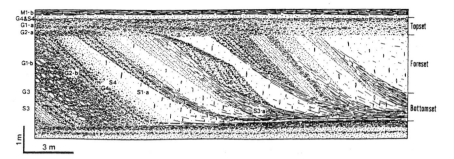

Figure 3.12. *An example of a diagram depicting sediments observed in the field: nested Gilbert-type foresets from the Duksung fan delta. Foreset height ranges from 1 to 10m (from Chough and Hwang, 1997, p. 732, fig. 9). Reprinted by permission of SEPM Society for Sedimentary geology.*

locally opposed, adjacent ripple sets may be dissimilar, bundled and chevron up-building, wavy lower bounding surface.

13) Angle: is the cross-bedding low angle? If so is it antidune or beach lamination?

3.3.2.5 Deformed Bedding

Folded bedding requires sketching of the fold structures in detail, labelling each end of the outcrop with a direction indicator (bearing) and placing a simple scale line by the sketch (e.g. Davis and Reynolds, 1996). Also, the folds should be photographed and the representative strike and dip attitudes of the folded layers measured. For large-scale folding, two or three readings on each limb, and three or four more on the hinge zone are required. For small-scale folding one reading on each limb and two readings in the hinge zone are sufficient. Record the orientations of the axial surface and the hinge line of the fold. If slump folds can be recognised, then the direction of movement can be calculated by determination of the mean downslope direction, using the mean axis method (Woodcock, 1979, Tucker, 1988, p.96). Similarly, faults should be recorded by sketching and photographing the fault. Also make a note of the strike and dip and the displacement along the dip of individual faults. If there are a large number of faults then a representative sample should be measured.

It may be useful to divide highly deformed sections using a grid system, whereby deformation can then be sketched more accurately using graph paper. To calculate the amount of deformation refer to Ramsay and Huber (1983, 1987). It is far easier to calculate the extent of deformation for sections that have undergone compressional deformation as opposed to extensional deformation. To calculate the amount of compressional deformation a balanced cross-section needs to be constructed (Dahlstrom, 1969), an accurate reconstruction of the succession prior to deformation. The sedimentology of the less deformed adjacent sections should be recorded when considering the construction of a balanced section (see Sections 8.2.4, 8.3.3.2).

Changes in length (of a bed) are referred to as 'longitudinal strains' and are recorded by measuring the extension (e) :

$$e = \frac{A'B' - AB}{AB}$$

Where:
A'B' is the deformed length
AB is the original length

A positive 'e' indicates extensional deformation and a negative 'e' indicates compressional deformation.

3.4 STRATIGRAPHIES

Researchers need to familiarise themselves with any stratigraphical scheme that may have already been established in their field area. If a new or revised stratigraphy is to be proposed then it is strongly recommended that the standard schemes are used (Hedberg, 1976, NACSN, 1983, Salvador, 1994). Some salient points are outlined below (see Section 2.3):

1) A **lithostratigraphic unit** should be mappable and defined on the basis of lithological character only, and not on any inference as to mode of origin or age (Bowen, 1978, Whittaker *et al.*, 1991). The formal name of a lithostratigraphic unit is compound, consisting of a geographic name with capital initials, combined with a descriptive lithic term. A newly-established or revised lithostratigraphic unit requires the following: exact location of the type section, unit-distinguishing lithological characteristics, relationship to other units, thickness and relationship to pre-existing classification (Whittaker *et al.* 1991). "*The local succession should be correlated, as far as is possible, with the international standard stratigraphical scale or with regional stratigraphical divisions*" (Whittaker *et al.*, 1991, p.813; for lithostratigraphy examples see Lunkka, 1994, Lubinski *et al.*, 1996 and Chapters 5 and 8).

2) A formal **allostratigraphic unit** must be "mappable at the scale practiced in the region where the unit is defined...genetic interpretation is an inappropriate basis for defining an allostratigraphic unit, but the unit should not be given the geographical name of the surface...inferred time spans, however measured, are not used to define an allostratigraphical unit. However, age relationships may influence the choice of the unit's boundaries...an

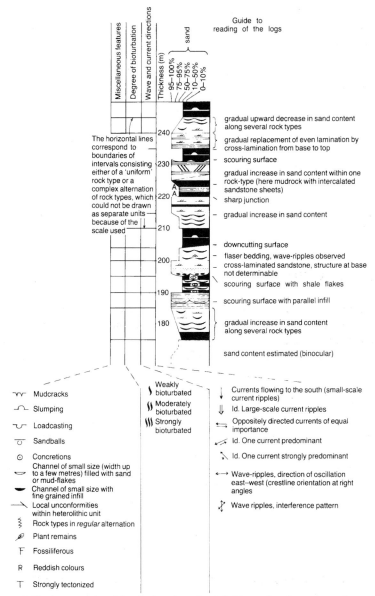

Figure 3.13. *An example of detailed and precise labelling taken from a complex scheme devised specifically for marginal marine sediments by De Raaf, Boersma, Leflef and Kuijpers, from Kuijpers, (1972). (Adapted from Graham, 1988, p.29, fig. 2.22a). Reprinted by permission of Blackwell Science.*

allostratigraphic unit is extended from its type area by tracing the boundary discontinuities or by tracing or matching the deposits between the discontinuities" (NACSN 1983, p.866).

3) A *"Formation should possess some degree of internal lithic homogeneity or distinctive lithic features. It may contain between its upper and lower limits (i) rock of one lithic type, (ii) repetitions of two or more lithic types, or (iii) extreme lithic heterogeneity which in itself may constitute a form of unity when compared to the adjacent rock units"* (NACSN, 1983). Formations are typically 10^1 - 10^3 m thick and may be associated with other adjacent and related formations, to form groups which are typically $> 10^3$ m thick.

4) Formations may be wholly or partially divided into **members** if some useful purpose is served (although some may have no members), and they are characterised by more specific lithological features that distinguish them from adjacent parts of the formation. A member may extend laterally from one formation to another and if there is a distinctive bed within a member this can also be labelled.

3.5 PUBLICATION STAGE

Presentation of field data is vitally important in terms of adding information to existing databases and relaying information to other workers for subsequent interpretations and correlations. One of the prime concerns of keeping descriptive and interpretative elements separated is that other researchers can make their own interpretations using the published descriptions.

3.5.1 Written Descriptions

Published accounts of field-section descriptions tend to fall into the following categories.

1) *Facies:* the largest proportion of publications describe field sections in terms of **facies** (e.g. Smith, 1988, Runkel, 1990, Bentham *et al.*, 1993, Lunkka, 1994, Yoshida 1994, Paim, 1995, Dardis *et al.*, 1995, Bentley, 1996, Hart, 1996, Horton and Schmitt, 1996, McCabe and Haynes, 1996, Boiano, 1997, Bruhn and Walker, 1997, Chamyal *et al.*, 1997, Fitzsimons, 1997, Gibson and Hickin, 1997, Nakayama and Yoshikawa, 1997); **facies associations** (e.g. Kelly and Olsen, 1993, Jennings and Weiner, 1996, McCabe and O'Cofaigh, 1996, Massari, 1996, Bondevik *et al.*, 1997); **facies groups** (e.g. Nakayama, 1996, Smith, 1987). and **facies assemblages** (e.g. Blair and McPherson, 1994). (See Sections 4.2.8, 6.5.5, 7.2.4, 9.3.2 and 10.6.2).

2) *Elements:* architectural elements are mentioned less frequently in the literature (e.g. Miall, 1985, 1988; Platt and Keller, 1992, Davis *et al.*, 1993, Tirsgaard, 1993, Dreyer, 1994, Eriksson *et al.*, 1995, Bruhn and Walker, 1997, Willis, 1997), (see Section 6.5.4).

3) *Stratigraphy:* where possible a number of field sections are described within an established stratigraphic framework (e.g. Hart, 1992, Glasser and Lewis, 1994, Hamblin and Moorlock, 1995, Krzyszkowski, 1995, Maddy *et al.*, 1995, Paul *et al.*, 1995, Gibbard *et al.*, 1997). (see Section 8.3.2).

4) *Units:* other terminologies used to describe and group sediments include: **macroforms** (e.g. Brennand, 1994, Brennand and Shaw, 1996), **complexes** (e.g. Hart *et al.*, 1996), **sedimentary units** (e.g. Bridgland and Harding, 1993) and **sequences** (Willis, 1997).

5) *Morphology:* a number of publications do not specifically identify any architectural elements or facies, but describe morphological units, fluvial terraces for example, in terms of their sediments exposed within field sections (e.g. Lewin *et al.*, 1991, Macklin *et al.*, 1992, Nemec and Postma, 1993, Tipping, 1994, Amorosi *et al.*, 1996, Chen *et al.*, 1996[6], Hereford *et al.*, 1996, Taylor and Lewin, 1996). This approach raises an important issue, namely how to relate sediments investigated in a vertical succession to surface morphologies. Gregory (1985) illustrated the need for such multidisciplinary research in the following image:

"in the period 1950-1980 confronted by a section in a Quaternary deposit there are physical geographers who would devote all their time to the analysis of the sediment characteristics and not look at the space relationships of the feature in which the deposit occurs, and there are others who would deliberate morphological evolution without closely investigating the sediment."

Ideally a publication should refer to facies, facies associations, architectural elements and associated morphologies. If a stratigraphy exists then the publication should make reference to this, but proposals of new or modified stratigraphies are less common and it is strongly recommended that the standard schemes are used (NACSN, 1983, Whittaker *et al.*, 1991).

3.5.2 Figures

Ideally, field-section descriptions should be accompanied by line diagrams, vertical profiles (see Figures 6.8 and 8.3) and photographs in publications (see Blikra and Nemec, 1998). The labelling of diagrams must be precise and detailed and be outlined fully in the key (Figure

---

[6] Palaeochannels.

3.13); also reference must be made to any existing schemes that are used. A number of journals offer the possibility of publishing fold-out line diagrams (e.g. Khan *et al.*, 1997, Zaleha, 1997, Gibson and Hickin, 1997). Colour figures are possible in some journals (e.g. Bondevik *et al.*, 1997, Krainer and Spötl, 1998) but the cost is usually met by the authors. However, it is recognised that difficulties do arise because of scale and spatial considerations and are even more salient when publications impose page-length and plate restrictions. This problem is being increasingly facilitated by the development of computer-based publications via the Web or on CD and there is the potential for even greater interactive material by using video (e.g., Hart and Martinez, 1997, Journal of Glacial Geology and Geomorphology (WWW)*, MTU volcanoes page (WWW)).

3.6 CONCLUSION

The collection of data from field sites has to be systematic and well organised and must follow a few basic rules that have been presented within this chapter. However, it is recognised that each site and scientific project will require its own set of additional specifications. Field sites of Quaternary sedimentology are often temporary and/or present logistical difficulties in terms of access. Therefore, the maximum amount of data needs to be collected in the time available and pre-fieldwork preparation plays an important role. It is also important that any data collected is made available for other scientists to use, from all subject-fields. The importance of storing field data is only just beginning to be recognised and a number of databases have been set up towards this end (e.g. INQUA, palaeohydrology, BGS, NGIS). Perhaps most importantly, this development further emphasises the need for standardisation with respect to stratigraphic field-section descriptions.

* Refer to QRA Web Page for this and other relevant sites: http://www.qra.org.uk
Glacial Geology and Geomorphology: http://www.ggg.qub.ac.uk/ggg/

AGER, D.V. 1993. *The Nature of the Stratigraphical Record*. Third Edition. J.Wiley. 151pp.

ALEXIS, S., ANASTAS, R.W., DALRYMPLE, N.J. and CAMPBELL, S.N. 1997. Cross-stratified calcarenites from New Zealand: subaqueous dunes in a cool-water, Oligo-Miocene seaway. *Sedimentology*, **44**, 869-891.

ALLEN, J.R.L. 1963. The classification of cross-stratified units, with notes on their origin. *Sedimentology*, **2**, 93-114.

ALLEN, J.R.L. 1964. Studies in fluviatile sedimentation: six cyclothems from the Lower Red Sandstone, Anglo-Welsh Basin. *Sedimentology*, **3**, 163-198.

ALLEN, J.R.L. 1965. A review of the origin and characteristics of recent alluvial sediments. *Sedimentology*, **5**, 89-191.

ALLEN, J.R.L. 1966. On bed forms and palaeoecurrents. *Sedimentology*, **6**, 153-190.

ALLEN, J.R.L. 1968. *Current Ripples*. North Holland, Amsterdam.

ALLEN, J.R.L. 1970. A quantitative model of grain size and sedimentary structures in lateral deposits. *Geol. Journal*, **7**, 129-146.

ALLEN, J.R.L. 1982. *Sedimentary structures: their character and physical basis*,Vol. 1-2. Elsevier Pub., 593 pp & 663 pp. (Developments in Sedimentology 30A & B).

ALLEN, J.R.L. 1983. Studies in fluviatile sedimentation: Bars, bar-complexes and sandstone (low sinuosity braided streams) in the Brownstones (L. Devonian), Welsh Borders. *Sedimentary Geology*, **33**, 237-293.

ALLEN, J.R.L. 1984. *Sedimentary Structures: Their Character and Physical Basis*. Unabridged one-volume edition. Elsevier, Amsterdam, 663 pp.

ALLEN, P.A. 1981. Sediments and processes on a small stream-flow dominated, Devonian alluvial fan, Shetland Islands. *Sedimentary Geology*, **29**, 31-66.

AMOROSI, A., FARINA, M., SEVERI, P., PRETI, D., CAPORALE, L. and DI DIO, G. 1996. Genetically related alluvial deposits across active fault zones: an example of alluvial fan-terrace correlation from the upper Quaternary of the southern Po Basin, Italy. *Sedimentary Geology*, **102**, 275-295.

ANDREWS, J.T. 1971. Techniques of till fabric analysis. *British Geomorphological Research Group Technical Bulletin* **No 6**.

ASHLEY, G.M. 1990. Classification of large-scale subaqueous bedforms: a new look at an old problem. *Journal of Sedimentary Petrology*, **60**, 160-172.

ASHLEY, G.M. and HAMILTON, T.D. 1993. Fluvial response to Late Quaternary climatic fluctuations, central Kobuk Valley, northwestern Alaska. *Journal of Sedimentary Petrology*, **63**, no.5, 814-827.

BAILEY, K.D. 1994. *Typologies and Taxanomies, an Introduction to Classification Techniques*. Sage Pub., 94 pp.

BAILEY, R.A., KING HUBER, M. and CURRY, R.R. 1990. The diamicton at Deadman Pass, central Sierra Nevada, California: A residual lag and colluvial deposit, not a 3 Ma glacial till. *Geological Society of America Bulletin*, **102**, 1165-1173.

BARRETT, P.J. 1980. The shape of rock particles. *Sedimentology*, **27**, 291-303.

BEATY, C.B. 1990. Anatomy of a White Mountains debris-flow - the making of an Alluvial fan. *IN*: Rachocki, A.H. and Church, M. (eds), *Alluvial Fans: A Field Approach*, 69-89. John Wiley and Sons Ltd.

BENN, D.I. and BALLANTYNE, C.K. 1993. The description and representation of particle-shape. *Earth Surface Processes and Landforms*, **18**, no.7, 665-672.

BENTHAM, P.A., TALLING, P.J. and BURBANK, D.W. 1993. Braided stream flood-plain deposition in a rapidly aggrading basin: the Escanillan Formation, Spanish Pyrenees. *IN*: Best, J.L. and Bristow, C.S. (eds), *Braided Rivers, Geological Society Special Publication 75*, 177-194.

BENTLEY, M. 1996. The role of lakes in moraine formation, Chilean Lake District. *Earth Surface Processes and Landforms*, **21**, 6, 493-508.

BEST, J.L. 1996. The fluid dynamics of small-scale alluvial bedforms, *IN*: Carling, P.A. and Dawson, M. (eds), *Advances in Fluvial Dynamics and Stratigraphy, 67-125*. Wiley, Chichester.

BLIKRA, L.H. and NEMEC, W. 1998. Postglacial colluvium in western Norway: depositional processes, facies and paleoclimatic record. *Sedimentology*, **45**, 909-959.

BLAIR, T.C. and MCPHERSON, J.G. 1992. The Trollheim alluvial fan and facies model revisited. *Geol. Soc. Amer. Bull.*, **104**, 762-769.

BLATT, H. 1982. *Sedimentary Petrology*. W.H. Freeman and Co, 514 pp.

BLATT, H., MIDDLETON, G. and MURRAY, R. 1980. *Origin of Sedimentary Rocks*. Second edition. Prentice Hall, 782 pp.

BLUCK, B.J. 1967. Deposition of some Upper Old Red Sandstone conglomerates in the Clyde area: a study in the significance of bedding. *Scott. J. Geol.*, **7**, 93-138.

BLUCK, B.J. 1974. Structure and directional properties of some valley sandur deposits in southern Iceland. *Sedimentology*, **21**, 533-554.

BLUCK, B.J. 1979. Structure of coarse grained braided stream alluvium. *Trans. of the Royal Society of Edinburgh*, **70**, 181-221.

BOGGS, S. Jr 1987. *Principles of Sedimentology and Stratigraphy*. Macmillan, 784 pp.

BOIANO, U. 1997. Anatomy of a siliciclastic turbidite basin: the Gorgoglione Flysch, Upper Miocene, southern Italy: physical stratigraphy, sedimentology and sequence-stratigraphic framework. *Sedimentary Geology*, **107**, 231-262.

BONDEVIK, S., SVENDSEN, J.I. and MANGERUD, J. 1997. Tsunami sedimentary facies deposited by the Storegga tsunami in shallow marine basins and coastal lakes, western Norway. *Sedimentology*, **44**, no. 6, 1115-1133.

BOUMA, A.H. 1962. *Sedimentary of Flysch deposits: a Graphic Approach to Facies Interpretation*. Elsevier, Amsterdam.

BOUMA, A.H. 1969. *Methods for the Study of Sedimentary Structures*. New York, Wiley.

BOWEN, D.Q. 1978. *Quaternary Geology "A stratigraphic framework for multidisciplinary work."* William Clawes and Son Ltd, 221 pp.

BRENNAND, T.A. 1994. Macroforms, large bedforms and rythmic sedimentary sequences in subglacial eskers, south-central Ontario: implications for esker genesis and meltwater regime. *Sedimentary Geology*, **91**, 9-55.

BRENNAND, T.A. and SHAW, J. 1996. The Harricana glaciofluvial complex, Abitibi Region, Quebec - its genesis and implications for meltwater regime and ice-sheet dynamics. *Sedimentary Geology*, **102**, no. 3-4, 221-262.

BRIDGE, J.S. 1993. Description and interpretation of fluvial deposits: a critical perspective. *Sedimentology*, **40**, 801-810.

BRIDGE, J.S. 1995. Reply to discussion by Miall, A.D. *Sedimentology*, **42**, 384-389.

BRIDGE, J.S. and MACKEY, S.D. 1993. A revised alluvial stratigraphy model. *IN:* Marzo, M. and Puigdefabregas, C. (eds), *Alluvial Sedimentation*, Special Publication no.17 of the Internat. Assoc. Sedimentology, 319-336. Blackwell Scientific Pub.

BRIDGLAND, D.R. (ed) 1986. *Clast Lithological Analysis*. Quaternary Research Association, Technical Guide, no.3, QRA London.

BRIDGLAND, D.R. 1988. Problems in the application of lithostratigraphic classification to Pleistocene terrace deposits. *Quaternary Newsletter*, **no.55**.

BRIDGLAND, D.R. and HARDING, P. 1993. Preliminary observations at the Kimbridge Farm Quarry, Dunbridge, Hampshire: Early results of a watching brief. *Quaternary Newsletter*, **69**, 1-9.

BRIERLEY, G. 1996. Channel morphology and element assemblages: a constructivist approach to facies modelling. *IN:* Carling, P. A. and Dawson, M.R. (eds), Advances in Fluvial Dynamics and Stratigraphy, 263-299. J. Wiley and sons.

BRITISH STANDARDS INSTITUTION, 1997. *Methods of Sampling and Testing of Mineral Aggregates, Sands and Fillers*. BS812, Part 1. British Standards Institute, London.

BRODZIKOWSKI, K. and VAN LOON, A.J. 1980. Sedimentary deformations in Saalian glaciolimnic deposits near WolstÛw (Zary area, western Poland). *Geologie en Mijnbouw*, **59**, 251-272.

BRODZIKOWSKI, K. and VAN LOON, A.J. 1991. *Glacigenic Sediments: Developments in Sedimentology*, 49. Elsevier Science Pub., 674 pp.

BROOKFIELD, M.E. 1977. The origin of bounding surfaces in ancient aeolian sandstones. *Sedimentology*, **24**, 303-332.

BRUHN, C.H.L. and WALKER, R.G. 1997. Internal architecture and sedimentary evolution of coarse-grained, turbidite channel-levee complexes, Early Eocene Regéncia Canyon, Espírito Santo Basin, Brazil. *Sedimentology*, **44**, 17-46.

CAILLEUX, A. 1947. L'indice d'emousse des grains de Sable et grès. *Revue Geomorph., dyn.,* **3**, 78-87.

CAMPBELL, C.V. 1967. Lamina, laminaset, bed and bedset. *Sedimentology*, **8**, 7-26.

CAMPBELL, C.V. 1976. Reservoir geometry of a fluvial sheet sandstone. *Bull. Am. Ass. Petrol. Geol.,* **60**, 1009-1020.

CARVER, R.E. (ed) 1971. *Proceedures in Sedimentary Petrology*. NewYork.

CAS, R.A.F. and WRIGHT, J.V. 1987. *Volcanic Successions*. Allen and Unwin.

CATT, J.A. 1986. *Soils and Quaternary geology*. Monographs on soil and resources survey no. 11. Oxford Science Publications.

CHAMYAL, L.S., KHADKIKAR, A.S., MALIK, J.N. and MAURYA, D.M. 1997. Sedimentology of the Narmada alluvial fan, western India. *Sedimentary Geology*, **107**, 263-279.

CHEN, W., QINGHAI, X., XIUQING, Z., and YONGHONG, M. 1996. Palaeochannels on the North China Plain: types and distributions. *Geomorphology*, **18**, 5-14.

COLLINSON, J.D. and LEWIN, J. 1983. Introduction. *IN:* Collinson, J.D. and Lewin, J. (eds), *Modern and Ancient Fluvial Systems*, Int. Ass. Sediment. Spec. Pub., 6, 1-4.

COLLINSON, J.D. and THOMPSON, D.B. 1989. *Sedimentary Structures*. Second edition. Allen and Unwin, 194 pp.

CONYBEARE, C.E.B. and CROOK, K.A.W. 1968. Manual of Sedimentary Structures: Department of National Development, Bureau of Mineral Resources. *Geology and Geophysics Bull.*, **102**, 327 pp.

CRITELLI, S., LE PERA, E. and INGERSOLL, R.V. 1997. The effects of source lithology, transport, deposition and sampling scale on the composition of southern Califonian sand. *Sedimentology*, **44**, no. 4, 653-671.

DAHLSTROM, C.D.A. 1969. Balanced cross sections. *Canadian Journal of Earth Sciences*, **6**, 743-757.

DARDIS, G.F., HANVEY, P.M. and COXON, P. 1995. Late-glacial resedimentation of drumlin till facies in Ireland. *IN*: Warren, W. and Croot, D.G. (eds), *Formation and Deformation of Glacial Deposits*. Balkema, Rotterdam.

DAVIS, J.M., LOHMANN, R.C., PHILLIPS, F.M., WILSON, J.L. and LOVE, D.W. 1993. Architecture of the Sierra Ladrones Formation, central New Mexico: depositional controls on the permeability correlation structure. *Geol. Soc. Amer. Bull.*, **105**, 998-1007.

DAVIS, G.H. and REYNOLDS, S.J. 1996. *Structural Geology of Rocks and Regions*. Second edition. J. Wiley and Sons. 776 pp.

DAWSON, M.R. and BRYANT, I.D. 1987. Three-dimensional facies geometry in Pleistocene outwash sediments, Worcestershire U.K. *IN*: Ethridge, F.G., Flores, R.M. and Harvey, M.D. (eds), *Recent Developments in Fluvial Sedimentology*, Society of Economic Palaeontologists and Mineralogists. Spec. Pub., 39, 391-396.

DE CELLES, P.G., LOGFORD, R.P. and SCHWARTZ, R.K. 1983. Two new methods of palaeocurrent determination from trough cross stratification. *Journal Sedimentary Petrology*, **53**, 629-642.

DOWDESWELL, J. A. and SHARP, M. 1986. Characterisation of pebble fabrics in modern terrestrial glacigenic sediments. *Sedimentology*, **33**, 699-711.

DREYER, T. 1994. Architecture of an unconformity-based tidal sandstone unit in the Ametlla Formation, Spanish Pyrenees. *Sedimentary Geology*, **94**, 21-48.

DUCK, R.W. 1994. Application of the QDa-Md method of environmental discriminator to particle size analyses of fine sediments by pipette and SediGraph methods: A comparative study. *Earth Surface Processes and Landforms*, **19**, 525-529.

DUNHAM, R.J. 1962. Classification of carbonate rocks. *Amer. Assoc. Pet. Geol.*, **1**, 108-121.

EHLERS, F.G. and BLATT, H. 1982. *Petrology, Igneous, Sedimentary and Metamorphic*. WH Freeman.

EMERY, D. and MYERS, K.J. 1996. *Sequence Stratigraphy*. Blackwell Science, 297 pp.

ERIKSSON, P.G., RECZKO, B.F.F., BOSHOFF, A.J., SCHREIBER, U.M., VAN DER NEUT, M. and SNYMAN, C.P. 1995. Architectural elements from Lower Proterozoic braid-delta and high energy tidal flat deposits in the Magaliesberg Formation, Transvaal Supergroup, South Africa. *Sedimentary Geology*, **97**, 99-117.

EYLES, N. 1983. *Glacial Geology, an Introduction for Engineers and Earth Scientists*. Pergamon Press, 409 pp.

EYLES, N., EYLES, C.H. and MIALL, A.D. 1983. Lithofacies types and vertical profile models; an alternative approach to the description and environmental interpretation of glacial diamict and diamictite sequences. *Sedimentology*, **30**, 393-410.

EYLES, C.H., EYLES, N. and GOSTIN, V.A. 1998. Facies and allostratigraphy of high-latitude, glacially-influenced marine strata of the Early Permian southern Sydney Basin, Australia. *Sedimentology*, **45**, no. 1, 121-163.

EYLES, N. and MIALL, A.D. 1984. Glacial facies. *IN*: Walker, R.G. (ed), *Facies Models*. Second edition. Geoscience Canada Reprint Series. Airworth Press Ltd., 15-38.

EYNON, G. and WALKER, R.G. 1974. Facies relationships in Pleistocene outwash gravels southern Ontario: a model for bar growth in braided rivers. *Sedimentology*, **21**, 43-70.

FAIRCHILD, I., HENDRY, G., QUEST, M. and TUCKER, M.E. 1988. Chemical analysis of sedimentary rocks. *IN*: Tucker, M.E. (ed), *Techniques in Sedimentology*. Blackwell Scient. Pub., 274-355.

FITZSIMONS, S.J. 1997. Entrainment of glaciomarine sediments and formation of thrust-block moraines at the margin of Sᵇrsdale glacier, east Antartica. *Earth Surface Processes and Landforms*, **22**, 175-187.

FLINT, R.F., SANDERS, J.E. and RODGERS, J. 1960. Diamictite: a substitute term for symmictite. *Geol. Soc. of Amer. Bull.*, **71**, 1809-10.

FOLK, R.L. 1974. *Petrology of Sedimentary Rocks*. Hemphill Pub. Co.

FOLK, R.L., ANDREWS, P.B. and LEWIS, D.W. 1970. Detrital sedimentary rock classification and nomenclature for use in New Zealand. *Newzealand Journal of Geology and Geophysics*, **13**, 937-968.

FRIEDMAN, G.M. 1967. Dynamic processes and statistical parameters compared for size frequency distributions of beach and river sands. *Journal of Sedimentary Petrology*, **37**, no.2, 327-354.

FRIEDMAN, G.M. and SANDERS, J.B. (eds) 1978. *Principles of Sedimentology*. Wiley and sons, New York, 792 pp.

FRIEND, P.F. 1983. Towards the field classification of alluvial architecture or sequence. *IN*: Collinson, J.D. and Lewin, J. (eds), *Modern and Ancient Fluvial Systems*. Int. Ass. Sediment. Spec. Pub. 6, 345-354.

FRIEND, P.F., SLATER, M.J. and WILLIAMS, R.C. 1979. Vertical and lateral buildings of river sandstone bodies, Ebro Basin, Spain. *Journal Geol. Soc. Lond.*, **136**, 39-46.

FROSTICK, L.E. and REID, I. 1980. Sorting mechanisms in coarse-grained alluvial sediments: fresh evidence from a basalt plateau gravel, Kenya. *Journal Geol. Soc. Lond.*, **137**, 431-441.

GALE, S.J. and HOARE, P.G. 1991. *Quaternary Sediments*, 114-121. Belhaven Press, 323 pp.

GALE, S.J. and HOARE, P.G. 1992. Bulk sampling of Coarse Clastic Sediments for Particle-Size Analysis, short communications. *Earth Surface Processes and Landforms*, **17**, no.7, 729-733.

GIBBARD, P.L., BOREHAM, S., ROE, H.M. and BURGER, A.W. 1996. Middle Pleistocene lacustrine deposits in eastern Essex, England and their palaeogeographical implications. *Journal of Quaternary Science*, **11(4)**, 281-298.

GIBSON, J.W. and HICKIN, E.J. 1997. Inter- and supratidal sedimentology of a fjord-head estuary, south-western British Columbia. *Sedimentology*, **44**, no.6, 1031-1053.

GLAISTER, R.P. and NELSON, H.W. 1974. Grain size distributions, an aid in facies identification. *Bulletin of Canadian Petroleum Geology*, **22**, 203-240.

GLASSER, N.F. and LEWIS, S.G. 1994. A report on recent excavation and conservation at Wolston Gravel Pit SSSI, Warwickshire. *Quaternary Newsletter*, **74**, 1-9.

GLEN, J.W., DONNER, J.J. and WEST, R.G. 1957. On the mechanism by which stones in till become orientated. *American Journal of Science*, **255**, 194-205.

GRAHAM, J. 1988. Collection and analysis of field data. *IN*: Tucker, M.E. (ed), *Techniques in sedimentology*, 5-63. Blackwell Scientific Pub.

GREEN, C.P. and MCGREGOR, D.F.M. 1978. Pleistocene gravel trains of the River Thames. *Proc. Geol. Ass.*, **89**, 143-156.

GREEN, C.P., MCGREGOR, D.F.M. and EVANS, A.H. 1982. Development of the Thames drainage system in Early and Middle Pleistocene times. *Geol. Mag.*, **119**, 281-290.

GREGORY, K.J. 1985. *The Nature of Physical Geography*. Edward Arnold, 262 pp.

GRESSLY, A. 1838. Observations geologiques sur le Jura soleurias. Neue Denkschr. Allg Schweiserische Gesellsch ges. *Naturw*, **2**, 1-112.

HAMBLIN, W.K. 1965. Internal structures of "homogenous" sandstones. *Kansas Geol. Survey Bull.*, **175**, pt.1, 1-37.

HAMBLIN, R.J.O. and MOORLOCK, B.S.P. 1995. The Kesgrave and Bytham sands and gravels of eastern Suffolk. *Quaternary Newsletter*, **77**, 17-31.

HAMBREY, M. 1994. *Glacial environments*. UCL press, 296 pp.

HARRISON, P. W. 1957. A clay-till fabric: its character and origin. *Journal of Geology*, **65**, 275-308.

HART, J.K. 1992. Sedimentary environments associated with glacial Lake Trimmingham, Norfolk, U.K. *Boreas*, **21**, 120-135.

HART, J.K. 1995. An investigation of the deforming layer/debris-rich ice continuum, illustrated from three Alaskan Glaciers. *Journal of Glaciology*, **41**, 619-633.

HART, J.K. 1996. Proglacial glaciotectonic deformation associated with glaciolacustrine sedimentation, Lake Pukaki, New Zealand. *Journal of Quaternary Science*, **11(2)**, 149-160.

HART, J.K. and BOULTON, G.S. 1991a. The interrelationship between glaciotectonic deformation and glaciodeposition within the glacial environment. *Quaternary Science Reviews*, **10**, 335-350.

HART, J.K., GANE, F. and WATTS, R.J. 1996. Deforming bed conditions on the Dänischer Wohld Peninsula. *Boreas*, **25**, 101-113.

HART, J.K. and ROBERTS, D.H. 1994. Criteria to distinguish between subglacial glaciotectonic and glaciomarine sedimentation: I - Deformational styles and sedimentology. *Sedimentary Geology*, **91**, 191-214.

HART, J.K. and MARTINEZ, K. 1997. *Glacial Analysis: An Interactive Introduction*. Routledge, London (CD-ROM).

HARVEY, A.M. 1990. Factors influencing Quaternary alluvial fan development in southeast Spain. *IN*: Rachocki, A.H. and Church, M. (eds), *Alluvial Fans: A Field Approach*. Wiley and Sons.

HEDBERG, H.D. (ed) 1976. *International Stratigraphic Guide*. Wiley Interscience, 200 pp.

HELLER, P.L. and PAOLA, C. 1996. Downstream changes in alluvial architecture: an exploration of controls on channel-stacking patterns. *Sedimentary Research*, **66**, no.2, 297-306.

HEREFORD, R., THOMPSON, K.S., BURKE, K.J. and FAIRLEY, H.C. 1996. Tributary debris fans and the late Holocene alluvial chronology of the Colorado River, eastern Grand Canyon, Arizona. *Geol. Soc. Amer. Bull.*, **108**, no.1, 3-19.

HICOCK, S.R., GOFF, J.R., LIAN, O.B. and LITTLE, E.C. 1996. On the interpretation of subglacial till fabric. *Journal of Sedimentary Research*, **66**, no.5, 928-934.

HOLMES, C.D. 1941. Till fabric. *Bull. Geol. Soc. Am.*, **52**, 1299-1354.

HORTON, B.K. and SCHMITT, J.G. 1996. Sedimentology of a lacustrine fan-delta system, Miocene Horse Camp Formation, Nevada, USA. *Sedimentology*, **43**, 133-155.

HUNT, C.B. 1959. Dating of mining camps with tin cans and bottles. *Geotimes*, **3**, 8-10.

HUNTER, L.E., POWELL, R.D. and SMITH, G.W. 1996. Facies architecture and grounding-line fan processes of morainal banks during deglaciation of coastal Maine. *Geol. Soc. of Amer. Bull.*, **108**, 1022-1038.

INGRAM, R.L. 1954. Terminology for the thickness of stratification and parting units in sedimentary rocks. *Geol. Soc. Amer. Bull.*, **65**, 937-938.

JACKSON, R.G.II 1975. Hierarchical attributes and a unifying model of bed forms composed of cohesionless material and produced by shearing flow. *Geol. Soc. Amer. Bull.*, **86**, 1523-11533.

JAMES, L.A. 1991. Quartz concentration as an index of sediment mixing: hydraulic mine tailings in the Sierra Nevada, California. *Geomorphology*, **4**, 125-144.

JENNINGS, A.E. and WEINER, N.J. 1996. Environmental change in eastern Greenland during the last 1300 years: evidence from foraminifera and lithofacies in Nansen Fjord, 68°N. *Holocene*, **6(2)**, 179-191.

JONES, A.P. 1995. *Provenance and Paleaoenvironments of Quaternary Sediments and their Associated Landforms*. Unpub. PhD thesis, U. W. Aberystwyth, 326 pp.

JONES, A.P. and OMOTO, K. submitted. Seismically induced soft-sediment deformation structures (seismites) in Late Pleistocene lacustrine sands and clays: Onikobe and Nakayamadaira Basins, northeastern Japan.

KAMB, W.B. 1959. Ice petrofabric observations from Blue Glacier, Washington, in relation to theory and experiment. *Journal of Geophysical Research*, **64**, 1891-1909.

KARROW, P.F. 1984. Lithofacies types and vertical profile models - an alternative approach to the description and environmental interpretation of glacial diamict and diamictite sequences, discussion. *Sedimentology*, **31**, no.6, 883-884.

KELLERHALS, R. and BRAY, D.I. 1971. Sampling procedures for coarse fluvial sediments. *Jour. Hydraulics Division, Proc. Amer. Soc. Civil Eng.*, 1165-1180.

KELLY, S.B. and OLSEN, H.O. 1993. Terminal fans - a review with reference to Devonian examples. *Sedimentary Geology*, **85**, 339-374.

KEMMIS, T.J. and HALLBERG, T.J. 1984. Lithofacies types and vertical profile models; an alternative approach to the description and environmental interpretation of glacial diamictite sequences, discussion. *Sedimentology*, **31**, 886-90.

KHAN, I.A., BRIDGE, J.S., KAPPELMAN, J. and WILSON, R. 1997. Evolution of Miocene fluvial environments, eastern Potwar plateau, northern Pakistan. *Sedimentology*, **44**, no. 2, 221-253.

KING, C.A.M. and BUCKLEY, J.T. 1968. The analysis of stone size and shape in arctic environments. *Journal of Sedimentary Petrology*, **38**, 200-214.

KONERT, M. and VANDENBERGHE, J. 1997. Comparison of laser grain size analysis with pipette and sieve analysis: a solution for the underestimation of the clay fraction. *Sedimentology*, **44**, no.4, 523-535.

KRAINER, K. and SP(TL, C. 1998. Abiogenic silica layers within a fluvio-lacustrine succession, Bolzano Volcanic Complex, northern Italy: a Permian analogue for Magadi-type cherts? *Sedimentology*, **45**, 489-505.

KRINSLEY, D.H. and DOORNKAMP, J.C. 1973. *Atlas of Quartz Sand Surface Textures*. Cambridge: Cambridge Univ. Press.

KRÜGER, J. 1994. Glacial processes, sediments, landforms and stratigraphy in the terminus region of Myrdalsjökull, Iceland. *Folia Geographica Danica*, **21**, 1-233.

KRUMBEIN, W.C. 1934. Size frequency distribution of sediments. *Journal of Sedimentary Petrology*, **4**, 65-77.

KRUMBEIN, W.C. 1941. Measurement and geological significance of shape and roundness of sedimentary particles. *Journal of Sedimentary Petrology*, **11**, 64-72.

KRUMBEIN, W.C. and PETTIJOHN, F.J. 1938. *Manual of Sedimentary Petrology*. Appleton-Century-Crofts-Inc. New York.

KRUMBEIN, W.C. and TISDEL, F.W. 1940. Size distributions of source rocks of sediments. *Am. Jour. Sc.*, **238**, no.4, 296-305.

KRZYSZKOWSKI, D. 1995. An outline of the Pleistocene stratigraphy of the KleszczÛw Graben, BelchatÛw outcrop, central Poland. *Quaternary Science Reviews*, **14**, 61-83.

KUENEN, P.D. 1956. Experimental abrasion of pebbles: Rolling by current. *Journal of Geology*, **64**, 336-368.

KUIJPERS, E.P. 1972. *Upper Devonian tidal deposits and associated sediments south and south-west of Kinsale (Southern Ireland)*. PhD thesis, University of Utrecht.

LEEDER, M.R. 1983. *Sedimentology: Process and Product*. Allen and Unwin, 344 pp.

LEWIN, J., DAVIES, B.E. and WOLFENDEN, P.J. 1977. Interactions between channel change and historic mining sediments. *IN*: Gregory, K.J. (ed), *River Channel Changes*. BGRG pub., 353-367. Wiley and Sons.

LEWIN, J. and MACKLIN, M.G. 1986. Metal mining and floodplain sedimentation in Britain. *IN*: Gardiner, V. (ed), *International geomorphology*, part I, 977-987.

LEWIN, J., MACKLIN, M.G. and WOODWARD, J.C. 1991. Late Quaternary fluvial sedimentation in the Voidomatis Basin, Epirus, northwest Greece. *Quaternary Research*, **35**, 103-115.

LINDHOLM, R. 1987. *A Practical Approach to Sedimentology*. Allen and Unwin, 276 pp.

LUBINSKI, D.J., KORSUN, S., POLYAK, L., FORMAN, S.L., LEHMAN, S.J. and

LUNKKA, J.P. 1994. Sedimentation and lithostratigraphy of the North Sea Drift and Lowestoft Till Formations in the coastal cliffs of northeast Norfolk, England. *Journal of Quaternary Science*, **9(3)**, 209-233.

MACKLIN, M.G. and LEWIN, J. 1986. Terraced fills of Pleistocene and Holocene age in the Rheidol valley, Wales. *Journal of Quaternary Science*, **1**, 21-34.

MACKLIN, M.G., RUMSBY, B.T. and HEAP, T. 1992. Flood alluviation and entrenchment: Holocene valley floor development and transformation in the British uplands. *Geol. Soc. Amer. Bull.*, **104**, 631-643.

MADDY, D., GREEN, C.P., LEWIS, S.G. and BOWEN, D.Q. 1995. Pleistocene geology of the Lower Severn Valley U.K. *Quaternary Science Reviews*, **14**, 209-222.

MAIZELS, J.K. 1987. Large-scale flood deposits associated with the formation of coarse-grained, braided terrace sequence. *IN*: Ethridge, E.G., Flores, R.M. and Harvey, M.D. (eds), *Recent Developments in Fluvial Sedimentology, Contributions from the Third International Fluvial Sedimentology Conference*, Soc. Econ. Pal. Mineral. Spec. Pub. no.39, 135-14.

MALTMAN, A. 1984. On the term 'soft-sediment deformation'. *Journal of Structural Geology*, **6**, 589-592.

MARK, D.M. 1973. Analysis of axial orientation data, including till fabrics. *Bull. Geol. Soc. Amer.*, **84**, 1369-1374.

MARTINI, I.P. and BROOKFIELD, M.E. 1995. Sequence analysis of Upper Pleistocene (Wisconsinan) glaciolacustrine deposits of the north-shore bluffs of Lake Ontario, Canada. *Journal of Sedimentary Research*, **B65**, 388-400.

MARZO, M., NIJMAN, W. and PUIGDEFABREGAS, C. 1988. Architecture of the Castissent fluvial sheet sandstones, Eocene, South Pyrenees, Spain. *Sedimentology*, **35**, 719-738.

MASSARI, F. 1996. Upper-flow regime stratification types on steep-face, coarse grained Gilbert-type progradational wedges (Pleistocene, southern Italy). *Journal of Sedimentary Research*, **66**, 364-375.

MCCABE, A.M. and HAYNES, J.R. 1996. A Late Pleistocene intertidal boulder pavement from an isostatically emergent coastline, Dundalk Bay, Eastern Ireland. *Earth Surface Processes and Landforms*, **21**, 6, 555-572.

MCCABE, A.M. and O'COFAIGH, C. 1996. Upper Pleistocene facies sequences and relative sea-level trends along the south coast of Ireland. *Journal of Sedimentary Research*, Section B-Stratigraphy and Global Studies, **66**, 376-390.

MCGREGOR, D.F.M. and GREEN, C.P. 1983. Post-depositional modification of Pleistocene catchment changes. *Boreas*, **12**, 23-33.

MCKEE, E.D. and WEIR, G.W. 1953. Terminology for stratification and cross-stratification in sedimentary rocks. *Geol. Soc. Amer. Bull.*, **64**, 381-390.

MCMANUS, J. 1988. Grain size determination and interpretation. *IN*: Tucker, M.E. (ed), *Techniques in Sedimentology*, 63-86. Blackwell Scientific Pub.

MENZIES, J. and MALTMAN, A.J. 1992. Microstructures in diamictons-evidence of subglacial bed conditions. *Geomorphology*, **6**, 27-40.

MIALL, A.D. 1977. The braided river depositional environment. *Earth Science Reviews*, **3**, 1-62.

MIALL, A.D. 1978. Lithofacies types and vertical profile models in braided river deposits: A summary. *IN*: Miall, A.D. (ed), *Fluvial sedimentology*: Can. Soc. Petrol. Geol. mem. 5, 597-604.

MIALL, A.D. 1985. Architectural-element analysis: a new method of facies analysis applied to fluvial deposits. *Earth Science Reviews*, **22**, 261-308.

MIALL, A.D. 1988. Reservoir heterogeneities in fluvial sandstones: lessons from outcrop studies. *American Association of Petroleum Geologists Bulletin*, **72**, no.6, 682-697.

MIALL, A.D. 1990. *Principles of Sedimentary Basin Analysis*. Second edition. Springer-Verlag, 667 pp.

MIALL, A.D. 1995. Description and interpretation of fluvial deposits: a critical perspective. *Sedimentology*, **42**, 379-389.

MIALL, A.D. 1996. *The Geology of Fluvial Deposits: Sedimentary Facies, Basin Analysis, and Petroleum Geology*. Springer-Verlag Berlin, 582 pp.

MIALL, A.D. 1997. *The Geology of Stratigraphic Sequences*. Springer-Verlag, Berlin, 433pp.

MOHINDRA, R. and BAGATI, T.N. 1996. Seismically induced soft-sediment deformation structures (seismites) around Sumdo in the lower Spiti valley (Tethys Himalya). *Sedimentary Geology*, **101**, 69-83.

MURPHY, C.P. 1986. *Thin Section Preparation of Soils and Sediments*. A B Academic Publishers, Berkhamsted.

NAKAYAMA, K. 1996. Depositional models for fluvial sediments in an intra-arc basin: an example from the Upper Cenozoic Tokai Group in Japan. *Sedimentary Geology*, **101**, 193-211.

NAKAYAMA, K. and YOSHIKAWA, S. 1997. Depositional processes of primary to reworked volcaniclastics on an alluvial plain; an example from the Lower Pliocene Ohta tephra bed of the Tokai Group, central Japan. *Sedimentary Geology*, **107**, 211-229.

NEMEC, W. and POSTMA, G. 1993. *Quaternary alluvial fans in southwestern Crete: sedimentation processes and geomorphic evolution*. Spec. Pub. Int. Ass. Sediment., 17, 235-276.

NORTH, C.P. 1996. The prediction and modelling of subsurface fluvial stratigraphy. *IN*: Carling, P.A. and Dawson, M.R. (eds), *Advances in Fluvial Dynamics and Stratigraphy*, 395-508. J. Wiley and Sons.

NORTH AMERICAN COMMISSION ON STRATIGRAPHIC NOMENCLATURE, 1983. North American Stratigraphic Code. *American Association of Petroleum Geologists Bulletin*, **67**, 841-875.

OWEN, G. 1995. Soft-sediment deformation in Upper Proterozoic Torridonian sandstones (Applecross Formation) at Torridon, northwest Scotland. *Journal of Sedimentary Research*, **A65**, no.3, 495-504.

PAIM, P.S.G. 1995. Alluvial palaeogeography of the Guaritas depositional sequence of southern Brazil. *Spec. Pub. Int. Ass. Sediment.*, **22**, 3-16.

PAUL, M.A., PEACOCK, J.D. and BARRAS, B.F. 1995. Flandrian Stratigraphy and sedimentation in the Bothkennar-Grangemouth area, Scotland. *Quaternary Newsletter*, **75**, 22-35.

PEAKALL, J., ASHWORTH, P. and BEST, J. 1996. Physical Modelling in Fluvial Geomorphology: Principles, Applications and Unresolved Issues. *IN*: Rhoads, B.L.

and Thorn, C.E. (eds), The Scientific Nature of Geomorphology: Proceedings of the 27th Binghamton Symposium in Geomorphology, 221-253. J. Wiley and Sons Ltd.

PEART, M.R. and WALLING, D.E. 1982. Fingerprinting sediment sources: the example of a small drainage basin in Devon, U.K. *IN: Drainage Basin Sediment Delivery Proceedings of the Albuquerque Symposium, IAHS Pub.*, 159, 41-55.

PENCK, A. and BRUCKNER, E. 1901-1909. *Die Alpen im Eiszeitalter, Tauchnitz*, Leipzig.

PETTIJOHN, F.J. 1957. *Sedimentary Rocks.* Second edition. Harper and Brothers.

PETTIJOHN, F.J. and POTTER, P.E. 1964. *Atlas and glossary of primary sedimentary structures.* Springer-Verlag. New York 370 pp.

PLATT, N.H. and KELLER, B. 1992. Distal alluvial deposits in a foreland basin setting - the Lower Freshwater Molasse (Lower Miocene), Switzerland: sedimentology, architecture and palaeosols. *Sedimentology*, **39**, 545-565.

POSAMENTIER, H.W. and JAMES, D.P. 1993. An overview of sequence-stratigraphic concepts: uses and abuses. *IN*: Posamentier, H.W., Summerhayes, C.P., Haq, B.U. and Allen, G.P. (eds), *Sequence stratigraphy and facies associations.* Spec. Pub. Int. Ass. Sediment., 18, 3-18. Blackwell Sci. Pub.

POSTMA, G. 1990. Depositional architecture and facies of river and fan deltas: a synthesis. *IN*: Colella, A. and Prior, D.B. (eds), *Coarse Grained Deltas. Spec. Pub. Int. Ass. Sediment.*, 10, 13-27.

POWERS, M.C. 1953. A new roundness scale for sedimentary particles. *Journal of Sedimentary Petrology*, **23**, 117-119.

RAMOS, A., SOPEÒA, A. and PEREZ-ARLUCEA, M. 1986. Evolution of Buntsandstein fluvial sedimentation in the northwest Iberian Ranges (central Spain). *Journal of Sedimentary Petrology*, **56**, 862-875.

RAMSAY and HUBER, M.I. 1983. *The Techniques of Modern Structural Geology*, Vol. I. Academic Press, London.

RAMSAY and HUBER, M.I. 1987. *The Techniques of Modern Structural Geology*, Vol. II. Academic Press, London.

READING, H.G. 1986. *Sedimentary Environments and Facies.* Second edition. Blackwell Scientific Pub. (*see also* the third edition).

REINECK, H.E. and SINGH, I.B. 1980. *Depositional sedimentary environments.* Second edition. Springer-Verlag New York, 223 pp.

RHEE, C.W., JO, H.R. and CHOUGH, S.K. 1998. An allostratigraphic approach to a non-marine basin: the north-western part of Cretaceous Kyongsang Basin, SE Korea. *Sedimentology*, **45**, no.3, 449-473.

RICCI LUCCHI, F. 1995. *Sedimentographica: Photographic Atlas of Sedimentary Structures.* Second, english edition. Columbia Uni. Press, 255 pp.

ROBERTS, D.H. 1991. Characterisation of microscale features of glacial sediments. *Quaternary Newsletter*, **68**, 6-8.

RUNDEL, A. 1985. The mechanism of braiding. *Zeit. für Geomorph.*, **55**, 1-13.

RUNKEL, A.C. 1990. Lateral and temporal changes in volcanogenic sedimentation; analysis of two Eocene sedimentary aprons, big bend region, Texas. *Journal of Sedimentary Petrology*, **60**, 747-760.

RUSNAK, G.A. 1975. The orientation of sand grains under conditions of "unidirectional" fluid flow. 1. Theory and experiment. *Journal of Geology*, **65**, 384-409.

RYDER, J.M. and CHURCH, M. 1986. The Lillooet terraces of Fraser river: a palaeoenvironmental enquiry. *Canadian Journal of Earth Science*, **23**, 869-884.

SALVADOR, A. (ed) 1994. *International Stratigraphic Guide.* Second edition, IUGS and Geological Society of America, 214 pp.

SELLEY, R.C. 1988. *Applied sedimentology.* Academic press, 446 pp.

SHENNAN, I. et al., 1996. Tidal marsh stratigraphy and the earthquake deformation cycle I: A 5000-year record in Washington, USA. *Quaternary Science Reviews*, **15**, 1-37.

SIMS, J.D. 1973. Earth-quake induced structures in sediments of Van Norman Lake, San Fernando, California. *Science*, **182**, 161-163.

SMART, P.L. and FRANCES, P.D. (eds) 1991. *Quaternary Dating Methods - a Users Guide.* Quaternary Research Association, Technical Guide no. 4. QRA Cambridge.

SMITH, G.A. 1987. The influence of explosive volcanism on fluvial sedimentation: the Deschutes Formation (Neogene) in central Oregon. *Journal of Sedimentary Petrology*, **57**, 613-629.

SMITH, G.A. 1988. Sedimentology of proximal to distal volcaniclastics dispersed across an active foldbelt: Ellensberg Formation (late Miocene), central Washington. *Sedimentology*, **35**, 953-977.

SNEED, E.D. and FOLK, R.L. 1958. Pebbles in the lower Colorado river, Texas - A study in particle morphogenesis. *Journal of Geology*, **66**, 114-150.

SPARKS, R.S.J. 1976. Grain size variations in ignimbrites and implications for the transport of pyroclastic flows. *Sedimentology*, **2**, 147-188.

TAIRA, A., BYRNE, T. and ASHI, J. 1992. *Photographic Atlas of an Accretionary Prism: Geological structures of the Shimanto Belt, Japan.* University of Tokyo Press.

TAYLOR, M.P. and LEWIN, J. 1996. River behaviour and Holocene alluviation: the River Severn at Welshpool, mid-Wales, U.K. *Earth Surface Processes and Landforms*, **21**, 77-91.

TEICHERT, C. 1958. Concepts of facies. *Bulletin of the American Association of Petroleum Geologists*, **42**, no.11, 2718-2744.

THOMAS, G.S.P., SUMMERS, A.J. and DACKOMBE, R.V. 1982. The Late Quaternary deposits of the middle Dyfi Valley, Wales. *Geological Journal*, **17**, 297-309.

THOMAS, R.G., SMITH, D.G., WOOD, J.M., VISSER, J., CALVERLEY, E.A. and KOSTER, E.H. 1987. Inclined heterolithic stratification-terminology, description, interpretation and significance. *Sedimentary Geology*, **53**, 123-179.

TIPPING, R. 1994. Fluvial chronology and valley floor evolution of the upper Bowmont valley, Borders Region, Scotland. *Earth Surface Processes and Landforms*, **19**, 641-657.

TIRSGAARD, H. 1993. The architecture of Precambrian high energy tidal channel deposits: an example from the Lyell Land Group (Eleonore Bay Supergroup), northeast Greenland. *Sedimentary Geology*, **88**, 137-152.

TODD, S.P. 1996. Process deduction from sedimentary structures. *IN*: Carling, P.A. and Dawson, M.R. (eds), *Advances in Fluvial Dynamics and Stratigraphy*. 299-350. J. Wiley and Sons.

TREWIN, N. 1988. Use of the scanning electron microscope in sedimentology. *IN*: Tucker, M.E. (ed), *Techniques in sedimentology*, 229-274. Blackwell Sci. Pub.

TROELS-SMITH, J. 1955. Characterization of unconsolidated sediments. *Danmarks Geologiske Undersøgelse*, Series IV, **3**, 38-73.

TUCKER, M. 1988. Introduction. *IN*: Tucker, M.E. (ed), *Techniques in Sedimentology, 1-5*. Blackwell Scientific Pub.

TUCKER, M.E. 1996. *Sedimentary rocks in the field*. Second edition. J. Wiley and Sons, 153 pp.

VAN DER MEER, J.J.M. 1993. Microscopic evidence of subglacial deformation. *Quaternary Science Reviews*, **12**, 553-587.

VAN DER MEER, J.J.M., RABASSA, J.O. and EVENSON, E.B. 1992. Micromorphological aspects of glaciolacustrine sediments in northern Patagonia, Argentina. *Journal of Quaternary Science*, **7(1)**, 31-44.

VAN DER MEER, J.J.M., VERBERS, A.L.L.M. and WARREN, W.P. 1994. The micromorphological character of the Ballycroneen Formation (Irish Sea Till). A first assessment. *IN*: Warren, W.P. and Croot, D.G. (eds), *Formation and Deformation of Glacial Deposits*. Balkema, Rotterdam.

VAN WAGONER, J.C.. MITCHUM, R.M., CAMPION, K.M. and RAHMANIAN, V.D. 1990. Siliciclastic Sequence Stratigraphy from Well Logs, Core and Outcrop. AAPG Methods in Exploration Series 7, 55 pp.

VISHER, G.S. 1969. Grain size distributions and depositional processes. *Journal of Sedimentary Petrology*, **39**, 1074-1106.

WADELL, H.A. 1932. Volume, shape and roundness of rock-particles. *Journal of Geology*, **40**, 443-451.

WALKER, R.G. (ed) 1984a. *Facies models*. Second edition. Geoscience Canada, reprint series, Airworth Press Ltd.

WALKER, R.G. 1984b. Shelf and shallow marine sands. *IN*: Walker R.G. (ed), *Facies models*. Second edition, 141-169. Geoscience Canada, reprint series, Airworth Press Ltd.

WALKER, R.G. 1995. An incised valley in the Cardium Formation at Rincus, Alberta: reinterpretation as an estuary fill, 47-74. *Spec. Pub. Int. Ass. Sediment.* 22.

WALTHER, J. 1894. Einleitung in die Geologie als Historische Wissenschaft, Bd. 3. Lithogenesis der Gegenwart, 535-1055. Fischer Verlag, Jena.

WEIMER, R.J., HOWARD, J.D. and LINDSAY, D.R. 1982. Tidal flats and associated tidal channels. *IN*: Scholle, P.A. and Spearing, D. (eds), Sandstone Depositional Environments, 191-245. The American Association of Petroleum Geologists, Tulsa, Oklahoma.

WELLER, J.M. 1958. Stratigraphic facies differentiation and nomenclature. *Bulletin American Association of Petroleum Geologists*, **42**, no.3, 609-639.

WENTWORTH, C.K. 1919. A laboratory and field study of cobble abrasion. *Journal of Geology*, **27**, 507-521.

WENTWORTH, C.K. 1922. A scale of grade and class terms for clastic sediments. *Journal of Geology*, **30**, 377-392.

WHITTAKER, A., COPE, J.W.C., COWIE, J.W., GIBBONS, W., HAILWOOD, E.A., HOUSE, M.R., JENKINS, D.G., RAWSON, P.F., RUSHTON, A.W.A., SMITH, D.G., THOMAS, A.T. and WIMBLEDON, W.A. 1991. A guide to stratigraphical procedure. *Journal of the Geology Society of London*, **148**, 813-824.

WHITTEN, D.G.A. and BROOKS, J.R.V. 1972. *The Penguin Dictionary of Geology*. Penguin Books.

WILGUS, C.K., HASTING, B.S., KENDALL, G.G.S.C., POSAMENTIER, H.W., ROSS, C.A. and VAN WAGONER, J.C. 1988. *Sea-level Changes and Integrated Approach*. SEPM Special Publication 42, pp. 407.

WILLIAMS, H., TURNER, F.J. and GILBERT, C.M. 1982. *Petrography, an Introduction to the Study of Rocks in Thin Sections*. Second edition. W.H. Freeman, San Francisco, 626 pp.

WILLIS, B.J. 1997. Architecture of fluvial-dominated Valley-fill deposits in the Cretaceous Fall River Formation. *Sedimentology*, **44**, no.4, 735-757.

WOLMAN, M.G. 1954. A method of sampling coarse river bed materials. *American Geophysical Union Transactions*, **35**, 951-956.

WOODCOCK, N.H. 1979. The use of slump folds as palaeoslope orientation estimators. *Sedimentology*, **26**, 83-99.

YOSHIDA, F. 1994. Interaction between alluvial fan sedimentation, thrusting, and sea-level changes: an example from the Komeno Formation (Early Pleistocene), southwest Japan. *Sedimentary Geology*, **92**, 97-115.

ZAHELA, M.J. 1997. Intra- and extrabasinal controls on fluvial deposition in the Miocene Indo-Gangetic foreland basin, northern Pakistan. *Sedimentology*, **44**, no. 2, 369-391.

ZINGG, T.H. 1935. Beiträge zur Schotteranalyse: Schweiz. *Mineralog. Petrog. Mitt.*, **15**, 39-140.

PART II

Chapter 4

ALLUVIAL FANS: A CASE STUDY FROM THE SORBAS BASIN, SOUTHEAST SPAIN

Anne E. Mather

4.1 INTRODUCTION

Alluvial fans are cone shaped depositional landforms which are found under a wide variety of climate zones and tectonic settings. They develop where confined streams emerge from mountain catchments into a zone of reduced stream power. This commonly occurs at a mountain front, intermontane basin or valley junction (Harvey, 1997). Fan development requires a high rate of sediment supply and this is common in mountainous catchments, particularly in semi-arid settings where sparse vegetation, intense rainstorms and abundant overland flow are common characteristics (Harvey, 1997). The alluvial fan system essentially comprises a sediment source area (the catchment) and a sediment dispersal and storage area (the fan). Thus, as long as the fan remains untrenched, the alluvial fan can store valuable palaeoenvironmental information about sedimentary processes, climate and catchment area characteristics, even where the latter is no longer attached through erosion or deformation.

Alluvial fans have recently formed the focus of dedicated volumes (e.g. Rachocki and Church, 1991) and conferences. There are many on-going debates in fan studies (see for example Lecce, 1990) but one current research concern appears to be what actually constitutes an alluvial fan and how to classify them (see discussions in Blair and McPherson, 1994b), with classifications being taken to extremes of complexity (Blair and McPherson, 1995). Not all alluvial fans will fit neatly into a classification and such classifications may be particularly difficult to apply to more ancient sediments where morphological information has been lost. Thus simple descriptions which describe the dominant processes which constructed the alluvial fan such as 'fluvial dominated', 'debris flow dominated' or 'mixed' (a combination of fluvial and debris flow processes) are more appropriate (e.g. Harvey, 1984).

i) *Fluvial Processes and Fans*: the transport of sediment by running water in the alluvial fan environment may occur i) in clearly defined channels, ii) in wide, ill-defined channels or iii) as unconfined flows (sheetfloods). Fluvial transport of sediment will dominate where there is a high water to sediment ratio, leading to transport of material as a Newtonian fluid. This will lead to the deposition of typically imbricated, sorted sediments (e.g. Nemec and Steel, 1984, Costa, 1988). Where sediment is of a suitable calibre and water depths are sufficient (i.e. in confined areas of flow), transverse (Smith, 1974) and lateral (Bluck, 1974) bars may develop. Elsewhere, particularly in less confined areas of flow, sediment movement will be predominantly as diffuse gravel sheets or longitudinal (Smith, 1974) bars. Fluvial processes will be encouraged where the supply of fine material is limited, typically in larger catchments where stream-side supply of sediment dominates. This indicates that fluvially dominated fans may be restricted to certain geological types such as high grade metamorphics (e.g. Harvey, 1984, 1987). In addition this means that the criteria for fluvial processes will become increasingly met with the progressive maturation of the catchment (i.e. as weathered slope material is progressively exhausted and larger, more open, lower relief catchments develop). In addition the spatial extent of fluvial deposits within the alluvial fan dispersal area will be greater than for debris flows as the potential transportation distance for the fluvial flows will be greater, but the gradient needed to maintain transport will be less. Thus fluvial dominated fans will tend to be larger and possess a gentler apex to toe gradient than their debris flow dominated counterparts (Harvey, 1987, 1990).

ii) *Debris Flow Processes and Fans*: the transportation and deposition of sediment by debris flow processes may be i) confined within channels or ii) as an unconfined lobe. Debris flows behave as a plastic (Costa, 1988) and may be channelised with levees in the upper parts of the fans, and more unconfined and lobate in the more distal parts of the fans. The types of flow will be determined by the water to sediment ratio and the type of fine sediment available. Essentially the flows can be i) cohesive or ii) non cohesive depending on the shear strength of the flow resulting from the sediment concentration (typically 70-90% by volume, Costa, 1988) and nature of fines. The resulting deposits of debris flows (see Section 6.5.5.3) typically lack sorting, may possess inverse grading (towards the base) and normal grading (towards the top), are matrix-supported and lack much in the way of internal structure, but will vary in their internal organisation depending on water content and cohesivity of the flow (see Nemec and Steel, 1984, Postma, 1986, Costa, 1988 for a discussion of mass flow processes). Debris flows are associated with catchments which generate sufficient fine material to lend shear strength to the flow and are supplied predominantly by slope material i.e. small, steep catchments (Harvey, 1990). These conditions are typically met when the catchment is developed on sedimentary and low grade metamorphic geologies (Harvey, 1990), and before the drainage network has had time to reduce relief in the fan catchment. Debris flows require a steeper gradient to maintain transport and tend to have a smaller run out distance than comparable fluvial flows, so that debris flow dominated fans are typically smaller and steeper than corresponding fluvial dominated fans.

iii) *Hyperconcentrated Flows and Fans*: as many alluvial fans are found in regions where sediment discharge is high, such as the semi-arid, it is worth noting here that many alluvial fan sediments are deposited from flows which are hyperconcentrated with sediment (40-70% by weight, Costa, 1988). These flows are intermediate between fluvial and debris flow processes. Flows may have some shear strength although there is some controversy as to the exact nature of these flows (Reid and Frostick, 1994). Resulting sediments (see

Sections 6.5.5.7, 7.5.4.4) may contain weak internal stratification, normal and reverse grading, weak imbrication and clasts may be matrix supported (Costa, 1988).

In general (i.e. in the absence of any major external influences such as climate) alluvial fans tend to be dominated by debris flows in the younger, more proximal parts of the fan. As the alluvial fan system matures, supplies of fine material become exhausted, the drainage network expands and the conditions for the generation of fluvial processes are increasingly met leading to the dominance of fluvial deposition in the fan dispersal area. As the fluvial processes require lower gradients than the debris flow processes to maintain transport, trenching of the fan surface is often a common feature associated with mature fans (Harvey, 1990).

The case study which forms the focus of this chapter will be taken from Plio/Pleistocene deposits of the Sorbas Basin in southeast Spain which are sourced from a combination of high grade metamorphic and carbonate lithologies and have produced a series of fluvially dominated fans. Most of the original morphology of the fans has been lost as a result of fan abandonment, deformation and subsequent erosion. Much of the evidence for the evolution of the palaeoenvironment is thus taken from the sedimentology of the deposits and remnant topography.

4.2 CASE STUDY: THE SORBAS BASIN, SOUTHEAST SPAIN.

4.2.1 Background to the Study Area

4.2.1.1 Regional Geological Setting
The Sorbas Basin is located in the internal zone of the Betic Cordillera of SE Spain. It is bounded by the Sierra de los Filabres and Bedar to the north and the Sierras Alhamilla and Cabrera to the south (Figure 4.1). The basin is part of the Trans-Alboran shear zone (Larouziére *et al.*, 1988), a left-lateral shear zone which has been active since the Neogene (Montenat *et al.*, 1990). During the late Tortonian the principal stress direction was dominantly NW-SE, but became NNW-SSE in the Pliocene to Holocene (Montenat and Ott d'Estevou, 1990, Mather and Westhead, 1993). The compression and fault orientations have combined to produce a series of compressional and extensional strains (Keller *et al.*, 1995) which have produced the modern topographic configuration of the region. In the Pliocene the basins underwent epeirogenic uplift as a function of the deformation (rates of uplift in excess of 130 m Ma^{-1} (Mather, 1991) in the study area) and the environment of deposition in the basin became continental. The area is still tectonically active with major earthquakes affecting the region over the historic time-scale (WWW, 1998).

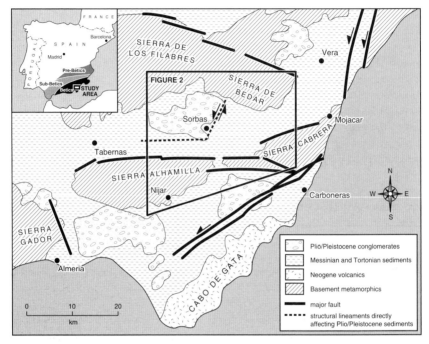

Figure 4.1. *Simplified geological map of the Almeria region showing lineaments affecting the Plio/Pleistocene sediments and the area covered by Figure 4.2 (boxed). Modified from Mather and Stokes (1996).*

4.2.1.2 Stratigraphy

Basin Fill

The sediments which form the focus of this study form part of the uppermost depositional fill of the Sorbas Basin, the Gochar Formation (Ruegg, 1964). No absolute dates are available for the sediments due to a lack of datable material, however stratigraphic reconstruction and the presence of *Iberus* towards the base of the sequence indicate a Pleistocene age for most of the sequence (Ott d'Estevou and Montenat, 1990). The sediments lie with local unconformity on the Cariatiz Formation (Mather, 1991, 1993b) and are locally capped with mid to Late Pleistocene fluvial terraces (Harvey and Wells, 1987, Harvey *et al.*, 1995) or calcreted erosional surfaces (Mather and Stokes, 1996). The contact between the terraces and Gochar Formation conglomerates may locally be unconformable.

The Gochar Formation can be divided into 4 main spatially distinct fluvial systems on the basis of sedimentology, palaeocurrent and provenance data (Mather, 1991, 1993a, b). These are 2 systems draining the Sierra de Los Filabres to the north of the basin (Gochar and Marchalico Systems), one draining the Sierra Alhamilla to the south (Mocatán System) and a fourth which axially drained the basin (Los Lobos System). It is the Marchalico system which drains the eastern end of the Sierra de Los Filabres/Sierra de Bedar which forms the focus of this case study.

Basin Margins

The stratigraphy of the basin margins is significant to this study as it provides the source area for the Plio/Pleistocene sediments. The study area is located in the northeast of the Sorbas Basin, adjacent to the Sierra de Bedar (Figures 4.1 and 4.2). The Sierra de Bedar comprises metamorphic basement geology of the higher Filabride Nappe (Weijermars, 1991), consisting dominantly of amphibole mica-schists, garnet mica-schists, chlorite mica-schists, amphibolite and tourmaline gneiss (Figure 4.2).

4.2.1.3 Climate

The climate record for the Plio/Pleistocene of southeast Spain is weak due to the poor preservation of pollen and fauna in the continental record. Gastropods such as *Iberus, Leuchocroa* and *Sphincterochila* found within the Gochar Formation of the Sorbas Basin indicate that the climate was dry for long periods. Sedimentological and paleontological data from stratigraphically equivalent mid Pliocene sediments in the Sorbas (Mather, 1991) and Vera (Stokes, 1997) Basins appear to indicate a more humid climate than present, with coastal conditions close to tropical, and with high magnitude flood events. Better preserved Quaternary records within the Mediterranean suggest a steppe vegetation during the later Pleistocene with extreme seasonal fluctuations (Prentice *et al.*, 1992, Rhodenburg and Sabelburg, 1980) and an inability to support a tree fauna during more arid European glacials (Amor and Florschutz, 1964). This has been seen as one of the major driving forces for aggradational and degradational phases in the later Pleistocene with more arid climates being associated with less slope stabilisation, enhancing slope erosion (Harvey, 1990). These data suggest that the climate varied significantly spatially within the mountains of the Betic Cordillera, was strongly seasonal and that it ranged from humid to more arid over the course of the Quaternary.

4.2.2 Methodology

The sediments (mainly conglomerates and subordinate (less volumetrically important) sands) which comprise the Marchalico System of the Gochar Formation range in thickness from 0-200 m (Mather, 1993a). To reconstruct the environment of deposition a basinwide analysis of the sediments was undertaken, using palaeosols, fauna, sedimentology, palaeocurrents and provenance (Mather, 1991).

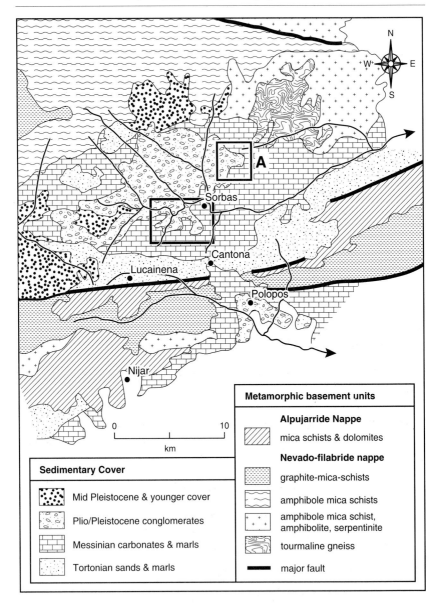

Figure 4.2. Simplified geological map of the Sorbas Basin. Box A highlights study area covered by Figure 4.5.

4.2.3 Source Area Identification

This was established by examining:

i) the direction of flow of palaeocurrents using measurements derived from imbrication of clasts in excess of 4 cm (long axis). Palaeocurrent observations are plotted on compass roses as percentages, scaled with respect to the modal class (the modal class is taken to the exterior circumference of the compass rose) using ROSE (ROCKWARE$_{TM}$). Where strata were dipping more than 5^0 the data were corrected using the methodology outlined in Appendix A of Collinson and Thompson (1989). Restricting the measurement of data to the larger clasts means that more reliable palaeocurrent measurements could be obtained as larger clasts will only be shifted by the main flow event and are less likely to reflect local reworking on waning flows (Bluck, 1974) (see Section 3.3.1.5).

ii) the provenance (see Section 2.2.1.6) of clasts over 4 cm long axis was determined using their metamorphic grade and lithology. A random selection of 100 clasts where taken from an individual bed. Clasts were marked with chalk to ensure that they were not duplicated in the count. Data are displayed in the form of pie charts plotted on EXEL$_{TM}$ (Figure 4.3).

4.2.4 Fan System Geomorphology

The fan system (source area and alluvial fan) morphological characteristics were reconstructed using the following data:

i) the spatial extent of the Gochar Formation, Marchalico System using 1:25 000 scale topographic maps and 1:30 000 black and white aerial photographs to map selected areas.

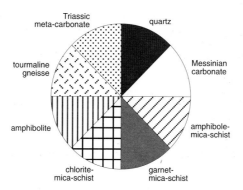

Figure 4.3. Key to pie charts used in Figures 4.8, 4.9 and 4.10.

All grid references are taken from the *Dirección General del Instituto Geográfico Nacional* map series. This included examining the deformation and where necessary plotting poles to bedding plane of the deposits onto a Schmidt Stereonet in order to determine the stratigraphy of the sediments. Area of the depositional fan bodies (F) could be obtained by careful geological and geomorphological mapping.

ii) the height and distribution of residual hills to reconstruct the end deposition land surface and fan gradient (G).

iii) by utilising fan area (F) and gradient (G) data from i and ii above to estimate fan catchment area (A, in km²), drainage basin slope (L, mean gradient between the highest and lowest points within the catchment area) and basin relief (B, the difference in elevation (m) between the highest and lowest points within the catchment), using equations 1, 2 and 3 below from Mather *et al.*, (in prep.). These equations have been formulated from a database subset of 31 fluvially dominated fans of mid to Late Pleistocene age in SE Spain and sourced from lithologies comparable to this case study.

$$A = 1.874 \, F^{1.28} \qquad \text{(equation 1)}$$

$$L = 1.186 \, G^{0.726} \qquad \text{(equation 2)}$$

$$B = 1000 \, A^{0.500} \, L^{0.778} \qquad \text{(equation 3)}$$

4.2.5 Depositional Processes

The identification of the processes of deposition operative in the Gochar Formation sediments was undertaken by careful field observations. Due to the extensive deformation sediment logs were only taken from areas of the sedimentary body where the stratigraphic relationships could be accurately identified. This restricted the sections that could be used to those where the base of the unit was clearly identifiable. The sediments at these sites were then described by:

i) vertical graphic sedimentary logs recorded from the base of the section and recording primary features such as bed thickness, 10 largest clasts (measured along the long-axis) in an individual unit, lithology, sediment fabric, presence of palaeosols, Munsell colour of soils (using a Munsell Soil Colour Chart) and degree of carbonate development where appropriate (using the nomenclature of Gile *et al.*, 1966, Birkeland, 1985), bed contacts, biogenic structures and secondary features such as faulting. Sections were measured using tapes and abney levels perpendicular to bedding. The sedimentological features examined and recorded on the sedimentary logs are detailed in Figure 4.4.

ii) sediment body (external) geometry using lateral sections, field sketches and the aid of photographic montages where appropriate.

4.2.6 Source Area

Earlier studies by Mather (1991, 1993a; Mather and Harvey, 1995) have indicated that the Marchalico System can be clearly distinguished from other systems within the Gochar Formation on the basis of provenance. In particular the system is characterised by a presence

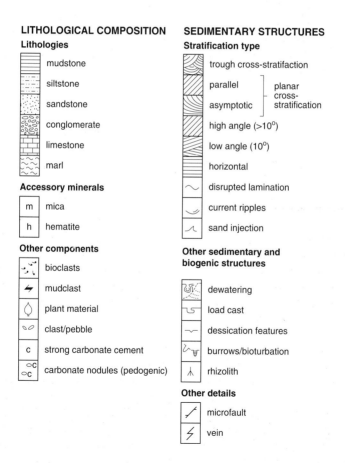

Figure 4.4. *Sedimentary features noted in the field and used in Figures 4.8, 4.9 and 4.10.*

of chlorite-mica-schist, amphibolite, garnet mica-schist and rare tourmaline gneiss which indicate a source area based in the Sierra Bedar on the north-eastern margin of the Sorbas Basin (Figure 4.2).

A summary of the clast count data is illustrated in Figure 4.5a. Using the data, two sub-systems can be determined within the Marchalico System:

i) a schist-rich system in the west of the study area with a typical assemblage dominated by mica-schists and amphibolite with only subordinate Messinian material and with palaeocurrents predominantly from the north/north-west together with

ii) a Messinian carbonate rich system dominated by the presence of Messinian reef and amphibolite with only subordinate mica-schist material and with palaeocurrents predominantly from the north/north-east.

Both systems show some degree of intermixing east of the Rambla Marchalico (Figure 4.5).

4.2.7 Palaeomorphology

Reconstruction of the palaeo-landsurface and extent of the Marchalico deposits indicates a fan-shaped feature with an apex around La Cerrada (GR 795 119) (Figures 4.5b and 4.6) which looses its definition towards the east where dissection and deformation have destroyed any relict features. Fan source area geomorphology could only be accurately reconstructed from the more complete sequence of the schist-rich system. This system has a relict surface gradient (G) of 0.031, and fan area (F) of 6.8 km^2. Using equations 1 to 3, this would indicate a catchment area (A) of 21.8 km^2, a basin slope (L) of 0.095 and a basin relief (B) of 748 m. Data for the Messinian carbonate-rich system is less complete but would suggest a fan surface gradient (G) of *ca.* 0.035, and fan area (F) of *ca.* 1.3 km^2. Using equations 1 to 3, this would indicate a catchment area (A) in the order of 2.6 km^2, a basin slope (L) of 0.104 and a basin relief (B) of 277 m.

Figure 4.5. *Detail of the study area: (a) provenance data (see Figure 4.3 for key) and palaeocurrents (averages taken from imbrication); (b) morphology reconstructed from the spatial extent of deposits, spot heights and aerial photographs; (c) schematic representation of facies distribution in vertical profile, across the study area. Asterisks denote areas of soft sediment deformation, bold lines indicate faults, numbers correspond to logs in Figures 4.8, 4.9 and 4.10, boxed area corresponds to Figure 4.14 (for location see Figure 4.2).*

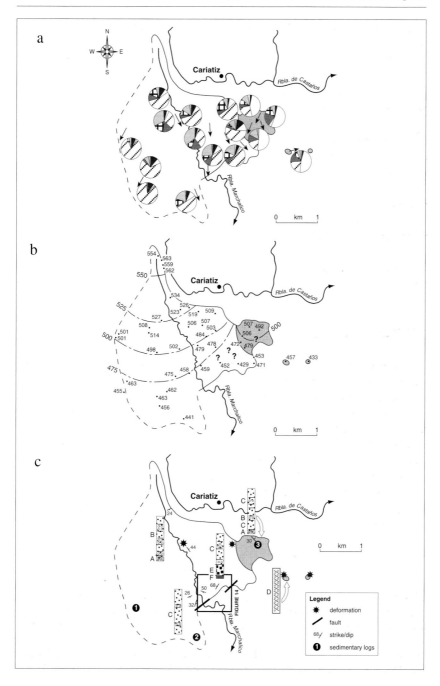

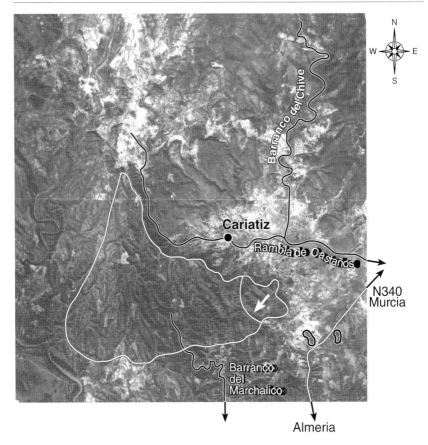

Figure 4.6. *Aerial photograph of study area showing location of deposits and surface morphology. Reprinted by permission of the Centro Nacional de Información Geográfica, Madrid. View is some 5 km across.*

4.2.8 Sedimentology

The sediments that comprise the Marchalico System can be grouped into a number of facies associations based on sedimentary structures, texture and lithology. In these descriptions sediment bodies with width to depth ratios of more than 15 are described as sheet-form (after Friend *et al.*, 1979). Figure 4.5c presents a schematic representation of the relative significance of the facies assemblages discussed below, in vertical profile. The characteristics and interpretation of the facies associations are summarised in Table 4.1.

Facies Association	Basic Description	Distribution	Environmental Interpretation
A	Bed thickness 0.5-2 m, sheet form, conglomerate dominated , poorly sorted, matrix-supported, outsize and subvertical clasts, non-erosive base	Basal parts of more proximal schist-rich and Messinian carbonate-rich sequence	Non-cohesive debris flow
B	Bed thickness 0.5-2 m, sheet-form, conglomerate dominated, clast to weakly matrix-supported conglomerate with crude grading, bedding and imbrication, overlain by poorly sorted sand unit	Dominates schist-rich sequence in west	More proximal hyper-concentrated sheet-floods
C	Bed thickness 0.1-0.5 m, conglomerate or sand dominated, sheet-form, clast to weakly matrix-supported conglomerates, laterally discontinuous	Dominates schist-rich sequence in south and Messinian carbonate-rich sequence	Distal hyper-concentrated sheet-floods
D	Low-angle, Cross-stratified gravels and conglomerates	Dominates Messinian carbonate-rich system in south and east	Poorly confined fluvial deposits
E	Massive red sands containing carbonate glaebules, increased redness and blue/grey mottling	Dominates basal southeast portions of schist-rich system	Pedogenic alteration of ?distal sheet-flood deposits
F	Laminated, bioturbated silts	Only found at the base of the schist-rich system in the south	Standing water

Table 4.1: *Summary of facies associations, their distribution and environmental interpretation.*

Figure 4.7. *Detail through Facies Association A (Proximal Messinian carbonate-rich system, GR 816 107).*

4.2.8.1 Facies Association A

Description: Facies association A comprises massive, poorly sorted, matrix-supported conglomerates containing outsized, commonly subvertical clasts (up to 90 cm long axis). Bed thickness ranges from 0.5-2 m. The sediments show no real evidence of grading or imbrication but may show a weak fabric in places (Figure 4.7). Locally the sand component may be rich in garnets with a high percentage of garnet-mica-schist clasts. The conglomerate beds may be draped with thin, structureless, poorly sorted sand units. The beds tend to have gently undulose bases onto underlying units and are rare within the sequence. They are mainly restricted to basal sections in both the schist-rich and Messinian carbonate rich systems (Figures 4.5c, 4.8 and 4.9).

Interpretation: the characteristic lack of sorting and internal fabric, presence of outsize and subvertical clasts, together with the matrix-supported nature of the conglomerates suggests deposition from a debris flow (Nemec and Steel, 1984). The weak clast alignment and absence of clay grade material suggests that this was most probably non-cohesive (nomenclature *sensu* Postma, 1986).

4.2.8.2 Facies Association B

Description: sheet-form, massive to crudely bedded conglomerates with some outsized clasts. Bases of the sheet forms may be locally scoured. The conglomerate beds range in thickness from 0.5-2 m and may show a crude grading and imbrication. The conglomerate beds are draped with a fine to medium red sand which is typically structureless, but may show a crude grading and lamination. The finer, reddened sands may contain scattered carbonate glaebules. This facies dominates the intermediate areas of the schist-rich system and is rare in the more proximal sections of the Messinian carbonate-rich system (Figures 4.5c, 4.8 and 4.9).

Interpretation: the presence of imbrication, crude grading and local scouring suggest a fluid flow. The sheet-form geometry suggests deposition by unconfined flow i.e. sheet flooding (*sensu* Hogg, 1982). The poor sorting suggests that the flow may have been hyperconcentrated with sediment (comparable with the D2 facies of Wells and Harvey, 1987 and 'fluidal sediments' of Nemec and Steel, 1984). The typical lack of internal structure suggests the conglomerates moved as sheets. The sands probably reflect the last element of flow within the sheetflood, with rapid deposition of material, or in some cases may represent a separate flow event. The typical lack of structure in the associated sand together with reddening and scattered carbonate glaebules suggest either weak *in situ* palaeosol development with pedoturbation destroying any previous structure, or reworking of palaeosols from the catchment area.

4.2.8.3 Facies Association C

Description: sheet-form, massive to crudely bedded conglomerates and sands with clasts ranging up to 20 cm (long axis), but more commonly much smaller. The percentage volume of conglomerate tends to be less in Association C than Association B (contrast Figures 4.8 and 4.10). Beds are 0.1-0.5 m thick and are moderately to well sorted and clast supported. Beds may be laterally continuous over 10's of metres or may pinch out laterally (Figure 4.11). They typically have width to depth ratios in excess of 15 and can thus be classified as sheet-form in geometry. They fine upwards rapidly into grey medium sands or red fine sands which are typically massive. The red sands (7.5YR5/6 - 5YR 7/4) may be associated with carbonate glaebule development and may contain mud rip-up clasts. The carbonate glaebules may be present as lags at the base of scour hollows within the sands. Association C dominates the most distal palaeocurrent areas of the schist-rich system (Figure 4.10) and most of the upper sections of the Messinian carbonate rich system (Figures 4.5c and 4.9).

Interpretation: the sheet-form geometry suggests deposition by weakly confined to unconfined flow. The finer nature of the sediments and thinner beds than Association B suggest shallower flows and probably a more distal location. The presence of imbrication, crude grading and local scouring suggest a fluid flow (Nemec and Steel, 1984). The poor sorting suggests that this may have been hyperconcentrated with sediment (Costa, 1988). The typical lack of internal structure suggests the conglomerates moved as sheets. Some of the sands probably reflect the last element of flow within the sheetflood. However, the presence of scour features and rip-up clasts within the sands also suggests that some of the

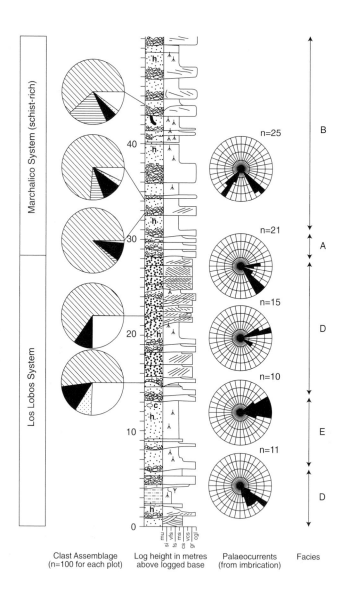

Clast Assemblage (n=100 for each plot)
Log height in metres above logged base
Palaeocurrents (from imbrication)
Facies

Figure 4.8. Graphic sedimentary log and associated data from the intermediate portion of schist-rich system (Casa Aguarico, GR 788 091) Note the Los Lobos System is the axial drainage system of Mather (1991).

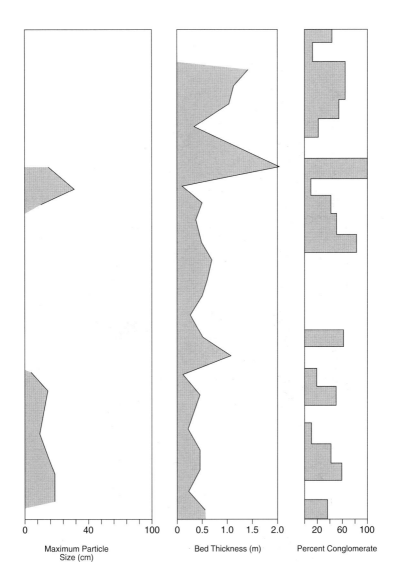

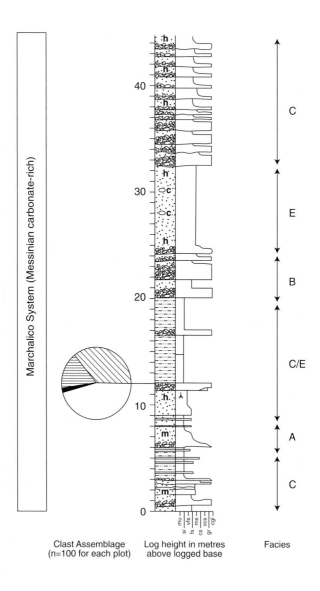

Figure 4.9. *Graphic sedimentary log and associated data from intermediate portion of Messinian carbonate-rich system (Los Sesares, GR 816 107).*

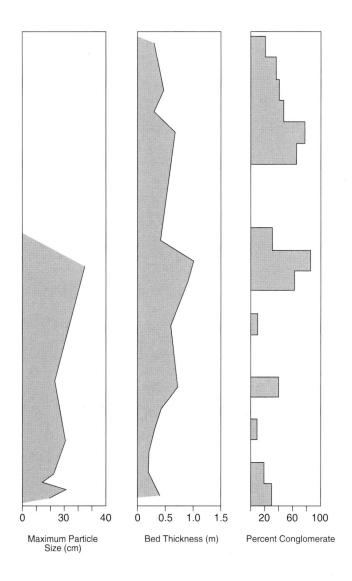

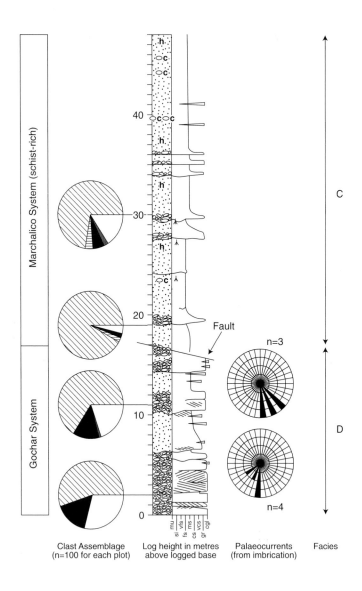

Figure 4.10. *Graphic sedimentary log and associated data from distal schist-rich system (Barranco Marchalico, GR 803 082). Note the Gochar System is the north-west fan/braided river system of Mather (1991).*

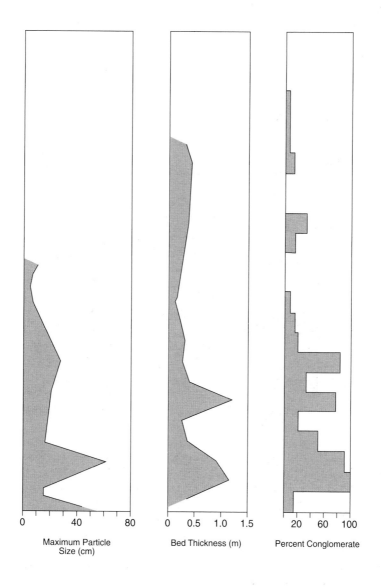

Maximum Particle
Size (cm)

Bed Thickness (m)

Percent Conglomerate

features may relate to reworking in later flow events. The typical lack of structure in the associated sand together with reddening and scattered carbonate glaebules suggest either weak *in situ* palaeosol development with pedoturbation destroying any previous structure, or reworking of palaeosols from the up-fan and catchment areas.

Figure 4.11. *Detail of Facies Association C (distal schist-rich system, GR 811 097).*
4.2.8.4 Facies Association D.

Description: typically well sorted, graded (on a dm-scale) and cross-stratified gravels (Figure 4.12). Clasts are typically imbricated. The stratification is generally low angle (less than 100) with the stratification picked out as pebble stringers in coarse sands or by the sedimentary fabric. In some sections the stratification is oblique to palaeoflow direction (obtained from imbrication). In the most southern and eastern exposures the cross-stratified gravels are contained within broad, shallow channels (*ca.* 10 m wide, 1.5 m deep). Locally small scour hollows contain sandstone rip-up clasts. This facies is only found in the stratigraphically highest and most distal part of the Messinian carbonate rich system in the east of the study area (Figure 4.5c).

Interpretation: the sorting and fabric is typical of deposition from braided fluvial processes. The bedding is typical of that associated with longitudinal bars (Smith, 1974). The development of low angle stratification may reflect modification on the waning flow or development of foresets as a result of bar migration. If the latter is true, it may be the result of a lower sediment discharge (increase in the water to sediment ratio) enabling the development of low-angle foresets rather than movement as gravel sheets (Associations B and C) which is typical of higher sediment and water discharges (Hein and Walker, 1977). Where flow is oblique to bedding this may reflect the development of lateral bars (Bluck, 1974).

Figure 4.12. *Detail of Facies Association D (distal Messinian carbonate-rich system, GR 823 098). ES = erosion surface; FU indicates fining upwards units).*

4.2.8.5 Facies Association E

Description: Facies Association E comprises a red, massive sand unit which may be up to 40 m thick. This overlies, and in places is lateral to, Association F in the southeast of the area to which it is restricted (Figure 4.5c). Association E contains small, cm-sized, randomly orientated carbonate glaebules which may be associated with increased reddening of the sediments (2.5YR 4/8). Locally the glaebules may form distinct horizons. Also apparent in the lower parts of the sequences are the presence of elongate, grey-blue mottles with red haloes, commonly with a rectilinear arrangement. In the finer sand units a finer grained carbonate is developed, forming distinct units which are traceable for up to a km. The carbonates are rubbly in appearance and contain vertical, well cemented tubes 0.5-0.7 cm in diameter. Association E is only found in the basal parts of the most distal schist-rich system in the east of the area (Figure 4.5c).

Interpretation: the carbonate accumulations are typical of the various stages of pedogenic carbonate development outlined by Gile *et al.* (1966) and discussed in Birkeland (1985).

The scattered nodules are typical of stage I development and the more continuous horizons of stages II-III. The lack of structure in the sands probably reflects destratification via pedoturbation (Wright and Allen, 1989). The presence of the rectilinear mottles in lower parts of the sequence suggests the development of pseudogley soils (Wright and Allen, 1989, Retallack, 1990). The rectilinear appearance is probably related to water stagnation in cracks in the sediments.

4.2.8.6 Facies Association F

Description: Facies Association F comprises finely laminated silts and very fine sands. Laminations are on a mm-scale and are commonly interrupted by unwalled burrows (Figure 4.13). This facies association is very rare and only accounts for a small thickness at the base of the schist-rich system in the east of the area (Figure 4.5c).

Figure 4.13. *Detail of Facies Association F (distal schist-rich system, GR 802 094).*

Interpretation: the well bioturbated units are lacking in any evidence of pedogenesis. The fine nature of the sediment suggests deposition in standing water with little current activity. The location of this sediment, above the last fully marine sediments (top Cariatiz Formation of Mather, 1991) and examination of stratigraphically equivalent horizons elsewhere in the basin (Mather, 1991) suggests that this may have been a marine/brackish environment, although no fauna were found at this site.

4.2.9 Secondary Modification

Particularly in the east of the area the sediments have been severely affected by deformation along a prominent structural lineament (discussed in Mather and Westhead, 1993, Mather and Stokes, 1996). This makes any correlation difficult. The sediments display a range of features from tilting and faulting (Figures 4.5c and 4.14) to soft sediment intrusions (Figures 4.5c). Much of the deformation occurred in a water rich environment and prior to lithification of the sediment. Local thickness variations suggest that the lineament may also have been active during deposition of the Marchalico System, dominating the local topography. The east of the area is also in contact with the gypsum of the Sorbas Basin. Some of the sediments overlying the gypsum show local deformation over doline structures (isolated hills in the east of the area, Figure 4.5c).

4.2.10 Environmental Reconstruction

Combining the source area, morphology and depositional data enables a reconstruction of the palaeoenvironment (Figure 4.15). These data suggest that there are 2 main components to the Marchalico System:

i) a larger (6.8 km^2), *schist-rich subsystem* which was fan-shaped (Figures 4.5b and 4.6) with a surface gradient of 0.031 and derived from the N/NW (Figure 4.5a) sourced from basement schists of the Sierra de Bedar (Figure 4.15). The system was dominated by hyperconcentrated, sheet-flood processes with only rare debris flows in the most proximal sections (Figure 4.5c). The sheet-flood deposits are more conglomerate dominated with thicker beds in the more proximal areas and more sand dominated with smaller clasts and thinner beds in the more distal areas (Figures 4.5c and 4.10). Palaeocurrents have a weak radial pattern (Figure 4.5a). This system appears to have prograded over the Gochar and Los Lobos fluvial system deposits in more marginal locations (Figures 4.8 and 4.10) and in the distal parts of the sequence to the east appears to have prograded over an area of shallow standing water associated with the withdrawal of the last marine incursion. The presence of palaeosols indicates an improvement in drainage conditions up the sequence with a progression from pseudogleys and calcretes (Facies Association E) to calcretes (in Facies Association C). The deposits were subjected to intense deformation throughout the sequence in the east of the area (Figures 4.5c and 4.14).

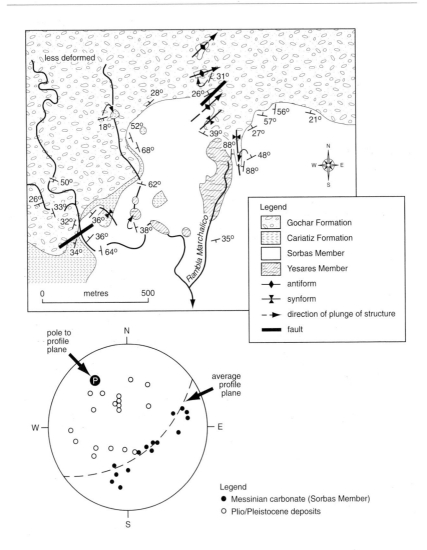

Figure 4.14. *Detailed map showing the deformation in the southeast region of the study area (see Figure 4.5c for location). Note consistency of main fault profile plane created by the Messinian carbonates compared with the scattered ones indicated by the Plio/Pleistocene sediments. This in part reflects the heterogenity of the Plio/Pleistocene sediments.*

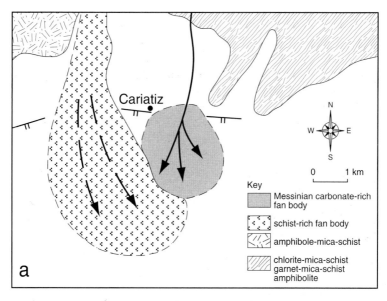

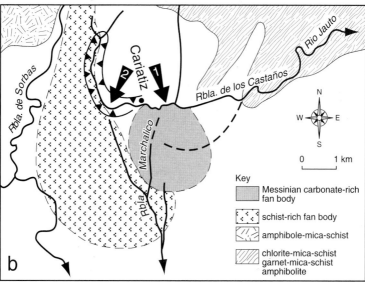

Figure 4.15. *Evolution of the Marchalico System: (a) Plio/Pleistocene; (b) Modern drainage setting and position of river captures (arrowed 1 for El Chive and 2 for La Cerrada).*

ii) a smaller ($ca.$1.3 km^2), *Messinian carbonate rich subsystem* derived from the NE (Figure 4.5a) with a source area mainly based on Messinian carbonates (Figure 4.15) but also tapping some basement schist in the foothills of the Sierra Bedar. Surface gradients were in the order of $ca.$ 0.035. The system was dominated by unconfined, hyperconcentrated flows in stratigraphically lower and more proximal section (Figure 4.5c). Proximal sections also contain rare debris flows (Figures 4.5c and 4.9). The sheet-floods appear to have been superseded by more fluvial, weakly channelised, less sediment charged braided channel flows in the later evolution of the sequence (Association D). The fluvial deposits are less deformed than other parts of the sequence.

The sedimentology and morphology of the deposits argue for an alluvial fan environment of deposition (Bull, 1972, 1977; Blair and McPherson, 1994a). In the case of the schist-rich system there is no evidence for confinement of flow. In the Messinian carbonate rich-system, however, there appears to be a change to more confined, fluvial flow towards the top of the sequence. In both cases there is little evidence for debris flow activity and the fans appear to be fluvial dominated. Using equations 1 to 3 it is possible to ascertain that the schist-rich system had the largest (21.8 km^2) and most rugged (748 m of basin relief) catchment, supplying a 6.8 km^2 fan body with a gradient of 0.031. In comparison, the least reliable data from the Messinian carbonate-rich fan suggests a smaller (about 2.6 km^2), less rugged (277 m of basin relief) catchment supplying a smaller ($ca.$ 1.3 km^2), steeper ($ca.$ 0.035) alluvial fan body.

4.2.10 Controls on Fan Development

The controls operative on the development of the alluvial fan can broadly be considered as those that are *internal* to the system (such as catchment area characteristics) and those which are controlled by factors *external* to the system (such as tectonics, climate and base level changes).

4.2.10.1 Catchment Area

The fluvial dominated nature of the fans reflects the water to sediment ratio of the catchment which may be in part determined by climate but also by the catchment lithology (Harvey, 1987). Fans derived from schist catchments commonly do not generate sufficient fine sediments for cohesive debris flow processes, resulting in a dominance of fluvial processes, producing a larger, lower gradient alluvial fan (Harvey, 1987).

The change from unconfined to more confined fluvial deposits in the Messinian carbonate rich fan may reflect an increase in the water to sediment ratio of the flows perhaps as a function of progressive changes in the catchment area through sediment exhaustion (Eckis, 1928) or river capture (Maizels, 1990, Mather, 1993a, Eliet and Gawthorpe, 1995, Mather and Stokes, 1996). Alternatively the weakly confined flow may reflect the threshold condition prior to trenching of the fan, which can occur as a result of fan maturity (Harvey, 1990).

4.2.10.2 Tectonics

Over the scale of the Plio/Pleistocene-recent tectonism is significant in that it can create (and maintains) the topographic niche for fan development (Schumm, 1977, Ahnert, 1970). In the source area rejuvenation may stimulate sediment delivery to the fan. In the dispersal area subsidence may govern the spatial extent of fans (Whipple and Trayler, 1996). Similarly fan tilting can stimulate incision (Rockwell *et al.*, 1984). The abundant evidence for syn and post depositional deformation in the east of the area may account for the limited extent of the Messinian carbonate-rich fan and could have contributed to increasing local gradients and promoting the onset of incision of the fan surface. Most of the deformation appears to be a function of the movement of the NNE-SSW strike-slip lineament outlined in Figure 4.1, but it should be noted that some of the deformation in the east of the area appears to be related to doline structures in the gypsum and could in part account for the anomolous palaeocurrents to the east (see Figure 4.5a) and the changes in palaeohydrology in the more distal parts of the fan that can be identified from palaeosols (i.e. poorly drained hydromorphic soils and better drained calcretes).

4.2.10.3 Climate

Climate controls appear to be more important over shorter time-scales than tectonics. Regional data appear to support an increasing aridification over the course of the Quaternary (Harvey, 1987). This is supported by data from palaeosols in the fan deposits with palaeosols becoming better drained up-sequence, with a change from pseudogleys to calcretes. The presence of the calcretes suggests that the climate was not sufficiently wet to leach carbonate out of soil profiles. The apparent increase in aridity may have affected vegetation in the catchment and thus indirectly the sediment and water yields. If the amount of effective runoff was increased without a parallel increase in sediment discharge this could have contributed in the change to more confined fluvial deposition in the Messinian carbonate-rich system.

4.2.10.4 Base level

Although the Marchalico fan systems were isolated from the affects of sea level, the uplift that led to the displacement of marine conditions from the Sorbas Basin also stimulated major base level changes via incision and river capture in the adjusting fluvial drainage network (Harvey and Wells, 1987, Mather and Harvey, 1995). These adjustments affected two main areas of the Marchalico fan system:

i) proximal effects - this largely relates to the incision of the Rambla de Castaños which is an aggressive subsequent developed from the main transverse drainage of the Rio Jauto

(Mather and Harvey, 1995). The progressive headward erosion of the Rambla de Castaños followed a structural lineament to the south of the Messinian reef complexes north of Cariatiz (Mather, 1991), progressively capturing the drainage of the Barranco del Chive (1 on Figure 4.15b) and north-south draining reach of the Rambla de Castaños near La Cerrada (2 on Figure 4.15b). These captures would have led to the abandonment of the fan surfaces and thus aided preservation of the relict fan morphology. One aspect of the capture cols which is difficult to explain is the difference in altitude. If El Chive was captured first, it would be realistic to assume that this col should have a higher elevation than La Cerrada in the west. In fact El Chive is some 100 m lower than the highest cols to the west. This most probably reflects the fact that the ancestral El Chive was already well incised into the fan sediments prior to capture, in the topographic low between the schist and Messinian carbonate-rich fans, in the area which was undergoing intense deformation.

ii) distal effects - the incision of the main drainage of the Rio Aguas as a function of river capture induced base level changes (Harvey and Wells, 1987) and stimulated incision of the distal parts of the abandoned fan systems.

4.3 CONCLUSIONS

This case study presents a field based approach to reconstructing an alluvial fan environment, combining information from the sedimentology and relict topography. The data enabled the identification of 2 fan systems based on palaeocurrents, provenance data and morphological evidence. These were i) a schist-rich fan derived from the northwest and ii) a Messinian carbonate-rich fan derived from the northeast. The remnant morphological evidence facilitated the reconstruction of the morphological characteristics (size, topographic ruggedness) of the catchment areas of the fan systems. The sediments stored in the alluvial fan body indicate that both fans were fluvially dominated and became isolated from their source areas as a function of river capture and fan abandonment. This occurred first in the carbonate rich system to the east. This latter fan was subject to considerable modification by deformation along a strike-slip fault and gypsum dissolution and collapse in its easternmost limits. This may account for locally anomalous palaeocurrent readings to the east. The schist-rich system continued as a less deformed and active fan until later into the Pleistocene and so retains more of its original topography.

ACKNOWLEDGEMENTS

Thanks to Dr. Adrian Harvey for reviewing early drafts of the manuscript, Lindy at Cortijo Urra Field Study Centre for providing accommodation, the University of Plymouth Research and Development Fund and the Centro Nacional de Información Geográfica, Madrid, for permission to reproduce the aerial photograph in Figure 4.6.

REFERENCES

AMOR, J.M. and FLORSCHUTZ, F. 1964. Results of the preliminary palynological investigation of samples from a 50m boring in Southern Spain. *Boletin de la Real Sociedad Espanola de Historia Natural (Geologia)*, **62**, 251-5.

AHNERT, F. 1970. Functional relationships between denudation, relief and uplift in large mid-latitude drainage basins. *American Journal of Science*, **268**, 243-263.

BIRKELAND, P.W. 1985. Quaternary soils of the western United States, *IN*: Boardman, J. *(ed)*, *Soils and Quaternary Landscape Evolution*, 303-324. Wiley.

BLAIR, T.C. and MCPHERSON, J.G. 1992. The Trollheim alluvial fan and facies model revisited *Geological Society of America Bulletin*, **104**, 762-769.

BLAIR, T.C. and MCPHERSON, J.G. 1994a. Alluvial fan processes and forms. *IN*: Abrahams, A.D. and Parsons, A.J. *(eds)*, *Geomorphology of Desert Environments*, 354-402. Chapman and Hall.

BLAIR, T.C. and MCPHERSON, J.G. 1994b. Alluvial fans and their natural distinction from rivers based on morphology, hydraulic processes, sedimentary processes and facies assemblages. *Journal of Sedimentary Research*, **A64**, 450-489.

BLAIR, T.C. and MCPHERSON, J.G. 1995. Alluvial fan terminology based on sedimentary process/facies. *IN*: Blair, T.C. and McPherson, J.G. (eds), *Proceedings and Abstracts Volume, SEPM Alluvial Fans Meeting*, Death Valley, California, 23-26.

BLUCK, B.J. 1974. Structure and directional properties of some valley sandur deposits in southern Iceland. *Sedimentology*, **21**, 533-554.

BULL, W.B. 1972. Recognition of alluvial-fan deposits in the stratigraphic record. *IN*: Rigby, J.K. and Hamblin, W. (eds), *Recognition of Ancient Sedimentary Environments*, 6-83. Society of Economic Paleontologists and Mineralogists, Special Publication **16**.

BULL, W.B. 1977. The alluvial-fan environment.: *Progress in Physical Geography*, **1**, 222- 270

COLLINSON, J.D. and THOMPSON, D.B. (1989) *Sedimentary Structures*. Second edition. George Allen and Unwin. 194 pp.

COSTA, J.E. 1988. Rheologic, geomorphic and sedimentologic differentiation of water floods, hyperconcentrated flows and debris flows. *IN*: Baker, V.R, Kockel, R.C. and Patton, P.C. (eds), *Flood Geomorphology*, 113-122. Wiley.

ECKIS, R. 1928. Alluvial fans of the Cucamonga District, southern California. *Journal of Geology,* **36**, 111-141.

ELIET, P.P. and GAWTHORPE, R.L. 1995. Drainage development and sediment supply within rifts, examples from the Sperchios basin, central Greece: *Journal of the Geological Society of London,* **152**, 883-893.

FRIEND, P.F., SLATER, M.J. and WILLIAMS, R..C. 1979. Vertical and lateral buildings of river sandstone bodies, Ebro Basin, Spain, *Journal of the Geological Society of London*, **136**, 39-46.

GILE, L.H., PETERSON, F.F. and GROSSMAN, R.B. 1966. Morphological and genetic sequences of carbonate accumulation in desert soils. *Soil Science*, **101**, 347-360.

HARVEY, A.M. 1984. Debris flows and fluvial deposits in Spanish Quaternary alluvial fans: implications for fan morphology. *IN*: Koster, E.H. and Steel, R.J. (eds), *Sedimentology of gravels and conglomerates*, 123-132. Canadian Society of Petroleum Geologists, Memoir **10**.

HARVEY, A.M. 1987. Patterns of Quaternary aggradational and dissectional landform development in the Almeria region, southeast Spain: a dry region tectonically active landscape, *Die Erde,* **118**, 193-215.

HARVEY, A.M. 1990. Factors influencing Quaternary alluvial fan development in southeast Spain. *IN*: Rachocki, A.H. and Church, M. (eds), *Alluvial Fans: A field approach*, 247-269. John Wiley and Sons.

HARVEY, A.M. 1997. The role of alluvial fans in arid zone fluvial systems. *IN*: Thomas, D.S.G. (ed), Arid Zone Geomorphology: Process, Form and Chnage in Drylands, 231-259. Wiley.

HARVEY, A.M., MILLER, S.Y. and WELLS, S.G. 1995. Quaternary soil and river terrace sequences in the Aguas/Feos river systems: Sorbas Basin, southeast Spain. *IN*: Lewin, J., Macklin, M.G. and Woodward, J.C. (eds), *Mediterranean Quaternary River Environments*, 263-282. Balkema.

HARVEY, A.M. and WELLS, S.G. 1987. Response of Quaternary fluvial systems to differential epeirogenic uplift: Aguas and Feos River systems, south-east Spain, *Geology*, **15**, 689-693.

HEIN, F.J. and WALKER, R.G. 1977. Bar evolution and development of stratification in the gravely, braided Kicking Horse River, British Columbia. *Canadian Journal of Earth Science*, **14**, 562-570.

HOGG, S.E. 1982. Sheetfloods, sheetwash, sheetflow or ....? *Earth Science Review*, **18**, 59 - 76.

KELLER, J.V.A., HALL, S.H., DART, C.J. and MCCLAY, K.R. 1995. The geometry and evolution of a tranpressional strike-slip system: the Carboneras fault, SE Spain, *Journal of the Geological Society of London*, **152**, 339-351.

LAROUZIÉRE, F.D. DE, BOLZE, J., BORDET, P., HERNANDEZ, J., MONTENAT, C. and OTT D'ESTEVOU, C. 1988. The Betic segment of the lithospheric Trans-Alboran shear zone during the late Miocene, *Tectonophysics*, **152**, 41-52.

LECCE, S.A. 1990. The alluvial fan problem. *IN*: Rachocki, A.H. and Church, M. (eds), *Alluvial Fans: A field approach*, 3-24. John Wiley and Sons.

MAIZELS, J. 1990. Long-term palaeochannel evolution during episodic growth of an exhumed Plio-Pleistocene alluvial fan, Oman. *IN*: Rachocki, A.H. and Church, M. (eds), *Alluvial Fans: A field approach*, 271-304. Wiley.

MATHER, A.E. 1991. *Caenozoic drainage evolution of the Sorbas Basin, SE Spain*. Unpublished Ph.D Thesis, University of Liverpool.

MATHER, A.E 1993a. Evolution of a Pliocene fan delta: links between the Sorbas and Carboneras Basins, SE Spain. *IN*: Frostick, L. and Steel, R. (eds), *Tectonic Controls and Signatures in Sedimentary Successions*, 277-290. IAS Special Publication **20**.

MATHER, A.E. 1993b. Basin inversion : some consequences for drainage evolution and alluvial architecture, *Sedimentology*, **40**, 1069-1089.

MATHER, A.E. and HARVEY, A.M. 1995. Controls on drainage evolution in the Sorbas Basin, SE Spain. *IN*: Lewin, J., Macklin, M.G. and Woodward, J.C. (eds), *Mediterranean Quaternary River Environments*, 65-76. Balkema.

MATHER, A.E., HARVEY, A.M. and STOKES, M. in prep. Quantitative reconstruction of ancient alluvial fan catchment areas.

MATHER, A.E. and WESTHEAD, R.K. 1993. Plio/Quaternary strain of the Sorbas Basin, SE Spain: Evidence from sediment deformation structures, *Quaternary Proceedings*, **3**, 57-65.

MATHER, A.E. and STOKES, M. 1996. Relative impact of deformation on Plio/Pleistocene drainage systems and subsequent landform development, Sorbas and Vera Basins, SE Spain. *IN*: Mather, A.E. and Stokes, M. (eds), *2nd Cortijo Urra Field Meeting, SE Spain: Field Guide*, 58-70. University of Plymouth, England.

MONTENAT, C., MASSE, P., COPPIER, G. and OTT D'ESTEVOU, P. 1990. The sequence of deformations in the Betic Shear Zone (SE Spain), *Annales Tectonicae*, **4**, 96-103.

MONTENAT, C. and OTT D'ESTEVOU, P. 1990. Eastern Betic Neogene Basins - a review, *Doc. et Trav. IGAL, Paris*, No.**12-13**, 9-15.

NEMEC, W. and STEEL, R.J. 1984. Alluvial and coastal conglomerates: their significant features and some comments on gravely mass-flow deposits. *IN*: Koster, E.H. and Steel, R.J. (eds), *Sedimentology of gravels and conglomerates,* 1-31. Canadian Society of Petroleum Geologists, Memoir **10**.

OTT D'ESTEVOU, P. and MONTENAT, C. 1990. Le Bassin de Sorbas - *Tabernas. Doc. et Trav. IGAL, Paris,* No.**12-13**, 101-128.

POSTMA, G. 1986. Classification for sediment gravity flow deposits based on flow conditions during sedimentation. *Geology*. **14**, 291-294.

PRENTICE, I.C., GUIOT, J. and HARRISON, S.P. 1992. Mediterranean vegetation, lake levels and palaeoclimate at the last glacial maximum. *Nature*, **360**, 658-660.

RACHOKI, A.H. and CHURCH, M. 1990. *Alluvial Fans: a Field Approach*. Wiley.

RETALLACK, G.J. 1990. *Soils of the Past: an Introduction to Palaeopedology*. Unwin.

REID, I. and FROSTICK, L.E. 1994. Fluvial sediment transport and deposition. *IN*: Pye, K. (ed), *Sediment transport and depositional processes,* 89-155. Blackwell.

RHODENBURG, H. and SABELBERG, U. 1980. Northwest Sahara Margin: terrestrial stratigraphy of the Upper Quaternary and some Palaeoclimatic implications. *IN*: Van Sinderen Bakker, E.M. Sr. and Coetsee (eds), *Palaeoecology of Africa and the surrounding Islands,* **12**, 267-276.

ROCKWELL, T.K., KELLER, E.A. and JOHNSON, D.L. 1984. Tectonic geomorphology of alluvial fans and mountain fronts near Ventura, California. *IN*: Morrisawa, M. and Hack, J.T. (eds), *Tectonic Geomorphology*, 183-207. Allen and Unwin.

RUEGG, G. J. H. 1964. Geologische onderzoekingen in bet bekken van Sorbas, S. E. Spanje. *Internal report Geol. Inst. Univ. Amsterdam*. 67 pp.

SCHUMM, S. 1977. *The Fluvial System*, Wiley, 338 pp.

SMITH, N.D. 1974. Sedimentology and bar formation in the Upper Kicking Horse River, a braided outwash stream. *Journal of Geology*, **82**, 205-224.

STOKES, M. 1997. *Plio/Pleistocene Drainage Evolution of the Vera Basin, SE Spain*. Unpublished PhD Thesis, University of Plymouth.

WEIJERMARS, R. 1991. Geology and tectonics of the Betic Zone, SE Spain. *Earth Science Review*, **31**, 153-236.

WELLS, S.G. and HARVEY, A.M. 1987. Sedimentological and geomorphic variations in storm-generated alluvial fans, Howgill Fells, northwest England. *Bulletin of the Geological Society of America,* **98**, 182-198.

WHIPPLE, K.X. and TRAYLER, C.R.1996. Geophysical controls on fan size: the importance of spatially variable subsidence rates. *Basin Research*, **8**, 351-366.

WRIGHT, V.P. and ALLEN, J.R.L.1989. Palaeosols in Siliclastic sequences. PRIS Short Course Notes 001, Reading University.

WWW 1998. Website for the the Andalusian Institute of Geophysics http://www.ugr.es/iag/iagpds.html

DESCRIPTION AND ANALYSIS OF QUATERNARY FLUVIAL SEDIMENTS: A CASE STUDY FROM THE UPPER RIVER THAMES, UK

Simon G. Lewis and Darel Maddy

5.1 INTRODUCTION

Fluvial deposits represent one of the most important archives of information available to Quaternary scientists concerning changing environments and the response of terrestrial geomorphic systems to climate change. In the UK the fluvial archive is unparalleled in its Pleistocene completeness, particularly in southern England where the records of the Rivers Thames (Bridgland, 1994, Gibbard 1985, 1994; Whiteman and Rose, 1992), Severn, Avon and Baginton (Maddy *et al.*, 1991, 1995) span back to at least the early Middle Pleistocene. Holocene fluvial archives also constitute a major resource for the study of changing environments and fluvial activity during the current interglacial (e.g. Macklin, 1993, Passmore *et al.*, 1993, Rumsby and Macklin, 1994, Frenzel, 1995).

Quaternary fluvial sediments record both changes in fluvial system dynamics and also contain important palaeoecological information (e.g. pollen, plant macrofossils, vertebrates including hominid remains, Mollusca, Insecta, Ostracoda etc.) and ample dateable materials, such as organics for radiocarbon age estimation, bone for U-series methods, teeth for electron spin resonance methods and ample quartz and feldspar-rich sediments for luminescence methods.

Such a rich and comprehensive archive requires a multidisciplinary approach to investigation. Often this will involve field investigations by a team of specialists which includes expertise in geomorphology, stratigraphy, sedimentology, palaeontology, archaeology and geochronology. Each of these disciplines has distinct field techniques and methods which require the recording of different attributes. This chapter is concerned mainly with the first three of these, with brief reference only made to the latter three.

5.2 THE FLUVIAL ENVIRONMENT

Fluvial systems respond to changing environmental conditions on differing spatial and temporal scales. As such their sedimentary archives offer important opportunities for the investigation of both short-term, high-resolution events as well as long-term responses. Fluvial successions (see also Chapters 4 and 5 and Section 6.5.5.2) contain evidence of both depositional and erosional episodes, though greater emphasis is usually placed on the depositional evidence. Site description must therefore include description of fluvial forms on a variety of scales, to reflect the response of the system over varying timescales represented by a range of micro-, meso- and macro-forms (Section 2.1.1).

5.2.1 Basin-Scale Studies

At the basin scale perhaps the most important fluvial landforms are terraces. River terraces (relatively flat surfaces) represent former river levels and can be either depositional (aggradational/constructional) or erosional (strath) features. Terraces are defined with respect to height above the present river and this enables the reconstruction of sediment-body geometry along longitudinal profiles. Terraces may vary in altitudinal separation from metres to many tens of metres, and separation is not always consistent along the length of the basin.

Terracing results from fluvial adjustment over a variety of timescales to internal and external controls causing the river to alter its gradient. Unfortunately the degree of altitudinal separation between terraces does not necessarily reflect the timescale of development, i.e. terraces close together could result from processes acting over a 10^2 - 10^5 year timescale. However, terraces which extend over the whole basin (or large proportions of it) most probably represent formation over the longer timescales (10^3-10^5 years) and are usually a result of system adjustment to uplift, either relative e.g. differential glacioisotatic rebound and outlet level lowering (Karrow, 1986), or absolute movement, related to tectonic activity (Maddy, 1997). In a Pleistocene context, it is these more extensive terraces which tend to be preserved.

However, terrace surfaces are not always underlain by fluvial deposits. A distinction should be made between the terrace landform and its underlying sediments. In certain tectonic situations fluvial sediments can be deposited in subsiding basins, for example in the lower Rhine valley (Brunnacker, 1975, 1986), to form thick accumulations of sediment. It may, however, be possible to relate this succession to terraced sequences upstream of the zone of subsidence.

The reconstruction of terrace long profiles is often the main tool for the correlation of these often very fragmentary former floodplain remnants. This method is, however, prone to difficulties as different responses may be recorded in upstream and downstream reaches of the basin, perhaps reflecting diversion, capture or differential tectonic uplift (cf. Maddy, 1997). This scale of investigation has more usually been undertaken where the primary focus lies in large-scale events with relatively low temporal resolution. Such an investigation is no different from investigations of pre-Quaternary rocks and hence where fluvial sedimentary units form discrete bodies of sediment that can be easily mapped they should be named using standard formal lithostratigraphy (see Section 2.3). Formations, which are the basic mappable unit (Hedberg, 1976) should be defined. Problems, however, arise when applying formal nomenclature, with various workers deploying formal lithostratigraphic terminology in different ways. As a consequence, in the UK there is little consistency in the usage of formations with respect to fluvial successions; in some situations the term is applied to the entire terrace sequence (eg. Gibbard, 1985, 1994; Maddy *et al.*, 1991, 1995), in others the term has been applied to individual terraces (Bridgland, 1994). An alternative scheme would be to use allostratigraphic units (North American Commission on Stratigraphic Nomenclature NACSN, 1983) which were specifically designed to overcome the difficulties in applying formal lithostratigraphical nomenclature or sequence stratigraphic principles (see Sections 2.3 and 3.4, for further discussion of these problems).

5.2.2 Floodplain and Reach-Scale Studies

The floodplain scale of investigation requires recording of sedimentological information from a large number of localities within the floodplain (or former floodplain in the case of sediments preserved beneath river terraces), each of which may reflect reach-scale responses. Detailed description of the sediments allows a potentially higher temporal resolution to be achieved. Investigations of this type are important both in a stratigraphic context and also in enhancing understanding of processes operating in the fluvial system over shorter (decadal to millennial) timescales.

Floodplains comprise horizontally and vertically stacked fluvial (channel and extra-channel), colluvial (valley slope derived) and possibly aeolian sediments. Each of these comprise distinct architectural elements (cf. Miall, 1985 see Section 2.1.2) within the body of sediment that makes up the (former) floodplain. Field description of these elements requires extensive exposure for accurate determination; alternatively, if the data quality permits, they may be defined from borehole reconstruction of gross facies changes, or from geophysical investigation, e.g. ground penetrating radar.

Fluvial sediments can be subdivided into channel and extra-channel types. Sediments within the channel are transported and deposited as a result of traction currents which lead to the formation of characteristic bedforms (the larger bedforms are referred to as bars). Bedforms vary depending on flow conditions and sediment type. Detailed discussion of relationships between bedform type, sediment calibre and flow regime may be found in, *inter alia*, Allen (1982), Ashley (1990) and Collinson (1986). The combination of sediment calibre and structure allows the identification of discrete lithofacies. Coding of these lithofacies (Table 5.1) greatly simplifies description and communication and allows otherwise complex sedimentary successions to be identified using a convenient short-hand (Miall, 1977, 1978, see also Sections 7.5, 7.6 and Table 3.2). Often these lithofacies are grouped into characteristic assemblages or associations (see Section 2.1.3). Implicit in this hierarchy of structures is the identification of a hierarchy of bounding surfaces (Table 5.2) which signify the scale of the events recorded.

The widespread adoption of lithofacies coding has been accompanied by the recognition of typical combinations of lithofacies which have been referred to as architectural elements. Architectural elements (Table 5.3) have been described for fluvial environments by Miall (1985, 1996). At the reach scale these elements help to define the familiar river planform types (Bridge, 1985) of straight, meandering (e.g. Bluck,1971), braided (Best and Bristow, 1993) and anastomosing (Smith, 1983), each of which may be associated with characteristic environmental conditions.

Facies code	Facies	Sedimentary Structures	Interpretation
Gms	massive, matrix supported gravel	grading	debris flow deposits
Gm	massive or crudely bedded gravel	horizontal bedding, imbrication	longitudinal bars, lag deposits, sieve deposits
Gt	gravel, stratified	trough cross-beds	minor channel fills
Gp	gravel, stratified	planar cross beds	longitudinal bars, deltaic growths for older bars
St	sand, medium to very coarse	solitary or grouped trough	dunes (lower flow regime)
Sp	sand, medium to very coarse, may be pebbly	solitary or grouped planar cross beds	linguoid , transverse bars, sand waves (lower flow regime)
Sr	sand, very fine to coarse	ripple cross lamination	ripples (lower flow regime)
Sl	sand, very fine to very coarse, may be pebbly	horizontal lamination, parting or streaming lineation	planar bed flow (upper flow regime)
Se	erosional scours with intraclasts	crude cross-bedding	scour fills
Ss	sand, fine to very coarse, may be pebbly	broad, shallow scours	scour fills
Fl	sand, silt, mud deposits	fine lamination, very small ripples	overbank or waning flood
Fsc	silt, mud	laminated to massive	backswamp deposit
Fcf	mud	massive, with fresh-water molluscs	backswamp pond deposit
Fm	mud, silt	massive, desiccation cracks	overbank or drape deposit

Table 5.1. *Facies classification and lithofacies codes for fluvial sediments (after Miall 1978, see also Miall 1996).*

Rank	Character of Bounding Surface	Depositional Unit	Example Process	Timescale of processes
0th Order	lamination surface	lamina	burst-sweep cycle	10^{-6}
1st Order	set bounding surface	ripple (microform)	bedform migration	$10^{-5} - 10^{-6}$
2nd Order	coset bounding surface	dune (mesoform)	bedform migration	$10^{-2} - 10^{-1}$
3rd Order	reactivation surface	macroform growth increment	seasonal events 10 yr flood	$10^{0} - 10^{1}$
4th Order	convex-up macroform top	macroform e.g. point bar	100 yr flood, bar migration	$10^{2} - 10^{3}$
5th Order	flat to concave-up channel base	channel	long term geomorphic process	$10^{3} - 10^{4}$
6th Order	flat, regionally extensive	channel belt sequence	Milankovitch cycles	$10^{4} - 10^{5}$

Table 5.2. *Hierarchy of bounding surfaces identifiable in fluvial sequences (modified from Miall, 1996).*

Element	Symbol	Principal Facies	Geometry and relationships
Channels	CH	any combination	finger, lens or sheet, concave-up erosional base, scale and shape highly variable; internal concave-up 3rd order erosion surface common
Gravel bars and bedforms	GB	Gm, Gp, Gt	lens, blanket, usually tabular bodies; commonly interbedded with SB
Sandy bedforms	SB	St, Sp, Sh, Sl, Sr, Se, Ss	lens, sheet, blanket, wedge, occurs as channel-fills, crevasse splays, minor bars
Downstream accretion macroforms	DA	St, Sp, Sh, Sl, Sr, Se, Ss	lens resting on flat or chanelled base, convex-up 3rd order internal erosion surface and upper 4th order bounding surface
Lateral-accretion macroforms	LA	St, Sp, Sh, Sl, Se, Ss, less commonly Gm, Gt, Gp	wedge, sheet, lobe; characterised by internal lateral-accretion 3rd order surface
Sediment gravity flow	SG	Gm, Gms	lobe, sheet, typically interbedded with GB
Laminated sand sheet	LS	Sh, Sl minor Sp, Sr	sheet, blanket
Overbank fines	OF	Fm, Fl	Thin to thick blankets; commonly interbedded with SB may fill abandoned channels

Table 5.3. *Architectural elements identifiable in fluvial successions (after Miall, 1985).*

5.3 METHODS FOR RECORDING FIELD INFORMATION

In the case of a geological investigation at the basin scale often only very basic descriptions may be required; for example, a generalised record of the deposits at the locality, thickness and lithological composition may be sufficient. However, in the case of an investigation of events at higher temporal resolution at the floodplain/reach scale it is usually more appropriate to make detailed internal structural observations on a number of adjacent faces in order to characterise the nature and variability of the sedimentology and to allow a detailed assessment of the fluvial activity represented at the site. In all instances it is desirable to record all available information which, if not of immediate use, may be of relevance at some point in the future in the context of different research objectives or when advances in understanding and techniques available may allow the data to be utilised. Published examples of such detailed studies of Pleistocene fluvial deposits include Bryant (1983), Dawson (1985), Rose *et al.* (1985), Dawson and Bryant (1987), Kasse *et al.* (1995), Krzyszkowski (1994) and Collins *et al.* (1996).

The approach adopted to record field information may also be dictated by the logistical problems presented by a particular site. Working gravel pits often have rapidly changing exposures as extraction progresses, giving the benefit of extensive exposure, but the problem of little time in which to make detailed observations. If possible when making the decision on which sections to record consideration should be given to provision of three dimensional coverage; it is inadvisable to restrict description to one or two parallel sections. Decisions also have to be made concerning the extent to which any one section is representative of the entire sequence and how many sections should be recorded. The physical scale of the exposure may also militate against detailed recording of all the available sections.

It is clear that field methods should be adapted to the prevailing circumstances and the quality of the available exposures. The following sections describe briefly those attributes of a site that should be considered when undertaking field work on fluvial sediments. Many of them are broadly applicable to any geological field investigation or are pieces of basic information that should not be, but occasionally are, overlooked. Useful additional information may be found in practical sedimentology texts such as Lindholm (1987) and Tucker (1988, 1996) and Chapters 2 and 3.

5.3.1 Plan of Working Faces

A map to show the position of recorded faces and other points within a site is essential. In working pits which change rapidly they provide an important record of the relative position of sections. In some instances base maps of working pits may be obtained from the extraction company, onto which detailed information can be added. A series of temporary benchmarks (located on buildings, entrance gates etc.) can be established close to the working area from a bench mark or spot height. These should be fixed points that will not be destroyed during further extraction. These allow rapid location of sections in working areas.

The altitude of the locality should also be accurately determined. Where the data are available this should be accomplished by surveying from a benchmark (in the UK these can be obtained from the Ordnance Survey) or where this is not possible from a spot height shown on at least a 1:25000 map. Once again in areas where no height information is readily available use of GPS to determine height is possible, though differential GPS would be required to achieve sub-metre accuracy.

5.3.2 Face Description

The process of recording sedimentary exposures is, to some extent, a matter of personal preference as to how this should be achieved. In the experience of the writers a combination of approaches has proved successful. If both vertical and lateral facies variability is to be assessed, which is desirable, a limited number of vertical profiles do not necessarily provide sufficient detail, unless closely spaced along a section. The disposition of facies along a face can be recorded using detailed field diagrams supplemented by photomosaics. This allows the major features to be recorded (bounding surfaces, major and minor channel features, laterally persistent unconformities, post depositional features, such as ice-wedge casts). The use of vertical sedimentary profiles can also be used to record detailed sedimentology at particular locations in the sequence.

When illustrating a particular section, the procedures used should allow the sedimentology to be recorded in detail. The resulting field diagram also serves as a base diagram for recording the position of samples taken for later analysis. Great detail can be recorded in geological sections using methods more often seen on archaeological excavations where sections are drawn in detail, often at a scale of 1:10 or 1:20. Recording of such detail may not be possible or appropriate for a purely geological record; however much can be gained from employing such methods. Adequately detailed drawing of lengthy sections can be done efficiently utilising an approach similar to that outlined below (see also Section 3.1).

Stage 1
Establish a horizontal datum. A string fixed on to nails driven into the face can be levelled using a line level and checked by surveying. The section can then be positioned accurately by surveying into the pre-existing temporary bench-marks. A 30 m tape can be fixed to this line for the purpose of recording the lateral section.

Stage 2

Draw the section. The section should be accurately drawn on to graph paper (though drawing film, while more expensive, has greater dimensional stability and is water-proof), denoting firstly any readily identifiable structures, such as channel features, major bounding surfaces, involutions etc, followed by more detailed inspection for more subtle form elements. Points are located by taking measurements along the reference line and heights above/below it. The scale of the diagram will depend on the size of the section; a scale of 1:50 is often sufficient for a face of several tens of metres in length.

Stage 3

Construct vertical profiles along the section. Vertical logs can be used to supplement the information contained on the drawn section and provide additional sedimentological detail (see Section 3.2.2). Logs may be positioned at regular intervals along the face (closer or wider spacing can be used as appropriate dependent upon the scale of exposure and the level of detail required). The sediments can be described using the lithofacies coding established by Miall (1977, 1996).

Stage 4

Photograph the section. A photographic record is an essential additional source of information when analysing the field sections. A photomosaic can be constructed by taking a series of overlapping photographs. Distortion around the edges of the image can create problems so a large overlap is desirable. These can be used to create a photomosaic to supplement the face diagrams. Miall (1996) suggested taking photomosaics into the field and using them as an underlay to detailed field recording and for the re-checking of recording accuracy (see Section 3.2.1).

The drawing of graphic logs, taking palaeocurrent measurements and sampling of sediments for analysis are discussed in detail in Chapter 3. It is worth noting here that sampling for palaeoecological and geochronological studies is often an important component of the field work. The sampling strategy will largely be determined by the availability of suitable materials and the particular requirements of the research. Accurate determination of plan position and the position of the sample locations within the sediments is critical and careful, systematic labelling of samples and their location on face diagrams to record their precise location will assist in their subsequent analysis.

5.4 CASE STUDY: THE UPPER THAMES

The case study chosen to illustrate the description and interpretation of Pleistocene fluvial sediments is from the site of Cassington (SP4810, Fig. 5.1) in the Upper Thames Valley where the deposits record significant changes in fluvial style over the last interglacial-

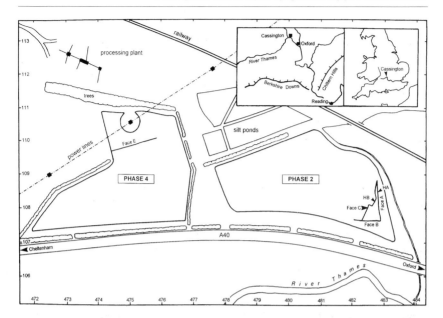

Figure 5.1. *Location of the quarry and the position of the sections recorded at Cassington.*

glacial cycle (the observations recorded here are reported fully in Maddy *et al.*, 1998). This case study has been selected as it illustrates the problems of recording extensive exposures and also the high quality of information that can be obtained from such exposures. For much of the Middle and all of the Upper Pleistocene the Upper Thames Valley remained outside the limit of ice advance and thus the main agent of landscape evolution has been the action of the River Thames and its tributaries. The river has successively incised into the landscape abandoning a series of terraces underlain by fluvial sediments at varying altitudes above the present river. This succession of river terraces (Table 5.4) was examined and each terrace named by Sandford (1924). Later work by Arkell (1947), Briggs and Gilbertson (1973) and Briggs *et al.* (1985) has tended to confirm this succession and enhanced its interpretation by distinguishing lithostratigraphic and biostratigraphic evidence for the further internal subdivision of units into cold and warm climate sediments. In addition a range of geochronological techniques has been applied to aspects of the succession (Briggs *et al.*, 1985, Bowen *et al.*, 1989). Recently these terrace sediments have been reclassified using formal lithostratigraphical nomenclature (Table 5.4).

The deposits at Cassington lie beneath the Floodplain Terrace (Northmoor Member of the Upper Thames Formation); the land surface is at a height of about 59 m OD and is some 1-2 m above the present river level.

Terrace stratigraphy			Lithostratigraphy		
	after Bridgland (1994)			after Gibbard (in press)	
	Member	**Formation**	**Member**	**Formation**	
Floodplain Terrace		Northmoor	Northmoor		
Sumertown Radley Terrace	Eynsham Gravel Stanton Harcourt Gravel Stanton Harcourt Channel Deposits	Sumertown-Radley	Sumertown-Radley	Upper Thames Valley	
Wolvercote Terrace	Wolvercote Channel Deposits	Wolvercote	Wolvercote Wolvercote Channel		
Hanborough Terrace		Hanborough	Hanborough		

Table 5.4. *Terraces of the upper Thames Valley and formal lithostratigraphic schemes for this succession*

5.4.1 Recording the Field Sections

During the initial phase of field work at the site extensive exposures were present at the eastern edge of the site. These were referred to as Faces A, B and C. For the purposes of this chapter the description given below is largely confined to the most extensive exposure, Face B, which was recorded during the period August-November 1991. At this time the portion of this working face selected for investigation was approximately 40 m in length.

The steps outlined in Section 5.3 were followed to produce a detailed field diagram of the lower part of the face, where there was considerable facies variability, both vertically and laterally. In order to record the upper part of the section, which consisted mainly of gravel-dominated facies, a total of 15 vertical sedimentary logs were recorded at 2 m intervals (part of the exposure was obscured by fallen debris). The vertical sedimentary logs were then combined with the detailed field diagrams of the lower part of the section to produce the final face diagram (Figure 5.2). This process was assisted by the use of a photomosaic (reproduced in Maddy *et al.*, 1998).

Figure 5.2. *View of Face B as exposed in the summer of 1991.*

5.4.1.1 Internal Structure

The deposits are up to *ca.* 4 m in thickness and sedimentary structures are generally well-preserved. The top *ca.* 1 m comprises modern alluvium and in all the sections examined it had been removed by the extraction company. The upper levels of the exposed sections show evidence of disturbance most probably due to the action of permafrost processes and the formation of involutions.

The approach to the interpretation of the sedimentology has been to identify "facies associations", or groupings of genetically related sedimentary facies (Reading, 1986 p.5). This approach has been utilised by other workers on fluvial sediments, for example Dawson (1985, 1987) in the interpretation of the deposits underlying the Main Terrace of the River Severn. The lithostratigraphy of the Cassington succession can be divided into a number of these facies associations (A-E). These are defined by 3rd-6th order bounding surfaces, defining distinct depositional phases and comprise individual lithofacies defined using the facies coding system of Miall (1977, 1996). The sedimentological properties of these associations are outlined in Table 5.5. Their generalised disposition is shown in Figure 5.2, which has been devised from the detailed face diagrams and vertical profiles constructed using the approach described above.

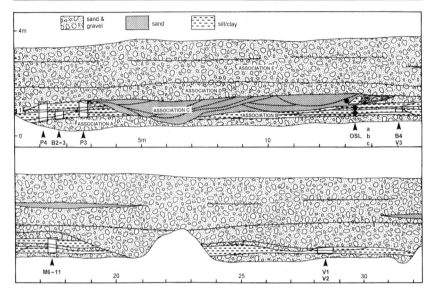

Figure 5.3. *Section diagram of Cassington, Face B, showing disposition of the five facies associations recognised, created from the section drawings and vertical logs.*

5.4.2 Description of the Field Sections

The sections described below present a two-dimensional view of the sediment body under investigation. Although useful, where practical this type of recording should be undertaken on more than one occasion as exposures change and preferably include exposures at a variety of angles, i.e. oblique to flow directions. This allows a comprehensive picture of three-dimensional structure to be determined. The interpretation of these deposits utilises the information presented here together with additional information from the site gained during description of additional exposures (Maddy *et al.*, 1998).

5.4.2.1 Facies Association A

Description: this comprises massive to crudely stratified, predominantly well-sorted limestone-dominated gravels, up to 1 m in thickness. It forms a near-continuous basal deposit at the eastern end of the pit, suggesting that sedimentation of this association is restricted to a relatively narrow zone, compared with the overlying coarse gravel deposits (Associations D and E).

Nature of the Lower Bounding Surface: the base of the succession constitutes a 6th order bounding surface (Table 5.3) forming the base of the Pleistocene succession on an eroded bedrock surface. Although this surface shows little relative relief it is punctuated by ellipsoidal scours which have formed in the lee of large septarian nodules.

5.4.2.2 Facies Association B

Description: this has been identified in a number of contexts, as isolated scour hollows and channel fills resting directly on the Oxford Clay, and as laterally persistent units of laminated sands and silts within the lower *ca.* 1 m of the succession (Figure 5.2). It is characterised by generally fine-grained, organic sediments. At the base of the succession a series of ellipsoidal scour hollows, formed in the lee of large septarian nodules are infilled with fine-grained sediments above a thin lag-gravel (Figure 5.4). The deposits lining these scours display bedding which is generally conformable with the scour forms and in places contain clasts of the underlying Oxford Clay bedrock. Large mammalian remains have also been recovered from these sediments (Figure 5.4). Higher in the succession, closely associated with gravels of Association A, are laterally persistent organic-rich, laminated and ripple bedded sands, silts and clays, up to *ca.* 1 m in thickness. These sediments overlie a sub-horizontal lower bounding surface and are over 30 m in lateral extent in Face B (Figure 5.3).

Figure 5.4. View of an excavation of a scour hollow at the base of the succession infilled with deposits of Facies Association B (position of scour marked HB on Fig. 5.1). Scale indicated by the drawing frame which is 1 m square. Pegs mark position of mammalian remains. (Excavation undertaken and photographed by Terry Hardaker).

Figure 5.5. *Close up of part of Face B, showing relationship between Facies Associations A, B and D. Pollen profile P3 is visible and spans ca. 80 cm through Association B.*

Nature of the Lower Bounding Surface: the lower bounding surface is a 3rd-order surface (Table 5.3). The nature of the contact may be sub-horizontal or scoured, the latter type is associated with the scour fills in the lee of septarian nodules at the base of the succession.

5.4.2.3 Facies Association C

Description: this comprises laterally discontinuous sand facies up to 1 m thick. The sands range from medium to fine grade. Multiple shallow channel fills are evident, with trough cross-bedded and massive sand facies. The channels commonly show high width-depth ratios.

Nature of the lower bounding surface: the base of the unit is a 5th-order (Table 5.3) channelled erosional contact (i.e. a concave-up bounding surface) with significant erosion into the underlying gravels (Figures 5.2 and 5.3).

5.4.2.4 Facies Association D

Description: this association comprises a predominantly coarse gravel, traceable over the entire worked area and is up to 2 m in thickness (Figures 5.2 and 5.3). The predominant facies consisits of laterally continuous, sub-horizontal, fining-upwards gravel sheets (10-15 cm in thickness). The gravel clasts range up to 15 cm long axis and fine upwards. Multiple shallow channel fills are evident, with channels showing high width-depth ratios.

Figure 5.6. *Face E, showing an ice wedge cast formed on the contact between Facies Associations D and E. Position of section shown on Figure 5.1.*

Nature of the lower bounding surface: the base of the unit is an erosional 5th-order bounding surface (Table 5.3), and is in many places channelled (a concave-up bounding surface) both into and through the underlying gravels, to rest directly on the Oxford Clay.

5.4.2.5 Facies Association E

Description: overlying Association D is a medium to fine gravel, 1.5 m in thickness (Figures 5.2 and 5.3). It is distinguishable from Association D in these exposures as it contains somewhat finer gravel particles. In one face they are clearly divisible by the presence of an ice-wedge cast associated with the bounding surface between them (Figure 5.6). The uppermost portion of this association displays disturbance with loading structures evident.

Nature of the lower bounding surface: this association lies on a 4th-order, planar lower bounding surface (Table 5.3), which, due to the sub-horizontal bedding of the upper parts of Association D, may appear in places to be conformable with it.

Facies Associations	Facies	Lower Bounding	Geometry
E	Gm, Sm, Ss	Planar and erosional (4th)	Tabular, laterally extensive planar bedded gravels up to 1.5 m in total thickness. Beds 10-15 cm. Isolated sets of planar cross-bedded sands.
D	Gm Gp, Sp	Planar and erosional. Locally concave up (5th)	Laterally persistent planar-bedded coarse gravel facies in excess of 20 m in length. Wedge units of tabular cross-bedded gravel orientated normal to channel axis and extending from channel sides. Tabular, laterally extensive units of massive to planar gravel up to 1.5 m in thickness. Tabular cross-bedded gravel units orientated parallel to transport direction (down-valley), interbedded with units of massive gravel. Lenticular beds of planar bedded sands up to 50 cm thick. Isolated sets of planar cross-bedded sand.
C	St, Sm	Concave-up (5th)	Trough cross-bedded and massive sands. Possibly some low-angle lateral accretion units.
B	Sm, Sl, Sr Fl, Fm, Fcf	Planar and Conformable (3rd)	Laminated and ripple-bedded sands, silts and clays. Thin pebble beds. Some low-angle lateral accretion units.
A	Gm	Planar and erosional (6th)	Laterally persistent planar-bedded gravels in excess of 20 m in length and up to 1 m in thickness.

Table 5.5. *Characteristics and interpretation of the facies associations identified at Cassington (after Maddy et al., 1998).*

Interpretation Planform	Element	Probable Surface (order)
Bar core (longitudinal) and bar top sedimentation. Slough channel fills.	CH, GB, SB	Braided
Vertical bar platform aggradation.	CH, GB, SB	Braided
Laterally down-filled channels.		
Agglomerated units of in-channel bar (longitudinal) deposition.		
Bar top and bar tail sedimentation.		
Channel-fill sequence	CH	Transitional
Bar top (supra-bar platform) sedimentation	SB	
Overbank fines	OF	
Agglomerated sequence of in-channel, bar deposition (bar platform). Lag deposits also present locally.	GB	Meandering

5.4.3 Interpretation of the Field Sections

Interpretation of this fluvial succession can best be achieved by consideration of the facies associations and their lateral variability rather than simple examination of individual facies and their vertical variability. Each facies association is considered briefly below and their interpretation is summarised in Table 5.5.

Facies Association A: this represents superimposed channel-fill sequences, where low-angle beds may represent lateral accretion surfaces albeit that no epsilon cross-beds were observed. Observations on other faces (see Maddy *et al.*, 1998) confirm the presence of asymmetrical channel fills, with evidence of undercut bank collapse, within this unit. These channels often display low width-depth ratios. Such geometry is consistent with formation in a sinuous channel. The widespread basal Gm facies probably represents bar-core sediment bar platform, (cf. Bluck, 1974).

Facies Association B: this suggests accumulation as a result of vertical accretion, most probably as overbank flood deposits. The succession generated is very similar to recent (Holocene) valley fills. The succession is consistent with deposition in a meandering, gravel-bed river (Bluck, 1974). The widespread preservation of low-energy facies would tend to support this interpretation. Frequent overbank flooding is consistent with a regime similar to that of the present-day River Thames.

Facies Association C: these medium to fine sands represent a changing fluvial style and higher stream power. The channels have relatively high width/depth ratios but bank collapse structures indicate some bank cohesion as the river undercut banks formed in the fine-grained sediments of Association B. It is likely that the planform is transitional (anastomosing?) between the sinuous planform of Associations A and B and the multi-channel planform of Association D.

Facies Association D: these coarse gravels are in complete contrast to those of Association A. The coarseness of the gravel suggests relatively high stream power. The laterally extensive nature of the unit indicates that deposition took place over a wider area than the underlying sediments and suggests considerably higher sediment supply. Major channels are infilled by coarse gravel facies, commonly on large progradational bedforms. The preservation and formation of relatively deep channel fills may be due to the channel bank stability afforded by the fine-grained sediments into which the channels were eroded. Later sedimentation would have been restricted to channels cut into coarse sediments which lack cohesion and hence form unstable banks.

Facies Association E: similar structures are recorded here to the underlying Association D. However, the gravels are distinctly finer (fine-medium) in texture. The planar lower bounding surface suggests an erosional contact and indicates a re-activation of sediment movement. The structures suggest deposition in a multi-channel system. Observations on an adjacent face (Face E) indicate the formation of intraformational ice wedges. This confirms deposition under cold climate conditions. Movement of the channel zone is indicated by the polymorphic nature of ice-wedge formation, demonstrating sedimentation on this part of the floodplain had become sporadic. The change from Facies Association D to E could simply therefore reflect a shift in the sedimentation zone.

5.4.4 Environmental Reconstruction

In order to establish a complete environmental reconstruction it is essential to utilise the additional information available from palaeontological and geochronological work. At Cassington work was undertaken on the Mollusca, Coleoptera and Vertebrata contained within the succession and luminescence and amino-acid geochronological techniques were applied to appropriate material. The results are reported fully in Maddy *et al.* (1998) and are summarised below.

5.4.4.1 Palaeoecology
In addition to the changing style of fluvial sedimentation indicated in this succession, particularly between Associations A-D, palaeoecological data also suggest major changes in environmental conditions. The evidence from vegetation, molluscan and coleopteran assemblages suggests cooling towards the top of the fine-grained sequence of Association B. The basal sediments were deposited in a temperate climate with an open forested canopy on the valley sides. Towards the top there is a distinct change to a cooler fauna (Tundra), with a more open herbaceous vegetation (Maddy *et al.*, 1998). Fauna and flora from organic fills on the Association D-E boundary indicate fully Arctic climatic conditions.

The recognition of a climatic change of this type is of particular significance in the interpretation of the fluvial succession and provides a possible causal mechanism to generate the changes in fluvial style observed at Cassington. Climatic deterioration would have had an impact upon discharge and sediment supply, which would have created a tendency for the river to switch from a single-thread, meandering system to a multi-thread, braided habit.

5.4.4.2 Geochronology
In order to establish wider significance for these changes it is necessary to determine a chronology of events. Results from Cassington allow the observed changes in environmental

conditions and river behaviour to be related to the fluctuations in climate through the last interglacial-glacial cycle represented in continuous terrestrial (Woillard, 1978), ice-core (Dansgaard *et al.*, 1993) and oceanic (Bond *et al.,* 1992) records.

Amino Acid Epimerisation: molluscan samples from organic-filled scour-hollows (Association B) were submitted to the Cardiff Geochronology Laboratory for amino acid epimerisation analysis. The results from two species, *Bithynia tentaculata* (0.081 ± 0.009 [6]) and *Valvata piscinalis* (0.136 ± 0.009 [5]) suggest these data can be correlated with localities attributed to a range of ages encompassing the last interglacial (oxygen isotope stage 5) (Bowen *et al.*, 1989).

Optically Stimulated Luminescence (OSL): samples were taken from three levels within Association A and B yielding ages (±1σ) of 78±20ka (865a), 84±19ka (865b) and 125±24ka (865c) (Rees-Jones and Tite, 1997, Maddy *et al.*, 1998). These age estimates would place the temperate interval indicated by the organic deposits in oxygen isotope stage 5.

The geochronological evidence would therefore suggest that the cooling indicated by floral and faunal evidence is most likely to have occurred during time equivalent to the marine oxygen isotope stage 5/4 transition. Such a major environmental change would also account for the changing fluvial style between Association A and D. Destabilisation of slopes consequent upon the disappearing vegetation cover would increase the sediment supply into the valley bottom. Furthermore, the major regional climatic instability associated with the 5/4 transition would also result in increased magnitude and frequency of depression tracks over the area leading to increased flood frequency and magnitude. The low-energy river responsible for Associations A and B would thus have to contend with increasing water and sediment supply. Such a change in regime would most likely lead to the development of a multi-channel system such as that identified in Association D, perhaps passing through the transitional phase represented by Association C. As the cold stage intensified it is probable that the river would be dominated by a more nival type regime, i.e. a pronounced spring flood. Similar climate-driven changes in fluvial response are well documented in other river systems (Vandenberghe, 1993, 1995; Starkel, 1990).

In exposures additional to those described above minor organic-rich channel fills occur at the bounding surface between Associations D and E. These scours are infilled with large quantities of plant macrofossil remains. However, they tend to be of one species, indicating a restricted vegetation. Age estimation on similar deposits in comparable stratigraphical position elsewhere in the upper Thames (Briggs *et al.*, 1985) suggests that Association D may relate to activity during the late-glacial (Loch Lomond) stadial. Hence the transition from Association D to E may reflect changing environmental conditions associated with the Devensian late-glacial oscillation rather than an intrinsic shift in sedimentation foci. The overall interpretation of the succession at Cassington is summarised in Figure 5.7.

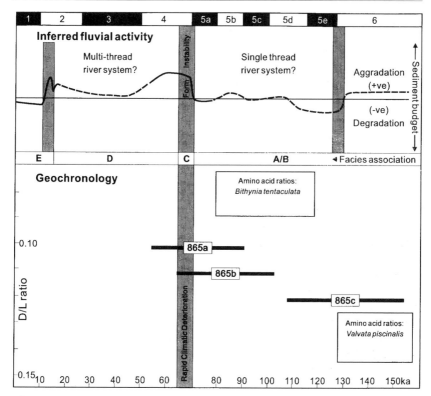

Figure 5.7. *Summary of the nature and timing of changes in river behaviour inferred from the sedimentological and palaeoecological investigations at Cassington.*

This interpretation is based upon detailed recording of the fluvial sedimentology at the site, together with detailed palaeontological information, which can be related to the observed changes in fluvial style. The importance of accurate recording of the sedimentology and its lateral variability cannot be over-emphasised. Though ultimately a fluvial succession may be generalised into architectural elements, facies associations or other similar genetically-related groupings of lithofacies (cf. Needham, 1992); this should be based upon identification of individual lithofacies and their relationship to one another. The archive of palaeoenvironmental information held in the fluvial sediments of major river systems such as the River Thames has considerable potential for understanding the response of terrestrial systems to climate forcing. Careful recording and interpretation of high resolution records, alongside detailed palaeoenvironmental and geochronological research are essential if this potential is to be realised.

ACKNOWLEDGEMENTS

This work was funded by an NERC research grant (GR9/01656). The assistance and co-operation of ARC Southern and the quarry manager, Bob Turner, is gratefully acknowledged, as is the work of all the specialists who have contributed to the research at Cassington.

REFERENCES

ALLEN, J.R.L. 1982. *Sedimentary Structures: their Character and Physical Basis*. Vol.1. Elsevier, Amsterdam.

ARKELL, W.J. 1947. *The Geology of Oxford*. Clarendon Press, Oxford.

ASHLEY, G.M. 1990. Classification of large-scale sub-aqueous bedforms: a new look at an old problem. *Journal of Sedimentary Petrology,* **60**, 160-172.

BEST, J. and BRISTOW, C. (eds) 1993. *Braided Rivers: Form, Process and Economic Applications.* Geological Society of London. Special Publication No.75.

BLUCK, B.J. 1971. Sedimentation in the meandering River Endrick. *Scottish Journal of Geology,* **7**, 93-138.

BLUCK, B.J. 1974. Structure and some directional properties of some valley sandur deposits in Southern Iceland. *Sedimentology,* **21**, 533-554.

BOND, G., HEINRICH, H., BROECKER, W., LABEYRIE, L., MCMANUS, J., ANDREWS, J., HUON, S., JANTSCHIK, R., CLASEN, S., SIMET, C., TEDESCO, K., KLAS, M., BONANI, G. and IVY, S. 1992. Evidence for massive discharges of icebergs into the North Atlantic ocean during the last glacial period. *Nature,* **360**, 245-249.

BOWEN, D.Q., HUGHES, S., SYKES, G.A. and MILLER, G.H. 1989. Land-sea correlations in the Pleistocene based on isoleucine epimerization in non-marine molluscs. *Nature*, **340**, 49-51.

BRIDGE, J.S. 1985. Perspectives: Paleochannel patterns inferred from alluvial stratigraphy. *Journal of Sedimentary Petrology*, **55**, 579-706.

BRIDGLAND, D.R. 1994. *Quaternary of the Thames*. Chapman and Hall, London.

BRIGGS, D.J. and GILBERTSON, D.D. 1973. The age of the Hanborough Terrace of the River Evenlode, Oxfordshire. *Proceedings of the Geologists' Association,* **84**, 155-173.

BRIGGS, D.J., COOPE, G.R. and GILBERTSON, D.D. 1985. *The Chronology and Environmental Framework of Early Man in the Upper Thames Valley.* BAR British Series **137**, Oxford.

BRUNNAKER, K. 1975. The Mid-Pleistocene of the Rhine Basin. *IN:* Butzer, K.W. and Isaac, G.L. (eds), *After the Australopithecines.* Mouton Publishers, The Hague, 189-224.

BRUNNAKER, K. 1986. Quaternary Stratigraphy of the Lower Rhine area and northern Alpine foothills. *Quaternary Science Reviews,* **5**, 373-379.

BRYANT, I.D. 1983. The utilisation of Arctic river analogues: studies in the interpretation of periglacial river sediments in Southern Britain. *IN*: Gregory, K.J. (ed), *Background to Palaeohydrology: A Perspective*. Wiley, New York, 413-431.

COLLINS, P.E.F., FENWICK, I.M., KEITH-LUCAS, D.M. and WORSLEY, P. 1996. Late Devensian river and floodplain dynamics and related environmental change in northwest Europe, with particular reference to a site at Woolhampton, Berkshire, England. *Journal of Quaternary Science*, **11**, 357-375.

COLLINSON, J.D. 1986. Alluvial sediments. *IN*: Reading, H.G. (ed), *Sedimentary Environments and Facies*, 20-62. Blackwell Scientific Publications, Oxford.

DANSGAARD, W., JOHNSON, S.J., CLAUSEN, H.B., DAHL-JENSEN, D., GUNDESTRUP, N.S., HAMMER, C.U., HVIDBERG, C.S., STEFFENSEN, J.P., SVEINBJÖRNSDOTTIR, A.E., JOUZEL, J. and BOND, G. 1993. Evidence for general instability of past climate from a 250-kyr ice-core record. *Nature*, **364**, 218-220.

DAWSON, M.R. 1985. Environmental reconstruction of a Late Devensian terrace sequence. Some preliminary findings. *Earth Surface Processes and Landforms*, **10**, 237-246.

DAWSON, M.R. 1987. Sedimentological aspects of periglacial river terrace aggradations: a case study from the English Midlands. *IN*: Boardman, J. (ed.), *Periglacial Processes and Landforms in Britain and Ireland*. Cambridge University Press, Cambridge, 265-274.

DAWSON, M.R. and BRYANT, I.D. 1987. Three-dimensional facies geometry in Pleistocene outwash sediments, Worcester, U.K. *IN*: Ethridge, F.G. (ed), *Recent Developments in Fluvial Sedimentology*. Society of Economic Paleontologists and Mineralogists, Special Publication **39**, 191-196.

FRENZEL, B. (ed.) 1995. *European river activity and climatic change during the Lateglacial and early Holocene*. Palaeoclimate Research, Special Issue: ESF Project European Palaeoclimate and Man 9. Gustav Fischer Verlag: Stuttgart.

GIBBARD, P.L. 1985. *The Pleistocene History of the Middle Thames Valley*. Cambridge University Press, Cambridge.

GIBBARD, P.L. 1994. *Pleistocene History of the Lower Thames Valley*. Cambridge University Press, Cambridge.

GIBBARD, P.L. in press. Upper Thames. *IN*: Bowen, D.Q. *et al*. (eds), Correlation of Quaternary Rocks in the British Isles. Special Report for the Geological Society of London.

HEDBERG, H.D. 1976. *International Stratigraphic Guide*. New York.

KARROW, P.F. 1986. Valley terraces and Huron basin water levels, southwestern Ontario. *Geological Society of America Bulletin*, **97**, 1089-1097.

KASSE, C., BOHNCKE, S.J.P. and VANDENBERGHE, J. 1995. Fluvial periglacial environments, climate and vegetation during the Middle Weichselian in the northern Netherlands with special reference to the Hengelo Interstadial. *Meded. Rijks Geol Dienst*, **52**, 387-414.

KRZYSZOWSKI, D. 1994. Sedimentology of Wartanian outwash near Belchatów, central Poland. *Boreas,* **23,** 149-163.

LINDHOLM, R. 1987. *A Practical Approach to Sedimentology.* Allen & Unwin, London.

MACKLIN, M.G. 1993. Holocene river alluviation in Britain. *Zeitschrift für Geomorphologie Supplement Band,* **88,** 109-122.

MADDY, D. 1997. Uplift-driven valley incision and river terrace formation in southern England. *Journal of Quaternary Science,* **12,** 539-545.

MADDY, D., KEEN, D.H., BRIDGLAND, D.R. AND GREEN, C.P. 1991. A revised model for the Pleistocene development of the River Avon, Warwickshire. *Journal of the Geological Society of London,* **148,** 473-484

MADDY, D, GREEN, C.P., LEWIS, S.G. AND BOWEN, D.Q. 1995. Pleistocene Geology of the Lower Severn Valley, UK. *Quaternary Science Reviews,* **14,** 209-222

MADDY, D, LEWIS, S.G. SCAIFE, R.G., BOWEN, D.Q., COOPE, G.R., GREEN, C.P., HARDAKER, T., KEEN, D.H., REES-JONES, J., PARFITT, S. AND SCOTT, K. 1998. The Upper Pleistocene deposits at Cassington, near Oxford, England. *Journal of Quaternary Science,* **13,** 205-231.

MIALL, A. D. 1977. The braided river depositional environment. *Earth Science Reviews,* **13,** 1-62

MIALL, A. D. 1978. Lithofacies types and vertical profile models in braided rivers: a summary. *IN*: Miall, A.D. (ed), *Fluvial Sedimentology.* Memoir of the Canadian Society of Petroleum Geologists, Calgary 5, 1-47.

MIALL, A. D. 1985. Architectural-Element Analysis: A new model of facies analysis applied to fluvial deposits. *Earth Science Reviews,* **22,** 261-308

MIALL, A. D. 1996. *The Geology of Fluvial Deposits - Sedimentary Facies, Basin Analysis and Petroleum Geology.* Springer-Verlag.

NEEDHAM, S. 1992. Holocene alluviation and interstratified settlement evidence in the Thames valley at Runnymeade Bridge. *IN*: Needham, S. and Macklin, M.G. (eds), *Alluvial Archaeology in Britain.* Oxbow Monograph **27,** Oxbow Books, Oxford, 249-260.

NORTH AMERICAN COMMISSION ON STRATIGRAPHIC NOMENCLATURE (NACSN) 1983, North American Stratigraphic Code. *American Association of Petroleum Geologists, Bulletin,* **67,** 841-875.

PASSMORE, D.G., MACKLIN, M.G., BREWER, P.A., LEWIN, J., RUMSBY, B.T. AND NEWSON, M.D. 1993. Variability of late Holocene braiding in Britain. *IN*: Best, J.L. and Bristow, C.S. *Braided Rivers.* Geological Society Special Publication No.**75,** 205-229.

READING, H.G. 1986. *Sedimentary Environments and Facies.* 2nd edition. Blackwell Scientific Publishers, Oxford.

REES-JONES, J. AND TITE, M.S. 1997. Optical dating results for British archaeological sediments. *Archaeometry,* **39,** 177-187.

ROSE, J., TURNER, C., COOPE, G.R. AND BRYAN, M.D. 1980. Channel changes in a lowland river catchment over the last 13,000 years. *IN*: Cullingford, R.A., Davidson, D.A. and Lewis, J. (eds), *Timescales in Geomorphology,* 159-175. John Wiley and Sons, Chichester.

RUMSBY, B.T. AND MACKLIN, M.G. 1994. Channel and floodplain response to recent abrupt climate change: The Tyne Basin, Northern England. *Earth Surface Processes and Landforms,* **19,** 499-515.

SANDFORD, K.S. 1924. The river gravels of the Oxford district. *Quarterly Journal of the Geological Society,* **80,** 113-79.

SMITH, D.G. 1983. Anastomosed fluvial deposits: modern examples from western Canada. *IN*: Collinson, J.D. and Lewin, J. (eds), *Modern and Ancient Fluvial Systems.* International Association of Sedimentologists Special Publication **6**, 155-168.

STARKEL, L. 1990. Fluvial Environment as an Expression of Geoecological Changes. *Zeitschrift für Geomorphologie Supplement Band,* **79,** 133-52.

TUCKER, M. 1988. *Techniques in Sedimentology.* Blackwell Scientific Publishers, Oxford.

TUCKER, M. 1996. *The Field Description of Sedimentary Rocks.* John Wiley, Chichester.

VANDENBERGHE, J. 1993. Changing fluvial processes under changing periglacial conditions. *Zeitschrift für Geomorphologie Supplement Band,* **88,** 17-28.

VANDENBERGHE, J. 1995. Timescales, climate and river development. *Quaternary Science Reviews* **14,** 631-638.

WHITEMAN, C.A. AND ROSE, J. 1992.Thames river sediments of the British Early and Middle Pleistocene. *Quaternary Science Reviews,* **11,** 363-375.

WOILLARD, G.M. 1978. Grande Pile peat bog: a continuous pollen record for the last 140,000 years. *Quaternary Research,* **9,** 1-21.

Chapter 6

PYROCLASTIC AND EPICLASTIC DEPOSITS: A CASE STUDY FROM THE UNZEN VOLCANO, KYUSHU, JAPAN

Alison P. Jones and Tadahide Ui

6.1 PYROCLASTICS

Active volcanic environments are among the most dynamic in the world and are continually supplying the field scientist with large volumes of fresh material to investigate (see MTU Volcanoes page: http://www.geo.mtu.edu/volcanoes/world.html). Pyroclastic deposits are just one, but nevertheless an important, product of this volcanism and have been the focus of increasing attention in the past two decades (e.g. Murai, 1961, Walker, 1971, Fisher and Schmincke, 1984, Cas and Wright, 1987, Roobol and Smith, 1990, Colella and Hiscott, 1997). Traditionally, given the nature of these environments and the logistical difficulties incurred, an inverse modelling approach is used whereby the scientist works backwards from specific observations, in this case stratigraphic field sections, to the causative events. In recent years there has been an intensified interest in the dynamic processes of volcanism, such as pyroclastic flows, and facies analysis is being increasingly used to answer specific questions on depositional-process dynamics. Direct observations and measurements of volcanic eruptions are notoriously difficult and understandably scarce; therefore new techniques are being developed to counteract this; for example physical modelling of flow behaviour (Freundt, 1998) and high-resolution video footage (Ui *et al.*, in press, Dolan, 1998a).

6.2 PYROCLASTIC DEPOSITS

Individual pyroclastic density currents produce varying proportions of fall deposits, flow deposits, and surge deposits.

Pyroclastic fall deposits include subaqueous fallout and subaerial fallout/airfall tephra, the former of which can be submarine or sublacustrine. Subaerial fallout is further divided into eruption-plume derived fall deposits which are ejected explosively from a vent, producing a plume of tephra and gas, and ash-cloud derived fall deposits, resulting in part from ash-clouds rising off a moving pyroclastic flow. Three main types of fall deposits can be distinguished by their genetic and lithological characteristics: scoria-fall, pumice-fall and ash-fall deposits. The buoyant part of ash clouds is believed to produce ash-fall deposits (Fisher, 1979, Yamamoto, 1993).

Pyroclastic flow deposits are the product of hot, gaseous, particulate density currents known as pyroclastic flows, which are emplaced rapidly with velocities between 20 m/sec and 100 m/sec being recorded (Blong, 1984). There are three main types of pyroclastic flow deposits: block-and-ash flow, scoria-flow and pumice-flow/ash-flow/ignimbrite deposits, distinguished by their dominant genetic and lithological characteristics (Cas and Wright, 1987).

Pyroclastic surge deposits result from highly expanded, turbulent, gas-water-solid density currents with low particle concentrations (e.g. Colella and Hiscott, 1997). Surges are associated with three main situations: phreatomagmatic and phreatic eruptions[1], pyroclastic flows, and pyroclastic falls (Cas and Wright, 1987). Phreatomagmatic and phreatic explosions generate base surges, and pyroclastic flows generate ground and ash-cloud surges. The dense parts of ash clouds are thought to result in the dilute gravity currents of ash-cloud surges (Fisher, 1979, Yamamoto, 1993).

6.3 EPICLASTIC DEPOSITS

The term "epiclastic" is often used within volcanic literature to refer to secondary sediments such as debris flow, debris avalanche and fluvial deposits, resulting from the reworking of primary volcanic deposits. The term "lahar" [2], originating from Indonesia, is often used in lieu of volcanic mudflow/debris flow; however, some researchers believe that this term should be restricted to mudflows where a direct link can be made to volcanic activity and that the term 'mudflow' be used for prehistoric deposits where this is not possible (e.g. Smith and Roobol, 1990). A number of studies have investigated the reworking of volcaniclastics by fluvial and mass-movement processes (e.g. Scott, 1985, Johnson, 1986, Smith 1986, 1987, 1988; Nakayama and Yoshikawa, 1997).

6.4 PHYSICAL PROPERTIES OF PYROCLASTICS AND EPICLASTICS

Pyroclastic deposits have a distinctive set of sedimentary properties as a direct result of: a) high density contrasts between clasts and the transport medium - hot gas/steam and air, compared with fluvial transport for example; b) intense and rapid post-depositional processes such as welding and alteration.

---

[1] The interaction between hot magma and water produces hydrovolcanic activity. Steam explosions are referred to as phreatic explosions and explosions occurring due to the interaction between external water and magma are referred to as phreatomagmatic.

[2] The term 'lahar' is often associated with volcanic areas and is defined by Fisher and Schminke (1984) as " a mass of flowing volcanic debris intimately mixed with water".

1) *Sedimentary Texture*

Pyroclastic deposits comprise varying proportions of juvenile fragments (pumice or scoria clasts), glass shards (fragments that are smaller than the average vesicle size), crystals and lithic fragments. Pyroclasts and tephra are collective terms used for pyroclastic fragments and pyroclastic deposits, respectively. Tephrochronology is an important tool in Quaternary research and is defined as "a dating method based on the identification, correlation and dating of tephra" (Thorarinsson, 1980, p.10). The term "tephra" was introduced by Thorarinsson in his thesis and is used as a collective term for pyroclasts (Thorarinsson, 1980).

Most sedimentary schemes can be applied to pyroclastic deposits, but grain-size classes differ from standard classification schemes (see Section 2.2.1.1) whereby the terms ash, lapilli and blocks are substituted for sand and silt, pebbles and cobbles/boulders respectively (Table 6.1). Commonly the description of the sorting parameter (e.g. $\sigma\phi$) for pyroclastic deposits differs from that of fluvial deposits (e.g. a well-sorted fall deposit is equivalent to a moderately poorly sorted fluvial deposit).

Grain size	Diameter (mm)
coarse-grained blocks	>256
fine-grained blocks	64-256
coarse-grained lapilli	16-64
medium-grained lapilli	4-16
fine-grained lapilli	2-4
very coarse-grained ash	1-2
coarse-grained ash	0.5-1
medium-grained ash	0.063-0.5
fine-grained ash	<0.063

Table 6.1. *Classification of grain size (after Chough and Sohn, 1990).*

Accretionary lapilli are defined as being "lapilli-sized pellets of ash commonly exhibiting a concentric internal structure" (Cas and Wright, 1987, p.126) and are thought to form by the accretion of ash around a nucleus of water or a particulate (Schumacher and Schmincke, 1991). They are found in all three types of pyroclastic deposit, but are commonly formed in wet (phreatic or phreatomagmatic) eruption columns and by fall-out from steam-rich plumes (e.g. Walker, 1981).

2) *Depositional Units*

The term 'depositional unit' refers to a single pyroclastic flow deposited in one lobe. When several very hot flow units pile rapidly one on top of the other, they may cool as a single 'cooling unit' (Fisher and Schmincke, 1984, p.195). Pyroclastic deposits exhibit a variety of grading-types (see Figure 3.11). Grading is thought to reflect properties of moving pyroclastic flows and be a function of grain size (Cas and Wright, 1987, p.188-189). Grading processes involving the coarse fraction of a facies are referred to as coarse-tail grading (see Section 3.3.2.3).

3) *Properties Associated with High Temperatures*
Some components of pyroclastic deposits indicate emplacement at high temperatures and are typically used to distinguish between pyroclastic and debris flow deposits, these include: carbonised wood, pink/red colouration due to thermal oxidation, dark colouration due to finely-disseminated microlites of magnetite, thermal remanent magnetism, radial cooling joints and gas escape structures (see Fisher and Schmincke, 1984, Cas and Wright, 1987, Smith and Roobol, 1990). However, recent observations in the aftermath of the Pinatubo eruption (1991, Philippines) have made doubtful some of these previously accepted discriminators (S. Self, pers com).

Gas escape structures, also referred to as fossil fumarole pipes or gas segregation pipes, locally occur in pyroclastic flow deposits, but can also form in hot mud-flow deposits; pipes off carbonising vegetation are very common. They are formed by escaping hot gases and are typically enriched in heavier crystals and lithics and depleted in fine-ash. They are generally vertical structures a few centimetres wide and a few tens of centimetres in length; however, many different structures and sizes have been recorded in the literature (see Cas and Wright, 1987, p.184). There are two main types of gas escape structure: (i) gases derived from juvenile material lead to secondary alteration in and around the pipe, due to high temperatures and acidity converting volcanic glass into clay and other secondary minerals, (ii) almost all of the gas is water vapour derived from either river water or wet sediments and no alteration is observed in and around the pipe. This variety is mechanically equivalent to spiracles formed within lava flows (Cas and Wright, 1987, p.73).

Welding is defined as "the sintering together of hot pumice fragments and glass shards under a compactional load," (Cas and Wright, 1987, p.251) and three main grades or zones are recognised: dense, partial, and non-welded.

6.5 CASE STUDY: THE UNZEN VOLCANO, KYUSHU, JAPAN

In 1990, after 198 years of dormancy the Unzen Volcano, in Kyushu erupted and a five year period of activity followed. The Unzen Volcano is reputed to be one of the most active volcanoes in Japan, and is recognised internationally as one of the most representative volcanoes in its class (Hoshizumi, *et al.*, 1997). The eruption was characterised by lava dome forming eruptions and pyroclastic flows of dome-collapse origin. Block-and-ash

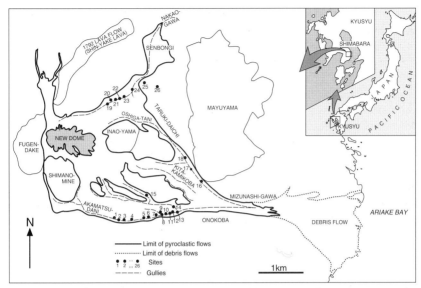

Figure 6.1. *Location map of the Unzen Volcano Field Area. Note that Kyusyu is Kyushu (both terms are used in Japan).*

flows were generated over 5,000 times between 1991 and 1995, and were limited in extent, with run out distances less than 3 km being common. Volumes of 10,000 m^3 for single flows were the most frequent and the maximum flow size was 1,000 000 m^3 (Ui *et al.*, 1997). Ash-cloud surges were commonly associated with block-and-ash flows and formed blast zones in the Nakao and Kamikoba areas. Flows were mainly confined to the existing valleys of the Akamatsudani, Mizunashi, Oshigadani and Nakao Rivers. However, volcanic activity has greatly altered the original topography, pyroclastic flows having obliterated valleys, waterfalls and manmade structures. The estimated total volume of this pyroclastic material is 1.2 x 10^8 m^3 (Ishikawa *et al.*, 1996). A system of deep gullies has developed which follow a similar course to the original valleys; this fluvial system is ephemeral, surface water being limited to storm events.

6.5.1 Volcano Monitoring and Data Collection

The activity of this eruption was intensively monitored by Shimabara Earthquake and Volcano Observatory (SEVO), Geological Survey of Japan (GSJ), Geographical Survey Institute (GSI), Japan Meteorological Agency (JMA), and the Joint University Research Groups (JURG). Measurements include deformation analysis (e.g. Ishihara *et al.*, 1997), TDEM (e.g. Kanda *et al.*, 1997), seismicity (e.g. Shimizu *et al.*, 1997), ERS ATSR and LANDSAT TM (e.g. Kaneko and Wooster, 1997), numerous sampling (e.g. Watanabe *et al.*, 1997), as well as widespread video coverage (e.g. Ui *et al.*, in press). This case study provides a detailed account of the sedimentary successions, which are in effect the products of the monitored activity. The evidence gathered can therefore be correlated to some extent with the specific real-time observations made during the eruption. This means that a direct link exists between the specific field observations, in this case stratigraphic sections, and the causative events, in this case documented by the monitoring evidence. However, opportunities to inspect field deposits during times of eruption are naturally, highly restricted due to safety considerations. As a result, detailed correlation is still limited and facies interpretation necessarily plays a major role.

6.5.2 Location

Geographically, Fugendake is located on the Shimabara Peninsula of western Kyushu, southern Japan (Figure 6.1) and geologically, it is situated on the western tip of the Central Kyushu Rift Valley (Beppu-Shimabara Graben) which cuts across the Island of Kyushu in a ENE-WSW direction (Okada, 1992). The Unzen Volcano comprises several lava domes, lava flows and pyroclastics, which are subdivided into Older Unzen and Younger Unzen Groups (Hoshizumi *et al.*, 1997). Futhermore, the Younger Unzen Group is subdivided into four volcanic bodies: Nodake, Myokendake, Fugendake and Mayuyama. The Older Unzen Group was active between *ca.* 0.25 Ma and 0.18 Ma and the Younger Unzen Group commenced activity *ca.* 0.10 Ma (Hoshizumi *et al.*, 1997).

6.5.3 Flow Mechanics and Eruptive History

Detailed accounts of the eruptive history of the Unzen Volcano have been presented by Yanagi *et al.* (1992), Ui *et al.* (in press) and Nakada *et al.* (in press).

1) *Initial Phase*
The initial phase of the 1990-95 eruption began with a series of phreatic explosions that started on November 17, 1990. A lava dome began to appear on May 20, 1991, and by November 1993, 12 exogenous flow lobes had emerged. The vent was located near the shoulder of a late Quaternary lava dome, and towards the east, flow lobes were seen to be hanging on the steep upper slopes. The maximum length of these flow lobes was 700 metres. Initial block-and-ash flows were generated 4 days after the appearance of the new lava dome on the 24th May, 1991.

2) *Flows*
Unzen flows are Merapi-type block-and-ash flows typified by hot avalanches of incandescent material from gravitational collapse of unstable coulées and lava domes (see Cas and Wright, 1987, p.352, Francis, 1993, p.253, Yamamoto *et al.*, 1993). The size (mass of material per

flow) of pyroclastic flows increased daily, and on the 3rd June 1991, one of the three largest flows overran the eastern foot of the volcano killing 43 civilians, including three volcanologists (Oshima, 1997). Large-scale flows of approximately 1 x 10^6 m^3 each, were discharged on 3rd June, 8th June and 15th September 1991: these flows comprised a series of successive flow phases that lasted between 8 to 20 minutes. Flow direction and mobility of block-and-ash flows varied during the 4 years of eruption at Unzen. Flow direction was controlled by the growth direction of the lava lobes and pre-existing valley channels. Runout distances of pyroclastic flows were generally less than 3 km from the source. During the course of the eruption, valleys were gradually filled with pyroclastic materials, creating a smoother and wider valley floor. As a result, runout distances of block-and-ash flows increased with time. Another factor controlling runout distances was flow volume, where larger flows tended to have greater runout distances.

3) Dome Growth
The lava dome reached 1200 x 600 m across and 250 m in height. Dome growth changed from exogenous to endogenous in November 1993 and thereafter, dome growth as well as block-and-ash flows were intermittent; pyroclastic flows were generated from exogenous rather than endogenous dome growth. The growth of a spine from which no block-and-ash flows were generated formed the final phase of the eruption between November 1994 and March 1995.

4) Secondary Processes
Heavy rains triggered off the reworking of pyroclastic deposits by secondary flows on a number of occasions (30th June 1991, 8-15th August 1992, and 28th April, 2nd May, 18th June, and 4th July 1993).

6.5.4 Techniques

The entire sedimentary fill of the eruption area was investigated with respect to the sedimentary facies, the associated geomorphologies and the relationships between them.

Unzen, typical of volcanic terrain, presents logistical problems in terms of scale and potential hazards. The field scientist in Unzen has to effectively describe and interpret a study area of unconsolidated volcaniclastics covering roughly 8 km^2. In addition, the study area was a designated 'danger zone' and special permission was needed to enter the area. Rock-falls were particularly common from stratigraphic sections, since loose blocks were supported by an easily eroded ash matrix, hence a hard hat was an essential part of the field kit, as well as radio communication in case of an emergency (see Section 3.1.1). Less frequent potential hazards included the collapse of the frontal (downslope) portion of the remnant lava dome, debris flows, and floods.

A thorough reconnaissance was made of the area during which stratigraphic sections were selected for further analysis, with the aim of including all the major gullies. Information was collected from the area as a whole and approximately 11 kms of stratigraphic field sections were logged and described in detail. Facies were gradually recognised during the field-work period, but were not designated until all the field data had been collected.

A Sony Pyxis GPS was also used for more accurate sitings of field sections. Sections were measured vertically with a metre ruler and laterally with a 30 m tape measure, which was laborious but necessary in an area with such lengthy sections and few landmarks. The textural characteristics measured in the field were: the maximum grain size of the 10 largest clasts, sediment colour using a Munsell's Soil Colour Chart, and clast lithology of at least 100 clasts per sample (Table 6.2). The largest 10 clasts were selected from an individual facies, taking care to discount any out-sized clasts and limit the sampling area to a few metres in width. The sampling area for clast lithological analysis was limited to a metre squared and clasts with intermediate axes greater than 1 cm were measured. All external and internal structures were recorded, drawn and where appropriate, photographed. Architectural elements were described using the method outlined in Section 3.2.4 and terminologies used for external geometry are outlined in Figure 6.2. Photomosaics were used in conjunction with field descriptions. Bulk samples of matrix were collected, weighing between 250g and 1kg relative to the grain size.

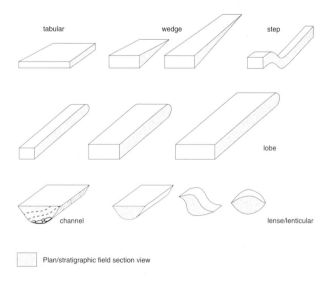

Figure 6.2. Terminology used for external geometry regarding architectural elements.

Lithology
G dom. by grey dacite blocks
R dom. by red dacite blocks
M mixed red & grey dacite blocks

Site	Facies or Facies Assemblage	Mean max. grain size cm	Sediment colour (Munsell)	Lithology
1	A	23,44,45,61,47	Brownish grey 7.5 YR 6/1	G Charcoal
2	A	17.45	Brownish grey 7.5 YR 6/1	G
2	B	12.0	Brownish grey 10 YR 6/1	M
3	A	60.67	Greyish brown 7.5 YR 6/2	R
8	C	74.1	Brownish grey 7.5 YR 5/1	M Debris
9	D	25.25	Brownish grey 10 YR 6/1	G Charcoal
10	G	14.17	Greyish brown 7.5 YR 5/2	M
11	C	45.9, 84	Greyish yellow brown 10 YR 6/2	M Debris
12	A	48.8	Brownish grey 10 YR 5/1	R
12	G	5.82, 14.17	Brownish grey 7.5 YR 5/1	M
13	B	4.0	Brownish grey 10 YR 6/1	M
14	D	18.1	Brownish grey 10 YR 6/1	G Charcoal
15	A	34.5,43.4,53.1		G and R
16	C	15.45	Reddish grey 10R 6/1	M Debris
16	A	27.36	Light grey 10 YR 7/1	G
18	A pre-eruption		Yellowish brown 10 YR 5/6	Weathered volcaniclastics
18	A	94.6	Brownish grey 10 YR 6/1	G
18	C		Greyish red 10 R 6/2	M Debris
19	A	45.27, 29	Dull reddish brown 7.5 R 4/3	R
20	A	14.9, 42	Dull reddish brown 7.5 R 4/3	R
20	B	15.4	Dull brown 7.5 R 5/3	R
21	A	44.3, 51.1, 63.55	Dark reddish brown 5 YR 3/4	R
			Dull reddish brown 5 YR 5/1	
22	A	37.6	Brownish grey 10 YR 5/1	R
23	A	49.27	Brownish grey 10 YR 5/1	R
25	E	19.1	Greyish red 10 R 4/2	G Red ash Charcoal
26	E	13.5	Greyish red 10R 4/2	G Red ash Charcoal

Table 6.2. *Sedimentary data of volcaniclastic facies from selected sites within the field area.*

6.5.5 Sedimentology

A number of distinctive facies are recognised within the field area, most of which can be grouped into facies associations where a more specific genetic and depositional relationship is established (see Section 2.1.3), and facies assemblages which represent a group of genetically similar facies whose depositional relationship is not known. For example, Facies Assemblage B represents a range of facies which have a broad similarity and are all interpreted as debris flow deposits. This approach was chosen in order to present a simple classification scheme for what is essentially a complex, multi-generic sedimentary fill. The facies assemblages are described and interpreted below and the facies associations are presented in Section 6.5.6 and Figure 6.8. Descriptions are based on the sediment properties, architectural elements and the morphological associations.

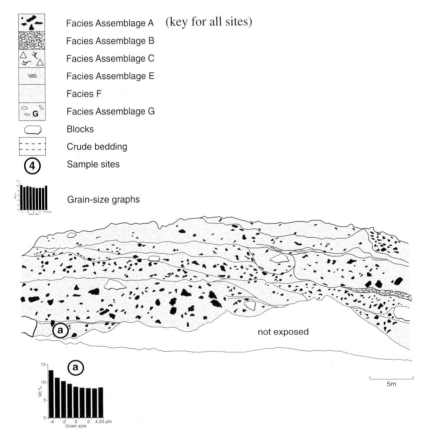

Figure 6.3. Annotated diagram of a field section at Site 1. The succession is dominated by Facies Association A with intermittent Facies Assemblage E and Facies F.

6.5.5.1 Facies Assemblage A

Description: Facies Assemblage A dominates the study area, and includes a number of facies that are generally made up of angular to subangular dacite blocks supported in a matrix of ash (Figure 6.3). There was a wide range in the roundness of clasts ranging from very angular to rounded. Facies vary from clast-supported, clast-dominated textures to the more common, matrix-supported, fines-dominated textures, but they are all very poorly sorted. The mean maximum grain-size of blocks ranges from 27.36 cm (Site 16) to 94.6 cm (Site 19), and in some sections block-diameters are seen to exceed 5 m (e.g. 6 m block at Site 23, 8 m at Site 17). The range in grain size within one particular unit varies, but the range tends to be relatively large since there is a marked bimodal grain-size distribution. These facies are dominated by ash and coarse gravel (blocks) and have the largest grain-size range of all the facies. The bimodal distribution is not reflected in the graphical grain-size distributions (see Figure 6.8) because these represent the matrix only ($< - 4 \phi$).

Larger blocks show well-developed post-depositional radial cooling joints (Figure 6.4) and a small number have a bread-crust outer surface. There appears to be an abundance of juvenile blocks with prismatic joints. Such juvenile blocks are common in Facies Assemblage A deposits produced in 1991, but less common in later deposits. These facies may be separated by erosional bounding surfaces or may grade into one another. Clast distribution is rarely even, this facies being poorly sorted, and changes in grain size (content and coarse-tail grading) are common both laterally and vertically: normal, reverse, and symmetric. Gas segregation pipes and carbonised wood are present, but to a limited extent.

Figure 6.4. *Post-depositional radial cooling joints in juvenile dacite lava block.*

The facies are monolithological, dominated by juvenile dacite clasts; however lithics are surface derived (overriding older pre-eruption Quaternary deposits) in the lower deposits (e.g. Site 17), although this is rare. The deposits including clasts and matrix are either grey, or reddened to some degree by oxidation which is controlled by the temperature of the lava at the time of inclusion into the flow. Some of the dacite clasts are vesicular, but most are dense.

Bed thickness ranges from 50 cm to 4 m and beds are sometimes separated by Facies E and F (thin beds of fine sediment). Lower boundaries are straight, wavy and uneven. Unit geometry includes straight, parallel and even beds, wedges and channel-shapes (Figure 6.2). Units are commonly seen to have overridden one another and individual boulders are often embedded at a boundary between two units. Small-scale cross-stratified fill units are sometimes found either side of big blocks and boulders, usually on their lee-side.

Architectural elements are varied and distinctive within this facies assemblage. Lower bounding surfaces of the elements are usually erosional, irregular and locally planar and quite often curved (concave up). The upper bounding surfaces tend to be curved (convex up), irregular or planar. A wide range of external geometries can be seen: wedges, lobes, and irregular sheets are all common. Less common are U-shaped fills, lenses and dishes (Figure 6.2). The tapering seen in wedges and lobes tends to be in a 'downstream' direction, although it is somewhat dependent on the underlying topography for specific units. The thickness of individual elements varies from 1 to 5 metres and the length/width of elements varies from 1 metre to 10's of metres. Elements tend to be dominated by one facies type, but second-order concordant and discordant bounding surfaces are seen in places. Internal bedding tends to be crude.

Depositional surface features are commonly associated with these facies, especially on the upper slopes. Surface morphologies include lobes with steep lobe fronts, levees, large surface blocks, gullies and terraces. The surface of the deposits, especially tongues and lobes, are littered with well sorted blocks. Many of these have been, and continue to be, rapidly degraded by fluvial erosion.

Interpretation: the textural characteristics and the presence of rare gas segregation pipes, together with the occurrence of carbonised wood and reddened clasts are typical of deposits having a pyroclastic flow origin (e.g. Cas and Wright, 1987, Fisher and Schminke, 1984). Dacite blocks are clasts of cooled juvenile magma and radial arranged cooling joints can be seen, indicating high-temperature emplacement. There is no evidence of secondary alteration in or around the segregation pipes, except possibly at Site 22. Therefore, the gas escape structures in Unzen are formed by escaping water vapour. Further evidence for this interpretation is that sites of fumarolic pipes were seen on aerial photographs taken 4 days after the June 3rd 1991 pyroclastic flow, and seen to be clearly originating from the pre-eruption river valley bottoms providing a source of water for the steam. Concerning the type of pyroclastic flow deposit, we know that Unzen flows were Merapi-type block-and-ash flows, and the field evidence is typical of these flow-types: low proportion of carbonised wood, dense juvenile fragments and gas segregation pipes. Many other features of these facies, for example, texture, monolithology, lack of vesiculated clasts, and no welding have also been identified in block-and-ash flow deposits (Cas and Wright, 1987, Smith and Roobol, 1990). Textural variation can be accounted for by differences in the rate of change of dome growth, the amount of volatiles in the flow and flow velocities.

Individual flow units are distinguished by the architectures within field sections; for example flow lobes are easily distinguished. The lobe-shaped elements with steep distal and/or marginal cliffs and surficial well-sorted blocks represent distal parts of pyroclastic flows which were observed at the upstream part of Akamatsudani and Taruki Daichi in 1992-93. The presence of large surface blocks and steep flow fronts indicates a high yield strength during flow (Cas and Wright, 1987). Erosional lower bounding surfaces of the flows are seen together with the resultant fill. Individual boulders are thought to be deposited on the surface of flows or with only a proportion of them actually embedded within flows: subsequent flows therefore incorporate or engulf the exposed part of the boulder. This effect is exaggerated by fluvial re-working of flow surfaces between eruption events. Local cross-stratified fill units commonly found in block-and-ash flow sequences are thought to represent fluvial fills of surface depressions, formed by local stream scouring around obstacles (boulders/blocks), during intervals between successive pyroclastic-flow depositional events.

There are a number of spatial and temporal variations in the sedimentary textures of block-and-ash flow facies. The change in style of dome growth during 1993 is reflected by a change in the facies: high temperature oxidation is a common characteristic of deposits which were emplaced during the endogenous dome growth stage of 1993-95. Juvenile blocks with prismatic joints are common in facies produced in 1991, but less common in later deposits. As for other pyroclastic deposits the existence of carbonised material depends largely upon the flow path. If the flow overrode previous flows then little if no plant material would have been available; on the other hand if the flow took a new course over vegetated areas, then a large amount of plant debris would have been available to be engulfed.

6.5.5.2 Facies Assemblage B
Description: this assemblage is dominated by thinly bedded, horizontal, even, parallel bedsets of relatively well-sorted fine-gravel, which exhibit normal grading and fining-up successions. Finer-grained granular, sand and ash beds are also common; however, there are few cobble and boulder sized clasts evident in this assemblage. The gravel is clast-

supported within a matrix of granules and a small proportion of ash. There are very few clasts with high A:B ratios and therefore clast alignment tends to be weak. Maximum grain-size ranges between 4 cm (Site 13) and 17.3 cm (Site 17). Clast roundness is similar to that of Facies Assemblage C and G, being sub-angular to sub-rounded; however, the clast lithology is polylithologic. Clast lithology, although dominated by dacite clasts is considered to be polylithological because it has a mixture of grey and reddened dacite clasts, as well as various amounts (<5%), of lithics, plant debris, rubble and carbonised material.

Bed thickness ranges from 10 cm to 1 m and can be seen to have high width/depth ratios and sheet architecture in three dimensional sections. Facies of horizontally stratified coarse-gravel, and fine-gravel/sand couplets between 10 to 20 cm thick are common; the finer fraction of the couplets overlies the coarser fraction. Facies within this assemblage tend to comprise bedsets or stacked units of thin to medium beds of gravel and sands. Some beds are inclined in a downstream direction, but most are planar, parallel and horizontally stratified. The other main structures are solitary sets and cosets of cross-bedding, and trough-shaped units of sand or gravel which vary in scale and have massive, normally graded horizontal bedsets or fining-up, fill units. Trough cross-stratification and parallel-curved bedding (Campbell, 1967) are also common in trough-fill units. These units often have discordant erosional boundaries with basal facies which are commonly cross-bedded. Planar cross-bedding (10 cm - 1 m thick sets) is common in bedsets of gravel and sand. Set thickness is small-scale ranging from 10 cm to 80 cm. Concordant, discordant, trough and tabular cross-beds are all present, as well as inclined bedding and dip angles range from 6° to 40°. Thin beds of well-sorted pebbles with very little matrix are also seen.

A number of architectural elements are recognised within this facies assemblage. Lower boundaries tend to be erosional, planar or curved (concave up) and upper bounding surfaces tend to be planar. External geometry includes sheets, which are the most common, channels, lenses and scoops. The elements are made up of bedsets of sand and gravel and tend to be small in scale with vertical and lateral scales ranging between 10's of cm to a few metres.

A variety of depositional landforms are commonly associated with this facies assemblage, and include channels, barforms and terraces with heights between 0.5 and 1 m. These facies are commonly found within stratigraphic field sections.

Interpretation: the bedding structures and sediment textures are typical of a fluvial environment (e.g. Blair and McPherson, 1994, Miall, 1996, see Sections 4.1, 4.2.8, Chapter 5 and 7.2). Trough fills represent either local scouring or single/multi-channel fill events (Figure 6.5). Sand beds represent both separate and waning flow events. Individual couplets resulted from the same sheet-flow events, the finer fraction deposited from suspension fall-out during waning flow. The polylithology of this assemblage can be explained by the

Figure 6.5. *Channel fill, Site 16. The fill (Facies Association B^1) is concordant, slightly asymmetrical and a fining-upward succession. The basal coarse gravel is thought to represent channel-floor lag deposits (mean maximum grain-size is 6.4 cm) and the finer units above represent suspended sediment fall-out during waning flow. The gravel is of mixed lithology. The lower boundary may be partly, but not wholly erosional, as depressions on the surface of block-and-ash flows are commonly filled. There is no particular fabric in the channel-floor lag clasts and very few clasts with ratios greater than 3:1 (the large clast at the base of the fill is part of the block-and-ash flow). The channel fill is thought to be perpendicular to the current flow and the fill is a frontal view of a single trough set of cross-bedding.* **Scale: knife, 22 cm in length.**

fact that the fluvial system is fed principally by Facies Assemblage A, which has both grey and reddened dacite facies.

6.5.5.3 Facies Assemblage C

Description: this assemblage is dominated by gravel-rich diamictons (see Section 3.3.1.1), although better-sorted gravel units are also common and a weak fabric is evident in some units. Clast roundness is sub-angular to sub-rounded, larger clasts tend to be more rounded than those of Facies Assemblage A. Clast lithology, although dominated by dacite clasts, is considered polylithologic because it has a mixture of grey and reddened dacite clasts, as well as various amounts (<25%) of other lithics, plant debris, rubble and fragments of carbonised material. Plant debris is common including tree trunks, most of which are not carbonised but have splintered surfaces. There is a lower proportion of carbonised material in this association than in the block-and-ash flow facies. Boulders and cobbles are supported in a matrix which has a large proportion of granules and smaller proportions of ash. The matrix on the whole is grey in colour, but the colour of individual granule grains is variable. Gravels on the whole are matrix-supported, but clast-supported units and gravel clusters are seen in places. Facies have a high proportion of pebbles and cobbles and the grain-size range is much smaller than that of Facies Assemblage A. Some facies, mainly those that are clast-supported, are highly consolidated, almost concreted. Units exhibit symmetric, reverse (usually basal) and normal grading, as well as typically massive bedding.

Units are between 30 cm to 1.5 m thick. Maximum grain-size ranges from 15.45 cm (Site 16) to 84 cm (Site 10). Architectural elements are very crude and not easily distinguished in this facies assemblage. Wedge and tongue shaped external geometries are seen having curved (concave up), or planar erosional lower boundaries and upper bounding surfaces are uneven and curved (convex up).

Facies within this assemblage are generally found within stratigraphic sections and rarely as depositional landforms (that have an exposed stratigraphic section). However, two good examples are found within the Akamatsudani at Sites 9 and 10. Surface morphologies comprise lobes of sediment with levees which may have been dissected by gullies. Plant debris litters the surface of these deposits, and dead trees that have not been carbonised are very common. Very little fine material exists on the surface of these deposits, which tend to be dominated by blocks. There is a marked difference in the surface morphology of the debris flow and block-and-ash flow zones within the Kita Kamikoba area: there is a much higher proportion of large blocks (diameters exceeding 1 m) on the surface of the block-and-ash flow deposits, making the surface morphology more uneven.

Interpretation: this facies is typical of a debris flow deposit in a number of respects: a sandy/granular matrix which supports clasts of all sizes, including large blocks, the occurrence of plant debris and wood, lack of stratification and basal reverse grading (e.g. Cas and Wright, 1987, Costa, 1988, Blair and McPherson, 1994, Chough and Hwang,1997, see Section 4.1, 4.2.8.1). Some of the facies have a high proportion of clasts and low proportion of clays, but still show basal reverse grading (Figure 6.7b). Reverse grading is reputed to be uncommon within volcanic debris flow deposits because of their low clay contents and correspondingly low cohesion and yield strength (e.g. Smith and Roobol, 1990). However, some researchers believe that as little as 5% clay can have a marked effect on sediment support within debris flows (e.g. Hampton, 1975, Naylor, 1980). Furthermore, basal reverse grading has been reported in some volcanic debris flow deposits (e.g. Smith, 1986).

However, alternative sediment support mechanisms are probably more significant in volcanic debris flows. Dispersive pressures (e.g. Bagnold, 1954) are important within high density flows of a coarse nature and will have played a major role in sediment support during flow events in Unzen. The coarse framework will allow coarse blocks to remain within and at the top of the unit in static flows (Rodine and Johnson, 1976). The high concentration of fine-grained sediment will have led to high pore pressures and buoyancy forces, especially in the matrix-rich debris flows. What is apparent is that sediment support mechanisms within the Unzen debris flows were effective enough to be able to move and support coarse blocks (Jones *et al.*, in prep.). Blocks with intermediate axes exceeding 1 m were seen to be moving on video films of the large debris flow events.

Sieve-like deposits are created by surface waters removing fines from surface gravels. Depositional and post-depositional depletion of fines may explain the low proportion of ash in this facies in comparison to block-and-ash flows. This will be more prevalent in debris flows with a higher fluid content (see also Section 6.5.5.7).

6.5.5.4 Facies D

Description: this facies, previously unidentified in the field area, is much less common than the block-and-ash flow facies within Facies Assemblage A and is significantly different, composed of boulders rarely exceeding 50 cm in diameter, supported in a friable, ash-rich matrix. Granules are also found within the ash-rich matrix which is always grey in colour. Mean maximum grain size of blocks ranges from 18.1 cm (Site 14) to 25.25 cm (Site 9). This facies unlike facies within Assemblage A, is always matrix rich and the boulders intermittent. This facies is monolithologic and very few of the clasts have been reddened by oxidation. Two key features of this facies are firstly, the large proportion of carbonised debris, with some of the smaller twigs exhibiting a fabric, and, secondly, the high proportion of ash. Gas segregation pipes are seen in some units and tend to be vertical and small in scale (e.g. Site 4). Units tend to be relatively thin, ranging from 10 cm to 1.5 m and bedding is evident at some sites. The bedding is wavy and uneven, locally exhibiting cross-stratification. Both the upper and lower boundaries are highly irregular, usually wavy and pinch and swell structures are common. Unit lengths are limited, rarely exceeding thirty metres. Lateral and vertical facies associations vary between block-and-ash flows, ash-cloud surge and aerial-fall deposits.

Interpretation: the presence of gas segregation pipes, the large proportion of carbonised material, a monolithology and the large proportion of ash suggests a pyroclastic flow rather than a debris flow origin. Turbulent grain-by-grain tractional transport is thought to occur in surges, which is reflected by the presence of cross-bedding for example (see Cas and Wright, 1987, p.205). Other evidence to support a surge interpretation is the large proportion of ash and the pinch and swell bedding. However, the coarsest blocks in places occur at the top of units and only typically laminar type flows with a high buoyancy force, which are thought to exist within debris flows and block-and-ash flows, will support blocks of this size. Therefore, this facies offers two conflicting groups of evidence, the first of which points to a surge origin and the second of which suggests a pyroclastic flow origin. It is thought that this facies may be an end-member of pyroclastic density currents, formed at the time of rapid rates of dome growth. An increase in volatiles and density cannot be offered as an explanation, since these two parameters were relatively constant after 1991 (T. Yamamoto pers. com.). However, the density within individual flows can vary spatially. High velocity pyroclastic flows are thought to occur on steep slopes (Yamamoto, 1993) and could account for proximal and medial emplacement of juvenile blocks (Facies Assemblage A); and distal fine grained, low density facies with some surge characteristics and a small number of blocks (Facies D). High density block-and-ash flows that have low density marginal flows which are surge-like in character, are known to occur (Francis, 1993).

Observations of the distal parts of block-and-ash flows were made on December 20th 1992, seven days after emplacement and the deposits were still soft and the matrix was a mixture of gas and ash particles (T. Ui pers com). Active fumaroles were observed and carbonised material in some instances. Although no direct correlations can be made, these observations suggest that matrix-rich distal flows did occur and lend support to the interpretation.

6.5.5.5 Facies Assemblage E
Description: this assemblage comprises coarse-grained to very coarse-grained ash units. Small fragments of carbonised wood are found within these facies (e.g. Site 3). Sediment colour varies. Granules are found at the base of facies at Sites 25 and 26, having mean, maximum grain-size diameters between 19.1 cm and 13.5 cm respectively. Lower boundaries are uneven and locally mantle underlying topography, but more often these facies are seen to thicken at depressions. At other times a break occurs in the facies when an obstacle, generally a boulder is encountered, forming discrete separated units. Bed thickness varies from 0.5 cm to 1.5 m and at some sites internal bedding is evident and is commonly in the form of cross stratification (e.g. Site 24). Some units have pinch and swell structures. Core type accretionary lapilli (e.g. Schumacher and Schmincke, 1991) are seen in places (e.g. Sites 8 and 25), with diameters between 0.1 and 0.5 cm, having coarse-grained cores and finer-grained ash envelopes. Upper units in the blast zone at Site 25 and 26 are vesiculated, as well as other units throughout the field area (e.g. Sites 14, 22, 24). Long (10-15 cm), thin (1 cm) gas escape structures which are infilled with fine granules are found at Site 20.

This assemblage is widespread in the field area and dominates the blast-zone areas near Nakao and Kamikoba. These areas are gently undulating with a covering of blasted, carbonised trees.

Interpretation: this facies assemblage has many of the characteristics used to classify ash-cloud surge deposits: pinch and swell structures, discrete separated units, and unidirectional

Figure 6.6. *Pyroclastic fall deposit, Site 18. Laminaset of ash between ash-cloud surge and debris flow deposits.* **Scale: knife, 22 cm in length.**

trough-cross-stratification (e.g. Fisher, 1979 and Yamamoto *et al.*, 1993). Other evidence supporting an ash-cloud surge interpretation is the presence of accretionary lapilli, vesiculation and carbonaceous material found in various units. The location of these facies is another supporting factor wherein they are always associated with block-and-ash flow facies and more importantly, they dominate zones which are known to have been blasted by ash-cloud surges.

6.5.5.6 Facies F
Description: this facies is relatively consistent across the field area and comprises thin beds of fine-grained to medium-grained ash (Figure 6.6). Small granules are found in some units and sediment colour varies. Grain size lies predominantly in the ash class. This facies is dominated by thin planar bedding, although wavy bedding is seen in places. Bed thickness between 0.5 cm and 5 cm are the most common, but thicker beds up to 40 cm are evident in places. Individual beds may occur discretely or within bedsets, but they always appear to be normally graded. Bedsets of wavy, parallel, even, thinly bedded ash are common (e.g. Site 20). Lower boundaries mantle the underlying topography. This facies, although contributing only a relatively small amount in terms of sediment volume, is widespread across the field area.

a)   b)

Figure 6.7. *(a) Hyperconcentrated flow deposit, Site 12. Grades upstream into debris flow deposits.* **Scale: knife is 22 cm.** *(b) Site 12, clast-rich debris flow deposit. Note the basal reverse grading.* **Scale: metre ruler.**

Interpretation: pyroclastic ash-fall typically produces deposits that mantle the underlying topography and as a result is used to distinguish it from fluvial sands and ash-cloud surge deposits. This facies is always found in association with block-and-ash flow facies. Other evidence supporting a fall-deposit interpretation is the fine nature of the facies, widespread coverage and the normal grading it exhibits (e.g. Walker, 1971, 1973). Because of the fine nature of this facies it is classified as an ash-fall deposit.

6.5.5.7 Facies Assemblage G
Description: this facies assemblage is composed of coarse gravel facies which are clast-supported in a matrix of granules and ash, and is intermediate between Facies Assemblage B and Facies Assemblage C, in terms of sorting, grain size and bedding structures (Figure 6.7a and b). In general, this facies has fewer fines than Facies Assemblage C, but more fines than Facies Assemblage B and like these two facies it is polylithological. Some facies are

finer grained and exihibit crude bedding. Grain sizes vary from coarse sand to cobbles which are moderately sorted, and out-sized clasts (Maizels, 1989) are found in every section where these facies are identified. Mean maximum grain-sizes range from 5.82 cm (Site 12) to 14.17 cm (Site 12). Larger clasts tend to be more rounded than those of Facies Assemblage A. Stratification is crude, discontinuous and most units are massive although at Site 12 the basal 35 cm of the unit is composed of fine granules which pass up into cobbles, producing basal reverse grading. Thin stringers of gravel and cobbles/boulders as well as pebble clusters also occur intermittently throughout. Facies often grade upstream and pass vertically into debris flow deposits (e.g. Sites 8 and 11). Groups of thin gravel lenses are evident in some units (e.g. Site 8) which are long and thin (3 cm thick by 20 cm long), tapered both ends and inclined (with downstream end highest). Units range between 30 cm to 2.5 m in thickness.

Surface forms are associated with debris flow and fluvial terrace deposits. Facies are also found in vertical sections.

Interpretation: the coarse, poorly sorted nature of these facies suggests rapid deposition from a high-capacity fluvial flow with a high sediment concentration (Beverage and Culbertson, 1964, Smith, 1986, Maizels, 1989, Brennand, 1994, see Sections 4.2.8.2 and 7.2.4.4). These facies are intermediate between fluvial and debris flow and are therefore interpreted as hyperconcentrated flow deposits (Jones *et al.*, in prep, see Section 4.1). There is a significant amount of evidence to support this interpretation, since the proportion of fines, sorting, crude stratification, reverse bedding and lateral grading into debris-flow deposits have all been identified as characteristic of hyperconcentrated flow deposits (e.g. Smith, 1986, Costa, 1988). Other evidence to support this view is the video footage and photographs of debris flow events in the Unzen field area during the eruption, which show flood events with very high sediment concentrations.

The lack of bedding within some of the facies suggests a lack of tractional transport and the presence of out-sized clasts, as well as basal reverse grading indicates that buoyancy forces were prevalent during flow. Dispersive pressures associated with high sediment concentration allow larger clasts to be supported in the upper parts of the flow and within, explaining the occurrence of cobbles and boulders towards the top of and within the facies (Bagnold, 1954, Costa, 1984, 1988, Schultz, 1984). However, the range in grain-size suggests that hyperconcentrated flow events were not capable of supporting large blocks.

Crude bedding and sorting mechanisms together with the high fluid content seen in video recordings suggest some of the flows were stream-driven, high density gravelly traction carpets (*sensu* Todd, 1989). Grading upstream into debris-flow deposits could be attributed to downstream dilution of debris flows.

6.5.6 Facies Patterns throughout the Field Area

Vertical and Lateral Facies Associations

Lateral facies changes are evident throughout the field area within relatively short distances. In general, the upper slopes of the 1991-95 volcanic deposits are dominated by block-and-ash flow units, with intermittent ash-cloud surge and ash-fall beds. Towards the middle and lower reaches epiclastics appear and become dominant beyond a distance of *ca.* 2 km. Within Facies Assemblage A itself, the average grain size decreases away from the lava dome. Block-and-ash flow units tend to override or overlap one another and in a number of areas the most recent flows are seen to override older deposits. Also in places debris flows are seen to override pyroclastic flows. Epiclastic deposits in the coastal region form fan like sheets which are made up of channel-fill elements comprising Facies Assemblage C deposits and the more widespread overbank elements comprising Facies Assemblage G which form the same unit (T. Yamamoto pers com). Mudflows and lahars have been reported as having overtopped stream banks in Mt. St. Helens - USA (e.g. Crandell and Mullineaux, 1978) and Pinatubo - Philippines (Dolan, 1998b). The fact that there is a lateral gradation from debris-flow deposits to hyperconcentrated flow indicates that the coarsest material is contained within the channel, behaving almost like a lag deposit, leaving a more dilute and mobile flow in the overbank areas. In general, hyperconcentrated flow and debris flow deposits are closely related in the field areas and indicate that individual events were bipartite having both Newtonian (fluid) and non-Newtonian (viscoplastic) portions (Jones *et al.*, in

Figure 6.8. Facies Assemblage is abbreviated as FA

(a) Site 8 (pre-cleaning): the basal facies comprises two wedge shaped units which thicken (1.8 m) in an upstream direction (to the RHS of photo) of diamicton (FAC). The clasts are matrix-supported in a matrix of granules, but at the tail end of the unit seen in the figure, they are clast-supported. The mean grain-size of the unit is 74.1 cm, and the lithology is mixed. Also, note the roundness of some of the large clasts. This facies is highly cemented and suggests that the debris flow had a very high sediment concentration (see Maizels, 1993). Overlying this facies is a small channel-fill unit (FAB) with a solitary set of cross-bedded gravels. This is a foreset, 23 cm thick with discordant, trough shaped, heterogenous, thin beds, having a dip angle of 40°. The unit above this is a poorly sorted diamicton (mean maximum grain-size is 19.8 cm) with mixed lithology and also containing plant debris. Coarse clasts occur at the top of this facies, supported within the matrix, suggesting a non-tractional transport process. This facies is reverse graded, the base being finer grained and is thought to be debris flow (FAC). The upper unit grades from FAG, to FAC (not seen on this figure). FAG comprises a composite bedset of sands and fine gravels with poorly defined contacts, parallel, wavy, discontinuous bedding and out-sized clasts. FAG coarsens upwards into fine gravels once again having out-sized clasts. Crude bedding is seen throughout this facies, but it is barely discernible. Upstream this unit overlies the basal debris flow facies. Similar successions were recorded by Smith (1986, 1987). Scale: file, 28 cm in length.

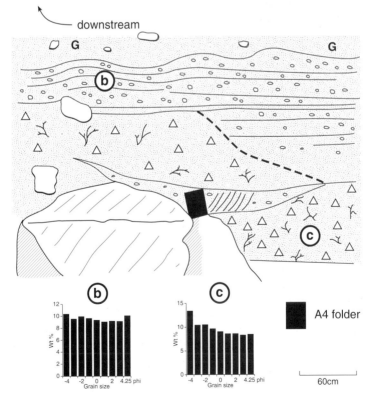

(b) Site 15: this section is dominated by FAA comprising a succession of diamicton units with various external geometries. The matrix is highly friable, dominated by ash, with some granules. Thin, uneven beds of ash-sized material (Facies E and F) lie between the diamicton units, as well as a thin bed of well sorted fluvial gravels. Towards the top of the section there are units of the 1993-95 eruption, FAA (labelled R) which have oxidised matrix and blocks (red in colour). This relates to a slow endogenous growth rate of the lava dome.
Scale: this succession is 6 m thick and 30 m in length. *LAA¹ refers to lithofacies Association A¹.*

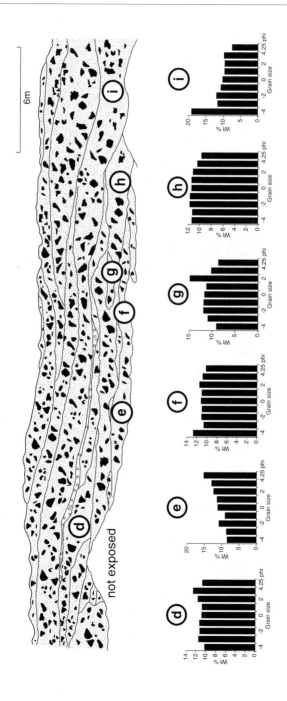

(c) Site 16: the basal unit of this section (FAC) exhibits reverse grading. This facies passes laterally into a block-and-ash flow facies which has an ash rich, highly friable matrix. A depression in the upper surface of this block-and-ash flow deposit has been infilled with fluvial sands and gravels (see Figure 6.5). The upper unit is a poorly sorted sand and gravel facies which has some out-sized clasts. This is thought to be debris flow which may pass laterally downstream into hyperconcentrated flow deposit. **Scale: shovel (metre).**

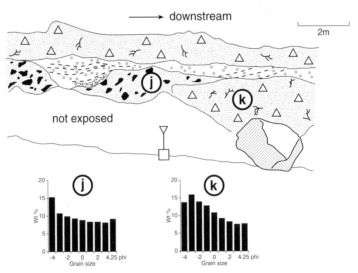

prep.).

Stratigraphical field sections typically comprise a number of different facies and facies associations (and at some sites include all recognised facies e.g. Site 18) within one vertical succession (Figures 6.8 a-d photos, diagram and explanation). Field evidence shows that block-and-ash flow, ash-cloud surge and ash-fall deposits were all generated from single pyroclastic density currents that were triggered by collapsing lava lobes; an important feature of the Unzen eruption is that ash-cloud surge and ash fall deposits never occurred independently of block-and-ash flow deposits. The relative proportions of these three types of deposits varied on the individual density current. Individual pyroclastic flow events therefore produce a distinctive fining-upward and thinning-upward Lithofacies Association A^1 (Figure 6.8b). The other main lithofacies association in the field area is the fining-up fluvial channel-fill successions (Figure 6.5).

6.5.7 Discussion

The Unzen Volcano field area has a number of distinctive facies and difficulties arise when attempts are made to interpret them. However, interpretation is important in terms of understanding the eruptive and depositional secondary processes occurring within the area.

Block-and-ash flow facies are notoriously difficult to distinguish from debris flow facies in such field areas. The presence of carbonaceous material and/or gas segregation pipes is often regarded as the best distinguishing field criteria between these deposits. However, carbonised material and gas segregation pipes were rarely found in the field area as a whole and therefore could not be widely used. Moreover, debris-flows are derived solely from pyroclastic flow deposits and therefore may well re-sediment the whole assemblage including carbonised wood. Other criteria often cited for distinguishing between block-and-ash flow and debris flow deposits proved to be useful, in particular matrix composition, clast lithology and the abundance of wood/plant debris. Hence, the debris flow facies are distinctive from the block-and-ash flow facies in a number of respects.

Further difficulties arose concerning the interpretation of epiclastic deposits and the continuum between fluvial - hyperconcentrated flow- debris-flows. Classification with respect to facies other than the two end members (fluvial and debris flow), is arbitrary to some extent, since the underlying process links are not fully understood. There are studies (albeit relatively few in number (e.g. Costa, 1988, Smith, 1986, Maizels, 1989, Wan and Wang, 1994)) that discuss flow rheology and transport mechanics within hyperconcentrated flow systems; however, these are largely based on inference and direct measurements of the flows themselves are lacking. Hence, there is a problem of how to define the boundaries between different epiclastic deposits.

*(d) Site 18: there is a basal weathered composite bedset of inclined sand and gravel beds which is a pre-1991, early Holocene alluvial fan deposit. The upper boundary of this fan deposit is inclined in a downstream direction. This passes up into a bed of relatively well sorted fluvial gravel of mixed lithology. A discontinuous bed of Facies E and F can be seen running through the middle of the section. Above this is a poorly sorted, gravel rich facies. The texture suggests that this is not a block-and-ash flow deposit and there is no evidence that this was produced by tractional currents. Therefore, this is either FAC or Facies G. This passes up into the finer grained Facies D which has some surge like flow structures. Overlying Facies D is a thin bed of Facies E. The top most unit is a block-and-ash flow facies (FAA). **Scale: this succession is 4 m thick and 24 m in length.***

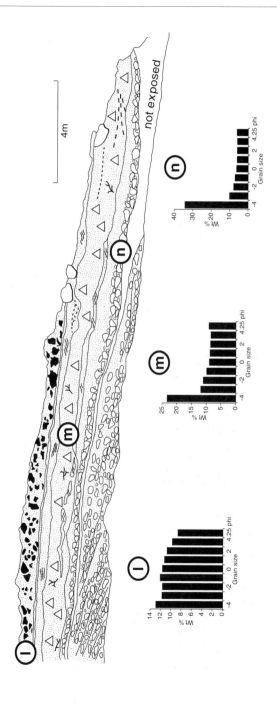

Large debris flows followed valley-bottoms especially in the mid and lower reaches as seen on video coverage and smaller debris flow events were seen to occur on top of existing deposits covering the volcanic slopes. The deposits from large debris flow events were relatively thin, rarely exceeding a few metres, and clast rich. Unfortunately in distal areas they have been removed by construction workers. These events have been uniformly labelled "debris flow", but there is substantial sedimentological evidence which is supported by video footage, to suggest that a number of them are in fact hyperconcentrated flows (Jones *et al.*, in prep.).

There appears to be significant textural differences between the facies assemblages. The block-and-ash flow facies are essentially the source facies which feed the secondary systems. This apparent difference in textures must therefore be related to the flow and depositional mechanics between the source facies and the secondary facies. High precipitation records are seen in this field area (Oshima, 1997, Nishida and Mizuyama, 1998), and lead to flood events, hyperconcentrated flows and debris flows. It would appear that the threshold between fluvial and hyperconcentrated flow is crossed relatively rapidly, given the fine nature of the fluvial facies. The large proportions of easily eroded ash could account for this, since high sediment concentrations (Beverage and Culbertson, 1964) could be achieved relatively quickly and in effect a conversion from fluvial to hyperconcentrated flow rheology would follow. Another consideration could be water temperature which is known to affect the fluid kinematic viscosity whereby higher temperatures decrease competence (Simons *et al.*, 1963, Smith, 1986).

The primary source material is characteristically bimodal in this basin. The nature of these source sediments means that there has to be a large increase in stream competence to transport the coarser block-sized material, as opposed to the easily eroded ash material. This could also mean that source materials gradually become depleted of fine material during intermittent fluvial events, leaving a coarser grained source material for debris flow and possibly hyperconcentrated flow events. The proportion of granular material is seen to increase in the secondary deposits and probably results from the erosion of dacite blocks during transport and sorting processes.

6.6 CONCLUSION

Pyroclastic eruptions present the scientist with a large area of unlithified and entirely exposed sediment, which is commonly reworked rapidly by a variety of secondary processes. Valuable evidence can be gathered through the investigation of stratigraphical field sections within these areas. This evidence can be used, for example, to reconstruct the depositional and eruptive history, record spatial and temporal variances, and determine transport mechanisms of volcanic and secondary systems. The Unzen eruption presents a superb opportunity to correlate the record of volcanic and epiclastic processes with field evidence, principally in the form of stratigraphic sections. This field evidence provides a useful documentation of volcaniclastic facies, and ultimately is an invaluable interpretation tool for pre-historic depositional successions.

ACKNOWLEDGEMENTS

Research at Unzen was carried out whilst the first author was receiving an EU/JSPS Postdoctoral Fellowship and we thank these two organisations for their financial contribution. Grateful acknowledgement is made to the Ministry of Construction for providing additional funding for this research and to Prof. Takahisa Mizuyama and Dr. Kenro Nishida for their assistance in many matters. Thanks also go to Dr. Takahiro Yamamoto, Prof. Maurice Tucker for reviewing the manuscript and to Prof. Steven Self for discussions on the depositional facies as well as reviewing the manuscript. We would also like to thank the cartographic unit at Southampton University and Dr. Ryuta Furukawa for excellent figure reproduction.

REFERENCES

BAGNOLD, R.A. 1954. Experiments on a gravity-free dispersion of large, solid spheres in a Newtonian fluid under shear. *Proc. Royal Society, London, Series A*, **225**, 49-63.

BLAIR, T. C. and MCPHERSON, J. G. 1994, Alluvial fans and their natural distinction from rivers based on morphology, hydraulic processes, sedimentary processes and facies assemblages: *Journal of Sedimentary Research,* **A64, No.3**, 450-489.

BRENNAND, T.A. 1994. Macroforms, large bedforms and rythmic sedimentary sequences in subglacial eskers, south-central Ontario: implications for esker genesis and meltwater regime. *Sedimentary Geology,* **91**, 9-55.

CAMPBELL, C.V. 1967. Lamina, laminaset, bed and bedset. *Sedimentology*, **8**, 7-26.

CAS, R.A.F. and WRIGHT, J.V. 1987. *Volcanic Successions.* Chapman and Hall. pp. 528

CHOUGH, S.K. and HWANG, I.G. 1997. The Duksung Fan Delta, SE Korea: growth of delta lobes on a gilbert-type topset in response to relative sea-level rise. *Journal of Sedimentary Research,* **67, No.4**, 725-739.

CHOUGH, S.K. and SOHN, Y.K. 1990. Depositional mechanics and sequences of base surges, Songaksan tuff ring, Cheju Island, Korea. *Sedimentology*, **37**, 1115-1135.

COLELLA, A. and HISCOTT, R.N. 1997. Pyroclastic surges of the Pleistocene Monte Guardia sequence (Lipari Island, Italy): depositional processes. *Sedimentology*, **44, No.1**, 47-67.

COSTA, J.E. 1984. The physical geomorphology of debris flows. *IN* : Costa, J.E. and Fleisher, P.J. (eds, *Developments and Applications of Geomorphology,* 268-317 Springer-Verlag, Berlin and New York.

COSTA, J. E. 1988, Rheologic, geomorphic and sedimentological differentiation of water floods, hyperconcentrated flows and debris flows. *IN*: Baker, V. R., Kochel, R. C., and Patton, P.C. *(eds), Flood Geomorphology*, 113-121 New York, Wiley.

CRANDELL, D.R. and MULLINEAUX, D.R. 1978. Potential hazards from future eruptions of Mount St. Helens Volcano, Washington. *Geol. Survey Bull.* 1383-C.

DOLAN, M.T. 1998a. Mudflows from Mt. Pinatubo volcano. WWW AGU 1992: http://www.geo.mtu.edu/volcanoes/world.html

DOLAN, M.T. 1998b. Mudflows from Mt. Pinatubo volcano. WWW AGU 1993: http://www.geo.mtu.edu/volcanoes/world.html

FISHER, R.V. 1979. Models for pyroclastic surges and pyroclastic flows. *Journal of Volcan. Geotherm. Res.*, **6**, 305-18.

FISHER, R.V. and SCHMINCKE, H.U. 1984. *Pyroclastic rocks*. Springer-Verlag.

FRANCIS, P. 1993. *Volcanoes, a Planetary Perspective*. Clarendon Press.

FREUNDT, A. 1998. The formation of high-grade ignimbrites, I: Experiments on high- and low concentration transport systems containing sticky particles. *Bulletin of Volcanology*, **59**, no.6, 414-435.

HAMPTON, M.A. 1979. Buoyancy in debris flows. *Journal of Sedimentary Petrology*, **49**, 753-758.

FUJII, T. and NAKADA, S. in press. The 15th September 1991 pyroclastic flows at Unzen (Japan): a flowing model. *IN*: Nakada, S. Shimuzu, H. and Ohta, K. (eds), *Journal of Volcan. Geotherm. Res., Unzen Special Issue*.

HAMPTON, M.A. 1975. Competence of fine-grained debris flows. *Journal of Sedimentary Petrology*, **45**, 834-844.

HOSHIZUMI, H., UTO, K. and WATANABE, K. 1997. Geology and K-Ar geochronology of the Unzen Volcano. *IN*: Nakada, S., Eichelberger, J. and Shimizu, H. (eds), *Procs. Unzen International Workshop: Decade Volcano and Scientific Drilling*, 22-25.

ISHIHARA, K., HENDRASTO, M., ETO, T., KIMATA, F. and MATSUSHIMA, T. 1997. Magma storage and injection related to the 1990-1995 activity at Mt. Unzen, inferred from ground deformation analysis. *IN*: Nakada, S., Eichelberger, J. and Shimizu, H. *(eds), Procs. Unzen International Workshop: Decade Volcano and Scientific Drilling*, 56-58.

ISHIKAWA, Y., YAMADA, T. and CHIBA, T. 1996. Topographic changes on the Unzen volcano due to volcanic activities from 1991 to 1995. *Journal Japan. Society of Erosion Control Engineering*, **204**, 38-44 (Japanese, Eng. Abstract).

JOHNSON, S.Y. 1986. Water-escape structures in coarse-grained, volcaniclastic, fluvial deposits of the Ellensburg Formation, south-central Washington. *Journal of Sedimentary Petrology*, **56, no.6**, 905-910.

JONES, A.P., HIRANO, M., NISHIDA, K. and MIZUYAMA, T. in prep. Sedimentary facies, hydraulic processes and morphologies associated with debris flow and hyperconcentrated flow events: Unzen Volcano, Kyushu, Japan.

KANDA, W., UTADA, H., KAGIYAMA, T. and TANAKA, Y. 1997. Resistivity model around Unzen Volcano inferred from TDEM experiments. *IN*: Nakada, S., Eichelberger, J. and Shimizu, H. (eds), *Procs. Unzen International Workshop: Decade Volcano and Scientific Drilling*, 50-55.

KANEKO, T. and WOOSTER, M.J. 1997. Infrared image analysis of the Unzen 1991-1994 activity using ERS ATSR and Landsat TM data. *IN*: Nakada, S., Eichelberger, J. and Shimizu, H. *(eds), Procs. Unzen International Workshop: Decade Volcano and Scientific Drilling*, 33-36.

LAJOIE, J., LANZAFAME, G., ROSSI, P.L. and TRANNE, C.A. 1992. Lateral facies variations in hydromagmatic pyroclastic deposits at Linosa, Italy. *Journal of Volcanology and Geothermal Research,* **54,** 135-143.

LOWE, D.R. 1979. Sediment gravity flows: their classification and some problems of application to natural flows and deposits. *IN*: Doyle, L.J. and Pilkey, O.H. (eds), *Geology of Continental Slopes, SEPM Spec. Pub.*, **no. 27**, 75-82.

MAIZELS, J.K. 1989. Sedimentology, paleoflow dynamics and flood history of Jökulhlaup deposits: palaeohydrology of Holocene sediment sequences in southern Iceland sandur deposits. *Journal of Sedimentary Petrology*, **59, no.2**, 204-223.

MIALL, A.D. 1996, *The Geology of Fluvial Deposits: Sedimentary Facies, Basin Analysis, and Petroleum Geology*, Springer-Verlag Berlin, pp582.

MURAI, I. 1961. A study of the textural characteristics of pyroclastic flow deposits in Japan. *Bulletin of Earthquake Research Inst.*, **39**, 133-254.

NAKADA, S. SHIMUZU, H. and OHTA, K. (eds.) in press. *Journal of Volcan. Geotherm. Res., Unzen Special Issue.*

NAKAYAMA, K. and YOSHIKAWA, S. 1997. Depositional processes of primary reworked volcaniclastics on an alluvial plain; an example from the Lower Pliocene Ohta tephra bed of the Tokai Group, central Japan. *Sedimentary Geology*, **107**, 211-229.

NAYLOR, M.A. 1979. The origin of inverse grading in muddy debris flow deposits - a review. *Journal of Sedimentary Petrology*, **50**, 1111-1116.

NISHIDA, K. and MIZUYAMA, T. 1998. Hydrological processes and topographic change on the slopes of Unzen Volcano. *IN*: Haigh, M.J., Krecek, J., Rajwar, G.S. and Kilmartin, M.P. (eds), *Headwaters Water Resources and Soil Conservation*, A. A. Balkema /Rotterdam/ Brookfield, 245-255.

OKADA, H. 1992. Geological and tectonic setting of Unzen Volcano. *IN*: Yanagi, T., Okada, H. and Ohta, K. (eds), *Unzen Volcano, the 1990-1992 Eruption*, The Nishinippon and Kyushu University Press, 29-34.

OSHIMA, O. 1997. A note on debris flow disasters in the 1990-95 eruption of Unzen Volcan. *IN*: Nakada, S., Eichelberger, J. and Shimizu, H. *(eds), Procs. Unzen International Workshop: Decade Volcano and Scientific Drilling*, 31-32.

RODINE, J.D. and JOHNSON, A.M. 1976. The ability of debris, heavily freighted with coarse clastic materials, to flow on gentle slopes. *Sedimentology*, **23**, 213-234.

SCHUMACHER, R. and SCHMINCKE, H.-U. 1991. Internal structure and occurrence of accretionary lapilli-a case study at Laacher See Volcano. *Bull. Volcan.*, **53**, 612-634.

SCOTT, K.M. 1985. Lahars and lahar-runout flows in the Toutle-Cowlitz River System, Mount St. Helens, Washington - origins, behaviour and sedimentology. *Geol. Surv. Prof. Pap. (U.S.)*, **85-500**, 1-202.

SHIMIZU, H., UMAKOSHI, K., MATSUWO, N., MATSUSHIMA, T. and OHTA, K. 1997. Seismic activity associated with the magma ascent and dome growth of Unzen Volcano. *IN*: Nakada, S., Eichelberger, J. and Shimizu, H. (eds), *Procs. Unzen International Workshop: Decade Volcano and Scientific Drilling*, 42-44.

SIMONS, D.B., RICHARDSON, E.V. and HAUSHILD, W.L. 1963. Some effects of fine sediment on flow phenomena. *U.S. Geol. Surv. Water-Supply Paper*, **1498-G**, pp.47.

SMITH, A.L. and ROOBOL, M.J. 1990. Mt. Pelee, Martinique; A study of an active island-arc Volcano. *Geol. Soc. of Amer.* Memoir 175.

SMITH, G.A. 1986. Coarse-grained nonmarine volcaniclastic sediment: Terminology and depositional processes. *Geol. Soc. of Amer. Bull.*, **97**, 1-10.

SMITH, G.A. 1987. The influence of explosive volcanism on fluvial sedimentation: the Deschutes Formation (Neogene) in central Oregon. *Journal of Sedimentary Petrology*, **57, No.4**, 613-629.

SMITH, G.A. 1988. Sedimentology of proximal to distal volcaniclastics dispersed across an active foldbelt: Ellensburg Formation (late Miocene), central Washington. *Sedimentology*, **35**, 953-977.

THORARINSSON, S. 1981. Opening address. *IN*: Self, S. and Sparks, R.S.J. (eds), *Tephra Studies*, 1-13. D. Reidel Pub. Co.

TODD, S.P. 1989. Stream-driven, high-density gravelly traction carpets: possible deposits in the Trabeg Conglomerate Formation, SW Ireland and some theoretical considerations of their origin. *Sedimentology*, **36**, 513-530.

UI, T, MATSUWO, N., SUMITA, M., FUJINAWA, A., SATO, H. and TAKARADA, S. 1997. Diversity of block-and-ash flow generations during 1990-96 eruption of Unzen Volcano. *IN*: Nakada, S., Eichelberger, J. and Shimizu, H. (eds), *Procs. Unzen International Workshop: Decade Volcano and Scientific Drilling*, 26-27.

UI, T., MATSUWO, N., SUMITA, M. and FUJINAWA, A. in press. Generation of block and ash flow during the 1990-95 eruption of Unzen volcano, Japan. *Journal Volcan.Geotherm.Res.*

WALKER, G.P.L. 1971. Grain size characteristics of pyroclastic deposits. *Journal of Geology*, **79**, 696-714.

WALKER, G.P.L. 1973. Explosive volcanic eruption - a new classification scheme. *Geol. Rundsch.*, **62**, 431-446.

WALKER, G.P.L. 1981. Characteristics of two phreatoplinian ashes, and their water flushed origin. *Journal Volcan. Geotherm. Res.*, **9**, 395-407.

WAN, Z. and WANG, Z. 1994. Hyperconcentrated flow. IAHR Monograph Series. Balkema.

WATANABE, K., WATANABE, K., DANHARA, T. and TERAI, K. 1997. Monitoring of juvenile material in ash before dome appearance during 1990-1991 eruption of Unzen volcano. *IN*: Nakada, S., Eichelberger, J. and Shimizu, H. (eds), *Procs. Unzen International Workshop: Decade Volcano and Scientific Drilling*, 76-77.

YAMAMOTO, T., TAKARADA, S. and SUTO, S. 1993. Pyroclastic flows from the 1991 eruption of Unzen Volcano. *Japan. Bull. Volcan.*, **55**, 166-175.

YANAGI, T., OKADA, H. and OHTA, K. 1992. *Unzen Volcano the 1990-1992 eruption*. The Nishinippon and Kyushu University Press.

Chapter 7

PROGLACIAL FLUVIAL SEDIMENTARY SEQUENCES IN GREENLAND AND ICELAND: A CASE STUDY FROM ACTIVE PROGLACIAL ENVIRONMENTS SUBJECT TO JÖKULHLAUPS

Andrew J.Russell and Philip M.Marren

7.1 INTRODUCTION, AIMS AND RATIONALE

This study examines the sedimentary characteristics of fluvial deposits of active proglacial environments within Greenland and Iceland (Figure 7.1). Attention is focused on the interpretation of sedimentary sections within proglacial fluvial systems subject to periodic glacier outburst floods or jökulhlaups. Although there have been numerous studies on the sedimentology of active proglacial rivers (Williams and Rust, 1969, Rust, 1972, Church, 1972, Fahnestock and Bradley, 1973, Gustavson, 1974, Bluck, 1974, Church and Gilbert, 1975), relatively few have focused specifically on the role of jökulhlaups in creating distinctive vertical sedimentary sequences (Jonsson, 1982, Maizels, 1989a, b, 1991, 1993a, b, 1995; Maizels and Russell, 1992). This paper aims to classify, describe and interpret vertical sections through jökulhlaup deposits within a variety of channel types and depositional settings.

There are many reasons for looking at the sedimentology of proglacial fluvial deposits in general and jökulhlaup deposits in particular. The rationale for the research, from which these case studies were selected, was to investigate the sedimentary expression of jökulhlaups within active and recently active proglacial river channels (Maizels, 1991, Maizels and Russell, 1992). Part of this case study deals with the relationship between flood flow hydrodynamics and fluvial sedimentology (Russell, 1989, 1993). Palaeohydrological reconstruction of the magnitude and frequency regime associated with former outwash systems may provide important information about the glacio-hydrological regime of former ice masses (Maizels, 1995). One might also be interested in reconstructing former flood events within active proglacial channel systems for hazard identification and mitigation (Sturm and Benson, 1985, Jones et al., 1985, Desloges et al., 1989, Matthews and Clague, 1993).

7.2 CASE STUDY: PROGLACIAL FLUVIAL SEDIMENTARY SEQUENCES IN GREENLAND AND ICELAND

7.2.1 A Variety of Local Depositional Settings

Interpretation of any sedimentary unit will depend upon its association with sedimentary structures and fluvial architecture as well as consideration of the type of channel in which the feature is found (Miall, 1985, Gregory and Maizels, 1991, Maizels, 1993) (Figure 7.2). This case study examines sedimentary successions within four channel types, three are from an active jökulhlaup-dominated channel in western Greenland and one is from the jökulhlaup-dominated proglacial area of the Skeiðarárjökull, Iceland (Figure 7.1). Examination of fluvial deposits within different proglacial channels provides scope for the interpretation of a wide range of lithofacies and architecture types. Interpretation of sedimentary sections often involves making inferences about flow conditions solely on the basis of empirical relationships between fluvial process and form. Studies which incorporate knowledge of flow conditions when interpreting sedimentary structures therefore provide a much sounder starting point for improved interpretation of the sedimentary record. It is for this reason that the first part of this case study is based within an active proglacial fluvial system in Greenland, chosen because of the presence of a range of distinctive channel types. Known hydraulic and channel morphological data are vitally important for the correct interpretation of sedimentary characteristics of the Greenland sections within each of the three distinctive channel types within a bedrock-confined fluvial system (Table 7.1). Consideration of factors such as the river flow discharge hydrograph, flow rheology and

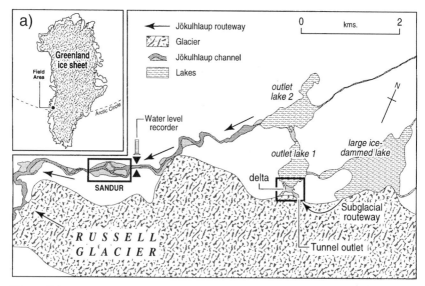

Figure 7.1. *Location of field sites in Greenland (a) and Iceland (b). (a) Note large ice-dammed lake which is the source of repeated jökulhlaups (Russell, 1989). Flood waters exit subglacially and form a delta into outlet lake 1 before pouring over a spillway into outlet lake 2 (see Figure 7.3). The jökulhlaup discharge hydrograph in Figure 7.6 was obtained from a water level recorder in a confined channel upstream of the sandur. (b) Section location relative to the present margin of Skeiðarárjökull and the active proglacial fluvial system.*

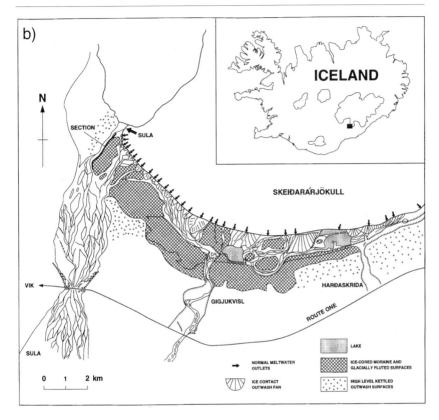

flow competence is absolutely essential for the interpretation of sections within active proglacial systems. Thicker Icelandic fluvial successions allow more detailed examination of the larger scale architecture of an unconfined proglacial fluvial system (Table 7.1). Interpretation of the Icelandic deposit is based solely upon section-derived information as surface morphology shows little relation to underlying sediments. Ignorance of available process information in the study of modern proglacial fluvial systems holds back advances in our understanding of ancient river systems.

7.2.2 Introduction to Fieldsites

7.2.2.1 Greenland

The first three river channel types under investigation form part of a river system which flows along the northern margin of the Russell Glacier 25-30 km north-east of Kangerlussuaq, west Greenland (Figure 7.1). The river is supplied by supraglacially-fed

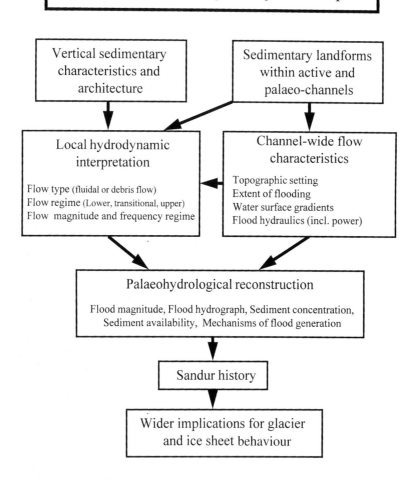

Figure 7.2. *Flow diagram illustrating what can be derived from the interpretation of sections within jökulhlaup channels. The role of additional channel morphological information for section interpretation is highlighted.*

Proglacial channel type controls	Main attributes of jökulhlaup flow and deposition within each channel type
Jökulhlaup-dominated fluvial delta topsets	Jökulhlaup drainage into a confined proglacial lake results in rapid flow deceleration upon flow expansion and deposition graded to a variety of temporary local base levels during jökulhlaups. Deltas commonly comprise boulder-sized sediment 'perched' above normal lake levels (Shakesby, 1985, Elfström, 1983,1987, Russell, 1994).
High gradient bedrock-controlled channels	Jökulhlaups within bedrock-controlled channels are generally characterised by: high flow velocities, high flood powers and a high degree of flow variability (Baker, 1984, Baker and Kochel, 1988b, Carling, 1989). Transition from supercritical to subcritical flows may produce violent, channel-scale, hydraulic jumps (Baker, 1984) (Figure 3). However, localised flow conditions within embayments or tributary channels may be tranquil in comparison to those within the main jökulhlaup channel (Baker *et al.*, 1983, Baker and Kochel, 1988a, O'Connor, 1993).
Valley-confined sandur	Valley-confined sandur may act as major stores of jökulhlaup sediment. Proximal sandur subject to jökulhlaups are characterised by rapid flow expansion whilst in distal sandur flow constriction may result in temporary backwater ponding. Jökulhlaups can inundate complete valley-floors generating relatively deep flows (Baker, 1973, Fahnestock and Bradley, 1973, Baker *et al.*, 1993, Rudoy and Baker 1993, Carling, 1996).
Unconfined sandur	Jökulhlaups unconfined by valley walls will form outwash fans with relatively uniform characteristics (Maizels, 1989a,b,1991). The Skeiðarársandur is the largest active proglacial outwash plain in the world, made up of a series of large coalescing fans which have been active within the last few centuries (Boothroyd and Nummedal, 1978, Maizels, 1991,1993a).

Table 7.1. Jökulhlaup flow conditions and depositional controls in each of the four channel types discussed in this study.

meltwater draining the northern flank of the Russell Glacier and the southern margin of the Isunguata Sermia (Figure 7.1). Local topography consists of ice-scoured bedrock with a relief of the order of several hundred metres. Periodic jökulhlaups result from the sudden subglacial drainage of a large ice-dammed lake on the northern flank of the Russell Glacier (Sugden *et al.*, 1985, Gordon, 1986, Scholz *et al.*, 1988, Russell, 1989, and Russell and de Jong, 1989) (Figure 7.1). The jökulhlaups drain into an outlet lake and have created a distinctive boulder delta (Figure 7.4). The confined valley sandur lies a further 7 km downstream and contains a series of large bars (Figure 7.5).

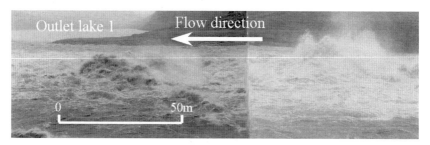

Figure 7.3. *Supercritical turbulent flows within high gradient Greenland spillway channel during 1987 jökulhlaup. Discharge is 1100 m³s⁻¹ and flood powers were up to 20,000 Wm⁻². This diagram illustrates the importance of local channel morphology in dominating the hydraulics of jökulhlaups.*

The magnitude and frequency regime of this proglacial river are distinctively bimodal, comprising high-frequency, low magnitude, ablation-controlled, diurnal events with maximum discharges of 40 m^3s^{-1} and jökulhlaups from the large ice-dammed lake with peak discharges in excess of 1000 m^3s^{-1} every 3-4 years (Figure 7.6). Jökulhlaups from the large ice-dammed lake therefore stand out as distinctive events within the proximal reaches of this catchment despite the fact that they only represent 0.0042% of the time over which non-jökulhlaup flows predominate and less than 0.04% of the total runoff volume. Jökulhlaups were observed in 1984 and 1987 (Sugden *et al.*, 1985, Russell, 1989). Evidence from aerial photographs suggest that at least 4 other jökulhlaups occurred between 1943 and 1982, but none since 1987. Review of the controls on the magnitude and frequency of jökulhlaups can be found in Maizels and Russell (1992), Evans and Clague (1994) and Maizels (1995).

Sediment volume and character are the two most important variables determining vertical sedimentary characteristics in proglacial fluvial systems, irrespective of flow magnitude and frequency regime (Maizels and Russell, 1992, Maizels, 1993). The relationship between sediment supply, hydrograph characteristics and vertical sedimentary characteristics is most clearly illustrated for jökulhlaups (Maizels, 1989a, b, 1991, 1993a, b).

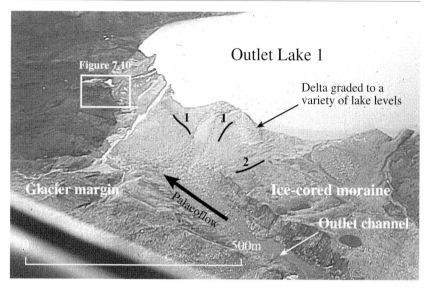

Figure 7.4. *Oblique air photograph of the Greenland jökulhlaup delta showing locations of sections relative to delta morphology and the jökulhlaup tunnel outlet. Note that the delta is 'perched' above the proglacial lake and graded to a variety of base levels.*

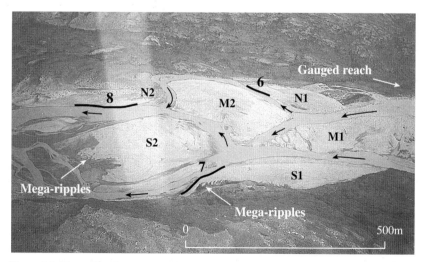

Figure 7.5. *View of Sandur 1 showing the locations of sections (6-7) relative to the main bars (N1, N2, M1, M2, S1 and S2). Note the presence of mega-ripples in the lee of bars S1 and S2. The discharge hydrograph in Figure 7.6 was obtained 100 m upstream of this sandur.*

Sediment is supplied to the Greenland channel mainly from the erosion of channel-margin glacial and fluvial deposits. However, the actual volume of coarse-grained sediment transported during jökulhlaups is low compared with the volume of water. For example, jökulhlaup sediment by volume over the Greenland delta topsets reached only 0.00016% of the total flood volume. Furthermore the two proglacial lake basins not only attenuated the jökulhlaup hydrograph but also acted as sediment traps, severely limiting downstream sediment supply. It is clear that parts of the Greenland jökulhlaup channel are starved of sediment, having no sediment input between jökulhlaups. In contrast, reaches adjacent to the glacier and with confluent meltwater fed tributaries are restocked with sand and gravel between jökulhlaups.

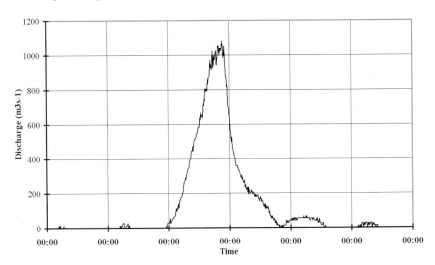

Figure 7.6. *Discharge hydrograph from July 16th - 21st 1987 obtained from a gauging station immediately upstream of Sandur 1. Note the bimodal nature of discharge events dominated by the jökulhlaup and lower magnitude diurnal variations.*

7.2.2.2 Iceland

The sandar of southern Iceland have long been a classic location for the study of glaciofluvial sediments, providing extensive, thick successions of sediment recording a long history of proglacial activity including a continuous record of jökulhlaups (Maizels, 1993b). Models of the development of the Skeiðarársandur were produced by a number of workers (Boothroyd and Nummedal, 1978, Maizels, 1991, 1993a) although to date only a small number of the available sedimentary sections have been discussed in the literature.

The Skeiðarársandur is subject to jökulhlaups from two sources; the subglacial geothermal lake Grímsvötn and the ice-dammed lake Graenalón. The two lakes drain with different frequencies and with markedly different magnitudes, resulting in a complex history of

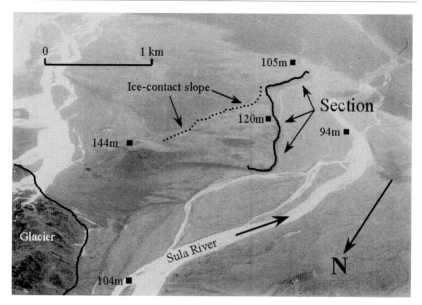

Figure 7.7. Oblique aerial photograph showing the location of the 2 km long Skeiðarársandur Section in relation to the present ice margin and river pattern.

jökulhlaup drainage over time. In addition, subglacial volcanic eruptions, either at Grímsvötn, or farther to the north at Bárðabunga can trigger large jökulhlaups (Björnsson, 1992). The November 1996 jökulhlaup from Grímsvötn occupied all of the rivers draining the Skeiðarárjökull, whereas those from Graenalón only occupy the Súla on the western margin of the Skeiðarársandur.

Since 1940, jökulhlaups from Grímsvötn have occurred every 4-6 years with peak discharges of between 2000 and 10000 m^3s^{-1}. Since 1939 only the November 1996 jökulhlaup was the product of a volcanic eruption, with a peak discharge of 45000 m^3s^{-1} (Björnsson, 1997, Russell, 1997). The only recorded jökulhlaups from Graenalón for the first half of this century occurred in 1898, 1935 and 1939 with peak discharges of between 4000 and 5000 m^3s^{-1} (Thorarinsson, 1939). Further jökulhlaups occurred in 1943, 1946, 1949 and 1951 (Björnsson, 1976); and since 1951, jökulhlaups from Graenalón have occurred at least once a year, with peak discharges between 1500 and 2000 m^3s^{-1} (Björnsson, 1992).

Information on sediment transport in jökulhlaups from the Skeiðarárjökull is sparse. Tómasson (1974) suggested suspended sediment variations and post-flood channel sedimentology for the 1972 jökulhlaup from Grímsvötn. Most of the fine-grained material, carried as suspended sediment, was derived from ice-wall melting of the subglacial jökulhlaup routeway. The bulk of this material was deposited in the flood channel where it was quickly reworked after the flood; some was deposited in the immediate offshore zone. A very small portion of the sand and gravel was derived from and transported by the flood in blocks of glacier ice. The majority of the sand and gravel was derived from flood channel widening and transported as bedload.

The Súla Section is located near the western margin of the Skeiðarárjökull (Figure 7.1) and, so far, has not been discussed in relation to the evolution of the Skeiðarársandur. The section extends for approximately 1.5 km on the eastern bank of the Súla, facing south-east for most of its length. Exposure is into a ridge-like block of sediment created by active erosion from the River Súla on its western flank and the presence of a distinctive ice contact slope on the eastern flank (Klimek, 1973). The river channel surface at the foot of the terrace lies at 95-100 m asl, whereas the highest points on the section lie at approximately 120 m asl. A distinctive erosional remnant at the north-eastern extremity of the terrace reaches a height of 144 m asl. Below the highest surface are two lower surfaces; one at approximately 120-125 m asl which is constructed of Units 1-6 (see below) and one at approximately 115 m asl which forms the upper surface of Unit 7. The 115 m asl surface extends across the present Súla channel; sediments with the same characteristics as those viewed on the eastern bank of the Súla could be seen on the western bank. Three distinct high points exposed in section act as convenient reference points, especially for Units 3, 4, 5 and 6. Working southwards these high points are referred to as HP1, HP2 and HP3 in the text (Figure 7.16).

7.2.3 Methods

Greenland jökulhlaup deposits were examined in a number of natural sedimentary sections into bar edges and pits excavated into bar surfaces and margins (Figures 7.4 and 7.5). Sections were logged in order to document: erosional contacts, bedding type and orientation, particle size and sorting, grading, overall architecture and clast imbrication. A modified version of Miall's (1978) lithofacies scheme was adopted in this study (Table 7.2). Jökulhlaup channel morphology was surveyed and mapped. Clast-sizes and palaeoflow directions were measured at intervals across the jökulhlaup channel. Fortunately, in this case a jökulhlaup was gauged in July 1987 at the head of the valley-confined sandur (Russell, 1989) (Figure 7.5). Hydrograph data and observations made during and immediately after the jökulhlaup proved invaluable for both the interpretation of sedimentary structures and the calculation of local hydraulic parameters such as stream power, boundary shear stress and Froude number. Baker and Costa (1987) discussed the calculation and value of these parameters for the study of floods and flood channels.

Lithofacies code	Description	Interpretation
Bm	Poorly sorted, heterogeneous, clast-supported imbricated boulder unit	Grain-by-grain deposition from traction load in a turbulent, high-energy flow.
Bms	Structureless boulder unit with finer-grained, poorly-sorted matrix.	Hyperconcentrated flow deposits
Gm	Poorly sorted, heterogeneous, structureless, imbricated cobble gravel: ungraded	Longitudinal bars, lag deposits, sieve deposits
Gms	Massive clast-supported gravel	Cohesionless debris flow
Gmm	Coarse, matrix supported boulders and rip-up clasts	Hyperconcentrated flow deposits
Gmuc	Poorly sorted, heterogeneous, structureless, imbricated cobble gravel: graded (upwards coarsening)	Depositional from fluidal flows on rising limb of flood event
Gh	Poorly sorted, heterogeneous, horizontally bedded gravel: ungraded. ugh: upwards fining uc; upwards coarsening	Deposition from fluidal flows. Transport in turbulent suspension prior to late-stage traction transport (Brennand 1994).
Gs	Massive, homogeneous, (well) sorted gravel: ungraded uf: upwards fining uc: upwards coarsening	Depositional from fluidal flow with high sediment concentration from single source.
Gt	Trough cross-stratified gravel	Channel fills
Gp	Planar cross-stratified gravel	Linguoid bars or deltaic units from dissection of bars
Sp	Planar cross-stratified sands	Linguoid bar front deposition. Upper or lower flow regime sand waves
Sr	Ripple marks	Ripples under lower flow regime conditions
Sh	Horizontally bedded sands	Planar bed flow upper and lower flow regime
St	Trough cross-stratified sands	Planar bed flow upper and lower flow regime
Dm	Homogeneous Diamict (massive)	Glacial till
Fh	Horizontally bedded silts	Planar bed upper and lower flow regime
(s)	Slumped and deformed examples	Deposition over buried ice
(b)	Bimodal size-distribution	Longitudinal sorting and/or flow separation on bedform

Table 7.2. *Lithofacies scheme used in this study after Miall (1979) and Maizels (1993).*

Where possible field sections were selected to provide information about the internal structure of major features within the jökulhlaup channel such as bars, delta surfaces and channel fills. Although only a small number of sections are described in this study, closely spaced or continuous sections provided the best information about bar composition. Similarly sections both parallel with and transverse to palaeoflow are particularly useful for interpretation. Sections were also purposely excavated into bar areas known to have been deposited or reworked by the 1987 jökulhlaup.

In the Iceland field area data were gathered in order to test the models of Skeiðarársandurs' evolution and to allow a local reconstruction of depositional events and glacier margin fluctuations. The geomorphology of the ridge was determined from basic field mapping and from the 1986 and 1991 aerial photographs of the area. The section was divided into distinctive units using large-scale sedimentary characteristics and architecture as criteria. Individual lithofacies were then recorded, classifying according to: grain-size, within unit grading, clast support type (i.e. matrix- or clast-supported), nature of matrix, and the type of contacts between units. This information was then used to group the sediments into distinct lithofacies associations. A (long) and b (intermediate) axis imbrication was used as an indicator of palaeoflow direction. Many lithofacies associations were closely related to the architectural units and are only found in one unit. Most sedimentary successions were dominated by coarse gravel and boulders, and fall under Miall's (1978) Gm or Gms lithofacies codes (see Section 2.1.3). Additional facies codes were created and used in this study in order to describe the detailed differences between the sediment packages present within the terrace (Table 7.2).

7.2.4 Description and Interpretation of Field Sections

Greenland

7.2.4.1. Fluvial Delta Topset

Massive Boulder Deposits Bm and Bms (Section 1)
Description: Section 1 forms an erosional face into the delta topset over a distance of 25-30 m (Figure 7.4). Sediment comprises a mixture of poorly sorted sand and gravel forming a matrix between the large boulders of up to 2 m diameter (Figure 7.8). Local open framework pockets can be identified (Figure 7.8). Although initially appearing structureless (Bms) closer observation revealed crude clast imbrication (Bm) (Figure 7.8). Open framework areas of the section are formed by boulder cluster structures where some clasts display a-axis imbrication, usually at high angles. Most of the clasts are, sub-angular/sub-rounded and because of their shape, imbrication is less prominent. The largest clasts are found just below the top of the section (Figure 7.8). The delta surface above this section

Figure 7.8. *Section 1 consists of massive boulder deposits (Bm) and (Bms). Sediment comprises a mixture of poorly sorted sand and gravel forming a matrix between the large boulders of up to 2 m diameter. Local open-framework pockets can be identified. Although initially appearing structureless (Bms), closer observation reveals crude clast imbrication (Bm). Open-framework areas of the section are formed by boulder-cluster structures where some clasts display a-axis imbrication, usually at high angles. Clustering and local high-angled imbrication indicate deposition from highly turbulent flows in a grain-by-grain mode from bedload (Brayshaw, 1985). The coarse grain-size and lack of sorting of these deposits indicate rapid deposition from a flow with high sediment transport capacity. An overall coarsening-upward trend within the section suggests deposition during the jökulhlaup rising limb.*

comprises a mixture of large boulders often in clusters, again locally showing imbrication. Sand and gravel sheets are deposited around boulder clusters, creating small obstacle marks and lee-side tail accumulations. Surface clusters often merge, forming large openwork areas. Openwork pockets are similar to clusters found on the delta surface.

Interpretation: the clustering and local high-angled imbrication indicate deposition from highly turbulent flows in a grain-by-grain mode from bedload (Brayshaw, 1985). Structureless, poorly sorted sediment between clusters was deposited around, against and in zones of flow separation in the lee of large boulders and cluster bedforms. The coarse grain size and lack of sorting of these deposits indicate rapid deposition from a flow with high sediment transport capacity. This interpretation is consistent with that of Brennand (1994) for similar heterogeneous unstratified gravel facies. An overall coarsening-upward trend within the section suggests deposition during the jökulhlaup rising limb (Maizels, 1991, 1993).

Sedimentation of the central portion of the delta succession occurred during an earlier jökulhlaup probably by rising stage flows to produce a coarsening-upward succession (Russell, 1991). The central delta surface shows signs of fluvial transport of boulder-sized sediment at high stages, and sand and gravel as sheets at lower stages. That the largest boulder-clusters on the main delta surface above this section were not moved during the 1987 jökulhlaup, indicates that the main delta surface was not disturbed to any great depth. Peak jökulhlaup flood powers, and velocities of 2846 Wm^{-2} and 5.2 ms^{-1} respectively, suggest boulder-size material was capable of being transported as bed or traction load from the jökulhlaup tunnel area to the proximal delta surface. Progressive reduction of flood powers from 2846 Wm^{-2} to 407 Wm^{-2} over the delta surface resulted in a marked reduction in delta surface grain size.

Coarsening-Upwards Horizontally Bedded Gravels Gh (Section 2)
Description: Section 2 extends for over 70 m from a relatively proximal position, only 30 m from the delta feeder channel, into a lobate bar leading towards a distal slipface into a lateral channel (Figure 7.4). Bar surface grain-size, decreases steadily away from the delta feeder channel. All of these deposits were poorly sorted, displaying crude near-horizontal stratification (Gh) within a generally coarsening-upward succession (Figure 7.9). A gradational contact at 40 cm depth separates a lower fine-grained unit from an upper coarser-grained unit. Lower units were characterised by thinner, compact laminae, consisting of coarse-grained sand inter-bedded with openwork gravel (Figure 7.9). The largest clasts are located near or on the deposit surface.

Interpretation: Section 2 contains sedimentary structures indicative of fluvial deposition. The crudeness and large-scale of the stratification together with poor sorting of deposits, suggests deposition during flows of high velocity and shear stress. Clast imbrication and cluster bedforms indicate grain-by-grain deposition of both large clasts (10 cm+) and coarse-grained sand. The sediments are similar to horizontally-bedded gravel units indicative of traction transport in fluidal flows (Brennand, 1994). Crude horizontal bedding indicates the deposition of laterally extensive gravel sheets. Progressive upward-coarsening of beds suggests deposition during the rising flow stage (Maizels, 1991,1995).

Comparison of pre- and post- 1987 jökulhlaup photographs, suggests that the sediments in Section 2 were deposited by the 1987 jökulhlaup. This is further supported by the fact that all grain sizes present in Section 2 (<10 cm) were capable of being transported in suspension within the nearby feeder channel by peak flood flows with powers of 2846 Wm^{-2}. Suspended load in the main feeder channel is thought to have been rapidly transferred to traction load within the backwater influenced area in the lee of an ice-cored moraine ridge (Figure 7.4). Progressively coarser sediment supplied to this location on the rising flood stage allowed the deposition of a series of progressively coarser-grained horizontal gravel sheets.

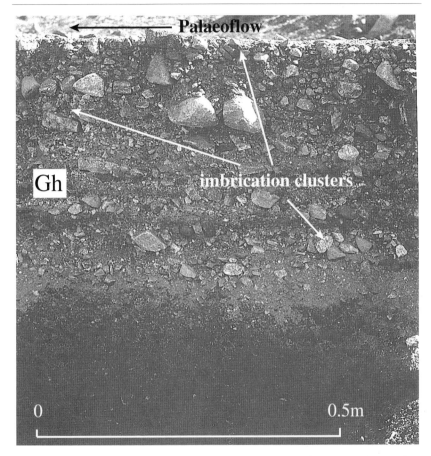

Figure 7.9. *Section 2 contains upwards-coarsening, horizontally bedded gravels (Gh) extending for over 70 m from a relatively proximal position, only 30 m from the delta feeder channel. This deposit is poorly sorted and displays crude near-horizontal stratification (Gh) within a generally coarsening-upward succession. A gradational contact at 40 cm depth separates a lower fine-grained unit from an upper coarser-grained unit. Lower units were characterised by thinner, compact laminae, consisting of coarse-grained sand, inter-bedded with openwork gravel. The largest clasts are located near or on the surface of the deposit. The crudeness and large-scale of the stratification together with poor sorting of deposits, suggests deposition during fluvial flows of high velocity and shear stress. Clast imbrication and cluster bedforms indicate grain-by-grain deposition of both large clasts (10 cm+) and coarse-grained sand. The sediments are similar to horizontally-bedded gravel units indicative of traction transport in fluidal flows. Crude horizontal bedding indicates the deposition of laterally extensive gravel sheets. Progressive upward-coarsening of beds suggest deposition during the rising flow stage.*

Coarsening Upward Units of Sand Sh,Sp and Sr (Section 3)

Description: a small tributary located near the delta edge on the western lake shore contains a sandy bar, thickest on the delta side of the tributary with its crest 20 m from the tributary mouth (Figure 7.4). Sections through the deposit show a coarsening-upward succession of medium to coarse-grained sand. Sedimentary structures include crude horizontal bedding (Sh) becoming better defined at higher levels within the section. At 0.35 m from the top of the section, laminae became coarser-grained containing local clasts of 2 mm diameter (Figure 7.10). The top 20 cm displays low angled cross-stratification (Sp). Local small-scale ripple trough cross-stratification (Sr) can be discerned. A sand layer near the bar surface contains soil and plant fragments, together with very angular, flake-like, clasts. Coarse-grained clasts on the surface are predominantly angular/very angular. The size of these clasts generally decreases with distance from the main channel. The clasts are nearly all platey or flake-like with a fresh non-weathered appearance.

Interpretation: the predominance of lithofacies Sh at this location represents the aggradation of plane-bedded sands and near vertical bar growth. The presence of pebbles within the Sh units suggests upper flow regime conditions. Small-scale (< 5 cm thick) Sp and Sr units suggest the development of ripples representing lower energy flow conditions. Very angular bedrock flakes found on the surface of the slackwater deposit were probably chipped from cobble-boulder sized sediment during traction transport. Their distinctive platey shapes would have allowed them to remain longer in suspension due to their high ratio of surface area to mass which would induce slow settling. The coarsening-upward trend suggests either an increase in flow energy or a change in sediment supply conditions.

The morphology of the sand bar is similar to that of slackwater deposits described by Baker and Kochel (1988a, b). Despite the presence of stratified sediments it is difficult to distinguish sediments deposited by individual jökulhlaups. However, as successive jökulhlaups extended the delta front into the lake basin, progressively coarser grained, more proximal sediments were likely to have been deposited producing the coarsening-upwards succession. During the 1987 jökulhlaup the sand bar was submerged by up to 1.4 m of water. The deposit was entirely submerged for 9 hours during which time flows over the nearby delta would have been subjected to backwater effects.

7.2.4.2 High Gradient Bedrock Controlled Channel

Bimodal Channel Fill Gp Capped by Boulder Lag (Section 4)

Description: downstream-dipping foreset sand and fine-grained gravel beds (Gp), are exposed within a 2 m high section through a boulder covered channel within a high gradient reach of the jökulhlaup channel (Figures 7.11a and b). Individual cross-strata of cm-scale thickness, show considerable variation of grain size and sorting (Figure 7.11b). This section

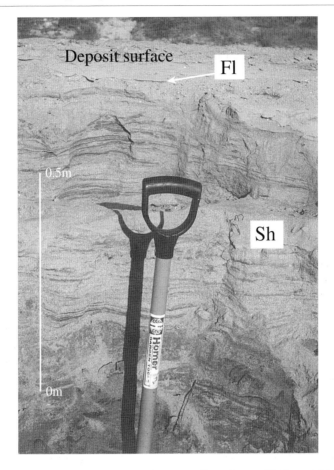

Figure 7.10. *Section 3 contains coarsening-upward sand units (Sh,Sp and Sr). A small tributary located near the delta edge on the western lake shore contains a sandy bar, thickest on the delta side of the tributary with its crest 20 m from the tributary mouth (Figure 7.4). Sections through the deposit show a coarsening-upward succession of medium to coarse-grained sand. Sedimentary structures including crude horizontal bedding (Sh) becoming better defined at higher levels within the section. At 0.35 m from the top of the section, laminae become coarser-grained containing local clasts of 2 mm diameter. The top 20 cm displays low angled cross-stratification (Sp). Local small-scale ripple trough cross-stratification (Sr) can be discerned. The predominance of lithofacies Sh at this location represents the aggradation of plane-bedded sands and near vertical bar growth. The presence of pebbles within the Sh units suggests upper flow regime conditions. Small scale (< 5 cm thick) Sp and Sr units suggest the development of ripples representing lower energy flow conditions. The coarsening-upward trend suggests either an increase in flow energy or a change in sediment supply conditions.*

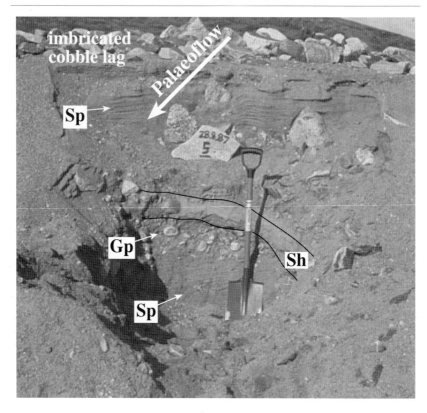

Figure 7.11a. *Section 4, bimodal channel-fill (Gpb) capped by an imbricated cobble lag. Downstream-dipping foreset sand and fine-grained gravel beds (Gp), are exposed within a 2 m high section through a boulder covered channel within a high gradient reach of the jökulhlaup channel. This section contains local boulder-size clasts (Gpb), orientated parallel to downstream cross-strata dips of 20-25°. Boulders outcropping in section have a mean b-axis (10 largest clasts) of 15 cm compared with 17 cm for the overlying imbricated surface boulder lag. The section contains two erosional contacts separating cross-stratified units with a total down-channel dip variation of 85°. Cross-strata exposed in Section 5 suggest the downstream migration of a series of foreset bedforms. Poor sorting of the sediments within foreset beds and the presence of out-sized clasts suggest that local jökulhlaup flows were able to transport a large range of grain-sizes and that deposition within the macroturbulent flow was too rapid for better sorting to develop. Erosional contacts indicate reworking associated with either bedform migration or fluctuations in local flow conditions such as direction, intensity or sediment flux. Similarity in the size and shape of surface boulders with those in section suggests the development of an armoured layer during the process of river bed erosion.*

contains local boulder size clasts (Gpb), orientated parallel to downstream cross-strata dips of 20-25° (Figure 7.11a). Boulders outcropping in section have a mean b-axis of the 10 largest clasts of 15 cm compared with 17 cm for the mean on the overlying imbricated surface boulder lag. The section contains two erosional contacts separating cross-stratified units with a total down-channel dip variation of 85°.

Interpretation: cross-strata exposed in Section 5 suggest the downstream migration of a series of foreset bedforms or sediment waves. Poor sorting of the sediments within foreset beds and the presence of out-sized clasts suggest that local jökulhlaup flows were able to transport a large range of grain-sizes and that deposition within the macroturbulent flow was too rapid for better sorting to develop. Erosional contacts indicate reworking associated with either bedform migration or fluctuations in local flow conditions such as direction, intensity or sediment flux. Similarity of size and shape between surface boulders and those within the section suggests the development of an armoured layer through river bed erosion.

It is suggested that sediments in Section 4 were deposited late on the rising jökulhlaup limb when a wide range of sediment sizes were available for transport and deposition. Plate-shaped boulders exposed in section and on the channel surface were all entrained from bedrock outcrops less than 300 m upstream. Finer-grained sand and gravel comprising the foresets travelled farther, having been transported through the upstream sandur. Channel incision occurred on the jökulhlaup waning stage removing sands and gravels but leaving the boulders to form the surface armoured layer.

Trough Cross-Bedded Sands St (Section 5)
Description: an embayment provides the location for a small sandy deposit which is sheltered from flows down the main channel, especially during the jökulhlaup waning stage (Figure 7.12). The surface of the deposit contains a series of well defined, low amplitude, three-dimensional dune bedforms transverse to the main flow direction (Figure 7.12). Excavation of the natural erosional face on the channel side of this deposit reveals repeated sets of moderate-angled (15-20°), sandy trough cross-strata (St) bounded top and bottom by erosional contacts, apparently dipping in an up-channel direction (Figure 7.12).

Interpretation: cross-strata (St) may represent eddy flow circulation within the embayment producing foreset beds locally dipping in an upstream direction. This hypothesis is favoured by the fact that cross-strata show significant variation in orientation rising vertically through the section and cross-strata dip angles are too steep for stoss-side development. It is suggested that these sandy cross-strata resulted from the development of a localised circulating flow cell during the jökulhlaup. Likely severe turbulence during peak flows, the fine unconsolidated nature of the sediment, and low elevation of this deposit relative to the

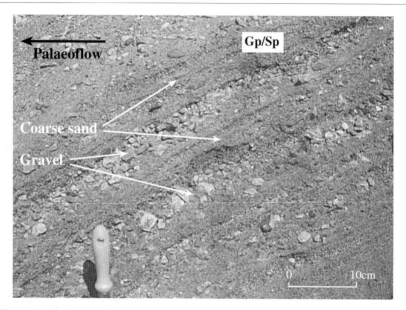

Figure 7.11b. *Section 4, sorting variations in gravel cross-strata (Gp) supporting local boulders/cobbles. Individual cross-strata of cm-scale thickness, show considerable variation of grain size and sorting.*

main channel, suggest that this deposit was laid down during waning jökulhlaup flows. The location and overall morphology of this deposit correspond with that of an eddy bar in Baker's (1984) classification scheme.

7.2.4.3 Valley Confined Sandur

Cross-Stratified Pebble-Rich Sands Sp Overlain by Very Poorly Sorted Cobble Unit Gm(s) (Section 6)
Description: ten small exposures were excavated over a distance of 35 m, on the downstream edge of a bar (Figure 7.13). All exposures contain generally upward coarsening units comprising: basal layers of poorly sorted, crudely planar cross-stratified, coarse-grained sands and gravels (Sp and Gp); very poorly sorted, almost structureless, upper gravelly units (Gm/Gms); and a surface sand sheet or imbricated cobble lag (Figure 7.13). Very poorly sorted, almost structureless, units varied in thickness from 0.1-0.85 m with the lower erosional contact dipping in a northerly direction (Figure 7.13). The upper poorly sorted unit contained turfs whilst the lower cross-stratified unit comprises alternating clast- and sandy matrix-supported strata with local, structureless, polymodal strata (Figure 7.13).

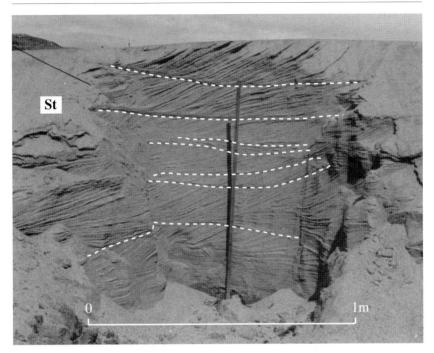

Figure 7.12. *Section 5, trough cross-stratified sands (St) deposited in an embayment within a confined reach of jökulhlaup channel. Excavation of the natural erosional face on the channel side of this deposit reveals repeated sets of moderate-angled (15-20°), sandy trough cross-strata (St) bounded top and bottom by erosional contacts, apparently dipping in an up-channel direction. Cross-strata (St) may represent eddy flow circulation within the embayment producing foreset beds locally dipping in an upstream direction. It is suggested that these sandy cross-strata are the result of the development of a localised circulating flow cell during the jökulhlaup. Dashed lines separate individual sets of cross-strata.*

Interpretation: the lowest unit represents the migration of successive bar fronts, perhaps slightly lobate, giving rise to the variation of dip directions found within these deposits. Large variations in grain size and sorting suggest either rapidly fluctuating sediment supply or flow conditions. Dip directions within these sections of between 200° and 340°, indicate a general flow direction towards bar M2 (Figure 7.5). Directional variation within an individual section is generally much lower (50°) suggesting consistent spatial variation of flow directions over time. The presence of the laterally extensive erosional contact at the base of the upper very poorly sorted unit suggests a phase of widespread scour. The very poorly sorted layer forms a channel fill, with greatest depth within the northern sections and thinning markedly southwards. A surface cobble lag indicates the winnowing action of waning stage flows.

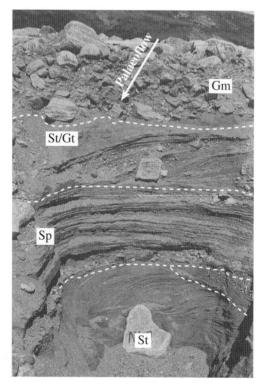

Figure 7.13. *Section 6, cross-stratified sands and gravels (Sp/St) overlain by poorly sorted structureless gravels (Gm). This section contains generally upward-coarsening units comprising: basal layers of poorly sorted, crudely planar cross-stratified, and coarse-grained sands and gravels (Sp and Gp); very poorly sorted, almost structureless, upper gravelly units (Gm/Gms); and a surface sand sheet or imbricated cobble lag. Very poorly sorted, almost structureless, units vary in thickness from 0.1-0.85 m with the lower erosional contact dipping in a northerly direction. The upper poorly sorted unit contained turfs whilst the lower cross-stratified unit comprises alternating clast- and sandy matrix-supported strata with local, structureless, polymodal strata. The lowest unit represents the migration of successive bar fronts, perhaps slightly lobate, giving rise to the variation of dip directions found within these deposits. Large variations in grain size and sorting suggest either rapidly fluctuating sediment supply or flow conditions. Dip directions within these sections of between 200° and 340°, indicate a general flow direction towards bar M2 (Figure 7.5). Directional variation within an individual section is generally much lower (50°) suggesting consistent spatial variation of flow directions over time. The presence of the laterally extensive erosional contact at the base of the upper very poorly sorted unit suggests a phase of widespread scour. The very poorly sorted layer forms a channel fill, with greatest depth within the northern sections and thinning markedly southwards. A surface cobble lag indicates the winnowing action of waning stage flows.*

Jökulhlaup flows over this section persisted for the 12 hours when discharges exceeded 300 m³s⁻¹. Peak jökulhlaup flows crossed the present river channel at 90° submerging the sections to a depth of 1-1.5 m. Section 6 shows evidence of down-sandur migration of low relief foreset bedforms or bars followed by high energy sheet flows and waning stage winnowing and consequent cobble lag formation. Multiple coarsening- and fining-upward units suggest that several jökulhlaups are recorded at this location.

Planar Cross-Stratified Gravels Gp Capped by Surface Gravel Sheet (Gm) (Section 7)
Description: the distal portion of bar S1 contains a 1.25 m high avalanche face dissected by numerous chute channels (Figure 7.5). Numerous ice block obstacle marks are found on the proximal side of this bar (Figure 7.14a) (Russell, 1993, Figures 7.8b and 7.12). Sections 7(a-i) are located on the north-western erosional edge of bar S1 (Figure 7.5). Frozen soil and vegetation present at the bottom of these sections represents the pre-jökulhlaup ground surface. Sections contain gravelly planar cross-stratification (Gp) overlain by massive gravel (Gm) (Figures 7.14a and 7.14b). The sections generally coarsen upwards to a surface gravel lag, although large clasts are found locally within foresets (Figure 7.14b). Foresets are interrupted by at least 7 reactivation surfaces found at relatively regular intervals of 1-2 m, marking the extent of former bar surfaces (Figure 7.14a) (Collinson, 1970).

Figure 7.14a. *Section 7, planar cross-stratified gravels (Gp) containing numerous reactivation surfaces. The distal portion of S1 (Figure 7.5) was subject to backwater effects during the 1987 jökulhlaup being submerged to a depth of 1-1.5 m on the bar crest and 2.5-3.5 m in the lee of the bar.*

Figure 7.14b. Section 7, detail of cross-stratified gravels showing erosional contacts marking former bar surfaces together with gravel sheet units (Gm).

Reactivation surfaces slope at angles of 5-10° laterally, across the bar surface, although local up-bar dipping surfaces occur (Figure 7.14a). Sediment immediately above each reactivation surface is coarser-grained than that in the underlying foresets.

Interpretation: the proximal portion of S1 comprises a series of low-amplitude gravel sheets migrating away from the main channel as a bar flank accretion deposit, similar to those described by Rust (1972). Numerous Gp units separated by reactivation surfaces indicate lateral and downstream bar migration into relatively deep water (Collinson, 1970, Rust, 1972). Large-scale planar cross-stratified gravel units are common in river channels associated with jökulhlaups (Fahnestock and Bradley, 1973, Dawson, 1989).

At least eight jökulhlaups are suggested by the reactivation surfaces (Figure 7.14a) which show the progressive bar development. Local up-bar dipping reactivation surfaces suggest rising stage bar migration and vertical aggradation. The distal portion of S1 was subject to backwater effects during the 1987 jökulhlaup being submerged to a depth of 1-1.5 m on the bar crest and 2.5-3.5 m in the lee of the bar. The 1987 jökulhlaup may only have slightly reworked the surface of the bar (Gm), leaving a significant depositional wedge on the distal portion of the bar (Gp).

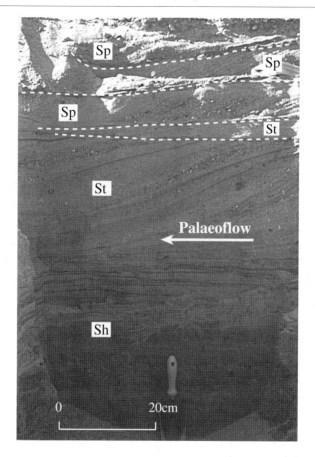

Figure 7.15. *Section 8, planar bedded sands (Sh) grading into cross-stratified sands (St). Two types of sandy cross-bedding are observed: firstly, those developed gradationally from plane beds (lower Section 8), and secondly, those with erosional bases in the upper parts of Section 8. The lower plane-bedded coarse-grained sand unit contains local gravel clasts and grades directly into sigmoidal cross-strata composed of coarse-grained sand and fine-grained gravel with scattered out-sized pebbles. Upper units 2-5 are all bounded by erosional contacts and characterised by cross-stratified sand displaying a variety of dip angles and directions. Erosional contacts at the base of Unit 5 and at the top of the section are marked by a gravel lag. Tabular cross-strata in Unit 3 increase in height downstream (left), as they replace lower angled cross-strata. The gradation from horizontally-bedded to cross-stratified sands is thought to represent deposition during progressively increasing flow depths whilst the upper cross-stratified sets represent the migration of bedforms with little net deposition. In the upper part of the photo, dashed lines separate individual sets of cross-strata.*

Horizontally-Bedded Sands Sh Grading into Cross-Stratified Sands St and Sp (Section 8)
Description: Section 8 was excavated by waning stage jökulhlaup flows into a distal bar parallel to the flow direction. Two types of sandy cross-bedding are observed: firstly, those developed gradationally from plane beds (lower Section 8), and secondly, those with erosional bases in the upper parts of Section 8 (Figure 7.15). When viewed from a distance the erosional contacts can be traced for up to 50 m. The lower plane-bedded, coarse-grained sand unit contains local gravel clasts and grades directly into sigmoidal cross-strata composed of coarse-grained sand and fine-grained gravel with scattered out-sized pebbles (Figure 7.15). Upper Units 2-5 are all bounded by erosional contacts and characterised by cross-stratified sand displaying a variety of dip angles and directions. Erosional contacts at the base of Unit 5 and at the section top are marked by a gravel lag (Figure 7.15). Tabular cross-strata in Unit 3 increase in height downstream (left), as they replace lower angled cross-strata (Figure 7.15).

Interpretation: the gradation from horizontally-bedded to cross-stratified sands is thought to represent deposition during progressively increasing flow depths whilst the upper cross-stratified sets represent the migration of bedforms with little net deposition. Alternatively, the gradation from Sh to St may reflect decreasing discharge on the waning flow stage. However, observations during the jökulhlaup suggest that bar incision was initiated during this period.

Extensive sub-horizontal erosional contacts suggest vertical bar growth as successive cross-stratified layers were deposited over large surface areas. The peak 1987 jökulhlaup flow stage was 4.2 m above the normal river channel and *ca.* 2 m above the surface of bar N2. Bar surface imbrication indicates that palaeoflow was in a southerly direction. Ripples indicate downbar flows parallel to the main channel (Figure 7.5).

Iceland

7.2.4.4 Icelandic Unconfined Sandur Deposits

Architecture
Five units based upon internal and external geometry were designated for the Súla River Section (Figure 7.16). These units were designated specifically for this one section for purely descriptive purposes and are not based upon any standard classification schemes. The units comprise various architectural elements (Miall, 1985; see Section 2.1.2) and six main lithofacies associations (see Sections 2.1.3, 3.2.4, 6.5.4 and 6.5.5). These are described below.

Lithofacies Association 1

Description: this lithofacies association consists of coarse-grained, clast-supported sand and gravel facies (Gm, Gmuc) and only occurs in Unit 1 (Figure 7.16). The sediments are poorly sorted and well imbricated containing numerous clusters of large boulders. All clasts are generally subangular to subrounded, the largest having b-axes of 0.6 m. The topmost metre contains a 0.3 m thick unit of medium-grained, horizontally-bedded gravels and sand overlain by coarser-grained gravel and a boulder lag of horizontally-bedded and massive gravel (Gh, Gm). The gravels are overlain for all of their length by up to 1 m of thinly bedded fine-grained sand and laminated silt (Sh, Fh).

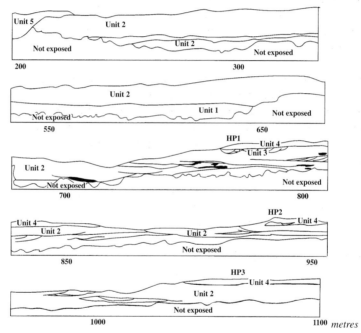

Figure 7.16. *Súla River Section. Units are designated by the letter U. High points along the section (HP1-3) are indicated for reference purposes. The units in the section (not depicted), between 300 m and 550 m are laterally continuous. Black areas indicate clusters or beds of large boulders. Unit 1 is laterally extensive and horizontal forming the base of the exposure and is dominated by gravel bar sediments and subsidiary, upper, laminated sands. Unit 2 consists of extensive successions of large-scale cross-cutting channels and low-angle bar forms which vary in size from approximately 30 m to nearly 100 m. Unit 3 consists of a small-scale set of cross-cutting channels infilled with finer-grained gravels. Unit 4 comprises horizontally bedded silts and sands and minor channels (infilled with gravel). Unit 5 consists of a variety of architectural elements (gravel bars, channels, laminated sands) and the overall geometry is generally horizontal or sub-horizontal .*

Interpretation: the coarsening-upwards gravel succession is thought to represent deposition on the rising limb of the flood. The minor changes in the style of sedimentation near the top of the gravel are interpreted as the product of localised changes in flow conditions, possibly during post-waning stage incision. The fine-grained capping of laminated silt and sand represents waning-stage deposition of fine-grained material. Lithofacies Association 1 (Unit 1) is therefore interpreted as representing a single flood event, with rising limb sedimentation, late stage reworking and falling limb sedimentation all preserved. This Lithofacies Association is the only flood deposit exposed within the section which is similar to flood sediments described elsewhere on the Skeiðarársandar (Maizels, 1991).

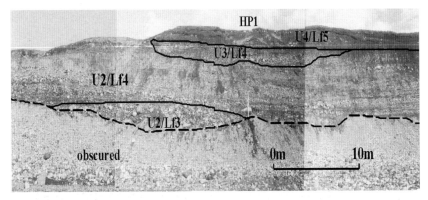

Figure 7.19. *The central section of the Súla River Section, beneath HP1.*

Lithofacies Association 2
Description: these facies form the upper part of Unit 1 (Figure 7.16), and although they are only exposed clearly in a small number of places, their geometry suggests that they are laterally extensive in the same way as Lithofacies Association 1. The association is dominated by a fine-grained silty diamicton (Dm) containing local angular to subrounded clasts, with b-axes of up to 0.2 m. Exposure of the diamicton is limited but it appears to be homogeneous throughout with no internal structure. The clasts within the diamicton are ungraded and do not display a preferred orientation.

Interpretation: the homogeneous nature of the sediment, with no obvious internal structure is suggestive of a non-fluvial deposit. The lack of stratification within the diamicton and the random clast orientation is not compatible with deposition into an ice-marginal lake. The absence of any grading and the laterally extensive nature of the sediments make a mass-flow origin unlikely. The diamicton is therefore interpreted as a subglacial till.

Lithofacies Association 3

Description: this association is characterised by an extremely poorly sorted boulder facies at the base of Unit 2 containing clasts with a-axes of up to 1 m supported by a fine-grained gravel matrix (Gmm) (Figures 7.16, 7.17 and 7.18). Local large clasts of diamicton, up to 0.8 m (a-axes, measured from a range of clasts after digging out the sides) are found incorporated within this package of sediment. These diamicton clasts are lithologically identical to the diamicton (Dm) in Lithofacies Association 2. In addition blocks of fluvially stratified fine- to medium-grained gravel are found locally, identified only when the bedding within the block is discordant to that of the surrounding sediment. The largest of these gravel blocks *ca.* 0.6 m in diameter has acted as a focus for cobble deposition.

Interpretation: Lithofacies Association 3 is interpreted as being the deposit of a flow with an extremely high sediment concentration. The association contains the coarsest-grained sediment preserved anywhere in the section, it is upwards coarsening and matrix-supported, allowing the largest clasts to be supported in the upper parts of the flow by dispersive pressure (Costa, 1984,1988). This association is therefore the product of a single extremely high-energy hyperconcentrated flood (see Sections 4.1 and 6.5.5.7). The possibility that the flood was an actual debris flow is discounted here as the presence of grain-to-grain contacts and local pebble and cobble clusters within the finer gravel which acts as a matrix, indicates that turbulent water flow processes were operating in parts of the flow.

Figure 7.18. *Lithofacies Association 3: rip-up clasts of horizontally bedded fluvial gravel (originally), redeposited with bedding at 90°. Note, imbricate cobbles stacked behind and above the rip-up clast.*

The presence of rip-up clasts of diamicton (Figure 7.18) and blocks of fluvial material suggest that sediments in the flood routeway were frozen, pointing to a winter flood event especially as there is no record of extensive permanently frozen ground in Iceland. Krainer and Poscher (1992) identified rip-up clasts from other proglacial sediment sequences suggesting that the diamicton blocks would not be able to survive journeys of more than a few kilometres. More recently, sheets of frozen river bed gravels were observed by the authors immediately following the November 1996 jökulhlaup in proximal areas of the Skeiðarársandar. Alternatively diamicton blocks could have been reworked from subglacial locations during a jökulhlaup. Whatever the source of the diamicton and fluvial rip-up clasts, their presence within the section indicates that deposition was relatively close to the ice margin. Lithofacies Association 3 is previously undescribed on the Skeiðarársandar.

Figure 7.19. Lithofacies Association 4: repeated upwards-coarsening (Gmuc), upwards-fining (Gmuf) and massive (Gm) units. These sediments are found within a large, cross-cutting channel system.

Lithofacies Association 4

Description: these sediments are found within Units 2 and 3 and as such lie within a large sequence of cross-cutting channels and bars (see Figure 7.16). The sediments of Lithofacies Association 4 consist of massive, ungraded or graded upward-coarsening and upward-fining units (Gs, Gsuc, Gsuf, Gm) (Figures 7.16, 7.19 and 7.20). The lower part of this association consists of distinctive homogeneous, well-sorted granule-sized basalt gravel (Gs) up to 3 m thick. Although the largest clasts are imbricated there is an absence of cluster bedforms as found in Associations 1 and 3. Strata above this are thinner and consist of local cobbles and coarse-grained gravel lenses overlain by fine- to medium-grained gravel. Indistinct foresets occur approximately halfway between HP1 and HP2 (Figure 7.16).

Interpretation: the presence of gravel bars, with associated lateral and frontal accretion units together with large-scale cross-cutting channels and upward-fining channel fills suggest a complex history of braided river aggradation and migration for Lithofacies Association 4 (upper part of Unit 2).

Lithofacies Association 4 sediments are dominated by granule-sized material of basaltic origin within channel fills. Clusters of coarser-grained, cobble-sized material are interpreted to represent bar cores (Williams and Rust, 1969, Eynon and Walker, 1974, Harms *et al.*, 1975, Hein and Walker, 1977). Lower ungraded or upward-coarsening units of 1-2 m thickness provide a marked contrast to the overlying upward-fining sequences. The lower sediments are also much more densely packed, and although they are imbricated, they do not display the strong imbrication and clustering seen in the higher sediments. The lower sediments are interpreted here as the product of heavily sediment laden 'hyperconcentrated flows' (Costa, 1984, 1988; Maizels 1989a, b) and as such are of high magnitude flood origin. The upper upward thinning and fining sediments near the top of the terrace (uppermost Units 2 and 3) are interpreted as 'normal' non-flood, fluidal flow sediments laid down during a period of glacier retreat and hence becoming more distal.

Lithofacies Association 5

Description: Lithofacies Association 5 (Figures 7.16 and 7.17) is found within Unit 4 and consists of horizontally bedded silt and sand, with local gravel beds (Fh, Sh, Gm) cut by small (2-3 m), gravel-filled channels (Gm). Below the topographic lows of the terrace surface, sediments are slumped (Fh(s), Sh(s)).

Interpretation: similar sediments were observed in the present proglacial area of the Skeiðarárjökull, occurring as small fans. As such, Unit 4 and Lithofacies Association 5 are interpreted as proglacial outwash fan sediments deposited gradually by successive diurnal meltwater flows.

Figure 7.20. *Lithofacies Association 4: massive (Gs) granular gravel with local cobble-sized, imbricated clasts. Palaeoflow from left to right. Trowel for scale is 25 cm long.*

Lithofacies Association 6

Description: Lithofacies Association 6 (Figure 7.16) is a chaotic assemblage of gravels, silts, sands and diamicton (Gm(s), Gh(s), Fh(s), Sh(s), Gm, Gh, Ghuf). The gravels are either horizontally bedded or massive, and poorly sorted, with a high fines content, occurring within channels up to 3 m wide which interfinger with silt and sand units. The finer-grained material is generally laminated. All of the sediments are locally slumped. Both the coarse and fine units are slumped into shallow depressions, 2-3 m wide. The finer sediments are also slumped locally into smaller (<1 m) depressions.

Interpretation: these sediments are similar to those found in the dead ice zone of the present margin of Skeiðarárjökull following the 1991 surge. Unit 5 and Lithofacies Association 6 may therefore represent ice-marginal supraglacial deposition. The finer-grained material is interpreted as proglacial fan and shallow pond sediments deposited in hollows formed by the melting of buried ice. The coarser-grained material is interpreted as representing small meltwater-outlet channels. The presence of slumping is indicative of deposition over buried ice. Normal faulting is commonly found associated with buried ice deposition but is extremely rare at this locality. Localised slumping suggests that deposition at this location occurred some way from the ice-margin and that the buried ice occurred as isolated blocks. The absence of compressive fold structures indicates that the features are not of a glaciotectonic origin.

7.3 SUMMARY AND CONCLUSIONS

7.3.1 Comparison of Greenland and Iceland Field Studies

The Greenland and Iceland case studies provide interpretation of sedimentary successions in a variety of depositional settings: deltaic topset, high gradient bedrock confined, valley confined, and unconfined sandar. In general, the Greenland examples reflect deposition within well-defined, confined and structurally controlled channels composed of highly resistant bedrock. Compared to the unconfined sandur in Iceland, patterns of deposition in the Greenland channel show much greater spatial variability of sediment size, sorting and depositional morphology. Complex channel morphologies create localised backwater effects and lakes act as sediment traps generating complex variations in both the amount of sediment in transport and local sediment transport capacities. By contrast, the Icelandic sedimentary succession reflects more uniform depositional conditions within a larger jökulhlaup channel. A much greater availability of sediment in the Iceland case study is reflected by the presence of non-Newtonian jökulhlaup deposits. The jökulhlaup sedimentary succession in Iceland is likely to represent a much longer history of both jökulhlaup and non-jökulhlaup deposition. The variety of lithofacies types present in the Súla River Section reflects changes in the glacier margin relative to the section as well as changes in sediment supply, flow regime and flood timing.

7.3.2 How to Distinguish Jökulhlaup from 'Normal' Braided Outwash

Proglacial outwash can take on many characteristics reflecting a complex interaction of flow regime, sediment supply characteristics and proglacial topography. Valley-confined braided sandar are commonly found in front of glacier snouts in many parts of the world. Although jökulhlaup sediments can vary considerably from 'normal' braided outwash, individual jökulhlaups can produce markedly different sedimentary successions. There is no single feature which can be used to distinguish flood from non-flood sediments. Rather, a suite of criteria have to be used and it is vital that as much as possible is known about the topographical setting and scale of the river system before an interpretation can be made.

The key criteria derived from this study are based on architecture, vertical sedimentary successions, sediment fabric and geomorphology.

1) Architecture
Non-flood sediments generally display a low lateral continuity relative to bar size. Cross cutting erosive contacts, and features such as small-scale channel scour and fill are common. Jökulhlaup-controlled sediments on the other hand tend to be laterally continuous within

individual flood channel or bar form. Waning stage flow around obstacles such as stranded ice-blocks can however severely modify the original flood deposit.

2) *Vertical Sedimentary Successions*
Jökulhlaup vertical successions reflect the flow conditions and the flood hydrograph. Maizels (1991, 1993a) suggested that upwards-coarsening gravels were deposited during the rising limb of the flood hydrograph, whilst cappings of fine-grained sediments were deposited on the waning stage. This study shows that although in some environments jökulhlaup deposits do indeed take this form, other distinctive sequences and successions can occur. Flood deposits can be either massive or upward-coarsening and there will be an absence of low flow sediments in the main unit. The vertical succession should be independent of scale but the units will be relatively thick. Non-flood sediments are typically repeated stacked, sequences of upwards-fining sediments although a much greater variety of grain sizes, bedforms and sedimentary structures can be expected. Again, non-flood successions should be scale independent but units will be relatively thin.

3) *Sediment Fabric*
In non-flood sediments, the flow regime will be almost entirely fluidal (turbulent), Newtonian flow. The resulting deposits will therefore almost always be clast-supported, with average to good sorting and imbrication. Flow directions will be unidirectional but with wide dispersion around the vector mean. Jökulhlaup deposits can display a variety of flow regimes. If flood flows are Newtonian, then the resultant sediments may be difficult to distinguish from non-flood sediments. Flow directions may have a lower dispersion around the vector mean. Hyperconcentrated or debris flow conditions are also common within floods. Although high sediment concentrations can occur in non-flood settings, they are rare, and in most circumstances, it can be assumed that sedimentary evidence of hyperconcentrated or debris flow is indicative of deposition during a jökulhlaup.

4) *Geomorphology*
A number of geomorphological features occur which are strongly indicative of jökulhlaup deposition and may be preserved for long periods of time after a flood. These include streamlined obstacle marks, densely kettled bar surfaces and extensive erosional wash limits. However, in many situations, flood deposits can be indistinguishable from ordinary braided river deposits, restricting the use of geomorphological criteria for distinguishing flood and non-flood sediments.

ACKNOWLEDGEMENTS

Research in Greenland was undertaken whilst AJR was in receipt of a NERC research studentship within the Department of Geography at the University of Aberdeen. Research in Iceland during summer 1996 was carried out as part of Keele University Iceland Expedition 1996 which received support from The Royal Geographical Society, The Gino Watkins Memorial Fund, and the Gilchrist Educational Trust. Dr. John F. Aitken, Prof. Maurice E. Tucker, Dr. Brian Turner and Dr. Alison P. Jones are thanked for constructive comments on previous versions of this manuscript. Andrew Lawrence, Peter Greatbach and David Wilde within the Department of Earth Sciences at Keele University are thanked for their cartographic skills.

REFERENCES

BAKER, V.R. 1973. Paleohydrology and sedimentology of lake Missoula flooding in Eastern Washington. *Geological Society of America Special Paper,* **144,** 79 pp.

BAKER, V.R. 1984. Flood sedimentation in bedrock fluvial systems. *IN*: Koster E.H. and Steel, R.J. (eds), *Sedimentology of gravels and conglomerates. Canadian Society of Petroleum Geologists Memoirs,* **10,** 87-98.

BAKER, V.R. and COSTA, J.E. 1987. Flood power. *IN*: Mayer, L. and Nash, D. (eds), *Catastrophic Flooding,* 1-25. Allen and Unwin.

BAKER, V.R. and KOCHEL, R.C. 1988a. Paleoflood analysis using slackwater deposits. *IN*: Baker, V.R. Kochel, R.C. and Patton P.C. (eds), *Flood Geomorphology,* 357-376. John Wiley and Sons Ltd.

BAKER, V.R. and KOCHEL, R.C. 1988b. Flood sedimentation in bedrock fluvial systems. *IN*: Baker, V.R., Kochel, R.C., and Patton, P.C. (eds), *Flood Geomorphology,* 123-137. John Wiley and Sons Ltd.

BAKER, V.R., KOCHEL., R.C., PATTON, P.C., and PICKUP, G. 1983. Palaeohydrological analysis of Holocene flood slackwater sediments. *IN*: Collinson, J.D. and Lewin, J. (eds), *Modern and Ancient Fluvial Environments, Special Publication of the International Association of Sedimentologists,* **6.,** 229-239.

BAKER, V.R., BENITO, G. and RUDOY, A.N. 1993. Paleohydrology of Late Pleistocene superflooding, Altay Mountains, Siberia. *Science,* **259,** 348-350.

BJÖRNSSON, H. 1976. Marginal and supraglacial lakes in Iceland. *Jökull,* **26,** 40-50.

BJÖRNSSON, H. 1992. Jökulhlaups in Iceland: prediction, characteristics and simulation. *Annals of Glaciology,* **16,** 95-106.

BJÖRNSSON, H. 1997. Grimvatnahlaup Fyrr og Nu. *IN*: Haraldsson, H. (ed), *Vatnajökull: Gos og hlaup.* Vegageroin, 61-77.

BLUCK, B.J. 1974. Structure and directional properties of some valley sandur deposits in southern Iceland. *Sedimentology,* **21,** 533-554.

BOOTHROYD, J. C. and NUMMEDAL, D. 1978. Proglacial braided outwash: a model for humid alluvial-fan deposits. *IN*: Miall, A. (ed), *Fluvial Sedimentology, Canadian Society of Petroleum Geologists Memoir,* **5,** 641-668.

BRAYSHAW, A.C. 1985. Bed microtopography and entrainment thresholds in gravel bed rivers. *Bulletin of the Geological Society of America,* **96,** 218-223.

BRENNAND, T.A. 1994. Macroforms, large bedforms and rhythmic sedimentary sequences in subglacial eskers, south-central Ontario: implications for esker genesis and meltwater regime. *Sedimentary Geology,* **91,** 9-55.

CARLING, P.A. 1989. Hydrodynamic models of boulder berm deposition. *Geomorphology,* **2,** 319-340.

CARLING, P.A. 1996. Morphology, sedimentology and palaeohydraulic sugnificance of large gravel dunes, Altai Mountains, Siberia. *Sedimentology,* **43,** 647-664.

COLLINSON, J.D. 1970. Bedforms of the Tana River, Norway. *Geografiska Annaler,* **52A,** 31-56.

COSTA, J.E. 1984. Physical geomorphology of debris flows. *IN*: Costa, J.E. and Fleisher, P. J. (eds), *Developments and Applications of Geomorphology,* 268-317. Springer-Verlag.

COSTA, J.E. 1988. Rheologic, geomorphic, and sedimentologic differentiation of water floods, hyperconcentrated flows, and debris flows. *IN*: Baker, V.R., Kochel K.C., and Patton, P.C. (eds), *Flood Geomorphology,* 113-122. John Wiley and Sons Ltd.

CHURCH, M. 1972. Baffin Island sandurs: a study of arctic fluvial processes. *Geological Society of Canada Bulletin,* **216,** 208 pp.

CHURCH, M. and GILBERT, R. 1975. Proglacial Fluvial and Lacustrine Environments. *IN*: Jopling, A.V. and McDonald, B.C. (eds), *Glaciofluvial and Glaciolacustrine Sedimentation, Society Economic Paleontologists and Mineralogists Special Publication,* **23,** 22-101.

DAWSON, M. 1989. Flood deposits within the Severn main Terrace. *IN*: Bevan, K. and Carling, P. (eds), *Floods, hydrological sedimentological and geomorphological implications: an overview,* 253-265. John Wiley and Sons Ltd.

DESLOGES, J.R., JONES, D.P. and RICKER, K.E. 1989. Estimates of peak discharge from the drainage of ice-dammed Ape Lake, British Columbia, Canada. *Journal of Glaciology,* **121,** 349-354.

ELFSTRÖM, A. 1983. The Baldakatj boulder delta, Lapland, Northern Sweden. *Geografiska Annaler,* **65A,** 201-225.

ELFSTRÖM, A. 1987. Large boulder deposits and catastrophic floods. *Geografiska Annaler,* **69A,** 101-121.

EVANS, S.G. and CLAGUE, J.J. 1994. Recent climatic change and catastrophic geomorphic processes in mountain environments. *Geomorphology,* **10,** 107-128.

EYNON, G. and WALKER, R.G. 1974. Facies relationships in Pleistocene outwash gravels, southern Ontario: a model for bar growth evolution in braided rivers. *Sedimentology,* **21,** 43-70.

FAHNESTOCK, R.K. and BRADLEY, W.C. 1973 Knik and Matanuska rivers, Alaska: a contrast in braiding. *IN*: Morisawa, M. (ed), *Fluvial Geomorphology, Binghampton International Symposia Series,* **4,** 220-250.

GORDON, J.E. 1986. Correspondence concerning glacial lake drainage near Søndre Strømfjord, West Greenland. *Journal of Glaciology,* **111,** 304.

GUSTAVSON, T.C. 1974. Sedimentation on gravel outwash fans Malaspina glacial foreland, Alaska. *Journal of Sedimentary Petrology,* **44,** 374-389.

GREGORY, K.J. and MAIZELS, J.K. 1991. Morphology and sediments: typological characteristics of fluvial forms and deposits. *IN*: Starkel, L., Gregory, K.J., and Thornes, J.B. (eds), *Temperate Palaeohydrology,* 31-57. John Wiley and Sons Ltd.

HARMS, J.C., SOUTHARD, J.B., SPEARING, D.R. and WALKER, R.G. 1975. Depositional environments as interpreted from primary sedimentary structures and stratification sequences. *SEPM Short Course,* **2,** 161 pp.

HEIN, F.J. and WALKER, R.G. 1977. Bar evolution and development of stratification in the gravelly, braided, Kicking Horse River, British Columbia. *Canadian Journal of Earth Sciences,* **14,** 562-570.

JONES, D.P., RICKER, N.E., DESLOGES, J.R. and MAXWELL, M. 1985. Glacier outburst flood on the Noeck River: the drainage of Ape Lake, British Columbia, October 20 1984. *Geological Survey of Canada, Open File Report,* **1139,** 92 pp.

JONSSON, J.1982. Notes on the Katla volcanoglacial debris flows, *Jökull,* **32,** 61-68.

KLIMEK, K. 1973. Geomorphological and glaciological analysis of the proglacial area of the Skeiðarárjökull: extreme eastern and western sections. *Geographica Polonica,* **26,** 89-113.

KRAINER, K. and POSCHER, G. 1992. Ice-rich, redeposited diamicton blocks and associated structures in Quaternary outwash sediments of the Inn valley near Innsbruck, Austria. *Geografiska Annaler,* **72A,** 249-254.

MAIZELS, J.K. 1989a. Sedimentology, paleoflow dynamics and flood history of jökulhlaup deposits: paleohydrology of Holocene sediment sequences in southern Iceland sandur deposits. *Journal of Sedimentary Petrology,* **59,** 204-223.

MAIZELS, J.K. 1989b. Sedimentology and palaeohydrology of Holocene flood deposits in front of a jökulhlaup glacier, South Iceland. *IN:* Bevan, K. and Carling, P. (eds), *Floods, hydrological, sedimentological and geomorphological implications: an overview,* 239-253. John Wiley and Sons Ltd.

MAIZELS, J.K. 1991. Origin and evolution of Holocene sandurs in areas of jökulhlaup drainage, south Iceland. *IN:* Maizels, J.K. and Caseldine, C. (eds), *Environmental change in Iceland: past and present,* 267-300. Kluwer.

MAIZELS, J.K. 1993a. Lithofacies variations within sandur deposits: the role of runoff regime, flow dynamics and sediment supply characteristics. *Sedimentary Geology,* **85,** 299-325.

MAIZELS, J.K. 1993b. Quantitative regime modelling of fluvial depositional sequence: application to Holocene stratigraphy of humid-glacial braid-plains (Icelandic sandurs). *IN:* North, C.P. and Prosser, D.J. (eds), *Characterisation of fluvial and aeolian reservoirs, Geological Society Special Publication,* **73,** 53-78.

MAIZELS, J.K. 1995. Sediments and landforms of modern proglacial terrestrial environments. *IN:* Menzies, J. (ed), *Modern glacial environments: processes, dynamics and sediments* (ed.), Butterworth-Heinemann, Oxford, 365-416.

MAIZELS, J.K. and RUSSELL, A.J. 1992. Quaternary perspectives on jökulhlaup prediction. *IN:* Gray, J.M. (ed), *Applications of Quaternary Research, Quaternary Proceedings,* **2,** 133-153.

MATTHEWS, W.H. and CLAGUE, J.J. 1993. The record of jökulhlaups from Summit Lake, northwestern British Columbia. *Canadian Journal of Earth Sciences,* **30,** 499-508.

MIALL, A. D. 1978. Lithofacies types and vertical profile models in braided river deposits: a summary. *IN:* Miall, A.D. (ed), *Fluvial Sedimentology, Canadian Society of Petroleum Geologists, Memoir,* **5,** 597-604.

MIALL, A.D.1985. Architectural element analysis: a new method of facies analysis applied to fluvial deposits, *Earth Science Reviews,* **22,** 261-308.

O'CONNOR, J. 1993. Hydrology, hydraulics, and geomorphology of the Bonneville Flood. *Geological Society of America, Special Paper,* **274,** Geol. Soc. of Am., Inc., Boulder

RUDOY, A.N. and BAKER, V.R. 1993. Sedimentary effects of cataclysmic late Pleistocene glacial outburst flooding, Altay Mountains, Siberia. *Sedimentary Geology*, **85,** 53-62.

RUSSELL, A.J. 1989. A comparison of two recent jökulhlaups from an ice-dammed lake, Søndre Strømfjord, West Greenland. *Journal of Glaciology,* **120,** 157-162.

RUSSELL, A.J. 1993. Obstacle marks produced by flows around stranded ice blocks during a jökulhlaup in West Greenland. *Sedimentology*, **40,** 1091-1113.

RUSSELL, A.J. 1994. Subglacial jökulhlaup deposition, Jotunheimen, Norway. *Sedimentary Geology,* **91,**131-144.

RUSSELL, A.J. and DE JONG, C. 1989. Lake drainage mechanisms for the ice-dammed Oberer Russellsee, Søndre Strømfjord, West Greenland. *Zeitschrift für Gletscherkunde und Glazialgeologie,* **24,** 143-147.

RUSSELL, A.J. Submitted. The morphology and sedimentology of a jökulhlaup delta, Kangerlussuaq, west Greenland. *Sedimentology.*

RUST, B.R. 1972. Structure and process in a braided river. *Sedimentology*, **18,** 221-245.

RUST, B.R. 1978. Depositional models for braided alluvium. *IN*: Miall, A.D. (ed), *Fluvial Sedimentology, Canadian Society of Petroleum Geologists, Memoir,* **5,** Calgary, Alberta, Canada. 605-625.

SCHOLZ, H. SCHREINER, B. and FUNK, H. 1988. Der einfluss von Gletscherlaufen auf die schmelzwasserablagerungen des Russell-Gletschers bei Søndre Strømfjord (WestGrönland). *Zeitschrift für Gletscherkunde Und Glazialgeologie,* **24,** 55-74.

SHAKESBY, R.A. 1985. Geomorphological effects of jökulhlaups and ice-dammed lakes, Jotunheimen, Norway. *Norsk Geografisk Tidskrift,* **39,** 1-16.

STURM, M. and BENSON, C.S. 1985. A history of jökulhlaups from Strandline Lake: Alaska. *Journal of Glaciology,* **31,** 272-280.

SUGDEN, D.E. CLAPPERTON, C.M. and KNIGHT, P.G. 1985. A jökulhlaup near Søndre Strømfjord, West Greenland , and some effects on the Ice sheet margin. *Journal of Glaciology,* **31,** 366-368.

THORARINSSON, S. 1939. The ice dammed lakes of Iceland with particular reference to their values as indicators of glacier oscillations. *Geografiska Annaler,* **21,** 216-242.

TÖMASSON, H. 1974. Grìmsvatnhlaup 1972, mechanism and sediment discharge. *Jökull,* **24,** 27-38.

WILLIAMS, P.F. and RUST, B.R. 1969. The sedimentology of a braided river. *Journal of Sedimentary Petrology,* **39,** 649-679.

Chapter 8

GLACIAL SEDIMENTOLOGY: A CASE STUDY FROM HAPPISBURGH, NORFOLK

Jane K. Hart

8.1 INTRODUCTION

The glacial environment is one of the most dynamic on Earth. In some ways it is similar to a volcanic environment in that both solid and liquid (and sometimes gaseous) phases of material exist side by side, and can rapidly change state. At the same time debris is being incorporated into the system and the glacier is continually advancing and retreating. Because of the dynamism of the glacial environment, glacial sediments are rarely deposited in a "layer - cake" manner, which makes stratigraphic interpretation difficult. Glacial sediments are more likely to be deposited in a series of interlocking lenses or discontinuous layers, which relate to different processes. Debris that passes through the glacial system can have a very complex transport history which means that on final deposition, individual debris elements may contain different data superimposed upon one another. Ideas about processes within the glacial environment have also changed in recent years which has meant that many sediments have been reinterpreted. The result of this is that in some areas of glacial sedimentology there is no definite agreement about distinguishing sedimentary criterion. Nevertheless, this chapter represents an attempt to outline a general synthesis, however, the reader is encouraged to refer to the texts quoted throughout the chapter for more specific details, as well as the recent text books on glacial geomorphology (e.g. Hambrey, 1994, Bennett and Glasser, 1996, Hart and Martinez, 1997, Benn and Evans, 1997).

One of the most common types of sediment within a glacial environment is called a *diamicton* (see Figure 2.6 and Sections 2.2.1 and 3.3.1.1). Glacial *tills* are a type of diamicton that have been deposited directly by the glacier. Other types of diamicton include those deposited by sediment gravity flows, gelifluction and glacio-aquatic processes.

Moraines are glacial landforms composed of glacial till and fluvioglacial sediment. *Debris* is the term used to describe sediment within and on top of the glacier before it is deposited. The only exception to this is a medial moraine, which is the name given to debris formed on the surface of a glacier where two lateral moraines form. This name is kept for traditional reasons.

8.2 GLACIAL PROCESSES

8.2.1 Movement and Thermal Regime

Glaciers move by three processes:

1) *internal deformation* (or *creep*) - due to the fact that ice is a semi-viscous fluid that flows under its own weight;

2) *basal sliding* - if the glacier is not frozen to its bed. This is facilitated if there is a film of water at the glacier base;

3) *subglacial deformation* - this includes movement in a saturated unconsolidated sediment layer underneath the glacier (deforming bed), and often in frozen debris at the glacier base (debris-rich basal ice) (Figure 8.1).

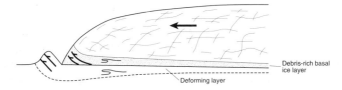

Figure 8.1. Schematic diagram to show proglacial (at the front of the glacier) and subglacial (beneath the glacier) deformation in both the deforming layer and the debris-rich basal ice layers.

Glaciers that are frozen to their beds are known as *cold-based glaciers* and can only move by internal deformation and movement in the debris-rich basal ice layer. As a result their movement is very slow and they are relatively inactive sedimentologically and geomorphologically. In contrast, glaciers that are not frozen to their beds (*warm-based or temperate glaciers*) can move by all three processes. These move much faster and have a far greater impact on the landscape.

Not all glaciers fit neatly into these two categories, most glaciers having more complex thermal regimes and being referred to as *polythermal* glaciers, e.g. many large ice sheets are mostly warm based with a frozen margin (cold toe).

8.2.2 Glacial Transport

These four processes are inherently linked together to produce the resultant complex sedimentology. Figure 8.2 shows the transport paths of sediment within ice.

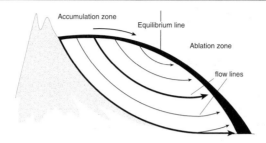

Figure 8.2. *Theoretical transport paths in a valley glacier.*

1) *Supraglacial and englacial transport paths* - debris will be eroded off the mountain peaks by non-glacial processes and fall on to the glacier surface. At the glacier margin englacial and subglacial material is brought up to the glacier surface.

2) *Subglacial transport paths* - debris will be brought into the subglacial environment by: i) basal erosion; ii) englacial sediment paths; iii) sediment falling into deep crevasses; iv) incorporation of the underlying sediment, and v) freezing-on of the underlying sediment by regelation, adfreezing and shearing. Once material is in the subglacial environment it can affect glacier motion (see above). Figure 8.3 shows the dynamic link between erosion, transport and depositional processes in the subglacial environment within the deforming layer and the subglacial deforming bed.

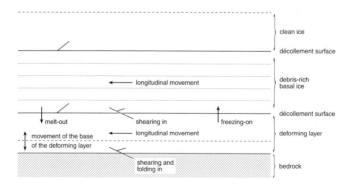

Figure 8.3. *Schematic diagram to show the theoretical interaction at the glacier base between the clean ice, debris-rich basal ice, deforming layer, and subglacial non-deforming strata (Hart, 1998).*

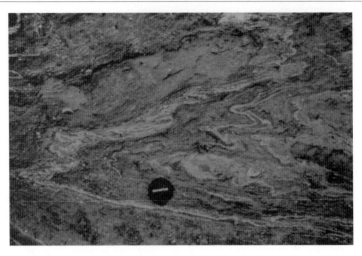

Figure 8.4. *Photograph of an example of subglacial deformation from West Runton in Norfolk, UK (for location see Figure 8.6).*

8.2.3 Different Till Types

These different processes will result in the formation of different types of till (see Table 8.1). Different types of till have been shown to have different eigenvalues (fabric strengths) shown in Figure 8.4. This has been examined in detail by Mark (1973), Dowdeswell and Sharp (1986), Hart (1994a) and Benn (1995).

1) *Supraglacial Till*
Debris on the surface of the glacier may collapse back onto the landscape once the ice beneath it melts. In the past this was called ablation till. This debris will rarely be deposited without alteration. As the ice melts, sediment gravity flows will occur to remobilize the debris (in the past this was known as flow till), and rivers will flow into hollows on the ice surface and lakes may form. So stratified sediments are commonly combined with supraglacial till.

Supraglacial till clasts may be angular as they have not been abraded by subglacial erosion, although some may be rounded from water action in supraglacial streams. Table 8.2 shows some examples of roundness (measured by RA) from different glacial environments (see Section 3.3.1.3).

Since supraglacial till is deposited by the melt-out of the ice, the fabric will mostly be chaotic. This means that it will have a low eigen value (fabric strength) and will not be oriented in the ice flow direction. Additionally there is a very high chance that this sediment

Till Type			Fabric	Shape	Other details
Supraglacial till			Weak fabric strength	Generally angular	Often contains discontinuous stratified units, very prone to debris flow re-mobilisation. A good example of a Quaternary supraglacial till is discussed in Benn (1992).
Subglacial till	*Lodgement till*		Strong fabric strength oriented in the ice flow direction	Generally rounded	Usually homogeneous and found either in rigid-bedded mountainous environments or areas where till has drained. Unequivocal description of lodgement tills in the literature are rare, however there is a very good paper describing the related process of ploughing by Clark and Hansel (1989). This process occurs when clasts held in the base of the ice are dragged through the till and come to rest because of a prow of till on the distal side. This process could be seen as intermediate between lodgement and deformation.
	Deforming bed till	Thick def. layer	Medium fabric strength	Generally rounded	May contain folds oriented in the direction of tectonic transport, in particular at the base of the sequence, may contain boudins and augens or may be homogeneous. Good examples of deforming bed till are described in Hart and Boulton (1991a), Hart (1995a) and Benn (1995).
		Thin def. layer	Strong fabric strength oriented in the ice flow direction	Generally rounded	Tills within flutes are a good example of a thin deforming layer, Hart (1995c), Eklund and Hart (1996), Benn (1994).
	Melt-out till		Fabric ranges from weak to strong	Generally rounded	Best location is in cavities, deformed melt-out a component of deforming bed till. The topic of melt-out is very controversial, a traditional view is provided in Haldorsen and Shaw (1982), whilst a more modern approach is discussed in Paul and Eyles (1990) and Hart (1995b).
Sediment gravity flow diamicton (flow till)			Fabric ranges from weak to strong	Any shape	All diamictons can be re-mobilised.

Table 8.1. Till types.

will be re-mobilised by debris flows. These will tend to flow down any available slope, and the strength of the fabric will depend on slope angle and water content. This process will probably orientate the particles down slope, but this will bear no relationship to ice flow direction.

A variant of this type of till is *sublimation till* (Shaw, 1977) formed when sublimation occurs in extreme polar regions.

2) *Subglacial Till*

Most tills in the glacial environment are formed by subglacial processes, in general subglacial till clasts may be more rounded than supraglacial till clasts as they may have been abraded by subglacial erosion and may also have been worn by subglacial melt-water (see Table 8.2). However, it must be remembered that the final shape of a clast will depend on the initial rock type (i.e. a soft/weaker rock is easier to erode than a hard rock), time within the glacier, and transport paths. Most clasts will have been in a number of glacial environments, e.g. initial weathering from a nunatak, via a rock fall to the glacier surface. From the glacier it may be carried by a supraglacial stream down a crevasse to the glacier base, frozen into the debris-rich basal ice and carried along, then melted out into the deforming layer, and finally deposited as till. In fact the number of possible routes are very high, and will be even greater if the glacier moves over till deposited during previous glaciations.

Sediment	RA at Matanuska, Alaska	RA at Slettmarkbreen, Norway
Supraglacial debris/till	36	86
Subglacial till	0	0

Table 8.2. *Examples of Roundness (RA = percentage of very angular and angular clasts) from Matanuska Glacier, Alaska (Hart, 1995b) and Slettmarkbreen, Norway (Benn and Ballantyne, 1993).*

There are three main types of subglacial till: a) lodgement till; b) deforming bed till; and c) melt-out till. All these tills can be altered by subsequent debris-flows, although this is much less likely to occur in the subglacial rather than the supraglacial environment. Each of these tills will now be discussed in turn.

a) *Lodgement Till*

This is formed by the frictional retardation of clasts, held in the base of the ice, against the bed. This type of till is formed when a glacier moves over a rigid bed; in either a hard rock environment (in the mountains), or associated with a well drained unconsolidated sediment. It can be seen from Figure 8.4 that lodgement tills tend to have a very strongly oriented fabric.

b) Deforming Bed Till

This is formed in association with an unconsolidated bed and a deforming bed glacier. Beneath this type of glacier subglacial deposition occurs through a combination of sedimentary and glaciotectonic processes (Hart and Boulton, 1991a, Hart, 1995a). This includes melt-out, sediment advection beneath the glacier, and changes in the thickness of the deforming layer.

If the amount of deformation is relatively low or the glacier moves over a visually distinctive lithology, then the resultant till will show visible evidence of deformation, e.g. West Runton, Norfolk (Hart and Boulton, 1991a, Hart and Roberts, 1994) (Figure 8.5). However, if the amount of deformation is high or the glacier passes over a homogeneous bedrock, then the resultant till will probably also be homogeneous. This is because the deformation process itself leads to the homogenisation of the deforming layer. Often the best place to observe visible evidence of deformation is at the base of the till where deformation is often low (when the glacier first advanced over the site), and closer to the bedrock (source of the lithologically distinct material) (Hart, 1995a).

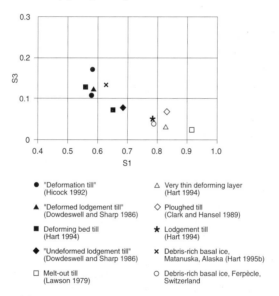

Figure 8.5. *Average fabric eigen values from different subglacial environments.*

Hart (1994a) and Benn (1995) have shown that deforming bed tills tend to have a range of fabric strength (see Section 3.3.1.5) dependant on the thickness of the deforming layer. Those tills deposited in association with a thick deforming layer tend to have a relatively weak fabric strength, whilst those associated with a thin deforming layer have a much stronger orientation (Figure 8.4). Good examples of the latter type are flutes (Benn, 1994, Eklund and Hart, 1996), which form by the deforming layer moving into low pressure areas found behind large clasts in the deforming layer.

c) Melt-Out Till

This is formed from the direct melting of the debris-rich basal ice layer (without subsequent deformation). Researchers have argued that this till will comprise stratification, high strength fabrics and specific grain size properties (Lawson, 1979, Haldorsen and Shaw, 1982). However, more recent studies suggest that the processes within the debris-rich basal ice layer and the deforming layer are very similar (Hart, 1995b) (including grain size and fabric - see Figure 8.4), and it may be unlikely that these sediments are released from the ice without re-orientation (Paul and Eyles, 1990) except into cavities associated with rigid bed environments. It is more likely, however, that in most cases melt-out is an important component of the formation of deforming bed till rather than a specific till type.

8.2.4 Deformation Structures

Folds are very common in glacial sediments and can provide further evidence about ice movement direction, the type of till, the nature of glacial deformation and glacial dynamics (e.g. Hart *et al.*,1990).

Deformation associated with active glaciers is known as glaciotectonic deformation (see Sections 2.2.2.5 and 3.3.2.5). Deformation at the glacier margin is known as proglacial glaciotectonic deformation, and deformation beneath the glacier is known as subglacial glaciotectonic deformation (Figure 8.1). Additionally, deformation associated with ice decay at the glacier margin is known as dead ice tectonics. This latter phenomenon is mostly associated with dead ice collapse features such as kettle holes, sediment gravity flows, and the injection of saturated subglacial sediments up through crevasses (known as crevasse infills or diapirs).

Proglacial deformation consists mostly of compressive styles of deformation, including open folds and reverse faults, resulting mostly from frontal pushing by the glacier. Proglacial deformation results in the formation of push moraines; these are commonly associated with both contemporary (e.g. *Spitsbergen:* Boulton, 1986, Etzelmüller *et al.*, 1996; *Iceland:* Croot, 1988; *Switzerland:* Eybergen, 1987) and Pleistocene glaciers (e.g. *UK:* Thomas, 1984, Hart, 1990; *Germany:* van der Wateren, 1987; Iceland: Ingólfsson, 1988, Hart, 1994b; New Zealand: Hart, 1996; Argentina: van der Meer *et al.*, 1992; *Canada:* Dredge and Grant, 1987). A full list of papers on glaciotectonics is available on the Internet at: http://www.soton.ac.uk/~jhart/wggt.htm.

Subglacial deformation is dominated by simple shear and longitudinal extension (Hart and Boulton, 1991a, Hart and Roberts, 1994). Characteristics of this type of environment are folds, tectonic laminations, augens and boudins (Figure 8.5). Modern examples of subglacial deformation have been described from: *Iceland:* Boulton, 1979; *Ice stream B*, Antarctica:

Alley *et al.*, 1986; and Pleistocene examples include: *UK*: Hart and Boulton, 1991a, Evans *et al.*, 1995, *Germany*: Hart *et al.*, 1996 and *North America*: Hicock and Dremanis, 1991, Alley, 1991.

8.3 CASE STUDY: THE EXAMINATION OF A QUATERNARY GLACIAL SITE, HAPPISBURGH, NORFOLK.

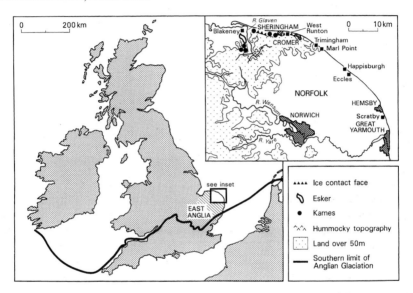

Figure 8.6. *Happisburgh site location map.*

8.3.1 Introduction

The cliff sections of the north-east Norfolk coast contain some of the most spectacular glacial geology and landforms in Britain. These were produced during the extensive Anglian glaciation (West, 1957, Perrin *et al.*, 1973, Hart and Peglar, 1990). The area south of the Walcott Gap at Ostend, Happisburgh and Eccles are the most southerly outcrops of the coastal exposures in north-east Norfolk and they lie to the south of the Cromer Ridge (Figure 8.6). South of this section from the North Gap at Eccles to Scratby, the cliffs are covered by sea defences and sand dunes and glacial sediments are not exposed.

There have been numerous studies of the Happisburgh area (e.g. Reid, 1882, Trimmer, 1895, Slater, 1927, Solomon, 1932, Banham and Ransom, 1965, Banham, 1968, 1977; Boulton *et al.*, 1984, Lunkka, 1988) mainly because of its contrast to the visually more deformed areas to the north (e.g. West Runton and Weybourne), where the highly deformed

"Contorted Drift" (Reid, 1882) (Laminated Diamicton - Hart and Boulton, 1991b) can be seen. Both Reid (1882) and Banham (1968, 1977) considered this site to be an undeformed version of the "Contorted Drift", and thus the site at the village of Happisburgh has been designated the type site[1] of the north-east Norfolk coastal glacial deposits. These workers suggested that the glacial history of north-east Norfolk consisted of three separate glacial advances, which deposited three distinct Cromer tills separated by non-glacial sediments (Table 8.3); these tills were distinguished on the basis of lithology, and by the fact that during the final advance the area to the north was "contorted". However, there are a number of objections to this hypothesis:

1) a "layer cake" approach is inappropriate for the study of glacial sedimentary environments and their deposits. Within these environments spatially varying, erosional and depositional processes occur, strongly influenced by ice marginal fluctuations, and produce complex lithofacies patterns. The purely lithostratigraphic approach used in the past has tended to ignore the evidence of complex sedimentology, palaeomorphology and structural geology.

2) a more recent study of the "Contorted Drift" indicated that it was not formed by the passive mixing of existing tills and outwash, but that it was formed by active subglacial deformation, which simultaneously deposited and deformed the till (Hart, *et al.*, 1990). By definition the tills would be expected to vary in lithology over the area, and thus additional evidence to that of lithology is needed to interpret the glacial history.

| GIMINGHAM SANDS |
| THIRD TILL |
| MUNDESLEY SANDS |
| SECOND TILL |
| INTERMEDIATE BEDS |
| FIRST TILL |

Table 8.3. *The Cromer Till Sequence (after Banham, 1968).*

Previous studies concentrated exclusively on the Happisburgh Section whereas this case study also investigated the stretch of cliff south of Eccles. In this Chapter specific localities are referred to by their position on the horizontal scale shown in Figure 8.7, although there are three main areas; the Happisburgh part of the sequence (0-1990 m), the large scale faulted zone (1990-2260 m) and the Eccles part of the sequence (2260-3600 m).

---

[1] The definition and name of stratigraphic units are established at a *type section* (or locality) that once specified, must not be changed (NACSN, 1983).The type section reflects the depositional history of an area. Since the glacial environment is so dynamic, they have limited use in glacial stratigraphy.

8.3.2 Stratigraphy and Sedimentology

A schematic stratigraphy of the section is shown in Figure 8.8 and a composite facies log of these units is shown in Figure 8.9. There are three major groups of glaciogenic sediment in the cliff sections: the Happisburgh Diamicton Unit, which consists of the Happisburgh Diamicton and the Ostend Sands, the Happisburgh Unit, and the Walcott Diamicton Unit, which consists of the Walcott Diamicton and the Upper Sands. There is also a unit of head at the top of the cliff.

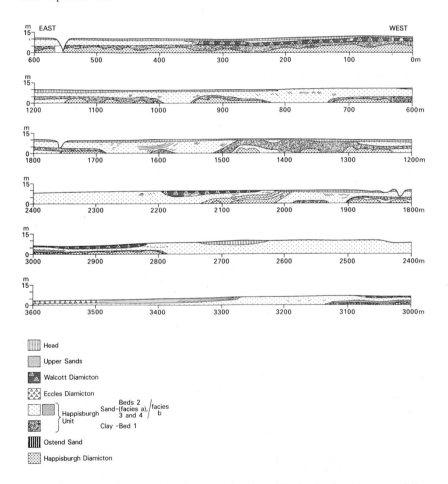

Figure 8.7. *Section diagram from the Happisburgh and Eccles Section (the gap at 560 m along the section is the Happisburgh Gap).*

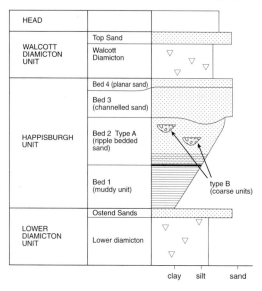

Figure 8.8. *Simplified stratigraphy at Happisburgh taken from the Happisburgh Gap area (560 m along the section shown in Figure 8.9).*

8.3.2.1 The Happisburgh Diamicton

Description: the lowest exposed deposit is a grey sandy clay diamicton which has brown weathering surfaces (Figure 8.9). It is largely homogeneous, up to 4 m thick, and contains ungraded sandy laminae which are frequently isoclinally folded. Additionally there are small deformed sand pods (*ca.* 10 cm wide). This diamicton contains erratic materials, including igneous and metamorphic pebbles, derived mostly from north-east Britain and the Midlands, although there are pebbles from Scotland and Scandinavia. Reid (1882) and Banham (1968) named this deposit the "First Till".

There is no direct folding evidence from within the Diamicton from which ice movement direction can be inferred. However, fabric analysis shows the clasts' orientation to be mainly NW/SE (Figure 8.9) although this is not statistically significant. The eigen value results indicate a very weakly oriented fabric with $S1 = 0.544$, $S3 = 0.146$.

Interpretation: the ungraded laminations and folded sand pods within a mainly homogenous diamicton, are typical diagnostic features of a subglacial deforming bed till (Hart, *et al.,* 1990, Hart and Boulton, 1991a, b). Similarly, the eigen value results are typical of deforming bed till with a relatively thick deforming layer (Hart, 1994a) (Figure 8.4). Other workers have interpreted these tills as waterlain (Eyles *et al.,* 1989) interpreting the laminae as sedimentary and not tectonic. Lunkka (1988) suggested the till is the product of both (firstly)

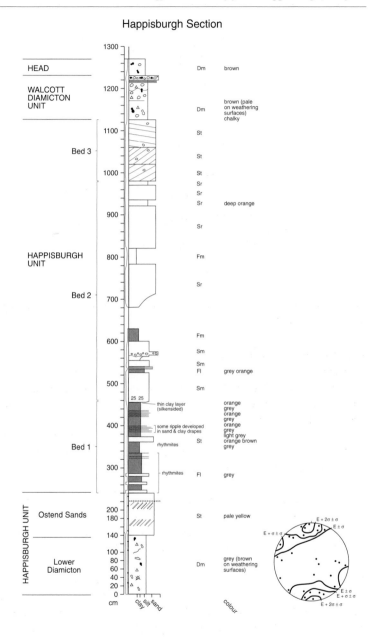

Figure 8.9. *Facies log from Happisburgh, taken at 550 m along the section (see Figure 8.7).*

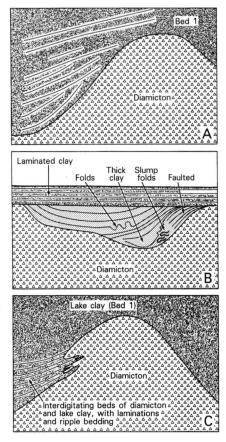

Figure 8.10. *Some schematic examples of the Happisburgh Diamicton/Happisburgh Unit (Bed 1) interface: a) Site 5, 460 m along the section; b) Site 13, 1870 m along the section; c) Site 2, 545 m along the section (see Figure 8.7 for section diagram).*

subaqueous and (then) subglacial processes, but failed to explain how evidence from the former environment could have survived the high strains involved during subglacial deformation.

The upper surface of the Happisburgh Diamicton

The surface of the Happisburgh Diamicton has been deformed into a series of folds (see Figure 8.7). The relationships between Bed 1 of the Happisburgh Unit and the Happisburgh Diamicton are as follows:

1) the muddy beds (Bed 1) of the Happisburgh Diamicton, which must have been deposited in a lake or pond, on-lap the sides of the diamicton antiforms (e.g. Figure 8.10a - Site 5, 460 m).

2) also at the side of the diamicton anticlines there are interlaminated beds of diamicton, clay and silts associated with slump folds, which reflect material slumping off the sides of the diamicton anticlines into the small lakes (e.g. Figure 8.10b - Site 2 (545 m). Additionally evidence of subsequent diapiric disturbance (Banham, 1977) has been recorded, which has in places altered the shape of the antiforms.

3) from the limited three dimensional outcrops of the moraines, they appear to be ridges. The strike of the ridges was measured where possible and found to have an average strike of 212°. Lunkka (1988) has suggested that these features are flutes, resulting from an ice flow towards the south-west.

8.3.2.2 Ostend Sand

Description: this a fine pale yellow to white sand which outcrops in small lenses above the Happisburgh Diamicton. At 160 m the Ostend Sand contains clasts of diamicton, erratics and broken shells. The bedding is planar at the base, with megaripple bedding higher in the section. The lower boundary between the diamicton and the sand is indistinct whereas the upper boundary is an erosional one.

Interpretation: the evidence of diamicton balls, erratics, broken shells, and a stratigraphic position immediately above the till, all suggest that this is a fluvial sediment deposited by streams flowing over a freshly exposed proglacial landscape and is most likely to be part of an outwash sequence.

8.3.2.3 Happisburgh Unit

Description: above the Lower Diamicton (and, where it is present, the Ostend Sand) there is a coarsening-upwards sequence which has been called the Happisburgh Unit in this study. It consists of four principal beds (labelled 1-4) (Figures 8.7 and 8.8). **Bed 1** (muddy bed) (maximum thickness 10 m) is equivalent to the "Intermediate Beds" of Reid (1882); named as such because they occur between two tills. North of 340 m the muddy beds are seen to lie between two diamicton units of glaciogenic origin. However, to the south of this, the uppermost diamicton is absent and where it does outcrop (2820 m - 3090 m), **Beds 2** (small-scale rippled bed - maximum thickness 5 m), **3** (channelled sands - maximum thickness 12 m) and **4** (planar bedded sands - maximum thickness 1 m) separate it and **Bed 1** of the Happisburgh Unit.

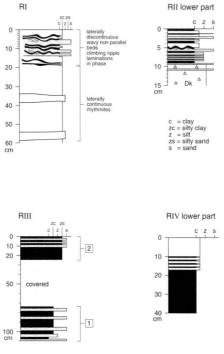

Figure 8.11. *Some examples of the rhythmitic sediments at the base of the Happisburgh Unit (Bed 1): a) Site 1 (RI), 550 m along the section; b) Site 11 (RII), 1050 m along the section; c) Site 10 (RIII), 895 m along the section; d) Site 13 (RIV), 1870 m along the section (see Figure 8.7 for section diagram).*

Bed 1 of the Happisburgh Unit consists of a coarsening upwards sequence of beds of clay, silt and fine sand. It is mostly horizontally bedded with some small-scale ripple lamination. There are some rhythmite beds of silt and clay, which become less continuous laterally, higher in the sequence. Examples of these rhythmitic beds are shown in Figure 8.11 (A: Site 1, 550 m; B: Site 11, 1050 m; C: Site 10, 895 m), which consist of a lower unit of silt (with an abrupt lower boundary) which grades up into a unit of darker silty clay. These couplets extend laterally for many metres.

Above the muddy bed (Bed 1) there are more sand rich beds. Figure 8.9 shows a detailed facies log of the sandy beds at Site 1 (550 m) and Figure 8.12 shows the sandy facies at a number of sites. At the base of the sandy beds at most of the sites there are fine laminations of clay and silt with de-watering structures. In places the boundary between the sandy and muddy parts of the Happisburgh Unit is erosive.

The main part of Bed 2 consists of fine or silty sand with small-scale ripple bedding. In places chalk flakes have collected along the bedding. Within the sand there are small beds of massive or laminated clay. Higher in the sequence there are climbing ripple beds of silty sand. These beds are silty in the east and become coarser in the west.

Bed 3 is slightly coarser and contains broken shells and occasional pebbles, some of which are erratics. There are large-scale cross-bedding, and horizontally bedded laminae. The cross-bedded sands consist of both tabular and planar cross-stratification, and have foreset beds up to 40 cm in height. Bed 3 outcrops in part, in the form of channels. Above this, Bed 4 comprises alternating planar-bedded orange fine sand and silty sand.

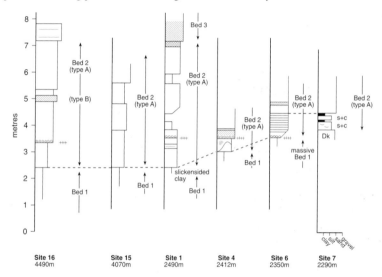

Figure 8.12. Some examples of the sandy facies of the Happisburgh Diamicton (for site locations along the section, see Figure 8.7).

Interpretation: Beds 1 to 3 of the Happisburgh Unit represent a coarsening-upwards sequence, with a transition from lake sediments to fluvial sediments. Within the lake sediments there is a vertical change from a basal distal facies (Smith, 1978) to an upper more proximal facies. This may reflect the progradation of a delta front towards the area. This pattern of sedimentation is very similar to glaciolacustrine delta sedimentation as described by Leckie and McCann (1982) and Jopling and Walker (1968). Thus, it is suggested that the Happisburgh Unit represents a prograding glaciolacustrine delta sequence. This was also suggested by Lunkka (1987). The lower beds relate to a series of small lakes (formed between the moraines) which coalesced into a larger glacial lake. These beds show evidence of a delta front (and probably a glacier front also) approaching. Higher in the sequence there is the delta front itself, which includes evidence of channels. Above this there are the channelled fluvial sediments. There is a general coarsening of sediment to the west and north, which suggests that the delta and the ice front prograded from the north towards the south.

8.3.2.4 Bush Estate Sands

Description: this is a large body of sand found in the south of the section, (large scale faulted zone and Eccles area, south of 1990 m) where the stratigraphy changes (see Figure 8.7) and much of the Happisburgh Unit has been eroded away and filled with a sand and gravel unit. Most of the unit is composed of fine sand although there are lenses of coarse gravel. There are also a number of large scale reverse fault structures in this unit that dip at 75° towards 196° (SSW).

Interpretation: because of the association of this sand with other glaciogenic deposits it is suggested that this is an outwash sand and that the faulting is due to glaciotectonic thrusting or the melting out of buried ice masses in the outwash zone (discussed in more detail in Section 8.3.3.2).

8.3.2.5 Eccles Diamicton

Description: the most southerly part of the section contains another lithological unit. This is a very coarse, clast-supported diamicton, with chaotic gravel in a clayey and sandy matrix. This grades westwards into a more stratified unit of cross-bedded sand and gravel. The western part of this unit has bedding structures similar to a mid-outwash fan and the sediments of the eastern part resemble a typical proximal till/outwash deposit.

Interpretation: it is suggested that this diamicton was laid near the snout of a glacier that advanced from the south-east (which is discussed in more detail in Section 8.3.3.2 below).

8.3.2.6 The Walcott Diamicton

Description: this is a brown, sandy diamicton, rich in chalk, although in places decalcification of this unit can be seen (e.g. at 270 m). Reid (1882) and Banham (1968) called this deposit the"Second Till". This contains similar erratics to those from the Happisburgh Diamicton except that the Walcott Diamicton is more chalk rich. It is mostly homogeneous, except at its base where there are ungraded laminations of sand and chalk.

Within the Walcott Diamicton no folds are observed from which it is possible to produce an estimate of ice movement direction. However, a fold consisting of the Walcott Diamicton and the Happisburgh Unit indicates ice movement from the north. Lunkka (1988) was able to find folds indicating an ice direction movement from the north-west. Additionally Banham (1970) produced fabric data to suggest that the ice direction was from the north-east.

Interpretation: this diamicton has a similar structure and texture to the other glaciogenic beds in the area. By analogy with these, it is suggested that the Walcott Diamicton is also a subglacially deformed till.

Banham (1970) correlated this till with other chalk-rich tills further north which contain folds. He proposed that this second till was deposited by an ice sheet flowing from the north-west. If the correlation is based on sedimentology and structural geology (discussed in detail in Hart and Boulton, 1991b), this till correlates with tills to the north which also contain folds indicating an ice direction from the north-west.

At 340 m Beds 2, 3, and 4 of the Happisburgh Unit are folded together with the Walcott Diamicton. Banham (1968) interpreted the sequence as one in which channels comprising Beds 2 - 4 formed, cutting into (i.e. above) the Walcott Diamicton, and that they were therefore younger. In fact the relationship at 340 m is more complex. The apparent superimposition of Beds 2 - 4 and the diamicton is the result of glaciotectonic activity. In the east of the section at 2860 m the undeformed sequence is seen and here the Walcott Diamicton is seen to overlie Beds 2 - 4. It is concluded that the upper sands of the Happisburgh Unit (Beds 2 - 4) are older than the Walcott Diamicton.

The fold at 340 m occurs at the western limit of the Happisburgh Unit sand above the upper surface of Bed 1. This may have acted as a décollement layer. At Site 1 (550 m) (shown in Figure 8.7) there is a slickensided layer of clay between Beds 1 and 2, indicating that there has been movement along this interface. This fold is typical of a subglacial fold and is further indication that the ice that deposited the Walcott Diamicton came from the north.

8.3.2.7 Upper Sand

Above the Walcott Diamicton there is a poorly exposed medium to fine-grained sand. This sand has been deformed and contains pods of diamicton. Any original bedding has been destroyed. It is therefore impossible to suggest its depositional environment or to estimate its original stratigraphic thickness, but its present vertical thickness ranges from 50 cm to 5 m.

8.3.2.8 Head

At the top of the cliff for much of the section there is a loamy diamicton, approximately 1 m thick. It is a highly weathered bed which contains local clasts of various sizes and composition, including flint and chalk. The base is marked by a layer of pebbles. The bed has a high silt content. It lies above a basal unconformity and is parallel to the present day landscape. The high silt content is suggestive of a loessic element, which may be mixed with a slope deposit.

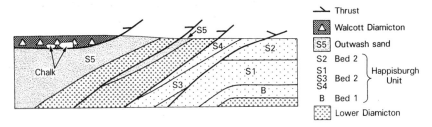

Figure 8.13. Schematic diagram to show the proglacial glaciotectonic thrust blocks (1980-2180 m along the section, see Figure 8.7).

8.3.3 Glacial History of the Site

8.3.3.1 The First Ice Advance from the North
The first ice advance with which the Happisburgh Diamicton is associated was from a generally northern direction, probably from the north-east.

8.3.3.2 The Ice Advance from the South
The sequence changes laterally in a southerly direction and between 1990 m and 2260 m there are number of faulted blocks separated by curved thrust planes that dip to the south (Figure 8.13). The section consists of three thrust block each composed of a basal sandy laminated diamicton and an upper coarse-sand and gravel. The angle of dip of each block is 20 - 25°. The lowermost block consists of sand (Happisburgh Unit -Bed 2), whereas the upper two blocks consist of a lower diamicton layer (Happisburgh Diamicton) and an upper medium to coarse-grained sand layer (Bush Estate Sands). The Happisburgh Diamicton within the thrust blocks is very highly deformed, with tectonic lamination and deformed sand pods. A fabric taken in this till indicates a tectonic movement direction of 195° with medium strength eigenvalues (S1 = 0.634; S3 = 0.116) (see Figure 3.8). The sands at the base of this diamicton are also highly deformed. The movement along the thrust blocks indicates a tectonic movement from the south.

The Walcott Diamicton at the top of the cliff contains a mass of disaggregated chalk, which is similar to the deformed chalk masses seen at West Runton. This diamicton contains laminae of chalk that string out towards the south, which is the opposite direction of movement from the thrust blocks below.

The most obvious explanation for such fault blocks is that they were produced by proglacial deformation (as discussed above in Section 8.2.4). Similar structures have been described at the nearby site at Trimingham (Hart, 1990), however those at Happisburgh are more brittle, probably due to the greater percentage of sandy sediments.

One immediately obvious feature of Zone B is that the fault blocks are dipping in the opposite direction to that expected if associated with an ice advance from the north. Although back thrusts have been seen in the Bride push moraine on the Isle of Man (Thomas, 1984), it is more likely that these faults were formed in front of a glacier moving from a southern direction.

To find the longitudinal strain associated with proglacial deformation, the equation from Section 3.3.2.5 is used. In order to do this, the original position of the beds must be known, and so a balanced cross-section needs to be constructed (Dahlstrom, 1969). There are problems with this as the beds beneath the faults have been highly deformed by the blocks moving over them. From a reconstruction of the balanced cross-section a shortening of 32% was calculated. This was similar to that calculated from the proglacial deformation at Trimingham - 32% (Hart, 1990).

The Bush Estate Sands are found in a large basin to the south of the thrust blocks. It is likely that the movement of large blocks of diamicton and sand must have left behind a hollow from which the sediments were removed, which were then subsequently infilled with outwash sands. This sediment unit grades southwards into the Eccles Diamicton. Thus this sediment/tectonic association is further evidence for an ice advance from the south.

8.3.3.3 The Readvance from the North

There is evidence for a second ice advance from the north in the presence of an upper chalky diamicton, the Walcott Diamicton. This ice advance did not deform most of the sediments below. It only caused erosion and deformation of the sandy beds of the Happisburgh Unit. Between the muddy and sandy beds of the Unit there is a slickensided layer which may have acted as a zone of décollement, and so prevented the deformation of underlying layers.

This diamicton is also present in the east of the section, extending eastwards until 3090 m indicating that the ice sheet associated with this diamicton advanced southwards of Eccles (as did the first northern advance). This advance occurred after the southern advance because the Walcott Diamicton is not associated with the deformation of the southern advance sediments. However, it should be noted that there is no site that contains both the Walcott Diamicton (second northern advance deposit) and the Eccles Diamicton (southern advance deposit).

8.3.4 Discussion

Both the structural and sedimentological evidence suggests that there were at least three ice advances in this area, an advance from the north, an advance from the south and a further advance from the north; the possible 'third till' of Reid and Banham was not observed. It has already been discussed that the sediments of the Happisburgh and Walcott Diamictons are related to similar diamictons throughout north-east Norfolk and it has been proposed that these form part of the North Sea Drift Formation shown in Table 8.4 (Hart and Boulton, 1991b).

	Happisburgh and Eccles	Mundesley	Trimingham	West Runton
Walcott Diamicton Member	Upper Sands Walcott Diamicton	Upper Sands Upper Diamicton	Outwash Sand D Upper Diamicton	Runton Sand & Gravel Laminated Diamicton
*Trimingham Member	Happisburgh Unit	Mundesley Sands	Trimingham Unit	Runton Sand & Gravel
*Eccles Diamicton Member	Bush Estate Sands/Eccles Diamicton			
Happisburgh Diamicton Member	Ostend Sands Happisburgh Diamicton	Lower Diamicton	Outwash Sand C Lower Diamicton Outwash Sand A	Laminated Diamicton

* = similar age = Trimingham sub-stage

Table 8.4. *The North Sea Drift Formation (after Hart and Boulton, 1991b).*

The first ice sheet advanced from the north and deposited the Happisburgh Diamicton. This ice sheet retreated north to Happisburgh and deposited an outwash sand (Ostend Sand) and small lakes between flutes (Happisburgh Unit). Eventually, the lake sediments built up to such an extent that the flutes became buried and one large lake was formed. The sedimentology of the lake reveals that the varves become more proximal with the glacier margin towards the north-west, and a delta prograded into the lake towards the south. At the same time there was an ice advance from the south, probably from the south-east. Fluvial outwash deposits were laid down on top of the deltaic deposits. Palaeocurrent analysis of fluvial outwash indicates flow direction from both south-east and north-west, which means that the outwash was fed from both ice sheets (also there may have been some non-glacial drainage rivers flowing north-east). Proglacial compressive thrusting towards the north occurred as a result of the southern ice sheet advancing into the southern part of the section. Following this the southern ice sheet retreated slightly, depositing an outwash sand immediately behind the push structures - the Bush Estate Sands. The proximal deposit outwash of the Eccles Diamicton was laid down close to an active margin of the southern ice sheet after this slight retreat. A second northern ice sheet reached the site and deposited the Walcott diamicton; the outwash sands deposited by this advance are possibly the Upper Sands.

8.4 CONCLUSION

This study has shown that although the site of Happisburgh cannot be used as a type site for the north Norfolk coastal drifts, it does record a dramatic record of glacial events. In particular it records the presence of two ice sheets in the area that interacted, to produce a complex set of sediments. This study has shown how the detailed investigation of the sedimentology and structural geology of this site can be used to reconstruct its glacial history.

ACKNOWLEDGEMENTS

I would like to thank Kirk Martinez for photography and field assistance, and Tim Aspden and his colleagues in the Cartographic Unit, University of Southampton for figure production. Thanks also go to D. McCarroll, M. E. Tucker and A. P. Jones for reviewing the manuscript.

REFERENCES

ALLEY, R. B. 1991. Deforming-bed origin for southern Laurentide till sheets? *Journal of Glaciology,* **37**, 67-76.

ALLEY, R. B., BLANKENSHIP, D. D., BENTLEY, C. R. and ROONEY, S. T. 1986. Deformation of till beneath ice stream B, West Antarctica. *Nature*, **322**, 57-59.

BANHAM, P. H. 1968. A preliminary note on the Pleistocene stratigraphy of north-east Nor folk. *Proceedings of the Geologists' Association*, **108**, 507-512.

BANHAM, P. H. 1970. *IN*: Boulton, G.S. (ed.) *Quaternary Research Association, Field Guide.*

BANHAM, P. H. 1971. Pleistocene beds at Corton, Suffolk. *Geological Magazine*, **108**, 281-285.

BANHAM, P. H. 1977. *IN*: West R. G. (ed.), *East Anglia*, X INQUA Congress Excursion Guide, Geoabstracts, Norwich, England.

BANHAM, P.H. and RANSON, C. E. 1965. Structural study of the Contorted Drift and disturbed chalk at Weybourne, north Norfolk. *Geological Magazine.*, **102**, 164-74.

BENN, D. I. 1992. The genesis and significance of "Hummocky Moraine": Evidence from the Isle of Skye, Scotland. *Quaternary Science Reviews*, **11**, 781-800.

BENN, D. I. 1994. Fluted moraine formation and till genesis below a temperate valley glacier: Slettmarkbreen, Jotunheimen, southern Norway. *Sedimentology*, **41**, 279-292.

BENN, D. I., 1995. Fabric signature of subglacial till deformation, Breidamerkurjökull, Iceland. *Sedimentology*, **42**, 735-747.

BENN, D. I. and BALLANTYNE, C. K. 1993. The description and representation of particle shape. *Earth Surface Processes and Landforms*, **18**, 665-672.

BENN, D. I. and EVANS, D. A. 1997. *Glaciers and Glaciation*. Arnold, London, 734 pp.

BENNETT, M. R. and GLASSER, N. F. 1996. *Glacial Geology, Ice Sheets and Landforms*. Wiley, Chichester.

BOULTON, G. S. 1979. Processes of glacier erosion on different substrata. *Journal of Glaciology*, **23**, 15-38.

BOULTON, G. S. 1986. Push-moraines and glacier-contact fans in marine and terrestrial environments. *Sedimentology*, **33**, 677- 698.

CLARK, P. U. and HANSEL, A. K. 1989. Clast ploughing, lodgement and glacier sliding over a soft glacier bed. *Boreas*, **18**, 201-207.

CROOT, D. G. 1988. Morphological, structural and mechanical analysis of neoglacial ice-pushed ridges in Iceland. *IN*: Croot, D. (ed.), *Glaciotectonics: Forms and Processes*, 33-48. Balkema, Rotterdam.

DAHLSTROM, C. D. A 1969. Balanced cross sections. *Canadian Journal of Earth Sciences*, **6**, 743-757.

DOWDESWELL, J. A. and SHARP, M. 1986. Characterisation of pebble fabrics in modern terrestrial glacigenic sediments. *Sedimentology*, **33**, 699-711.

DREDGE, L. A. and GRANT, D. R. 1987. Glacial deformation of bedrock and sediment, Magdalen Islands and Nova Scotia, Canada: Evidence for a regional grounded ice sheet. *IN*: van der Meer, J.J.M. (ed.), *Tills and Glaciotectonics*, 183-195. Balkema, Rotterdam.

EKLUND, A. and HART, J. K. 1996. Glaciotectonic deformation within a flute from the glacier Isfallsglaciären, Sweden. *Journal of Quaternary Science*, **11**, 229-310.

ETZELMÜLLER, B., HAGEN, J. O., VATNE, G., ÖDEGÅRD, R. S. and SOLLID, J. L. 1996. Glacier debris accumulation and sediment deformation influenced by permafrost: examples from Svalbard. *Annals of Glaciology*, **22**, 53-62.

EVANS, D. J. A., OWEN, L. A., and ROBERTS, D. 1995. Stratigraphy and sedimentology of Dimlington stadial glacial deposits, East Yorkshire. *Journal of Quaternary Science*, **10**, 241-265.

EYBERGEN, F. A. 1987: Glacier snout dynamics and contemporary push moraine formation at the Turtmannglacier, Wallis, Switzerland. *IN*: van der Meer, J. J. M. (ed.), *Tills and Glaciotectonics*, 217-234. Balkema, Rotterdam.

EYLES, N., EYLES, C. H. and MCCABE, A. M. 1989. Sedimentation in an ice-contact subaqueous setting: The mid-Pleistocene 'North Sea Drifts' of Norfolk, UK. *Quaternary Science Reviews*, **8**, 57-74.

HALDORSEN, S. and SHAW, J. 1982. The problem of recognising melt-out till. *Boreas*, **11**, 261-277.

HAMBREY, M. J. 1994. *Glacial Environments*. UCL Press.

HART, J. K. 1990. Proglacial glaciotectonic deformation and the origin of the Cromer Ridge push moraine complex, North Norfolk, UK. *Boreas*, **19**, 165-180.

HART, J. K. 1994a. Till fabric associated with deformable beds, *Earth Surface Processes and landforms*, **19**, 15-32.

HART, J. K. 1994b. Proglacial glaciotectonic deformation at Melabakkar-Ásbakkar, west Iceland. *Boreas*, **23**, 112-121.

HART, J. K. 1995a. Glacial erosion, deposition and deformation associated with a deformable bed. *Progress in Physical Geography*, **19**, 173-191.

HART, J. K. 1995b. An investigation of the deforming layer/debris-rich ice continuum, illustrated from three Alaskan glaciers. *Journal of Glaciology*, **41**, 619-633.

HART, J. K. 1995c. Drumlins, flutes and lineations at Vestari-Hagafellsjökull, Iceland. *Journal of Glaciology*, **41**, 596-606.

HART, J.K. 1996. Proglacial glaciotectonic deformation associated with glaciolacustrine sedimentation, Lake Pukaki, New Zealand. *Journal of Quaternary Research*, **11**, 149-160.

HART, J. K. in press. The deforming bed / debris-rich basal ice continuum and its implications for the formation of glacial landforms (flutes) and sediments (melt-out till). *Quaternary Science Reviews.*

HART, J. K. and BOULTON, G. S. 1991a. The interrelationship between glaciotectonic deformation and glaciodeposition within the glacial environment. *Quaternary Science Reviews*, **10**, 335-350.

HART, J. K. and BOULTON, G. S. 1991b. The Glacial Geology of north east Norfolk. *IN*: Rose, J., Gibbard, P. L. and Elhers, J. (eds.), *The Glacial Deposits of Britain and Ireland*, 233-244. Balkema, Rotterdam.

HART, J. K. and PEGLAR, S. M. 1990. Further evidence of the timing of the Middle Pleistocene Glaciation in Britain. *Proceedings of the Geologists' Association.*

HART, J. K. and ROBERTS, D. H. 1994. Criteria to distinguish between subglacial glaciotectonic and glaciomarine sedimentation: I - Deformational styles and sedimentology. *Sedimentary Geology*, **91**, 191-214.

HART, J. K., HINDMARSH, R. C. A. and BOULTON, G. S. 1990. Different styles of subglacial glaciotectonic deformation in the context of the Anglian ice sheet. *Earth Surface Processes and Landforms,* **15**, 227-241.

HART, J. K., GANE, F. and WATTS, R. 1996. Evidence for deforming bed conditions on the Dänischer Wohld peninsula, northern Germany. *Boreas*, **25**, 101-113.

HART, J. K. and MARTINEZ, K. 1997. *Glacial Analysis: An Interactive Introduction*. Routledge, London (CD-ROM).

HICOCK, S. R. and DREIMANIS, A. 1992. Deformation till in the Great Lakes region: implications for rapid flow along the south-central margin of the Laurentide Ice Sheet. *Canadian Journal of Earth Sciences,* **29**, 1565-79

INGÓLFSSON, Ó. 1988. Large-scale glaciotectonic deformation of soft sediments: A case study of a late Weichselian sequence in western Iceland. *IN*: Croot, D. (ed.), *Glaciotectonics: Forms and Processes*, 101-107. Balkema, Rotterdam.

JOPLING, A. V. and WALKER, R. G. 1968. Morphology and origin of ripple-drift cross lamination, with examples from the Pleistocene of Massachusetts. *Sedimentary Petrology*, **38**, 971-984.

LAWSON, D. E. 1979. A comparison of the pebble orientations in ice and deposits of the Matanuska Glacier, Alaska. *Journal of Geology*, **87**, 629-645.

LECKIE, D. A. and MCCANN, S.B. 1982. Glaciolacustrine sedimentation on low slope prograding delta. *IN*: Davidson-Arnott, R., Nickling, W. and Fahey, B.D. (ed), *Research in Glacial, Glacial-fluvial and Glacio-lacustrine Systems*. Proceeding of the 6th Guelph Symposium on Geomorphology 1980, 261-278. Geobooks, Norwich.

LUNKKA, J. P. 1988. Sedimentation and deformation of the North Sea Drift Formation in the Happisburgh area, North Norfolk. *IN*: Croot, D.G. (ed.), *Glaciotectonics: Forms and Processes*, 109-123, Balkema, Rotterdam.

MARK, D. M. 1973. Analysis of axial orientation data including till fabrics. *Bull. Geol. Soc. Am.*, **84**, 1369-1374.

MEER, J. J. M. van der 1993. Microscopic evidence of subglacial deformation. *Quaternary Science Reviews*, **12**, 553-587.

MEER, J. J. M.. van der, RABASSA, J. O., and EVENSON, E. B. 1992. Micromorphological aspects of glaciolacustrine sediments in northern Patagonia, Argentina. *Journal of Quaternary Science*, **7**, 31-44.

PAUL, M. A. and EYLES, N. 1990. Constraints on the preservation of Diamict Facies (Melt-Out Tills) at the margins of Stagnant Glaciers. *Quaternary Science Reviews*, **9**, 51-71.

PERRIN, R. M. S., DAVIES, H. and FYSH, M. D. 1973. Lithology of the Chalky Boulder Clay. *Nature*, **245** (146), 101-104.

REID, C. 1882. *The Geology of the country around Cromer*. Memoirs of the Geological Survey of England and Wales.

SHAW, J. 1977. Tills deposited in arid polar regions. *Canadian Journal of Earth Sciences*, **14**, 1239-1245.

SLATER, G. 1926. Glacial tectonics as reflected in disturbed drift deposits. *Proceedings of the Geologists' Association*, **37**, 392- 400.

SMITH, N. D. 1978. Sedimentation processes and patterns in a glacier fed lake with a low sediment input. *Canadian Journal of Earth Science.*, **15**, 741-756.

SOLOMON, J. D. 1932. The glacial succession of the North Norfolk Coast. *Proceedings of the Geologists' Association*, **32**, 241-271.

THOMAS, G. S. P. 1984. On the glacio-dynamic structure of the Bride Moraine, Isle of Man. *Boreas*, **13**, 355-364.

TRIMMER, J. 1895. On the cliffs of Northern Drift on the coast of Norfolk. *Quarterly Journal of the Geological Society of London*, **1**, 218-19.

WATEREN, van der F. M. 1987. Structural geology and sedimentology of the Dammer Berge push moraine, FRG. *IN*: van der Meer, J.J.M. (ed.), *Tills and Glaciotectonics*, 157-182, Balkema, Rotterdam.

WEST, R. G. 1957. Note on a Preliminary Map of some features of the Drift Topography around Holt and the Cromer Area, Norfolk. *Transactions of the Norwich and Norfolk Naturalists Society*, **18**, 24-30.

Chapter 9

ICE FACIES: A CASE STUDY FROM THE BASAL ICE FACIES OF THE RUSSELL GLACIER, GREENLAND ICE SHEET

Peter G.Knight and Bryn P. Hubbard

9.1 INTRODUCTION

Glaciers are composed of a variety of different types of ice, each reflecting a different mechanism of initial formation and/or subsequent alteration. This compositional variability has led to the identification of ice facies, each defined on the basis of an assemblage of physical characteristics that is both spatially prevalent and distinctive from those of other facies. The adoption of such a classification provides a research framework within which each ice facies may be investigated under the assumption of a fundamentally different origin or history from all other facies. The identification and diagnosis of ice facies thereby provides a means of cross-glacier comparison of form and, more significantly, process.

Although the application of the facies concept (see Section 2.2.3) to the study of glacier ice has been inherited from a geological background, it has developed largely independently of these origins over some decades. This is partly due to the existence of distinctively glaciological process-form relationships, and partly because not all scientists working in glaciology have remained *au fait* with developments in sedimentology. A consequence is that facies terminology in glaciology offers a rather unusual case study for this guide; rather like island evolution deviating from that of a parent ecosystem. This report will briefly review some of the facies classifications that have been used in the description and interpretation of ice in glaciers, and provide a case study of the interpretation of facies associations from the margin of the Greenland ice sheet.

9.2 ICE FACIES SCHEMES

At the broadest level, a distinction is commonly drawn between ice facies present in three stratigraphic zones; supraglacial, englacial and basal, each of which is summarised below.

9.2.1 Supraglacial Zone

This zone includes snow and ice forms that are exposed at the glacier surface. Benson (1961) offered one of the best-known, early applications of the facies concept to supraglacial snow and ice located in the accumulation area of glaciers. Benson defined four main facies in terms of their thermal and physical properties:

1) *Dry-snow facies*. This facies is comprised of snow that is unaffected by melting at anytime of year. Dry-snow compaction and recrystallisation therefore occurs in a perennially dry environment that is characterised by continuously low temperatures. The dry-snow facies is therefore restricted to locations at high altitudes or latitudes.

2) *Percolation facies*. This facies includes snow that has experienced surface melting, but in insufficient quantities to raise the pack temperature to 0 °C. Meltwaters therefore percolate through the snow and refreeze entirely at depth, releasing latent heat and forming ice lenses or layers.

3) *Wet-snow facies*. This facies includes snow that has experienced sufficient melting to raise its bulk temperature to 0 °C for at least part of the year. The wet-snow facies is therefore generally isothermal (0 °C) at the end of the melt-season, when any additional heat input exclusively fuels snow-melt.

4) *Superimposed facies*. Superimposed facies-ice forms from the refreezing of meltwaters generated within the wet-snow zone. Refreezing may occur on the glacier surface, either beneath or downglacier of the snowpack.

When Paterson (1994), in what is widely regarded as the standard glaciological reference text, reported Benson's classification, he explicitly replaced the term 'facies' by the term 'zone'. This inconstancy of commitment to the facies concept is typical of the term's history in glaciology.

Material	Density (Kg m^{-3})
Fresh snow	50 - 70
Settled snow	200 - 300
Wind-packed snow	350 - 400
Firn	400 - 830
Very wet snow and firn	700 - 800
Ice	830 - 910

Table 9.1. Density of snow, firn and ice.

9.2.2 Englacial Zone

The predominant mechanism of ice formation at most ice-masses is via the progressive compaction and recrystallisation of snow as it is buried at the glacier surface. This process of firnification involves sequential density changes that culminate in the formation of ice, as air passages are sealed off to form bubbles, at a density of about 830 kg m⁻³ (Table 9.1). Firnified glacier ice is typically bubble-foliated at a scale of tens of centimetres, contains very low concentrations of included debris and comprises the bulk of most ice masses. Lawson (1979), in his benchmark study of ice facies at Matanuska Glacier, Alaska, termed this the *englacial diffused* facies (Figure 9.1 and 9.3). This facies contrasts with Lawson's *englacial banded* facies which is less prevalent and contains coarse angular debris supplied supraglacially in the accumulation area of the glacier. This bipartite classification has largely been adopted unaltered by subsequent investigations.

The englacial zone extends from the glacier surface (or lower surface of any supraglacial facies present) to close to the glacier bed, where it may be replaced by basal zone facies.

Figure 9.1. *Hand-specimen of englacial diffused facies ice, showing high bubble-content and low debris content. In this photograph the bubbles appear white, the clear ice dark, when held against a dark background. Sample is ca.10 cm across.*

9.2.3 Basal Zone

The basal zone is composed of ice that has been affected by direct or close contact with the glacier bed. Many glaciers have a distinctive 'basal ice layer' (BIL), in which ice is formed either by the net accretion of material (such as ground ice or refrozen meltwaters) or by the alteration of pre-existing ice by processes operating close to the glacier bed. Of the three zones outlined here, the greatest research effort has been expended on identifying and diagnosing basal zone ice facies. This focus reflects, firstly, the wide variety of ice forms that characterise this zone, and secondly, the potential such studies have to yield information relating to physical conditions and processes operating at the glacier bed (from where direct observations are largely precluded by restricted accessibility).

However, glaciologists working at different glaciers have not always defined basal zone facies according to standardised criteria and terminology. For example, different schemes have combined different degrees of genetic and descriptive classification, and the adoption of different scales of analysis represents a particular problem where BILs are comprised of a nested hierarchy of distinctive ice forms. Some workers therefore refer to the whole BIL as a single facies, while others divide it into several discrete facies. Those facies are in turn divided into constituent sub-facies by other researchers. Precisely which physical characteristics define such facies and sub-facies may also vary widely between different glaciological investigations: some researchers, for example, focus on the sedimentology of included debris and others on a range of physical characteristics including the chemical properties of the ice. This flexibility has no doubt contributed to the current co-existence of a number of complementary basal ice facies schemes. The first and most important of these was developed by Lawson (1979) on the basis of research at Matanuska Glacier. In addition to the two englacial facies outlined above, Lawson identifies two basal facies and three basal sub-facies at this polythermal glacier (Table 9.2).

Figure 9.2. *Hand specimen of basal stratified laminated sub-facies ice, showing debris laminae separated by layers of debris-free, bubble-free ice. Sample is ca. 15 cm across (thumb nail in bottom right-hand corner for scale).*

The two basal facies identified by Lawson are *basal dispersed* and *basal stratified* (Figure 9.2). The basal dispersed facies ice contains a relatively uniform distribution of polymodal debris at concentrations of 0.04 to 8 % by volume. In contrast, basal stratified facies ice is composed of bands of debris-rich and clean ice of variable thickness and lateral extent. Lawson defined three stratified sub-facies: (a) the *basal stratified suspended* sub-facies contains suspended particles and aggregates ranging from 0.02 to 55 % by volume and "includes the relatively pure ice that occurs throughout the stratified facies" (Lawson, 1979, p.11); (b) *the basal stratified solid* sub-facies is composed of well-defined layers of sediment-rich ice (> 50 % by volume), often characterised by the preservation of internal structures; (c) *the basal stratified discontinuous* sub-facies contains irregular aggregates of predominantly fine-grained sediment and varies in thickness laterally between 0.05 to 2.0 m. Separate units of basal stratified discontinuous sub-facies ice may overlap to form more continuous debris-rich zones.

Zone	Facies	Sub-facies	Origin
supraglacial			surface phenomena
englacial	diffused		surface firnification
	banded		surface firnification
basal	dispersed		combined firnification and basal regelation
	stratified	stratified *discontinuous*	basal relegation
		stratified *suspended*	basal regelation
		stratified *solid*	basal regelation

Table 9.2. *Facies classification of Matanuska Glacier, Alaska, according to Lawson (1979).*

Lawson's classification has been widely adopted and built upon by other glaciological researchers, and descriptions of glaciers from a range of other locations have been couched in Lawson's terminology. However, not all features observed at other glaciers fit comfortably into Lawson's scheme, necessitating a degree of adaptation and, in some cases, new definitions. Knight (1987), for example, largely followed Lawson's scheme, but also recognised the importance of tectonic disturbance in the basal layer at the margin of the Greenland ice sheet (Table 9.3; case study below). Despite terminological differences, the two facies codes are in fact closely related (Knight, 1994, Souchez and Lorrain, 1991), the principal difference between the two being that Lawson's scheme does not explicitly recognise the effects of debris-band formation by folding or thrusting.

Figure 9.3. *Vertical section exposing coarse-grained englacial diffused facies ice overlying very fine-grained snow in the process of transformation to ice. The snow has been overridden by advancing ice at the glacier margin. Section shown is ca. 50 cm from top to bottom.*

Basal Ice Family	Origin of Family	Facies Description	Origin
clotted	clotted ice	clotted ice	basal entrainment in interior of ice sheet
banded	tectonic intercalation facies of clotted and solid families	clotted ice between debris bands	basal entrainment in interior of ice sheet, and transport towards margin
		debris bands	basal entrainment (solid family) and folding/ thrusting
solid	basal entrainment	stratified ice frozen till old snow	regelation congelation/overriding overriding

Table 9.3. Knight's (1987) classification of basal ice facies.

Sharp *et al.* (1994) also developed a facies scheme similar to that of Lawson's on the basis of research at surge-type Variegated Glacier, Alaska. These authors defined two basal facies, *basal diffused* and *basal stratified*. Basal diffused is tectonically incorporated glacier ice (the basal equivalent of Lawson's englacial diffused facies) while basal stratified, characterised by a higher debris content and more variable ice characteristics, is divided into three sub-facies: clear, laminated and solid (Table 9.4). *Basal stratified clear* sub-facies ice contains low concentrations of incorporated debris and gas and is hypothesised to form via metamorphism of glacier ice under variable pressure close to the glacier bed. In contrast, units of *basal stratified solid* and *basal stratified laminated* sub-facies ice are respectively composed of massive units of frozen debris and repeated laminations of clear and debris-rich ice. They are closely equivalent to Lawson's basal stratified discontinuous and basal stratified solid sub-facies, and their widespread presence at Variegated Glacier testifies to the capacity of predominantly temperate-based, surge-type glaciers for basal accretion.

Recently, Hubbard and Sharp (1995) extended the facies-based approach to the analysis of basal ice at warm-based glaciers. These authors identified seven basal ice facies and two sub-facies (Table 9.5), many of which are unique to this classification scheme. These new facies largely reflect distinctive processes operating at or close to the beds of predominantly temperate-based glaciers. They include: (a) *basal laminated* facies ice, defined by debris laminae repeated at a scale of 0.1 to 1 mm and associated with pressure-induced melting and refreezing around bedrock hummocks; (b) *basal interfacial* facies ice, located within

Zone	Facies	Sub-facies	Origin
englacial	englacial diffused		firnification
	englacial banded		supraglacial debris
basal	basal stratified	*basal stratified - laminated*	incremental basal accretion
		basal stratified - clear	metamorphism of englacial or basal diffused facies
		basal stratified - solid	en-masse basal accretion
	basal diffused		tectonically incorporated englacial ice

Table 9.4. *Ice facies of the Variegated Glacier, Alaska, according to Sharp et al. (1994).*

cavities formed between the glacier bed and the solid substrate; (c) *basal dispersed* facies ice, containing dispersed basal debris and hypothesised to form by the incorporation of interfacial facies ice; and (d) *basal planar* facies ice, composed of thin layers of fine debris that cut across existing foliation, formed as healed crevasses.

Each of the classifications outlined above associates the physical characteristics of individual facies with processes of formation, thereby allowing inference of subglacial conditions upglacier of marginal basal ice exposures. It is also possible to go one stage further, and consider the process implications of associations and/or sequences of basal ice facies. The geography and geometry of the association/sequence as a whole has the potential to reveal more about the spatial distribution of subglacial processes upglacier of exposure locations than does the analysis of individual facies. The following section considers a case study of the process-interpretation of associations of basal ice facies exposed at the margin of the Greenland Ice Sheet.

9.3 CASE STUDY: BASAL ICE FACIES OF THE RUSSELL GLACIER, GREENLAND ICE SHEET

The Russell Glacier (67° 06' N, 50°15'W) is one of the many outlet glaciers and lobes that form the western margin of the Greenland Ice Sheet. Basal ice is exposed along several tens of kilometres of the ice-sheet margin in the area of the Russell Glacier. The basal ice

Facies	Sub-facies	Origin	Implication
clear		stress-induced metamorphism close to the bed; Lliboutry (1993) regelation	basal interface at melting point. Bedrock roughness decimetres-metres
laminated		Weertman (1957,1964) regelation	base at melting point, cm-dm bed roughness, low basal melt rate, compressive strain
interfacial	*interfacial layered*	freezing of flowing basal water	sub-freezing base, metre-scale bed roughness, cavitation, linked cavity hydrology
	interfacial continuous	freezing of standing basal water	
dispersed		incorporation and transport of interfacial facies	sub-freezing base, metre-scale bed roughness, cavitation, linked cavity hydrology, variable sliding rate
solid		adfreezing of saturated sediment	unconsolidated sedimentary substrate
stratified		any basal facies tectonically thickened and interstratified with glacier ice	marginal compression
planar		closure of ice-marginal fracture planes incorporating aeolian debris	marginal fracturing / crevassing.

Table 9.5. Hubbard and Sharp's (1995) classification of basal ice facies from glaciers in the Western Alps.

characteristics described here are derived partly from data previously presented by Knight (1987, 1989, 1994), Sugden *et al.* (1987), Knight *et al.* (1994) and Souchez and Lorrain (1991).

This description takes an ice facies to be a body of ice created by a distinctive set of processes that are reflected in a suite of observable characteristics. This might involve several different processes at different locations over an extended period of time. Therefore, a single facies might be made up of several different sub-facies, each with a distinctive origin. The facies unit is defined in terms of the summative result of a series of events creating a visible unit. Therefore individual ice types or sub-facies might occur in more than one individual facies.

Associations of basal ice facies are highly variable from site to site around the glacier margin, depending on the processes operating at the margin and up-flow in the glacier interior. However, it is possible to compare individual sites with a 'complete' facies assemblage where all the different basal ice types are present. This complete assemblage would involve three facies.

9.3.1 Facies

Stratified Facies
This forms a layer up to *ca.* 5 m thick at the base of the succession, comprising old snow, frozen unconsolidated sediment, and finely laminated layers of ice and debris. These components are frequently jumbled and contorted, and occur in widely varying proportions between sites. The facies originates by the overriding of proglacial material and by entrainment and deformation of material at the glacier bed, including material incorporated from subglacial cavities. This is equivalent to Lawson's stratified facies and can include as sub-facies several of the facies described by Hubbard and Sharp (1995) including their laminated, interfacial, dispersed and solid facies. In the stratified facies at Russell Glacier these sub-facies are frequently so intermingled by deformation that their original stratigraphic relationship is hard to distinguish.

Banded Facies
This can be up to 30 m thick, and comprises distinct layers or bands of material from the stratified facies intercalated with either non-basal ice or clotted ice (see below). The intercalation occurs as a result of compressive deformation that raises stratified facies ice into the overlying facies either by folding or by thrusting. The debris bands can be up to several tens of centimetres in thickness, and can be traced laterally for tens of metres around the margin. They are commonly separated by cleaner layers up to several metres

thick. The bands tend to dip upglacier at angles of 20-60°. Bands can consist of massive debris with only interstitial ice, or mm-scale laminae of ice and debris. The banded facies overlies the stratified facies.

Clotted Facies

The clotted facies occurs in the upper part of the basal succession and is characterised by dispersed debris particles and lenticular particle-aggregates up to several centimetres in length surrounded by generally clean and bubble-poor ice. The clotted ice is formed by a combination of basal regelation and the metamorphism of englacial ice during transport close to the bed (Knight and Knight, 1994).

The principal sub-facies which occur within these facies are given in Table 9.6, their distinction based on visible characteristics of debris in the ice.

Basal ice facies *(sub-facies)*	**Code**	**Description**
solid	s	massive debris with only interstitial ice
basal stratified solid	Bs_s	occurring in the stratified facies
basal banded solid	Bb_s	occurring in debris bands in the banded facies
laminated	l	interlayered ice and debris, with individual layers at the mm scale
basal stratified laminated	Bs_l	occurring in the stratified facies
basal banded laminated	Bb_l	occurring in debris bands in the banded facies
distributed	d	debris particles or particle aggregates distributed in otherwise clean ice.
basal stratified distributed	Bs_d	occurring in the stratified facies
basal banded distributed	Bb_d	occurring in debris bands in the banded facies
basal clotted distributed	Bc_d	occurring in the clotted facies
planar	p	individual planes of debris particles or particle aggregates.
basal stratified planar	Bs_p	occurring in the stratified facies
basal banded planar	Bb_p	occurring in debris bands in the banded facies
basal clotted planar	Bc_p	occurring in the clotted facies

Table 9.6. Sub-facies observed in the basal ice at Russell Glacier, Greenland.

9.3.2 Facies Associations and their Interpretation

On the basis of the three facies described above, seven possible basal ice facies associations can be identified, and interpreted, as follows:

9.3.2.1 Facies Association Type 0
Description: no basal ice is present.

Interpretation: either no basal ice is formed upglacier of the point of observation, or whatever has been formed has subsequently been removed by melting (Knight *et al.*, 1994).

9.3.2.2 Facies Association Type 1
Description: the basal layer comprises only basal stratified facies ice.

Interpretation: a zone of basal accretion exists upglacier of the observation point. If laminated sub-facies ice exists then incremental freezing of basal water is implied. If solid sub-facies ice exists, en-masse accretion of sediment by freezing on or tectonic processes is implied.

9.3.2.3 Facies Association Type 2
Description: the basal layer comprises only banded facies ice, with debris bands intercalated with englacial ice.

Interpretation: this reflects thrusting within the lower layers of a glacier that transports basal sediment upwards along the thrust plane. This association implies compressive flow, the existence of material in basal transport, but the absence of bulk accretion close to the margin.

9.3.2.4 Facies Association Type 3
Description: the basal layer comprises only clotted ice.

Interpretation: if the clotted ice comprises only distributed sub-facies ice, then one interpretation is that ice flowed close to the melting point with regelation and/or inter-granular water flow (Lawson, 1979, Sugden *et al.*, 1987). An alternative interpretation could be that the ice has experienced substantial total strain and that basal debris has been dispersed by the strain process (Hart, 1995). If there is planar sub-facies ice in the clotted facies, this implies strongly attenuated thrust layers intruding from below, with implications similar to those of Association Type 2. Such an association also implies that, while the environment close to the glacier margin is not characterised by net accretion, basal ice formed in the interior of the ice mass can survive passage through this zone without removal (Knight *et al.*, 1994).

9.3.2.5 Facies Association Type 4

Description: the basal layer comprises stratified and banded facies ice.

Interpretation: this association implies an accretionary marginal environment with compressive flow, but with no survival to the margin of basal ice formed in the interior of the ice mass. This association may typically characterise sub-polar and surge-type glaciers, and was observed at Jakobshavn Isbrae by Sugden *et al.* (1987).

9.3.2.6 Facies Association Type 5

Description: the basal layer comprises stratified and clotted facies, with no banded facies (e.g. Lawson, 1979).

Interpretation: as for Association Type 3, but with an accretionary margin as in Association Type 1.

9.2.3.7 Facies Association Type 6

Description: the basal layer comprises banded and clotted facies, but no stratified facies ice.

Interpretation: basal ice formed close to the pressure melting point in the interior of the ice mass, with regelation and/or inter-granular water flow and/or major total strain, survives the journey to the ice margin without melting, and experiences strong compressive flow, possibly with some basal freezing, close to the margin (Knight *et al.*, 1994).

9.3.2.8 Facies Association Type 7

Description: the basal layer comprises stratified, banded and clotted facies.

Interpretation: basal ice formed close to the pressure melting point in the interior of the ice mass, with regelation and/or inter-granular water flow, is affected by freezing-on and compression close to the glacier margin (Knight, 1994).

9.4 CONCLUSION

Ice facies in glaciers reflect the processes of their formation. Supraglacial and englacial facies reflect primarily the processes of accumulation of snow and its progressive transformation to ice, along with dynamic and hydrological processes operating during the flow of the glacier. Basal ice facies reflect processes and conditions operating at and close to the bed of the glacier, so the interpretation of basal facies permits the reconstruction of subglacial conditions and processes.

The facies concept sits uneasily in glaciology, and its use is uneven. A clear and universal terminological and methodological framework for the description and interpretation of ice facies remains elusive. In part this is because the processes by which ice facies evolve are as yet incompletely understood.

ACKNOWLEDGMENTS

The authors are pleased to acknowledge the helpful comments made by Prof. W. Theakstone, Dr. A. P. Jones, Dr. J. K. Hart and Prof. M. E. Tucker during the preparation of this chapter.

REFERENCES

BENSON, C.S. 1961. Stratigraphic studies in the snow and firn of the Greenland Ice Sheet. *Folia Geographica Danica*, **9**, 13-37.

HART, J.K. 1995. An investigation of the deforming layer/debris-rich basal-ice continuum, illustrated from three Alaskan glaciers. *Journal of Glaciology* **41**, 139, 634-641.

HUBBARD, B. and SHARP, M. 1995. Basal ice facies and their formation in the western Alps. *Arctic and Alpine Research*, **4**, 301-310.

KNIGHT, P.G. 1987. Observations at the edge of the Greenland ice sheet; boundary condition implications for modellers. *IN: The Physical Basis of Ice Sheet Modelling*, 359-366. International Association of Hydrological Sciences Publication, **170**.

KNIGHT, P.G. 1989. Stacking of basal debris layers without bulk freezing-on: isotopic evidence from West Greenland. *Journal of Glaciology*, **35**, (120), 214-216.

KNIGHT, P.G. 1994. Two-facies interpretation of the basal layer of the Greenland ice sheet contributes to a unified model of basal ice formation. *Geology*, **22**, (11), 971-974.

KNIGHT, P.G. and KNIGHT, D.A. 1994. Glacier sliding, regelation water flow, and development of basal ice. *Journal of Glaciology*, **40**, (136), 600-601.

KNIGHT, P.G., SUGDEN, D.E. and MINTY, C. 1994. Ice flow around large obstacles as indicated by basal ice exposed at the margin of the Greenland ice sheet. *Journal of Glaciology*, **40**, (135), 359-367.

LAWSON, D.E. 1979. Sedimentological analysis of the western terminus of the Matanuska Glacier, Alaska. *U.S. Army Cold Regions Research and Engineering Laboratory*. Report 79-9. Hanover, New Hampshire. 112 pp.

PATERSON, W.S.B. 1994. *The Physics of Glaciers.* Third edition. Pergamon, Oxford. 480 pp.

SHARP, M., JOUZEL, J., HUBBARD, B. and LAWSON, W. 1994. The character, structure and origin of the basal ice layer of a surge-type glacier. *Journal of Glaciology* **40**, (135), 327-340.

SOUCHEZ, R.A. and LORRAIN, R.D. 1991. *Ice Composition and Glacier Dynamics.* Springer-Verlag, Berlin. 207 pp.

Chapter 10

PERMAFROST: A CASE STUDY IN CRYOSTRATIGRAPHY, PLEISTOCENE MACKENZIE DELTA, WESTERN CANADIAN ARCTIC

Julian B. Murton

10.1 INTRODUCTION

About one fifth of the Earth's land surface is underlain by permafrost, that is, ground (soil or rock) which remains at or below 0°C for at least two years (Permafrost Subcommittee, ACGR, 1988). Permafrost may contain moisture in the form of water and/or ice. Where the ice volume exceeds the pore volume that the ground would naturally have when unfrozen, the permafrost contains *excess ice* and is termed *ice-rich*. As ice-rich permafrost grows (aggrades) and thaws (degrades) it forms distinctive structures and facies of ice, sediment and/or bedrock (e.g. Katasonov, 1969, 1975, 1978; French *et al.*, 1982, 1986; Murton and French, 1994). These features are described by way of a *cryostratigraphic* approach that integrates sedimentology, stratigraphy and geocryology.

Variation in the amount and distribution of ice within sediment or bedrock produces distinct cryostratigraphic units, the interpretation of which permits reconstruction of ground thermal and hydrological conditions, and thus of permafrost history (e.g. Harry and French, 1988). Where ice-rich permafrost no longer exists, its former cryostratigraphy can sometimes be inferred from structures indicating the former occurrence of perennial ground ice, for example ice-wedge casts (e.g. Demek, 1978, Ballantyne and Harris, 1994) and some brecciated bedrocks (e.g. Murton, 1996a).

In areas of contemporary permafrost, cryostratigraphy provides a framework for regional studies of perennially frozen sediments (e.g. Katasonov and Ivanov, 1973, Sellmann and Brown, 1973, Péwé, 1975, Sher *et al.*, 1979), palaeoenvironmental studies of inactive ice wedges (e.g. Mackay, 1975, 1976; French *et al.*, 1982, Black, 1983, Harry *et al.*, 1985), studies of climate change (e.g. Mackay, 1978, Burn *et al.*, 1986, Burn, 1997), genetic studies of massive ice and icy sediments (e.g. Mackay, 1971, Astakhov and Isayeva, 1988, French and Harry, 1990, Mackay and Dallimore, 1992), stratigraphic studies of near-surface segregated ice (e.g. French *et al.*, 1986, Burn, 1988) and sedimentological studies of permafrost degradation (e.g. Murton, 1996b, Murton and French, 1993a, 1993b). In areas of former permafrost in mid-latitudes, cryostratigraphic interpretations provide a framework for studies of Quaternary stratigraphy and periglacial palaeoenvironments (e.g. Van der Hammen *et al.*, 1967, Gozdzik, 1973, Kolstrup, 1980, Rose *et al.*, 1985, Worsley, 1987, Vandenberghe and Pissart, 1993, Ballantyne and Harris, 1994, Van Vliet-Lanoë, 1996) and former cryogenic processes (e.g. Dylik, 1964, Vandenberghe and Van den Broek, 1982, Murton, 1996a).

10.2 GROUND ICE

Ground ice can be defined as ice within the ground (soil or rock), irrespective of the origin or form of occurrence of the ice (cf. Shumskii, 1964, National Academy of Sciences, 1974).

Ground ice may be classified descriptively or genetically. Descriptive classifications distinguish *cryotextures* and *cryostructures* of ice and sediment or bedrock. Cryotextures can be distinguished microscopically according to non-ice grain and/or ice-crystal size and shape, and the nature of the contacts between grains and crystals (cf. Shumskii, 1964).

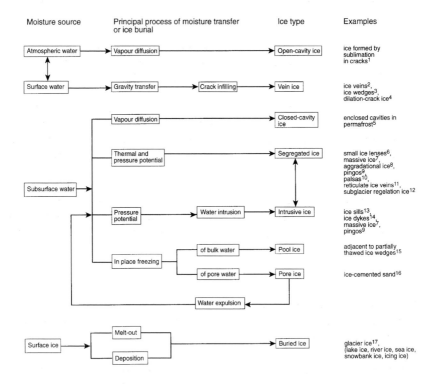

Figure 10.1. *Genetic classification of ground ice, based on Mackay (1972, 1988) and Shumskii (1964).* [1](*Mackay, 1972);* [2](*Mackay and Matthews, 1983);* [3](*citations in Mackay, 1995);* [4](*Mackay, 1985);* [5](*Mackay, 1965);* [6](*Taber, 1929; Penner, 1972);* [7](*Rampton and Mackay, 1971; Mackay, 1971, 1989; Mackay and Dallimore, 1992);* [8](*Mackay, 1972; Cheng, 1983; French et al., 1986; Burn, 1988);* [9](*Mackay, 1979, 1985);* [10](*Seppälä, 1986);* [11](*Mackay, 1974; Murton and French, 1994);* [12](*Knight, Section 9.2);* [13](*Lawson, 1983);* [14](*Mackay, 1989);* [15](*Shumskii, 1964; Mackay, 1988);* [16](*Kudriavtsev, 1978, pp. 301-304);* [17](*Knight, Section 9.2).*

Examples include contact, film and pore-filling types of ice cement (e.g. Kudriavtsev, 1978, p.301-304). Cryostructures are distinguished megascopically according to the shape, distribution and proportions of ice and non-ice material within frozen ground. A cryostructural classification of ground ice (discussed below) is more practical for field description of permafrost because cryostructures are visible to the naked eye.

Genetic classifications of ground ice provide the basis for subsequent interpretation of cryostratigraphy. An example shown in Figure 10.1 has as its principal criteria (i) the source of moisture and (ii) the processes of moisture transfer to the freezing plane (Mackay, 1972) or of burial of surface ice (Shumskii, 1964). Large, usually tabular bodies of ground ice with gravimetric ice contents exceeding 250% (i.e. *massive ice*; Permafrost Subcommittee, ACGR, 1988) are genetically either *buried* or *intrasedimental* ice (Mackay and Dallimore, 1992). Buried ice forms by burial of glacial or non-glacial (e.g. snowbank) ice, whereas intrasedimental ice forms in place by freezing of water within sedimentary sequences (Mackay, 1971), and includes pore, segregated and intrusive ice.

Ground ice forms either during (syngenetic) or after (epigenetic) deposition of the material in which it occurs. Examples of *syngenetic* ground ice include pore ice, segregated ice and ice-wedge ice formed during aggradation of loess (e.g. Carter, 1988); examples of *epigenetic* ground ice include the same three ice types formed in a non-aggrading substrate.

Permafrost field sections can be described in terms of cryostructures, cryofacies and ice contacts (Murton and French, 1994). The terms are reviewed below and details of the background literature are summarised in English by Katasonov (1969, 1975, 1978), Harry and French (1988), Mackay (1989) and Murton and French (1994).

10.3 CRYOSTRUCTURES

The shape, distribution and proportions of ice and sediment (or bedrock) within frozen ground constitute its cryostructure (cf. Murton and French, 1994). Six cryostructures are distinguished in Figure 10.2 and summarised below.

Structureless (Sl): frozen sediments in which ice is not readily visible lack a cryostructure and are termed *structureless*. This seemingly illogical term avoids confusion with the term massive (as in *massive ice*), which denotes large size. Structureless cryostructures are common in sand and gravel containing little silt or clay, forming where pore water freezes in place around mineral grains.

Lenticular (Le): lens-shaped bodies of ice in sediment, or vice-versa, are described as *lenticular.* Lenses vary from horizontal to vertical. They are described by inclination, thickness, length, shape and relationship to each other (planar, wavy or curved, and parallel

Cryostructure and code	Sediment	Ice	Occurrence as or within
 structureless (Sl)	sand gravel	pore	ice in sand + gravel
 lenticular (Le)	muddy peat mud (fine sand) / sand	segregated / crack infill	ice/sediment lenses massive ice icy sediments / (ice wedges) (composite sand-ice wedges) (dilation-crack ice)
 layered (La)	muddy peat mud (fine sand) / sand	segregated intrusive / crack infill	ice/sediment layers massive ice icy sediments / ice wedges composite sand-ice wedges dilation-crack ice
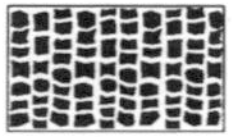 regular reticulate (Rr)	mud	segregated	ice in mud
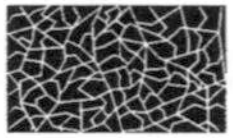 irregular reticulate (Ri)	mud	segregated	ice in mud
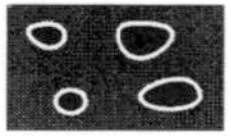 crustal (Cr)	mud frost-susceptible clasts	segregated	
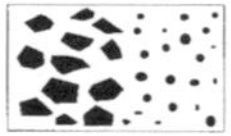 suspended (Su)	mud sand gravel	segregated intrusive	icy layer at top of permafrost ice dykes in mud / ice lenses massive ice icy sediments ice dykes

Figure 10.2. *Cryostructure classification (from Murton and French, 1994). Ice is shown in white, and sediment (or bedrock) in grey or black. In lenticular and layered cryostructures, lenses and layers may comprise either ice or sediment.*

or non-parallel; Figure 3.10). Lenticular cryostructures are common in silt, sand and massive ice. The orientation of ice lenses reflects the orientation of freezing fronts and (or) the structural properties of the sediment (e.g. bedding).

Layered (La): continuous bands of ice, sediment or a combination of both are termed *layered*. Individual layers are described in the same way as lenses. Layered cryostructures occur in massive ice, icy sediments, ice wedges and composite wedges. Their thickness varies from millimetres to metres. Vertical to subvertical layers commonly result from infilling of thermal contraction and dilation cracks with ice, clastic sediment and (or) organic material. Horizontal to gently dipping layers are commonly associated with segregated and intrusive ice.

Reticulate (R): a three-dimensional, net-like structure of ice veins surrounding mud-rich blocks is termed *reticulate*. Reticulate cryostructures may be *regular* or *irregular*. The regular reticulate form (Rr) is an oriented network of ice surrounding rectangular to rhombic, mud-rich blocks. Reticulate ice veins vary in thickness from a few millimetres to *ca*.10 cm and in length from *ca*. 1 to 100 cm. The irregular reticulate form (Ri) is an irregular network of ice veins surrounding sediment blocks a few millimetres to *ca*. 25 cm long. Reticulate cryostructures probably form in a semi-closed freezing system by infilling of shrinkage cracks in muddy sediments with water (ice) derived from adjacent muddy blocks (Mackay, 1974). Why some reticulate cryostructures are regular and others irregular is unclear.

Crustal (Cr): an ice crust or rim around a rock clast is termed *crustal*. Crustal cryostructures are common just beneath the permafrost table, where ice crusts up to a few centimetres thick may envelop pebbles and wood fragments, typically within silt-rich sediment. Crustal cryostructures probably form by localised ice segregation around frost-susceptible clasts (cf. Mackay, 1984).

Suspended (Su): grains, aggregates and rock clasts suspended in ice are described as *suspended*. Individual grains vary from silt to boulder size. Aggregates of for example sandy mud are termed *mud aggregates* and range in diameter or length from ≤1 mm to several centimetres or more. Mud aggregates vary in roundness from angular to rounded and in shape from equant to elongate. The sides of angular mud aggregates are commonly *matched* across ice bodies. Rounded mud aggregates are typically equant, with diameters ranging from ≤0.5 mm to 20 mm or more. Suspended cryostructures are common in massive ice and also just beneath the permafrost table. Suspended sediment aggregates have been observed in segregated ice (e.g. aggradational ice), intrusive ice (e.g. ice dykes), vein ice and glacier ice. Suspended rock clasts can occur in both glacier ice and massive intrasedimental ice.

The classification above depicts cryostructures individually. In reality, however, many cryostructures are transitional or composite. For example, transitional cryostructures can be partly suspended and partly irregular reticulate, or partly irregular reticulate and partly lenticular. Composite cryostructures include (i) structureless and crustal in pebbly sand and (ii) lenticular and layered within composite (sand-ice) wedges. Hierarchical cryostructures also exist, for example, large irregular-shaped blocks separated by thick irregular reticulate ice veins may be subdivided into smaller blocks and thinner veins. Different cryostructures may also be organised hierarchically, for example, where reticulate or suspended cryostructures are layered near the permafrost table, or within massive ice and icy sediments.

10.4 CRYOFACIES

Facies of ice and non-ice material (*cryofacies*) can be divided into five categories according to arbitrarily defined classes of volumetric ice content (Murton and French, 1994). These comprise (i) pure ice (100% ice); (ii) sediment-(or bedrock) poor ice (>75-≤100% ice); (iii) sediment-rich ice (>50-≤75% ice); (iv) ice-rich sediment (>25-≤50% ice); and (v) ice-poor sediment (≤25% ice). The categories are subdivided according to features like sediment grain size or bedrock type and cryostructure, depending on the aims of a particular study.

Cryofacies may occur individually or collectively. A group of cryofacies that occur together as a distinctive cryostratigraphic unit and are thought to be genetically or environmentally related is referred to here as a *cryofacies association* (cf. Reading, 1986, p.5), and a group whose genetic relationship is unclear is referred to as a *cryofacies assemblage* (see Section 2.1.3).

10.5 ICE CONTACTS

Ice contacts between cryofacies or cryostratigraphic units may be sharp or gradational; planar, curved or irregular; and conformable or unconformable.

Ice contacts form by freezing, thawing or erosion. Freezing contacts develop when ground ice forms in freezing or frozen ground. Examples of sharp freezing contacts include the unthawed sides of ice wedges and cryostructural discontinuities between sediments of contrasting frost susceptibility (e.g. sand and silt). Examples of gradational freezing contacts include (i) the downward increase in size and frequency of ice lenses above certain bodies of massive intrasedimental ice; (ii) suspended sediment fragments below the contact of intrusive ice with host sediment; and (iii) the downward gradation of segregated ice in the overburden of some pingos into intrusive ice of the pingo core (Mackay, 1989). Gradational contacts develop only where the ice is similar in age or younger than the enclosing material; they should rarely exist with buried ice, which predates its overburden (Mackay, 1989).

Thaw contacts (*thaw unconformities*; Mackay, 1975) mark the position of thawing fronts (past or present) in seasonally or perennially frozen ground. Examples include the tops of ice wedges and the base of previously-deeper active layers that have subsequently refrozen (e.g. Mackay, 1975, 1978; Büdel, 1982, Burn *et al.*, 1986, Harry and French, 1988, Burn, 1997); in the case of the latter, ground ice below the unconformity must pre-date thaw, whereas ground ice above it must post-date it. Downward thaw through ice-sediment mixtures can form melt-out deposits above thaw unconformities (Murton and French, 1993c).

Erosional contacts in ice-rich permafrost commonly result from thermal erosion (i.e. the combined thermal and mechanical action of moving water; Permafrost Subcommittee, ACGR, 1988). Examples include those where glaciofluvial deposits unconformably overlie massive ice (e.g. Murton *et al.*, 1997, fig. 3f), and often where pool ice overlies partially-thawed ice wedges (e.g. Murton and French, 1993b, fig. 6). Erosional contacts, unlike thaw unconformities, should rarely be overlain by *in situ* melt-out deposits because such deposits are commonly eroded away.

Ice contacts may be primary or secondary in origin. Primary contacts are those where the initial contact formed between two cryofacies or cryostratigraphic units is preserved. Secondary contacts are those where the initial contact has been destroyed by thaw or erosion (cf. Mackay, 1989).

10.6 CASE STUDY: CRYOSTRATIGRAPHY, PLEISTOCENE MACKENZIE DELTA, WESTERN CANADIAN ARCTIC

The case study is from ice-rich permafrost exposed in coastal bluffs at Crumbling Point, Summer Island, in the Pleistocene Mackenzie Delta, Western Canadian Arctic (e.g. Murton and French, 1993a, 1993b, 1993c, 1994; Murton *et al.*, 1997) (Figure 10.3). The area is part of the Tuktoyaktuk Coastlands (Rampton, 1988), a region underlain by thick, commonly ice-rich Quaternary sediments. In the Tuktoyaktuk Coastlands the permafrost thickness ranges from <100 m to 750 m (Taylor *et al.*, 1996). Mean annual air temperatures are typically *ca.* -10°C to -12°C, and mean annual ground temperatures *ca.* -8°C to -10°C (Mackay, 1979). The vegetation is that of the low-arctic tundra zone (Ritchie, 1984).

The Tuktoyaktuk Coastlands were last extensively glaciated during either the early Wisconsinan (Rampton, 1988) or the late Wisconsinan (Dyke and Prest, 1987). The area experienced regional permafrost degradation at *ca.* 12-8 ka BP. This thermokarst activity

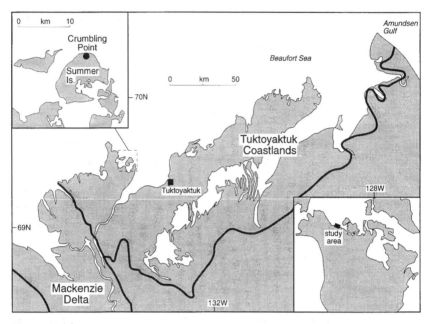

Figure 10.3. *Location map of the Tuktoyaktuk Coastlands.*

was expressed by the development of numerous thermokarst basins, retrogressive thaw slumps and a regional deepening of the active layer (Rampton, 1974, Mackay, 1978, Burn, 1997). The case study below illustrates the cryostratigraphy associated with the latter.

10.6.1 Methods

Methods used in this study include sedimentological logging, isotopic analysis of ground ice, measurement of volumetric ice content and radiocarbon dating. The logs record cryostructures, cryofacies, ice contacts and sedimentary structures. Logging of ice-rich permafrost was carried out during times when surface thaw was absent or minimal, so that ground ice could be examined carefully. The oxygen isotope analysis of ground ice relies on the fact that the $\partial^{18}O$ value of water (or ice) is strongly influenced by the temperature at which precipitation condenses: the lower the temperature, the more negative (isotopically lighter) is the resulting $\partial^{18}O$ value of precipitation (e.g. Bradley, 1985, p.124-134, Johnsen *et al.*, 1989, fig. 3). Providing no major isotopic changes occur (by mixing, evaporation or fractionation) between precipitation and freezing, or by diffusion after freezing, the $\partial 18O$ values of the ice will reflect the palaeoclimate at the time of precipitation (e.g. Michel and Fritz, 1982, Mackay, 1983). Oxygen isotope analysis of ground ice can sometimes also be used to detect thaw unconformities (e.g. Mackay and Lavkulich, 1974, Burn *et al.*, 1986, Burn, 1997). The volumetric ice content is the ratio of the volume of ice in a sample to the volume of the whole sample, expressed as a percentage. Age control is provided by AMS ^{14}C dating of *in situ* rootlets in permafrost.

10.6.2 Description

Ice-rich permafrost exposed between 1989 and 1993 at Crumbling Point comprised two cryostratigraphic units penetrated by sand wedges and ice wedges, and separated by a sharp contact (Figures 10.4 and 10.5). The lower horizon (at least 15 m thick) is referred to as the *layered cryofacies assemblage*, being dominated by layers of diamicton-poor ice (>75% volumetric ice content), diamicton-rich ice (>50-≤75% ice) and ice-rich sand (>25-≤50% ice). The sediment comprises sandy mud diamicton, and the average volumetric ice content is *ca.* 84% (s = 8%; n = 10). Although most layers (*ca.* 0.01-0.4 m thick and *ca.* 2-60 m or more long) are horizontal to moderately inclined and parallel to subparallel, the assemblage is highly deformed, containing numerous recumbent folds.

The upper horizon is named the *sand and diamicton cryofacies assemblage*. The sand is fine grained and moderately well sorted, similar to that within the adjacent sand wedges. The diamicton comprises granule to cobble clasts supported in a matrix of sandy mud texturally identical to that in the underlying layered assemblage. The diamicton is massive and contains fragments of wood and charcoal, and abundant rootlets. Within this assemblage the volumetric ice content of the sand is *ca.* 35-40% and that of the diamicton *ca.* 35-80%; hence the following cryofacies are distinguished: ice-rich sand, ice-rich diamicton, diamicton-rich ice and diamicton-poor ice (see Section 3.3.1.1).

The sand and diamicton assemblage forms a widespread cryostratigraphic unit present only above the layered assemblage. Diamicton is absent, however, above sand wedges or beneath thick (>*ca.* 1.5 m) units of sand. The assemblage is typically at least twice as thick (0.9-3.2 m) as the modern active layer (0.23-0.90 m). The basal 10-30 cm of the assemblage generally contains more ice ($\bar{x}$ = 72% vol. ice content; s = 5%; n = 6) than the major part of the assemblage ($\bar{x}$ = 46%; s = 8%; n = 6; Figure 10.6). The proportions of sand and diamicton vary; where both are present, the sand generally overlies or occurs within the upper metre of the diamicton. Sand overlying the diamicton occurs as a veneer (Figure 10.5a) contiguous with the tops of some sand wedges (Figure 10.5b).

The sand and diamicton assemblage contains abundant involutions. The involutions comprise sand load casts, pseudo-nodules, ball-and-pillow structures, and diamicton diapirs and flame structures (Murton and French, 1993a). The most common are ball-and-pillow structures (Figure 10.6), on average 17 cm wide, 10 cm high and generally asymmetrical,

Figure 10.4. *Cryostratigraphy at Crumbling Point, Summer Island. Composite sand-ice wedges penetrate a sand and diamicton cryofacies assemblage (S) and underlying layered assemblage (L). The assemblages are separated by a sharp ice contact (large arrow) that marks a thaw unconformity at a depth of ca. 2 m. Thermokarst involutions (small arrow) occur above the contact and below the modern active layer, the base of which is marked by tops of the ice wedges. 1.8 m tall person for scale.*

with concave-up bases and convex-up tops. Their average depth below the ground surface ($\bar{x}$ = 111 cm; n = 95) and their average height above the base of the assemblage ($\bar{x}$ = 68 cm; n = 70) are highly variable (s = 44 cm and 23 cm, respectively). The involutions are commonly grouped into an upper horizon of diapirs, flame structures and load casts, and a lower horizon of ball-and-pillow structures or, more rarely, pseudo-nodules. Undeformed involutions are the most common, and underlie flat ground, their long axes variably inclined with respect to the base of the assemblage. Deformed involutions underlie gently sloping ground, their long axes aligned oblique to the base of the assemblage and dipping upslope. Some 5 m wide sections contain more than fifty involutions; others, none.

Within the sand and diamicton assemblage, the tops of sand wedges may be irregular or folded (Murton and French, 1993b). Irregular tops show small-scale features similar to adjacent involutions, for example, load casts and flame structures. Folded tops are restricted to gently sloping terrain and are folded downslope. They are commonly associated with deformed involutions and locally penetrated by vertical ice wedges.

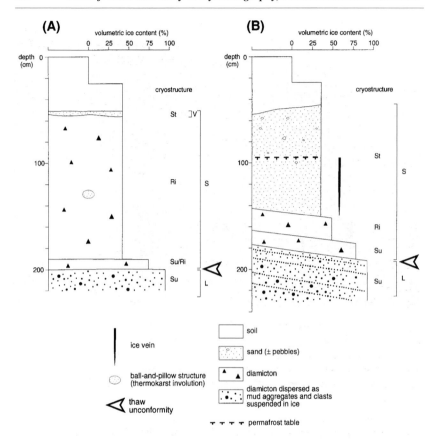

Figure 10.5. *Graphic logs through sand and diamicton cryofacies assemblage (S) and top of the layered assemblage (L), Crumbling Point. Cryostructure codes are shown in Figure 10.2. V = sand veneer. Depth of permafrost table in (a) is not known because the section was examined in early June but is estimated to be ca. 0.4 - 0.7 m, based on measurements of the depth of the late-summer frost table in nearby diamicton-rich sections. The sand in (b) is an oblique section through the top of a sand wedge.*

The base of the assemblage is marked by a sharp, generally planar, horizontal ice contact (Figure 10.6). The contact is locally undulatory, and near to sand wedges, it may be slightly downturned, or near to large ice wedges, upturned. The contact is typically conformable with layers in the underlying assemblage, but in places forms an angular unconformity (Figure 10.6). The contact is at an average depth of *ca.* 1.9-2.0 m beneath flat ground, and *ca.* 2.3 m beneath sloping ground. The contact coincides with discontinuities in cryofacies,

Figure 10.6. *Thaw unconformity (arrow) between the layered cryofacies assemblage (L) and the sand and diamicton assemblage (S), Crumbling Point. Aggradational ice (A; dark grey) within diamicton (light grey) overlies the thaw unconformity. Thermokarst involutions (ball-and-pillow structures of sand (I)) occur within the sand and diamicton assemblage. Section is ca. 1.3 m high.*

cryostructures and oxygen isotopes. Cryofacies beneath the contact are generally more ice-rich than those above it (Figure 10.5). In addition, composite wedges terminate upward at the contact (Murton, 1996c). The cryostructural discontinuity is typically expressed by an abrupt change from small (<1 to *ca.* 10 mm), rounded mud aggregates suspended in ice beneath the contact, to large (few mm to several cm long), angular mud aggregates suspended in, or thinly separated by ice above it (Figure 10.6). Isotopic profiles show an abrupt increase in $\partial^{18}O$ values of ground ice above the contact (Figure 10.7). Ground ice in the layered assemblage is isotopically lighter ($\bar{x} = -29.6^{o}/oo$; $s = 1.1^{o}/oo$; $n = 13$) than that in the sand and diamicton assemblage ($\bar{x} = -24.2^{o}/oo$; $s = 1.1^{o}/oo$; $n = 8$). Ground ice in the latter becomes isotopically heavier towards the modern active layer: Figure 10.7 shows an isotopic trend from $-24.8^{o}/oo$ in ground ice immediately above the contact to $-22.8^{o}/oo$ immediately beneath the active layer.

The cryostratigraphy described above is unrelated to present-day conditions because the modern active layer at Crumbling Point varies in depth from 23 cm to 90 cm (Murton *et al.*, 1995).

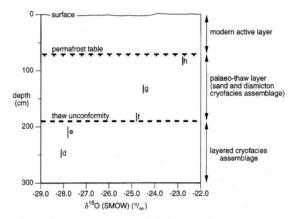

Figure 10.7. *∂18O profile through ground ice in the sand and diamicton assemblage and the top of the underlying layered assemblage, Crumbling Point. The contact between the assemblages (thaw unconformity) coincides with an isotopic discontinuity.*

10.6.3 Interpretation

The sand and diamicton assemblage is attributed to melt-out and deformation during former, active-layer deepening. Downward thaw to greater depths than the base of the present active layer explains the stratigraphic position of the sand and diamicton assemblage above the layered assemblage. Melt-out of diamicton from the layered assemblage would account for the textural similarity between diamicton in both assemblages. Melt-out likely initiated soft-sediment deformation, producing thermokarst involutions and deforming the tops of sand wedges (cf. Murton and French, 1993a, 1993b). Downward thaw probably caused some mixing between meltwater from the layered assemblage and surface water derived mainly from contemporaneous precipitation. Given that the average $\partial^{18}O$ value is -29.6‰ for ground ice in the layered assemblage, and assuming $\partial^{18}O$ values of -14.0‰ to -16.0‰ for latest Wisconsinan- early Holocene precipitation (cf. Michel and Fritz, 1982), then the average $\partial^{18}O$ value of -24.2‰ for the sand and diamicton assemblage is consistent with mixing between these two water sources.

The lower contact of the sand and diamicton assemblage is a thaw unconformity. Thaw is indicated by an angular unconformity with the layered assemblage and by discontinuities in cryofacies, cryostructures and oxygen isotopes. For example, the cryostructural discontinuity (Figure 10.6) probably reflects different conditions of freezing: the ice above the contact is aggradational ice formed by upfreezing associated with a rising permafrost table (cf. Mackay, 1972) and/or repeated [ice] segregation (Cheng, 1983); the ice beneath the contact is of unknown origin. Thaw had probably commenced by *ca.* 11,000-10,400 cal yr BP. This is because AMS ^{14}C dates of 9770 ± 160 14C yr BP (TO-4237) and 9420 ± 110 14C yr BP (TO-4238) have been obtained from *in situ* rootlets in the basal 30 cm of the sand and diamicton assemblage and the upper 60 cm of the underlying ice (Murton *et al.*, 1997). In all probability, the rootlets grew during a time of thaw associated with active-layer deepening.

10.7 CONCLUSIONS

Field description of ice-rich permafrost requires an understanding of ground ice in order to define cryostructures, cryofacies and ice contacts. As illustrated in the case study, these features serve to identify cryostratigraphic units, the interpretation of which permits reconstruction of ground thermal and hydrological conditions, and thus of permafrost history.

At least three avenues of cryostratigraphic research merit further study:

1) development of morphogenetic classifications of cryostructures, as pioneered in Siberia by E. M. Katasonov, to interpret the depositional and freezing histories of Quaternary sediments (e.g. formation of syngenetic permafrost in aggrading fluvial, loessic and colluvial deposits versus formation of epigenetic permafrost in stable substrates);

2) description of more cryostratigraphic sections through ice-rich permafrost, particularly buried glacier ice and frost-susceptible bedrocks (e.g. shales and marly limestones), to assist interpretation of massive ice and icy sediments, and to provide a stronger, comparative basis from which to interpret Pleistocene periglacial sections in the mid-latitudes;

3) experimental work on the preservation potential of relict cryostructures following permafrost degradation, in order to identify relict cryostructures in sequences no longer frozen.

ACKNOWLEDGEMENTS

Fieldwork was supported by The Polar Continental Shelf Project, The Science Institute of the Northwest Territories (now Aurora College) and The Geological Survey of Canada. Constructive comments on the chapter were provided by Professor H. M. French.

REFERENCES

ASTAKHOV, V.I. and ISAYEVA, L.L. 1988. The "Ice Hill"; an example of "retarded deglaciation" in Siberia. *Quaternary Science Reviews*, **7**, 29-40.

BALLANTYNE, C.K. and HARRIS, C. 1994. *The Periglaciation of Great Britain*. Cambridge University Press, Cambridge, 330 pp.

BLACK, R.F. 1983. Three superposed systems of ice wedges at McLeod Point, Northern Alaska, may span most of the Wisconsin stage and Holocene. *IN: Proceedings, Fourth International Conference on Permafrost*, Fairbanks, Alaska, vol. 1, National Academy Press, Washington D.C., 68-73.

BRADLEY, R.S. 1985. *Quaternary Paleoclimatology: Methods of Paleoclimatic Reconstruction*. Allen and Unwin, Boston, 472 pp.

BÜDEL, J. 1982. *Climatic Geomorphology*. Princeton University Press, Princeton, N.J., 443 pp.

BURN, C.R. 1988. The development of near-surface ground ice during the Holocene at sites near Mayo, Yukon Territory, Canada. *Journal of Quaternary Science*, **3**, 31-38.

BURN, C.R. 1997. Cryostratigraphy, paleogeography, and climate change during the early Holocene warm interval, western Arctic coast, Canada. *Canadian Journal of Earth Sciences*, **34**, 912-935.

BURN, C.R., MICHEL, F.A. and SMITH, M.W. 1986. Stratigraphic, isotopic and mineralogical evidence for an early Holocene thaw unconformity at Mayo, Yukon Territory. *Canadian Journal of Earth Sciences*, **23**, 794-803.

CARTER, L.D. 1988. Loess and deep thermokarst basins in Arctic Alaska. *IN: Permafrost, Fifth International Conference, Proceedings, vol. 1*, Tapir, Trondheim, 706-711.

CHENG, G. 1983. The mechanism of repeated segregation for the formation of thick-layered ground ice. *Cold Regions Science and Technology*, **8**, 57-66.

COLLINSON, J.D. and THOMPSON, D.B. 1989. *Sedimentary Structures*. Unwin Hyman, London, 207 pp.

DEMEK, J. 1978. Periglacial geomorphology. *IN*: Embleton, C., Brunsden, D. and Jones, D.K.C. (eds), *Geomorphology: Present Problems and Future Prospects*, 139-155, Oxford University Press, Oxford.

DYKE, A.S. and PREST, V.K. 1987. Paleogeography of northern North America, 18 000-5 000 years ago. *Geological Survey of Canada Map* **1703A**, scale 12 500 000, 1 sheet..

DYLIK, J. 1964. Le thermokarst, phénomène négligé dans les études du Pléistocène. *Annales de Geographie*, **73**, 523-533.

FRENCH, H.M., and HARRY, D.G. 1990. Observations on buried glacier ice and massive segregated ice, western Arctic coast, Canada. *Permafrost and Periglacial Processes*, **1**, 31-43.

FRENCH, H.M., HARRY, D.G. and CLARK, M.J. 1982. Ground ice stratigraphy and late-Quaternary events, southwest Banks Island, Canadian Arctic. *IN*: French, H.M. (ed), *The R.J.E. Brown Memorial Volume, Proceedings of the Fourth Canadian Permafrost Conference*, 81-90. National Research Council of Canada, Ottawa.

FRENCH, H.M., BENNETT, L. and HAYLEY, D.W. 1986. Ground ice conditions near Rea Point and on Sabine Peninsula, eastern Melville Island. *Canadian Journal of Earth Sciences*, **23**, 1389-1400.

GOZDZIK, J.S. 1973. Geneza i pozycja stratygraficzna struktur peryglacjalnych w srodkowej Polsce (Origin and stratigraphical position of periglacial structures in middle Poland). *Acta Geographica Lodziensia*, **31**, 119 pp. (Polish with English summary).

HARRY, D.G. and FRENCH, H.M. 1988. Cryostratigraphic studies of permafrost, Northwestern Canada. *IN: Permafrost, Fifth International Conference, Proceedings, vol. 1*, Tapir, Trondheim, 784-789.

HARRY, D.G., FRENCH, H.M. and POLLARD, W.H. 1985. Ice wedges and permafrost conditions near King Point, Beaufort Sea coast, Yukon Territory. *IN: Current Research, Part A, Geological Survey of Canada, Paper* **85-1A**, 111-116.

JOHNSEN, S.J., DANSGAARD, W. and WHITE, J.W.C. 1989. The origin of Arctic precipitation under present and glacial conditions. *Tellus*, **41B**, 452-468.

JOHNSTON, G.H. 1981. *Permafrost: Engineering Design and Construction*. John Wiley and Sons, Toronto, 540 pp.

KATASONOV, E.M. 1969. Composition and cryogenic structure of permafrost. *IN: Geologische Dienst*, **31-15**, 181-153.

KUDRIAVTSEV, V.A. (ed) 1978. *Obshcheye Merslotovedeniya (Geokriologiya)* (General Permafrost Science) Izd. 2, (edu 2) moskva (Moscow), Izdatel'stvo Moskovskogo Universiteta (Moscow University Editions), 404 pp. (In Russian)

LAWSON, D.E. 1983. Ground ice in perennially frozen sediments, Northern Alaska. *IN: Permafrost: Fourth International Conference, Proceedings*, Fairbanks, Alaska, National Academy Press, Washington D.C., 695-700.

MACKAY, J.R. 1965. Gas-domed mounds in permafrost, Kendall Island, N.W.T. *Geographical Bulletin*, **7**, 105-115.

MACKAY, J.R. 1971. The origin of massive icy beds in permafrost, western Arctic coast, Canada. *Canadian Journal of Earth Sciences*, **8**, 397-422.

MACKAY, J.R. 1972. The world of underground ice. *Annals of the American Association of Geographers*, **62**, 1-22.

MACKAY, J.R. 1974. Reticulate ice veins in permafrost, Northern Canada. *Canadian Geotechnical Journal*, **11**, 230-237.

MACKAY, J.R. 1975. Relict ice wedges, Pelly Island, N.W.T. *IN: Current Research, Part A, Geological Survey of Canada, Paper* **75-1A**, 469-470.

MACKAY, J.R. 1976. Pleistocene permafrost, Hooper Island, Northwest Territories. *IN: Current Research, Part A, Geological Survey of Canada, Paper* **76-1A**, 17-18.

MACKAY, J.R. 1978. Freshwater shelled invertebrate indicators of paleoclimate in northwestern Canada during late glacial times: Discussion. *Canadian Journal of Earth Sciences*, **15**, 461-462.

MACKAY, J.R. 1979. Pingos of the Tuktoyaktuk Peninsula area, Northwest Territories. *Géographie physique et Quaternaire*, **33**, 3-61.

MACKAY, J.R. 1983. Oxygen isotope variations in permafrost, Tuktoyaktuk Peninsula area, Northwest Territories. *IN: Current Research, Part B, Geological Survey of Canada, Paper* **83-1B**, 67-74.

MACKAY, J.R. 1984. The frost heave of stones in the active layer above permafrost, with downward and upward freezing. *Arctic and Alpine Research*, **16**, 439-446.

MACKAY, J.R. 1985. Pingo ice of the western Arctic Coast, Canada. *Canadian Journal of Earth Sciences*, **22**, 1452-1464.

MACKAY, J.R. 1988. Catastrophic lake drainage, Tuktoyaktuk Peninsula area, District of Mackenzie. *IN: Current Research, Part D, Geological Survey of Canada, Paper* **88-1D**, 83-90.

MACKAY, J.R. 1989. Massive ice: some field criteria for the identification of ice types. *IN: Current Research, Part G, Geological Survey of Canada, Paper* **89-1G**, 5-11.

MACKAY, J.R. 1995. Ice wedges on hillslopes and landform evolution in the late Quaternary, western Arctic coast, Canada. *Canadian Journal of Earth Sciences*, **32**, 1093-1105.

MACKAY, J.R. and DALLIMORE, S.R. 1992. Massive ice of the Tuktoyaktuk area, western Arctic coast, Canada. *Canadian Journal of Earth Sciences*, **29**, 1235-1249.

MACKAY, J.R. and LAVKULICH, L.M. 1974. Ionic and oxygen isotopic fractionation in permafrost growth. *IN: Current Research, Part B, Geological Survey of Canada, Paper* **74-1B**, 255-256.

MACKAY, J.R. and MATTHEWS, J.V. Jr. 1983. Pleistocene ice and sand wedges, Hooper Island, Northwest Territories. *Canadian Journal of Earth Sciences*, **20**, 1087-1097.

MICHEL, F.A. and FRITZ, P. 1982. Significance of isotope variations in permafrost waters at Illisarvik, N.W.T. *IN*: French, H.M. (ed), *The R.J.E. Brown Memorial Volume, Proceedings of the Fourth Canadian Permafrost Conference*, 173-181. National Research Council of Canada, Ottawa.

MURTON, J.B. 1996a. Near-surface brecciation of Chalk, Isle of Thanet, southeast England: a comparison with ice-rich brecciated bedrocks in Canada and Spitsbergen. *Permafrost and Periglacial Processes*, **7**, 153-164

MURTON, J.B. 1996b. Thermokarst-lake-basin sediments, Tuktoyaktuk Coastlands, Western Arctic Canada. *Sedimentology*, **43**, 737-760.

MURTON, J.B. 1996c. Morphology and paleoenvironmental significance of Quaternary sand veins, sand wedges, and composite wedges, Tuktoyaktuk Coastlands, Western Arctic Canada. *Journal of Sedimentary Research*, **66**, 17-25.

MURTON, J.B. and FRENCH, H.M. 1993a. Thermokarst involutions, Summer Island, Pleistocene Mackenzie Delta, western Canadian Arctic. *Permafrost and Periglacial Processes*, **4**, 217-229.

MURTON, J.B. and FRENCH, H.M. 1993b. Thaw modification of frost-fissure wedges, Richards Island, Pleistocene Mackenzie Delta, western Canadian Arctic. *Journal of Quaternary Science*, **8**, 185-196.

MURTON, J.B. and FRENCH, H.M. 1993c. Sand wedges and permafrost history, Crumbling Point, Pleistocene Mackenzie Delta, Canada. *IN: Permafrost, Sixth International Conference, Proceedings*, 5-9.07.93, Beijing, China, 482-487. South China University of Technology Press, Wushan Guangzhou.

MURTON, J.B. and FRENCH, H.M. 1994. Cryostructures in permafrost, Tuktoyaktuk Coastlands, Western Arctic Canada. *Canadian Journal of Earth Sciences*, **31**, 737-747.

MURTON, J.B., WHITEMAN, C.A. and ALLEN, P. 1995. Involutions in the Middle Pleistocene (Anglian) Barham Soil, Eastern England: a comparison with thermokarst involutions from arctic Canada. *Boreas*, **24**, 269-280.

MURTON, J.B., FRENCH, H.M. and LAMOTHE, M. 1997. Late Wisconsinan erosion and eolian deposition, Summer Island area, Pleistocene Mackenzie Delta, Northwest Territories: optical dating and implications for glacial chronology. *Canadian Journal of Earth Sciences*, **34**, 190-199.

NATIONAL ACADEMY OF SCIENCES, 1974. *Priorities for Basic Research on Permafrost.* National Academy of Sciences, Washington D.C., 54 pp.

PENNER, E. 1972. Soil moisture redistribution by ice lensing in freezing soils. *IN: Proceedings 17th Annual Meeting*, Canadian Society of Soil Science, Lethbridge, Alberta, July 1971, 44-62.

PERMAFROST SUBCOMMITTEE, ASSOCIATE COMMITTEE ON GEOTECHNICAL RESEARCH, 1988. *Glossary of Permafrost and Related Ground-ice Terms*, National Research Council of Canada, Technical Memorandum **142**, 156 pp.

PÉWÉ, T.L. 1975. *Quaternary Geology of Alaska*. United States Geological Survey, Professional Paper **835**, 145 pp.

RAMPTON, V.N. 1974. The influence of ground ice and thermokarst upon the geomorphology of the Mackenzie-Beaufort region. *IN*: Fahey, B.D and Thompson, R.D. (eds), *Research in Polar and Alpine Geomorphology*, Proceedings of the Third Guelph Symposium on Geomorphology, Geo-Abstracts, Norwich, 43-59.

RAMPTON, V.N. 1988. *Quaternary Geology of the Tuktoyaktuk Coastlands, Northwest Territories*. Geological Survey of Canada, Memoir **423**, 98 pp.

RAMPTON, V.N. and MACKAY, J.R. 1971. Massive ice and icy sediments throughout the Tuktoyaktuk Peninsula, Richards Island, and nearby areas, District of Mackenzie. *Geological Survey of Canada, Paper* **71-21**, 16 pp.

READING, H. G. 1986. Facies. *IN*: Reading, H.G. (ed), *Sedimentary Environments and Facies*, 4-19. Blackwell, Oxford.

RITCHIE, J.C. 1984. *Past and Present Vegetation of the Far Northwest of Canada*. University of Toronto Press, Toronto, 251 pp.

ROSE, J., BOARDMAN, J., KEMP, R.A. and WHITEMAN, C.A. 1985. Palaeosols and their interpretation of the British Quaternary stratigraphy. *IN*: Richards, K.S., Arnett, R.R. and Ellis, S. (eds), *Geomorphology and Soils*, 348-375. George Allen and Unwin, London.

SELLMANN, P.V. and BROWN, J. 1973. Stratigraphy and diagenesis of perennially frozen sediments in the Barrow region, Alaska. *IN*: *Permafrost; North American Contribution to the Second International Conference,* Yakutsk, USSR, National Academy Press, Washington D.C., 177-181.

SEPPÄLÄ, M. 1986. The origin of palsas. *Geografiska Annaler*, **68A**, 141-147.

SHER, A.V., KAPLINA, T.N., GITERMAN, R.E., LOZHKIN, A.V., ARKHANGELOV, A.A., KISELYOV, S.V., KOUZNETSOV, YU. V., VIRINA, E.I. and ZAZHIGIN, V.S. 1979. *Late Cenozoic of the Kolyma Lowland*. Tour XI Guidebook, XIV Pacific Science Congress, August 1979, Khaborovsk, Academy of Sciences, USSR, Moscow, 115 pp.

SHUMSKII, P.A. 1964. *Ground (subsurface) Ice*. National Research Council of Canada, Technical Translation **1130**, 118 pp.

TABER, S. 1929. Frost heaving. *Journal of Geology*, **37**, 428-461.

TAYLOR, A.E., DALLIMORE, S.R. and JUDGE, A.S. 1996. Late Quaternary history of the Mackenzie-Beaufort region, Arctic Canada, from modelling of permafrost temperatures. 2. The Mackenzie Delta - Tuktoyaktuk Coastlands. *Canadian Journal of Earth Sciences*, **33**, 62-71.

VANDENBERGHE, J. and VAN DEN BROEK, P. 1982. Weichselian convolution phenomena and processes in fine sediments. *Boreas*, **11**, 299-315.

VANDENBERGHE, J. and PISSART, A. 1993. Permafrost changes in Europe during the last glacial. *Permafrost and Periglacial Processes*, **4**, 121-135.

VAN DER HAMMEN, T., MAARLEVELD, G.C., VOGEL, J.C. and ZAGWIJN, W.H. 1967. Stratigraphy, climatic succession and radiocarbon dating of the last glacial in the Netherlands. *Geologie en Mijnbouw*, **46**, 79-95.

VAN VLIET-LANOË, B. 1996. Relations entre la contraction thermique des sols en Europe du Nord-Ouest et la dynamique de l'inlandsis weichsélien. *C.R. Académie des Sciences Paris*, t.**322**, série II a, 461-468.

WORSLEY, P. 1987. Permafrost stratigraphy in Britain: a first approximation. *IN*: Boardman, J. (ed), *Periglacial Processes in Britain and Ireland*, 89-99. Cambridge University Press, Cambridge.

Chapter 11

COASTAL STRATIGRAPHY: A CASE STUDY FROM JOHNS RIVER, WASHINGTON, U.S.A.

Antony J. Long, James B. Innes, Ian Shennan, and Michael J. Tooley

11.1 INTRODUCTION

At the height of the last glaciation eighteen thousand years ago, sea level was up to *ca.* 120 m below its current level (e.g. Barbados, Fairbanks, 1989); extensive tracts of the world's continental shelves were exposed to subaerial processes, and land bridges connected countries and continents that are now separated by sea. As the ice sheets melted and water returned to the oceans, so sea level rose, flooding the continental shelves and reworking their sediment mantles. The record of sea-level change since this time has varied and many regional factors, such as glacio-isostasy and the effects of hydro-isostatic loading, sediment supply and climate change have modified the underlying global trend (e.g. Clarke *et al.*, 1978, Pirazzoli, 1991, Lambeck, 1993). A physical manifestation of these changes in relative sea level (RSL) is preserved in the coastal stratigraphic record. Although it is now routine to employ an array of laboratory analytical techniques to complement and extend field stratigraphic data, nevertheless careful and systematic field descriptions still lie at the heart of many Quaternary coastal studies.

This Chapter provides a review of the techniques of stratigraphic data collection from free-face sections and boreholes, focusing on the Troels-Smith (1955) scheme of sediment description. An example is provided of this scheme in operation, with reference to a recent investigation of the coastal sediments recorded in Johns River, Washington, U.S.A. (Shennan *et al.*, 1996).

11.2 FREE-FACE SECTIONS AND BOREHOLES

Natural free-face sections in which more than a few metres of Holocene intertidal sediment are exposed are unusual in the UK, being restricted to areas with a high tidal range (such as in the Severn Estuary). Free-face exposures are much more common during deep excavations for construction work. Notable examples of the latter include the early descriptions of the Thames Holocene sequences made by Whitaker (1899) and Spurrell (1899) during the construction of the London Docks, and more recently the work of Devoy (1979) undertaken during the building of the Dartford Tunnel. Indeed, all the pioneering work of the Geological Survey of the United Kingdom in the nineteenth century (Reid, 1913) was done from open-face engineering excavations or ditch sections, for example de Rance (1869) and Reade (1871) in north-west England. Face sections allow examination of the lateral and vertical relationship between different facies, often over tens or hundreds of metres (e.g.

Allen, 1987). They enable the identification of stratigraphic anomalies and also facilitate the easy collection of large sediment samples for laboratory analysis (such as required for plant macrofossil analysis). Where larger sections are exposed, such as in some of the dykes of the East Anglian Fenland, a more expansive approach to field data collection may be possible. In these cases, a level and staff can be used to trace the height of the main stratigraphic units over several kilometres (e.g. Godwin, 1940, Waller, 1994). The choice between the collection of extensive or intensive stratigraphic descriptions involves a compromise between, on the one hand, generating palaeogeographic information at a landscape scale, and on the other, collecting very detailed local information from a single site. Ideally, a combination of both techniques of data collection should be employed; lengthy sections or borehole transects, supplemented by detailed stratigraphic descriptions of representative sections and/or sample cores chosen for further laboratory analysis.

Unless commissioned (such as in archaeological investigations at some expense), face sections tend to be in areas not ideal for the scientific programme in hand. For this reason, hand coring using a gouge sampler is the most frequent way in which coastal stratigraphic data are collected, certainly in Northwest Europe at least (e.g. Tooley, 1974, 1978; Shennan, 1986, Plater, 1992, Waller, 1994). The technique provides a flexible, cheap and relatively rapid means of obtaining stratigraphic data to depths of *ca.* 10 m below ground surface (for details of different corers, see Tooley (1981)). The sampling interval between cores will depend on the degree of stratigraphic variability present and the objectives of the study. In some cases, laterally persistent stratigraphic units may allow a sampling interval between cores of 100 m (e.g. Long and Innes, 1995); in others where stratigraphic variability is high, the interval may be <1 m (e.g. van de Plassche, 1995). However, gouge coring is not without its problems, the more common of which include: i) contamination of sediment in the open chamber during recovery; ii) loss of sediment from the corer (especially very wet near-surface salt marsh sediment or saturated sand); iii) depth measurement error due to non-vertical coring and/or rod bending; iv) compaction of soft sediments; and v) non-penetration of some deposits (sands/gravel/wood).

11.3 STRATIGRAPHIC DESCRIPTIONS

Any scheme for the stratigraphic description of coastal sediments must be broad enough to cover the range of organic and inorganic deposits likely to be encountered, flexible enough to allow quantification of the separate components of what may be a heterogeneous deposit, and yet simple enough not to hinder extensive data collection. Many schemes have been proposed, and their merits debated (West 1968, Walker and James, 1992). One scheme which fulfils these criteria and which is commonly used by coastal stratigraphers (and other Quaternary scientists) is that proposed by Troels-Smith (1955), although this itself is a simplified version of the earlier scheme of Granlund and von Post (1926). The Troels-

Smith scheme (see Section 2.2) is based on the semi-objective classification of unconsolidated sediments according to a tried and tested set of guidelines which, once learnt, are easy and quick to use. The scheme is descriptive and independant of any knowledge of depositional processes, and its structured approach enables direct comparison of results collected by different investigators. Its logical structure also makes it ideal for use with students, requiring them to examine in detail the various physical attributes of the sediment under investigation. It requires almost no field equipment.

11.4 FIELD SAFETY

Field safety (see Section 3.1.1) must be carefully addressed before embarking on any programme of stratigraphic data collection. In the UK, the Health and Safety Executive issues guidelines covering aspects of this type of work, but the coastal zone has its own peculiar set of field dangers which include; the remoteness of some sites, rapid tidal changes, soft sediments from which it can be difficult to extract oneself, unstable cliff and creek sections, as well as sediment and water pollutants. Work should never be conducted alone. Additional dangers can arise during handling of heavy sampling equipment and incorrect lifting posture can easily cause injury - back problems are no indicator of age amongst the Quaternary fraternity!

11.5 PROCEDURE

The procedure for field stratigraphic descriptions using the Troels-Smith scheme is discussed here with reference to a hypothetical face section (see Section 3.1.1).

Stage 1
Before commencing, ensure that all necessary safety precautions are adhered to (see above). Once a section has been identified, cut it as near vertically as possible, or in steps, and clean the section face with a spade, flat trowel, knife or spatula, working across the face from the top downwards to avoid contamination. It is useful to photograph the sequence at this point, including an appropriate scale.

Stage 2
Visually identify discrete stratigraphic units or layers and mark on the face using a blade, pins or pegs. If time and access permit, a grid of string may be hung across the sediment face to allow the drawing of an accurate field sketch (see Tooley, 1981). Alternatively, a baseline can be levelled and unit boundaries measured relative to this baseline. The latter has the advantage of being relatively quick, something which is sometimes necessary where work can only be undertaken between tides.

Name	Code	Sediment type	Field characteristics
Argilla steatodes	As	Clay <0.002mm	May be rolled into a thread < or = 2mm diameter without breaking. Plastic when wet, hard when dry.
Argilla granosa	Ag	Silt 0.06-0.002mm	Will not roll into thread without splitting. Will rub into dust on drying (such as on hands). Gritty on back of teeth.
*Grana minora**	Gmin	Fine, medium and coarse sand (0.06-2.0mm)	Crunchy between teeth. Lacks cohesion when dry. Grains visible to naked eye.
*Grana majora**	Gmaj	Fine, medium and coarse gravel (2-60mm)	
Testae (molluscorum)	test.(moll)	Whole mollusc shells	
Particulae testarum (molluscorum)	part. test. (moll)	Shell fragments	
Substantia humosa	Sh	Humified organics beyond identification	Fully distintegrated deposit lacking macroscopic structure, usually dark brown or black.
Turfa herbacea	Th^{0-4}	Roots, stems and rhizomes of herbaceous plants	Can be seen vertically aligned or matted within sediment in growth position.
Turfa bryophytica	Tb^{0-4}	The protonema, rhizods, stems, leaves etc. of mosses	Can be seen vertically aligned or matted within sediment in growth position.
Turfa lignosa	Tl^{0-4}	The roots and stumps of woody plants and their trunks, branches and twigs.	Can be seen vertically aligned or layered within sediment in growth position.
Detritus lignosus	Dl	Detrital fragments of wood and bark >2mm	Non-vertical or random alignment. may be laminated, not in growth position.
Detritus herbosus	Dh	Fragments of stems and leaves of herbaceous plants >2mm	Non-vertical or random alignment. may be laminated, not in growth position.
Detritus granosus	Dg	Woody and herbaceous humified plant remains <2mm >0.1mm that cannot be separated.	Non-vertical or random alignment. may be laminated, not in growth position.
Limus detrituosus	Ld^{0-4}	Fine detritus organic mud (particles <0.1mm).	Homogeneous, non-plastic, often becomes darker on oxidation and will shrink on drying. Most shades of colour.
Limus ferrugineus	Lf	Mineral and/or organic iron oxide	Forms mottled staining. Can be crushed between fingers. Often in root channels or surrounding Th.
Anthrax	Anth	Charcoal	Crunchy black fragments
Stirpes	Stirp	Tree stump	
Stratum confusum	Sc	Disturbed stratum	

Table 11.1. *A selective list of the commonest sediment types recorded in coastal sediments (after Troels-Smith (1955)) incorporating the modifications (denoted by *) suggested by Aaby and Berglund (1986).*

Stage 3

Record the depth and nature of the upper and lower boundary, which can be either sharp or diffuse, of each stratigraphic unit and number in ascending order from the base of the sequence. Having cut a block of sediment from the face, break open horizontally and vertically to determine the sediment composition and structure (see below). Using waterproof paper is a help here, especially when working with wet sediment, and ensures that the field notes can be deciphered on return to the laboratory.

Stage 4

Further examine the sediment sample and describe its physical components. The most common sediment types encountered in coastal stratigraphic sequences are listed in Table 11.1, together with their abbreviated code for field use and ways in which they can be identified. The components are given descriptive Latin names in order to avoid confusion with other classification schemes and to allow universal application.

In the Troels-Smith (1955) scheme each layer is characterised by its components and physical properties. The components of a layer are recorded on a 4 point scale, where 1 is 25% and 4 is 100% of the layer. Thus, a peat which comprises 100% herbaceous roots with attached stems and leaves (*turfa*) would be recorded as Th4, whereas a peat with 50% clay and 50% herbaceous stems and roots as As2, Th2. Additional minor components (<25%) which do not contribute to the main component totals can be recorded by a '+'. For organic deposits, the degree of humification is also recorded on a five point scale as a superscript from 0 (no humification) to 4 (totally humified) (Table 11.2). Hence, partly humified but distinct plant structures in a peat comprising 100% *turfa* would be described as $Th^2 4$. Troels-Smith (1955) provided a guideline for assessing the degree of humification based on the colour of the liquid released by sediment on squeezing, as well as the strength of the material (see Table 11.2). Colourless water yielded after squeezing indicates a humification value of 0, whereas a turbid liquid characterises value 3. Humification provides a rough indicator of sediment oxidation, which in coastal sequences may point to a lowering of the watertable, and perhaps also sea level.

Stage 5

Describe the physical properties of the sediment. Here information regarding the degree of darkness (or *nigror*) of the sediment, its stratification (*stratificatio*), dryness (*siccitas*), and its elasticity (*elasticitas*) are recorded. As with the component descriptions, each physical attribute is measured on a scale from 0 to 4 (Figure 11.1). Unless already done in stage 3, record the nature of the lithological contact between the unit under examination and the one immediately above (*limes superior*) on a 0 to 4 scale (Figure 11.1). The Troels-Smith scheme provides no formal guidance in contact description beyond this simple five point scale, and where face sections are available, an expanded description of the contact, for example how it varies laterally, can be made in the written summary which accompanies each unit. Colour should also be noted using a Munsel Soil Colour Chart. The general structure of the sediment, whether granular, laminar, fibrous or felted, and how plastic or cohesive, may also be recorded, although the scheme is relatively poor in this respect.

Humicity	Comment
0	Plant structure fresh. Yields colourless water on squeezing.
1	Plant structure well-preserved. Squeezing yields dark coloured water. 25% deposit squeezes through fingers.
2	Plant structure partially decayed though distinct. Squeezing yields 50% deposit through fingers.
3	Plant structure decayed and indistinct. Squeezing yields 75% deposit through fingers.
4	Plant structure barely discernable or absent. 100% passes through fingers on squeezing.

Table 11.2. Key for the measurement of humicity (after Troels-Smith (1955)).

Stage 6
Lastly, a written description of the sediment can be added, providing any further descriptive information not already described, such as bedding structures.

The Troels-Smith scheme is, on the whole, relatively easy to learn and administer. However, there are a few areas of difficulty where care is required, the most common being in the identification of *Limus* and the classification of some of the more humified organic deposits. For example, the term *Limus detrituosus*, (Ld¹ to Ld³), is a non-generic term used to describe an homogeneous organic deposit of microscopic structure with a varying admixture of humous substance. Its most humified form Ld⁴ - termed *Limus humosus*, however, refers to a deposit which is generally inelastic, very greasy and adhesive, and consists entirely of a humous substance. Troels-Smith (1955) explicitly uses *Limus humosus* to describe a water-lain organic mud (termed dy), and therefore the term is generic (which is contrary to the spirit of the scheme). Another term, *Substantia humosa*, also describes a fully disintegrated organic deposit which lacks macrofossil structure, and this definition clearly overlaps with that for *Limus humosus*, which is composed fundamentally of *Substantia humosa*. Where this particular uncertainty occurs, Troels-Smith (1955) recommended that *S. humosa* (which does not presuppose depositional origin) is used, at least until laboratory analysis can further determine the depositional origin of the sediment in question. In the field, distinction between Ld and Sh may be very difficult, but disaggregation of the sediment in KOH may provide a good indication, *Substantia humosa* virtually dissolving and staining the liquid, *Limus detrituosus* falling slowly from suspension.

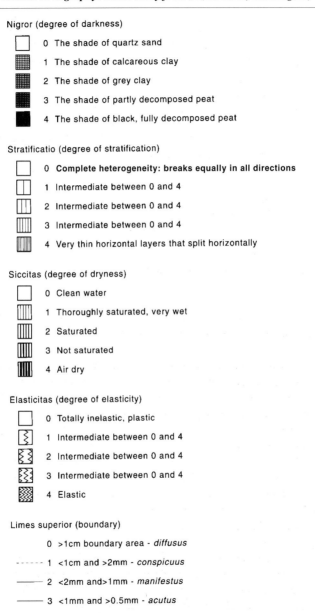

Figure 11.1. *Physical properties of a sediment, as well as boundary classifications (after Troels-Smith (1955)). The symbols representative of each element are also shown.*

Another problem with the scheme is that the size classifications for the mineral sediments originally proposed by Troels-Smith (1955) are now out of date. Aaby and Berglund (1986) have addressed this issue by revising this part of the scheme by i) combining *Grana arenosa* and *Grana saburralia* (fine and coarse sand) as *Grana minora* (0.06 to 2.0 mm), and ii) combining *Grana glareosa minora* and *Grana glareosa majora* as *Grana majora* (2.0 to 60 mm).

Finally, in some cases the guidelines provided by Troels-Smith for classifying the physical characteristics of a sediment are at best general (Figure 11.1). For example, an *elasticitas* of 1, 2 or 3 is defined as being intermediate between *elasticitas* 0 (totally inelastic) and 4 (fully elastic) - hardly the most explicit definition! Whilst appearing vague on paper, in the field one quickly develops the ability to discriminate between these levels, but this is one example of how the Troels-Smith scheme is never purely objective. Indeed, Troels-Smith (1955, p.43) clearly recognised this subjectivity when, in providing an introduction to the scheme, he stated "It is important to emphasize that this is not a question of exact characterization, but of non-quantitative estimation....As a result identical conditions may be estimated more or less differently in practice, not only by different investigators, but also by the individual investigator at different times".

One of the appealing features of the Troels-Smith scheme is a key which allows graphical quantification of the original stratigraphic data. Although strict adherence to this part of the scheme is rare (e.g. Tooley and Switsur, 1988), partly due to difficulties in reproduction and interpretation of densely overlaid symbols (e.g. Tooley, 1978a, Long and Tooley, 1995), nevertheless a simplified scheme such as that developed by Everett and Shennan (1987) and more recently by Waller *et al.* (1995) enables a quantifiable link to be made between the original field descriptions and the stratigraphic plots. A lithostratigraphic option which produces high-quality overlain Troels-Smith symbols is also available in the TILIA plotting program of Grimm (1993).

11.6 CASE STUDY: COASTAL STATIGRAPHY IN WESTERN NORTH AMERICA

Alternating organic and clastic deposits, termed peat and mud in the North American literature, are found in many estuaries in Washington and Oregon and have been interpreted as evidence for the repeated earthquakes connected to the accumulation and release of strain on the Cascadia subduction zone (e.g. Atwater, 1987, 1992, Darienzo and Peterson, 1990, Darienzo *et al.*, 1994, Nelson, 1992). The pattern of land- and sea-level movements accompanying these earthquakes is described by the 'earthquake deformation cycle' which has two stages. Stage one involves RSL fall as strain accumulation causes land uplift. Coastal wetlands become infilled with sediment during this period and widespread marsh development occurs. This is followed (Stage 2) by strain release and coseismic subsidence, which causes sudden RSL rise and drowning of the coastal marshes. In some instances, thin sand layers immediately above the peats suggest tsunami sedimentation accompanying coseismic subsidence (Atwater, 1987, Darienzo and Peterson, 1990). Spatial and temporal correlation of these deposits has enabled estimates to made of the timing (Atwater *et al.*, 1991), recurrence interval (Darienzo and Peterson, 1990, Atwater and Hemphill-Haley, 1996) and magnitude (Atwater, 1992, Nelson, 1992, Mathewes and Clague, 1994) of Holocene earthquakes along the Cascadia subduction zone.

Previous stratigraphic descriptions in Washington and Oregon have been collected in a non-standard manner, with individual authors developing their own schemes of sediment description and display. In Atwater's (1987) seminal paper, for example, the different stratigraphic units identified in his gouge cores and sections are depicted using a series of symbols (squares, triangles, circles etc.) positioned against vertical lines which represent the borehole locations. In contrast, Nelson (1992) used a combination of lithofacies codes developed by fluvial and glacial sedimentologists, as well as some from the Troels-Smith (1955) scheme. Nelson (1992) argued that this combination of codes and symbols allows better identification of lithofacies changes, especially those recorded by thin (<10 cm) but important stratigraphic units.

It was the clear need for the standardisation of sediment description and classification in Northwest Europe which prompted Troels-Smith (1955) to develop his scheme of symbols and notation. In the following section we use the Troels-Smith scheme to present a simplified model of contemporary and fossil sedimentary environments in Washington and Oregon. We then describe and interpret a stratigraphic log collected during part of a recent study of the coastal stratigraphy recorded at Johns River, Washington (Shennan *et al.*, 1996) using the Troels-Smith scheme.

11.6.1 Contemporary and Fossil Environments

Figure 11.2 is a schematic representation of the contemporary and fossil environments present in the estuaries of Washington and Oregon States. This type of stratigraphic sequence is superficially similar to that found on passive coastal margins, such as those of Eastern North America and Northwest Europe. However, a closer inspection reveals a number of features which, although not in themselves peculiar to the coastal stratigraphy of Washington and Oregon, have in association been attributed to the earthquake deformation cycle (Long and Shennan, 1994, Nelson *et al.*, 1996). These features include:

1) abrupt stratigraphic contacts (often *Limes superior* 4) between the peats and overlying clastic sediments, contrast gradational contacts (*Limes superior* 0 or 1) between the base of the peats and the underlying sediment. This stratigraphic asymmetry suggests gradual

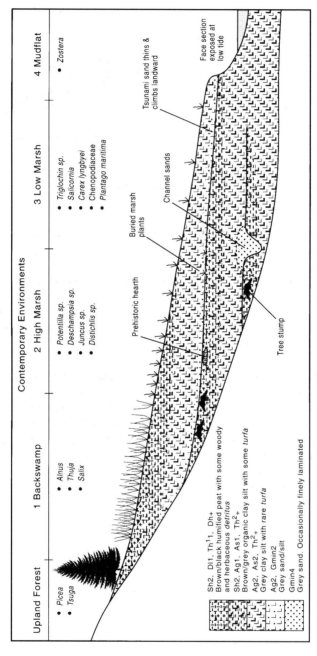

Figure 11.2. *Schematic diagram of contemporary and fossil sedimentary environments recorded in the coastal marshes of Washington and Oregon. The stratigraphic symbols used are based on the Troels-Smith (1955) scheme. Physical characteristics are not included, since they are likely to vary spatially.*

emergence followed by sudden drowning, as predicted by the earthquake deformation cycle (see above).

2) thin units of sand or coarse silt may occur immediately above the peat. These have been interpreted as possible tsunami deposits which accompanied coseismic subsidence.

3) rooted stems of saltmarsh plants with still attached leaves (*Turfa herbacea*) may extend from the peat tops into the overlying minerogenic sediments. The good macrofossil preservation suggests rapid inundation and burial by sediment (Atwater and Yamaguchi, 1992).

4) peats rise in altitude towards the pre-Holocene surface but do not coalesce. This implies rapid submergence of the entire marsh accompanying coseismic subsidence.

5) well-preserved outer rings in trees rooted in the upper parts of buried peats also suggest rapid submergence and burial with sediment.

6) presence of sand dykes caused by strong ground shaking and liquefaction (Atwater, 1992).

11.6.2 Johns River, Washington

Shennan *et al.* (1996) examined the late-Holocene sea-level history at Johns River, a small estuary which drains into Grays Harbour, Washington (Figure 11.3). A combination of gouge cores and face section descriptions establish the sedimentary architecture of the study area. In total, eight buried peats are identified (JR93 I-VIII). The following section focuses on the lithostratigraphy of the top five of these peats (JR93 I-V) exposed in a bank section (JR93-1) located on the west side of Johns River. The detailed stratigraphic description of the face section is provided in Table 11.3, and a graphical summary of these data using the Troels-Smith symbols is provided in Figure 11.4.

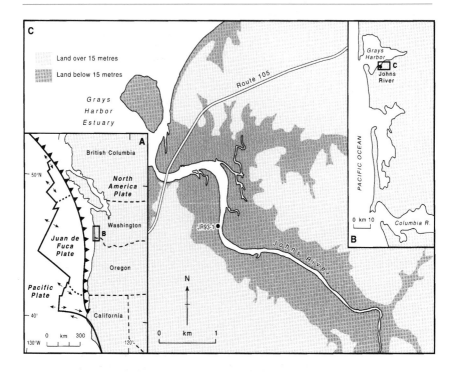

Figure 11.3. *Site map of Johns River, Washington, showing the location of the sample site described in the text, JR93-1.*

11.6.3 Interpretation

JR93-V

The lower sediments (Unit 1-4) record a progressive transition from predominantly inorganic to organic sediments. Comparison with contemporary depositional environments (Figure 11.2) suggests that this change reflects a transition from a low marsh or mudflat to a high marsh. Unit 4 is abruptly overlain (*Limes superior* 4) by a clayey silt with some *Limus ferrugineus* and *Turfa herbacea* (Unit 5). Similar abrupt changes in lithostratigraphy occur elsewhere in Washington and Oregon and are interpreted as evidence for coseismic subsidence and the instantaneous lowering of the marsh surface into the intertidal zone (see above).

JR93-IV

Unit 5 fines upwards into a clayey silt with some *Turfa herbacea* (Unit 6) and then an organic clay with silt (Unit 7). Although the organic content of Unit 7 does not exceed

Depth	Unit	Description
41-69	18	$Ag3$, $As1$, Th^2+, $Lf+$, nig.2, strf.0, elas.0, sicc.2 lim.sup.0 Blue grey clayey silt with herbaceous roots and iron staining.
69-75	17	$Th^3 2$, $Sh1$, $Ag1$, nig.4, strf.0, elas.0, sicc.2 lim.sup.4 Black *turfa* peat with some humous substance and silt.
75-79	16	$Sh2$, $Ag2$, Th^2+, nig.3, strf.0, elas.0, sicc.2 lim.sup.0 Silty humous substance with herbaceous roots.
79-109	15	$As2$, $Ag2$, Th^2+, $Lf+$, nig.2, strf.0, elas.0, sicc.2 lim.sup.0 Blue grey clayey silt with herbaceous roots and iron staining.
109-113	14	$As3$, $Ag1$, $Sh+$, Th^2+, nig.2, strf.0, elas.0, sicc.2 lim.sup.4 Silty clay with humous material and herbaceous roots.
113-145	13	$As2$, $Ag2$, Th^2+, nig.2, strf.0, elas.0, sicc.2 lim.sup.0 Blue grey silty clay with herbaceous roots
145-156	12	$Ag4$, Th^2+, nig.2, strf.0, elas.0, sicc.2 lim.sup.0 Blue grey silt with herbaceous roots
156-160	11	$Ag4$, $Gmin+$, Th^2+, $Dh+$, nig.2+, strf.0, elas.0, sicc.2 lim.sup.2 Blue grey slightly sandy silt with herbaceous roots and rare herbaceous detritus.
160-172	10	$Th^3 1$, $Sh2$, $Ag1$, nig.4, strf.0, elas.0, sicc.2 lim.sup.4 Black *turfa* peat with humous material and silt.
172-178	9	$Ag2$, $As1$, $Sh1$, Th^3+, nig.2, strf.0, elas.0, sicc.2 lim.sup.0 Grey humous material with clay, silt and herbaceous roots.
178-209	8	$Ag3$, $As1$, Th^2+, $Lf+$, nig.2, strf.0, elas.0, sicc.2 lim.sup.0 Blue grey clayey silt with herbaceous roots and some iron staining.
209-212	7	$As3$, $Ag1$, $Sh+$, Th^3+, nig.2, strf.0, elas.0, sicc.2 lim.sup.4 Organic silty clay with rare herbaceous roots.
212-239	6	$Ag2$, $As2$, Th^3+, nig.2, strf.0, elas.0, sicc.2 lim.sup.0 Blue grey clayey silt with herbaceous roots.
239-257	5	$Ag3$, $As1$, $Gmin+$, Th^2+, $Lf+$, nig.2, strf.0, elas.0, sicc.2 lim.sup.0 Grey slightly sandy clay silt with rare roots and some iron staining.
257-264	4	$Th^3 2$, $Sh1$, $Ag1$, nig.4, strf.0, elas.0, sicc.2 lim.sup.0 Black *turfa* peat with humous substance and some silt.
264-271	3	$Sh2$, $Ag1$, $Th^3 1$, nig.3, strf.0, elas.0, sicc.2 lim.sup.0 Silty organic material with some herbaceous roots.
271-274	2	$Sh2$, $Ag2$, Th^3+, nig.3, strf.0, elas.0, sicc.2 lim.sup.0 Silty organic material with some herbaceous roots.
274-277	1	$Ag3$, $As1$, $Sh+$, Th^2+, nig.2, strf.0, elas.0, sicc.2 lim.sup.0 Blue grey clayey silt with rare herbaceous roots.

Table 11.3. Partial stratigraphic log from a free-face section exposed at Johns River, Washington (JR93-1), described using the Troels-Smith (1955) scheme of stratigraphic notation.

25%, nevertheless the change from Unit 5 to Unit 7 indicates a fining-upwards sequence suggestive of progressive shallowing, sediment accumulation and the development of a low marsh. Unit 7 is abruptly overlain by a 31 cm thick silt with some clay, indicating sudden submergence and an increase in tidal energy. Assessing the magnitude of submergence here is difficult in the absence of further macro or microfossil data. For example, in other studies (e.g. Atwater, 1987), the presence of *Triglochin* remains in the mineral-rich sediments above the high marsh peat have been used to infer RSL rise of at least 0.5 to 2 m.

JR93-III
Above Units 7 and 8 is a further transition to organic sediments enriched in *Turfa herbacea* (Units 9 and 10). This suggests the development of high marsh once more. Unit 10 is abruptly overlain by a 4 cm unit of sandy silt (Unit 11) containing *Turfa herbacea* and *Detritus herbosus*. The contact between Unit 10 and 11 is not transitional (*Limes superior* 4) and the end of peat accumulation appears sudden with a marked reduction in organic sedimentation, probably due to an increase in water depth and tidal energy at the sample site. The presence of *Turfa herbacea* in Unit 11 indicates initial deposition in a low marsh or upper mudflat environment.

JR93-II
Units 11-14 record a sequence of sediments similar to that described for JR93-IV. Organic enrichment never exceeds 25% of the sediment by volume, but the presence of *Turfa herbacea* and *Substantia humosa*, together with an accompanying progressive reduction in grain size, suggests a gradual removal of marine conditions and the development of a low marsh. As for JR93-IV, the upper contact of Unit 14 is abrupt (*Limes superior* 4) but in this instance the accompanying change in grain size is less pronounced than previously recorded. Unit 15 is a grey clayey silt with herbaceous roots, and probably accumulated in a mudflat environment.

JR93-I
The uppermost part of the section includes one more peat abruptly buried by intertidal sediments (Units 15 to 18). The change in lithostratigraphy recorded here is similar to that described above, with the lower mineral-rich sediments becoming increasingly enriched in organic matter. The high percentage of organic matter including *Turfa herbacea* in Unit 17 (Th^{3}2, Sh1) suggests that a high marsh developed on the site. The transition to Unit 18 is abrupt (Limes superior 4) and the overlying sediment is a clayey silt with some *Turfa herbacea*, indicating sediment accumulation in low marsh or mudflat conditions.

11.6.4 Comparison of Troels-Smith and Laboratory Results

The Troels-Smith scheme was designed to provide a reliable field estimate of the relative proportions of the major sediment components of a deposit and to record the presence of the minor components. It was never intended to supersede accurate laboratory measurement as a scientific method for detailed sediment analysis. At their different scales of resolution, however, both methods should yield broadly compatible results. It is interesting, therefore, to compare the Troels-Smith description of the Johns River lithological section shown in Table 11.3 with the results of particle size analyses (PSA) and loss on ignition measurements (LOI) made on the same sediments in the laboratory, which are shown as Figure 11.4.

The most significant contrast within the deposit is in the relative proportions of organic and fine-grained clastic sediment. The PSA results show that within the predominantly clastic sediments, which account for the great majority of the section, there is a consistent background organic component of about 10% of the total. The Troels-Smith description agrees well with this, and in every stratigraphic unit a trace of organic material is recorded, usually as *Turfa herbacea*. Some discrepancy occurs, however, with the description of highly organic marsh peats. In the field the Troels-Smith notation recorded 75% organic sediments, whereas the LOI results show the organic component of these peats to be 50% at best. The most likely explanation for this difference is that the Troels-Smith scheme describes sediment by volume, whereas the LOI and PSA data are based on weight. Thus, clastic sediments may represent a high proportion of the deposit by weight, but a comparatively small proportion by volume.

Within the clastic components there is generally good agreement between the field and laboratory descriptions, given that percentage fluctuations of ten to fifteen percent are too small to be recognised at the scale of resolution of the Troels-Smith scheme and peaks in the LOI data at individual levels are meaningless in relation to the Troels-Smith signatures. Where silt (Ag) is the dominant component the degree of comparability between description and analysis is very high, as in Units 1, 5, 11, 12 and 18 for example. Where clay (As) is substantial, however, it has tended to be overestimated. In Unit 6 for example, As has been described as half of the sediment whereas the LOI data show it in reality to comprise only about 35%, or in Unit 14 where the field description has it as three quarters but in reality it is only 30%. While the relative clastic proportions recorded using the Troels-Smith scheme may on occasion be inaccurate, however, the trend of change within the Ag/As ratio is always correctly described, and in agreement with, rises and falls in the LOI pecentage data. Interpretation of changes in the sedimentary environment are therefore consistent under both methods.

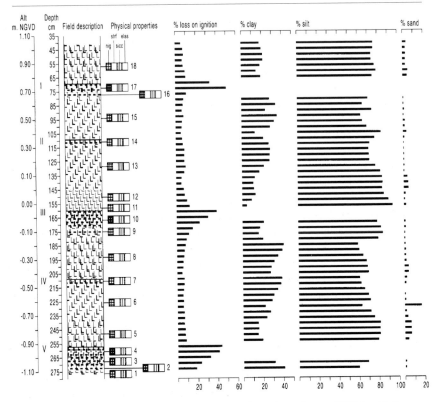

Figure 11.4. *Stratigraphic profile of the exposed creek section at JR93-1 with loss on ignition and particle size data. Stratigraphic symbols are after Troels-Smith (1955). Each buried soil is numbered I-V. NGVD is the National Geodetic Vertical Datum of the U.S.A.*

11.7 CONCLUSIONS

Many elements of the lithostratigraphy described above from Johns River are broadly similar to those attributed previously to the earthquake deformation cycle (Figure 11.1). Comparison with the sediments found in the contemporary intertidal zone suggests that burial of three of the peats was accompanied by a rapid change from high marsh to mudflat, with the other two recording small amounts of submergence, probably from low marsh to mudflat.

Long and Shennan (1994) drew attention to the fact that much previous work in Washington and Oregon was based on the examination of lithostratigraphic data alone. They argued that rigorous testing of the earthquake deformation cycle would only be possible with the assistance of microfossil analytical techniques. Pollen and diatom data collected from contemporary and fossil sediments in Johns River (Shennan *et al.*, 1996) support the pattern of vegetation changes predicted by the earthquake deformation cycle (Long and Shennan, 1994) in most of the Johns River peat-mud couplets. Moreover, the combination of litho- and biostratigraphic data from fossil and contemporary environments enables quantification of the magnitude of submergence accompanying inundation for each peat studied; of those described above, JR93-V, JR93-III and JR93-I experienced intermediate submergence of 1.0+/-0.5m, and JR93-IV and JR93-II submergence of *ca.* 0.35m (Shennan *et al.*, 1996).

The widespread use of the Troels-Smith scheme by Quaternary scientists in Northwest Europe over the last 40 years reflects its ability to describe in a quantitative and semi-objective manner a plethora of Quaternary unconsolidated sediments. For the coastal stratigrapher, the scheme is of particular value because of its ability to characterise the palimpsest of organic and inorganic sediments which typify the stratigraphic record in coastal lowlands. Although never designed to replace sophisticated laboratory analysis, the Troels-Smith scheme represents a critical first stage in any systematic investigation of coastal stratigraphy. Differences between the field and laboratory classification of sediments are inevitable and users of this scheme are encouraged, therefore, to calibrate their field descriptions on a regular basis.

An important aspect of the Troels-Smith scheme is that it requires field scientists to get their hands dirty, to consider carefully the composition and physical characteristics of the sediment under study and to record these observations in a systematic manner. The (largely) non-generic nature of the sediment descriptions avoids over-interpretation in the field and underscores the need for a combination of field and laboratory techniques in Quaternary palaeoenvironmental reconstruction. As such, the Troels-Smith (1955) scheme should be seen as an essential field technique for any Quaternary scientist, and an integral part of any programme of undergraduate and postgraduate training.

ACKNOWLEDGEMENTS

We thank Andy Plater and Jane Sidell for helpful comments on this paper, and Arthur Corner, Steven Allan and David Hume for drafting the figures.

REFERENCES

AABY, B. and BERGLUND, B.E. 1986. Characterization of peat and lake sediments. *IN*: Berglund, B.J. (ed), *Handbook of Holocene Palaeoecology and Palaeohydrology*, 231-246. John Wiley and Sons, Chichester.

ALLEN, J.R.L. 1987. Late Flandrian shoreline oscillations in the Severn Estuary; The Rumney formation at its type site. *Philosophical Transactions of the Royal Society of London* B, **315**, 157-184.

ATWATER, B.F. 1987. Evidence for great Holocene earthquakes along the outer coast of Washington State. *Science*, **236**, 942-944.

ATWATER, B.F. 1992. Geological evidence for earthquakes during the past 2000 years along the Copalis river, southern coastal Washington. *Journal of Geophysical Research*, **97**, 1901-1919.

ATWATER, B.F. and HEMPHILL-HALEY, E. 1996. Preliminary estimates of recurrence intervals for great earthquakes of the past 3500 years at northeastern Willapa Bay, Washington. *U.S. Geological Survey Open-File Report* 96-001, 88 pp.

ATWATER, B.F. and YAMAGUCHI, D.K. 1991. Sudden, probably co-seismic submergence of Holocene trees and grass in coastal Washington State. *Geology*, **19**, 706-709.

ATWATER, B.F., STUIVER, M. and YAMAGUCHI, D.K. 1991. A radiocarbon test of earthquake magnitude at the Cascadia subduction zone. *Nature*, **353**, 156-158.

BERGLUND, B.E. 1971. Littorina transgressions in Blekinge, South Sweden - a preliminary survey. *Geologiska Foreningens i Stockholm Forhandlingar,* **93**, 623-652.

CLARK, J.A., FARRELL, W.E. and PELTIER, W.R. 1978. Global changes in postglacial sea level: a numerical calculation. *Quaternary Research*, **9**, 265-278.

DARIENZO, M.E. and PETERSON, C.D. 1990. Episodic tectonic subsidence of late Holocene salt marshes, northern Oregon coast, central Cascadia margin, U.S.A. *Tectonics*, **9**, 1-22.

DARIENZO, M.E., PETERSON, C.D. and CLOUGH, C. 1994. Stratigraphic evidence for great subduction-zone earthquakes at four estuaries in northern Oregon, U.S.A. *Journal of Coastal Research*, **10**, 850-876.

DEVOY, R.J.N. 1979. Flandrian sea-level changes and vegetation history of the lower Thames Estuary. *Philosophical Transactions of the Royal Society of London* B, **285**, 355-407.

DIGERFELDT, G. 1975. A standard profile for Littorina transgressions in Western Skåne, South Sweden. *Boreas*, **4**, 125-142.

EVERETT, R.J.C. and SHENNAN, I. 1987. *STRAT: a computer program for Quaternary stratigraphic data display and management.* Occasional Publication (New Series), **no. 20**. Department of Geography, University of Durham.

FAIRBANKS, R.G. 1989. A 17,000 year glacio-eustatic sea-level record: influence of glacial melting rates on the Younger Dryas event and deep-ocean circulation. *Nature*, **342**, 637-642.

GODWIN, H. 1940. Studies of the post-glacial history of British vegetation. III. Fenland pollen diagrams. IV. Post-glacial changes of relative land- and sea-level in the English fenland. *Philosophical Transactions of the Royal Society* B, **230**, 239-303.

GRANLUND, E. and VON POST, L. 1926. Sodra sveriges torvtillgangar. I. *Sveriges Geologiska Undersokning*, Ser. C. No. 335. Arbok 19 (1925) No.2. Stockholm.

GRIMM, E. 1993. *A Pollen Program for Analysis and Display*. Illinois State Museum, Springfield.

LAMBECK, K. 1993. Glacial rebound of the British Isles-I. Preliminary model results. *Geophysical Journal International*, **115**, 941-959.

LONG, A.J. and INNES, J.B. 1995. The back-barrier and barrier depositional history of Romney Marsh and Dungeness, Kent, UK. *Journal of Quaternary Science*, **10**, 267-284.

LONG, A.J. and SHENNAN, I. 1994. Sea-level changes in Washington and Oregon and the 'earthquake deformation cycle'. *Journal of Coastal Research*, **10**, 825-838.

LONG, A.J. and TOOLEY, M.J. 1995. Holocene sea-level and crustal movements in Hampshire and Southeast England, United Kingdom. *Journal of Coastal Research Special Issue* **no. 17**, 299-310.

MATHEWES, R.W. and CLAGUE, J.J. 1994. Detection of large prehistoric earthquakes in the Pacific Northwest by microfossil analysis. *Science*, **264**, 688-691.

NELSON, A.R. 1992. Holocene tidal-marsh stratigraphy in south-central Oregon-evidence for localized sudden submergence in the Cascadia subduction zone. *SEPM Special Publication*, **48**, 287-301.

NELSON, A.R., SHENNAN, I. and LONG, A.J. 1996. Identifying coseismic subsidence in tidal-wetland stratigraphic sequences at the Cascadia subduction zone of western North America. *Journal of Geophysical Research*, **101**(B3), 6115-6135.

PIRAZZOLI, P.A. 1991. *World Atlas of Holocene Sea-level Changes*. Elsevier, Amsterdam, 300 pp.

PLATER, A.J. 1992. The late Holocene evolution of Denge Marsh, southeast England: a stratigraphic, sedimentological and micropalaeontological approach. *The Holocene*, **2**, 63-70.

RANCE, C.E. de 1869. The Geology of the Country between Liverpool and Southport. *Memoirs of the Geological Survey UK*. HMSO, Harpenden.

READE, T.M. 1871. The geology and physics of the post-glacial period as shown in deposits and organic remains in Lancashire and Cheshire. *Proceedings of the Liverpool Geological Society* **2**, 36-88.

REID, C. 1913. Submerged Forests. Cambridge University Press, 129 pp.

SHENNAN, I. 1986. Flandrian sea-level changes in the Fenland I. The geographical setting and evidence of relative sea-level changes. *Journal of Quaternary Science*, **1**, 119-154.

SHENNAN, I., LONG, A.J., RUTHERFORD, M.M., GREEN, F.M.L., INNES, J.B., LLOYD, J.M., ZONG, Y. and WALKER, K. 1996. Tidal marsh stratigraphy and the earthquake deformation cycle I: A 5000 year record in Washington, USA. *Quaternary Science Reviews*, **15**, 1-37.

SPURRELL, F.C. 1889. On the estuary of the Thames and its alluvium. *Proceedings of the Geology Society,* **11**, 210-230.

TOOLEY, M.J. 1974. Sea-level changes during the last 9,000 years in north-west England. *Geographical Journal*, **140**, 18-42.

TOOLEY, M.J. 1978a. *Sea-level changes in north-west England during the Flandrian Stage*. Oxford, Clarendon Press.

TOOLEY, M.J. 1978b. Interpretation of Holocene sea-level changes. *Geologiska Foreningens i Stockholm Forhandlingar,* **100**, 203-212.

TOOLEY, M.J. 1981. Methods of reconstruction. *IN*: Simmons, I.G., and Tooley, M.J. (eds), *The environment in British prehistory, 1-48*. Duckworth, London.

TOOLEY, M.J. and SWITSUR, V.R. 1988. Water level changes and sedimentation during the Flandrian Age in the Romney Marsh area. *IN*: J. Eddison, J. and Green, C. (eds), *Romney Marsh: Evolution, Occupation, Reclamation*. Oxford, Oxford University Committee for Archaeology Monograph **24**, 53-71.

TROELS-SMITH, J. 1942. Geologisk Datering af Dryholm-Fundet. *Det Kongelige Dansk Videnskebernes Selskab Arckaeologisk-Kunsthistoriske Skrifter*, **1**(1), 137-212.

TROELS-SMITH, J. 1955. Characterization of unconsolidated sediments. *Danmarks Geologiske Undersøgelse*, Series IV, **3**, 38-73.

VAN DE PLASSCHE, O. 1995. Periodic clay deposition in a fringing peat swamp in the Lower Rhine-Meuse river area, 5,400-3,400 Cal BC. *Journal of Coastal Research Special Issue,* **no. 17**, 95-102.

WALKER, R.G. and JAMES, N.P. 1992. *Facies Models Response to Sea-level Change.* Geological Association of Canada.

WALLER, M. J. 1994. *The Fenland Project, Number 9: Flandrian Environmental Change in Fenland.* East Anglian Archaeology Report No 70; Cambridge Archaeological Committee.

WALLER, M.J., ENTWISTLE, J.A. and DULLER, G.A.T. 1995. TSPPlus - A menu driven program for the display of stratigraphic data. *Quaternary Newsletter*, **77**, 32-39.

WHITAKER, W. 1889. Geology of London. *Memoirs of the Geological Survey*, **1**, 454-477.

Appendix 1

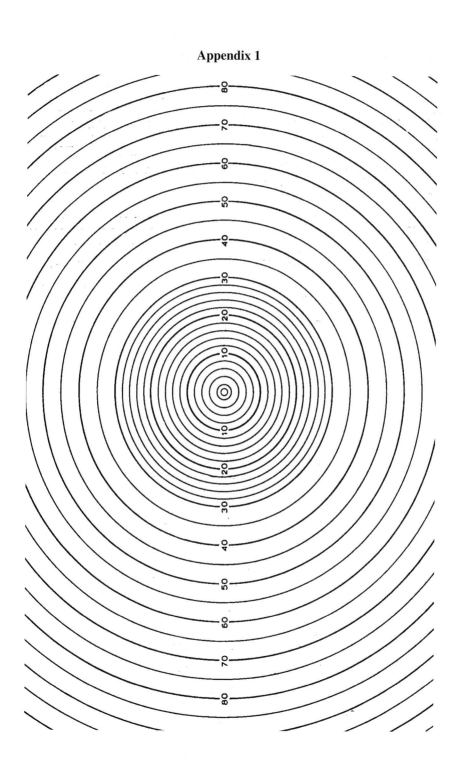

Appendix 2

Comments were received on various issues from the following: P. Brewer, D. Bridgland, A. Cullum, T. Fisher, H. Hobbs, A. Long, D. Maddy, A. Mather, J. Murton, T. Oguchi, K. Rijsdijk, A. Russell, I. Shennan, M. Stokes, B. Van Vilet-Lanoe, and I. West.

Regarding	Comment
Objectivity	All of the researchers agreed that section descriptions should be primarily objective in the field, but stressed that this was sometimes difficult. A number of researchers added a brief interpretative summary in the field. One researcher suggested, given time and logistical constraints, a sample strategy can be devised post-interpretation. However, all of the researchers were in favour of objective terminology, although there were criticisms of some existing terminology, e.g. hollow. Most of the researchers used the term diamicton, although most of them did not particularly liked it.
Indices	Grain size, sedimentary structures, tectonic structures, orientation of tectonic structures, clast fabrics, clast shapes, sedimentary contacts, occurrence of erratics, striations, percussion marks, clast clusters, stone lines, estimation of consolidation, palaeocurrent measurements, colour, bed thickness, clast lithology, channel/scour dimensions, preserved fauna/ flora, deformation structures, micromorphology, ESR and TL tube collection. Other criteria that were measured include: time, weather, elevation, map sheet, geomorphic landform, orientation of the exposure.
Measurement of indices	All of the researchers logged from the base of the section, using it as the zero mark unless they were: coring and describing individual palaeosols; working with archaeologists; requiring a stable position that could be found on return visits (zero at top). *Grain size*: all of the researchers measured the ten largest clasts and used a grain size comparator for sand-size sediment and finer. *Grain roundness and shape*: most researchers estimated particle roundness but did not record particle shape. *Colour*: all of the researchers used the Munsell Soil Colour Chart. One researcher described only fresh, humid samples. The Troels-Smith scheme was also used for core descriptions.
Sampling strategy	All of the researchers said that they tried to use a systematic sampling strategy that accounted for any discontinuities and avoided any cross-boundary sampling. One researcher pointed out that it was not always viable to sample a section at regular intervals because of the inaccessibility of some parts. Also, most of the researchers would select sampling sites after surveying the section. One researcher pointed out that their sampling strategy differed according to the research goals, i.e. sedimentological sampling strategy may well differ from a geochemical one.

Sample size	*Grain size*: ten largest clasts or bulk samples of 50 grams (till) - 5kg (coarse grain) bulk sample. In most cases researchers used *ca.* 500g for finer sediments; *Grain form*: 25 - 250 clasts; Fabric: 25-50 clasts; Clast lithology: 50 - 400+ clasts. One of the researchers compared his results (50 gram samples) to that of a colleague who collected much larger samples: his colleague's texture analysis cluster was much better, which suggests that there is a small-scale component of variability in tills. He pointed out however, that this may give a misleading impression w.r.t. the uniformity of tills.
Facies	Some of the researchers used the facies scheme and almost all of them divided the succession into facies and facies associations in the laboratory, after field work. Most used Miall's facies codes, or adapted it, although for facies other than fluvial and alluvial fan they used descriptive terms or labelled facies, objectively.
Architectural elements	This system was not employed by many of the researchers. Those that had used it followed Friend (1983) and Friend *et al.* (1989) and Miall (1983 and his later modifications) and Krüger (1994), for glacial diamicts.
Stratigraphy	None of the researchers used allostratigraphy and sequence stratigraphy has yet to make an impact in Quaternary studies. A few had used lithostratigraphy, one researcher preferring the original Hedberg (1976) format rather than the more recent adaptions. Most of the researchers used the NACSN scheme. Other types of stratigraphy used were: pedostratigraphy, chemostratigraphy and event-lithostratigraphy.

INDEX